INDIAN PHILOSOPHY : PAST AND FUTURE

INDIAN PHILOSOPHY : PAST AND FUTURE

Edited by

S. S. RAMA RAO PAPPU

and

R. PULIGANDLA

South Asia Books

SOUTH ASIA BOOKS
Box 502, Columbia, Missouri, 65205

Indological Publishers & Booksellers
Head Office : 41-U.A., Bungalow Road, Delhi-110 007
Branches : 1. Chowk, Varanasi-1 (U.P.)
2. Ashok Rajpath, Patna-4 (BIHAR)

ISBN 0 8364 0670 2

First Edition : Delhi, 1983

Printed in India
By Shantilal Jain, at Shri Jainendra Press,
A-45, Phase I, Industrial Area, Naraina, New Delhi-110 028
Published by Narendra Prakash Jain, for Motilal Banarsidass,
Bungalow Road, Jawahar Nagar, Delhi-110 007.

Preface

During the past decade (1970-80) there appeared three collections of essays on Contemporary Indian Philosophy—K. S. Murty and K. R. Rao (ed) *Current Trends in Indian Philosophy* (1972); M. Chatterjee (ed) *Contemporary Indian Philosophy*, Second Series (1974); and N. K. Devaraja (ed), *Indian Philosophy Today* (1975). These three volumes present a sample of contemporary philosophical thinking in India. The reviewers and editors of the above books complained that philosophical thinking in India, as represented in the above volumes, is at cross-roads, that many of the essays in the above books are indistinguishable from "Western" philosophical thinking and that Indian philosophy needs a goal and direction.

We have, therefore, undertaken the task of inviting over twenty eminent Indian philosophers (many of whom also contributed to the three volumes referred to above) to share with the philosophical world what they consider to be the meaning and essence of the *Indian* philosophical tradition, the role of tradition in modernity and the future of Indian philosophy. The present book is thus not another collection of essays on Contemporary Indian Philosophy. Rather, it is a meta-philosophical work that our contributors have undertaken.

The contributors to this volume represent a cross-section of the Indian philosophers. Some of them live and teach Indian philosophy in Indian universities; others live and teach Indian philosophy in Great Britain, Canada and U.S.A. This gives the present volume a rich perspective—whereas Indian philosophers living in India take an 'internal' point of view concerning their role and future, Indian philosophers living abroad take an 'external' point of view about the tradition and future of Indian philosophy in their homeland and abroad. Many of our contributors are very influential thinkers who have made their mark in Indian and world philosophic scene. But we have also included in our book contributions from some brilliant young Indian philosophers. Just as the contents of the book bring together tradition and modernity, our contributors also belong to the older and the younger generations of Indian philosophers.

All the essays which appear in this volume (except part of P. T. Raju's article) are original and written specially for this volume. Professor Raju's article "The Western and the Indian Philosophical Traditions" first appeared in *The Philosophical Review* (Vol. LVI, No. 2, March 1947). Due to failing health, Professor Raju could not write an original essay to our volume, but he was kind enough to write a long postscript to this article explaining his present views. We are grateful to Professor Raju and *The Philosophical Review* for granting permission to reprint the above article.

We would also like to thank the Miami University Research Office and the University of Toledo for giving us a modest grant to defer the xeroxing expenses of the manuscript.

Finally, we would like to thank the publishers of this volume, especially J. P. Jain of Motilal Banarsidass, Delhi, and N. G. Barrier of South Asia Books, Columbia, Missouri, for their constant help and assistance in the preparation and printing.

S. S. RAMA RAO PAPPU
R. PULIGANDLA

ACKNOWLEDGEMENTS

We would like to thank the publishers listed below for giving us permission to include here excerpts from the following books and journals:

The Philosophical Review for P. T. Raju's article "The Western and the Indian Philosophical Traditions;"

George Allen and Unwin for excerpts from *Contemporary Indian Philosophy* edited by Margaret Chatterjee (1974) and *Indian Philosophy* by S. Radhakrishnan (1923);

Princeton University Press for excerpts from *A Sourcebook in Indian Philosophy*, edited by Sarvepalli Radhakrishnan and Charles A. Moore [copyright © by Princeton University Press]; *Philosophy East and West* edited by Charles A. Moore [copyright © 1972 by Princeton University Press], and *Philosophies of India* by Heinrich Zimmer (1971);

The University of Hawaii Press for excerpts from J. A. B. van Buitenen, "Dharma and Moksa" in *Philosophy East and West*, Vol. VII (1957) and R. Prasad, "Tradition, Progress and Contemporary Indian Philosophy," *Philosophy East and West*, Vol. XV, 1965;

Houghton Mifflin, for excerpts from *A Biography of the Greek People* by Cecil F. Lavell (1934);

Philosophy and Phenomenological Research for excerpts from R. Prasad, "The Concept of Moksa," in *Philosophy and Phenomenological Research*, Vol. 62 (1979);

Mouton Publishers, for excerpts from *Epistemology, Logic and Grammar in Indian Philosophical Analysis*, by B. K. Matilal (1971).

CONTENTS

PAGE

PART III : THE FUTURE OF INDIAN PHILOSOPHY

Editors' Introduction

Every beginning student of philosophy asks the question: "What is philosophy?" and every philosophy teacher is puzzled to answer this innocent-looking, simple-minded question. If a philosophy teacher does not straightaway give a "definition" of philosophy, he at least tries to calm the inquiring student by saying that "The definition of philosophy is itself a philosophical problem" or "A definition of 'philosophy' comes, not at the beginning of our inquiry, but at the end of it" or "Don't ask for a definition of 'philosophy'—philosophy is what philosophers do in their professional moments" and so on. If the student persists in his questioning, most of the philosophy teachers give a single-sentence definition of philosophy, such as "Philosophy is the science which investigates being as being" (Aristotle) or "Philosophy shows the fly the way out of the fly-bottle" (Wittgenstein) or "Philosophy delves below the apparent clarity of common speech" (Whitehead) or Philosophy concerns itself "with concepts, with the ways in which and the means by which we think and communicate" (Warnock) or Philosophy is "rational discussion" (Karl Popper), etc. If the student still insists that the teacher elaborate and explain these definitions, the teacher asks him to read the Great Philosophers themselves or some for the specialized books on the concept of philosophy, such as Stephen Korner's *What is Philosophy? One Philosopher's Answer* (1969), Arthur Danto's *What Philosophy Is: A Guide to the Elements* (1968), Henry W. Johnstone (ed) *What is Philosophy* (1965), etc.

The problem of defining and understanding the nature of philosophy becomes even more acute when we come to Indian philosophy or Chinese philosophy or Greek philosophy, etc. In our classes on Indian philosophy and in our discussions on Indian philosophy—especially in Western universities and also in our encounters with Western philosophers—many a second-order questions are repeatedly asked about Indian philosophy. These are, for example, "What is 'Indian' about Indian philosophy?" or "Does the 'Indianness' of Indian philosophy merely consist of the fact that certain modes of thought (which are sometimes similar to and sometimes different from, say, Western philosophy) developed in the Indian sub-continent ?" or' "Ist here an 'essence' of Indian philosophy ?" or "Does Indian philosophy merely mean the "schools" of philosophy which have historically developed in the Indian sub-continent ?" or "When is a philosopher doing *Indian* philosophy ?" and so on.

Many modern writers on Indian philosophy seem to think that although Indian philosophy is, first and foremost, philosophy, yet it is not merely philosophy. There is, according to these thinkers, the spirit of Indian philosophy. "If we can abstract from the variety of opinion and observe the general spirit of Indian thought," says S. Radhakrishnan, "we shall find that it has a disposition to interpret life and nature in the way of monistic idealism."[1] "In India," says M. Hiriyanna, "philosophy becomes a way of life, not merely a way of thought."[2] Some other essential features, attributed to Indian philosophy, are that it is *mokṣa*-oriented; that it believes in some kind of *ātman* (self), *karma*, rebirth, *dharma*, etc.; that it is synthetic, practical, optimistic about the ultimate goals, life-oriented as contrasted to nature-oriented, and so on.[3]

Other contemporary Indian writers like Debiprasad Chattopadhyaya, Daya Krishna and Rajendra Prasad, question the above characterizations of Indian philosophy. According to Debiprasad Chattopadhyaya,

> "however much one may inflate the academic myth concerning Indian spiritualism and Indian idealism, the Indian people remain the inheritors and the custodians of Indian materialism. It is also for them to enrich it with the ever-growing wealth of scientific knowledge. We have thus to reassert the elemental truth of our ancient materialism, though of course on an immeasurably higher level."[4]

1. S. Radhakrishnan, *Indian Philosophy*, Vol. I (London : George Allen and Unwin, 1923), p. 32.

2. M. Hiriyanna, *Outlines of Indian Philosophy* (London : George Allen and Unwin, 1932), p. 18.

3. For a summary of these characteristics, see R. Puligandla, *Fundamentals of Indian Philosophy* (Nashville : Abingdon Press, 1975), pp. 24-26, and C. A. Moore (ed), *The Indian Mind* (Honolulu : University of Hawaii Press, 1967), pp. 12-16.

4. Debiprasad Chattopadhyaya, *Indian Philosophy : A Popular Introduction* (New Delhi : People's Publishing House, 1972), p. 199.

Whereas Chattopadhyaya holds a materialistic interpretation of Indian philosophy, Daya Krishna thinks that Indian philosophy is indistinguishable from "philosophy proper" and, therefore, there is no essence of Indian philosophy.

> "Indian philosophy," says Daya Krishna, "is neither exclusively spiritual nor bound by unquestionable infallible authority nor constricted and congealed in the frozen moulds of the so-called 'schools,' all of which is supposed to constitute the essence of Indian philosophy by everyone who has written on the subject. These are just plain myths and unless they are seen and recognized as such, any new fresh look at Indian philosophy will be impossible. The dead, mummified picture of Indian philosophy will come alive only when it is seen as a living stream of thinkers who grappled with difficult problems, which are, philosophically, as alive today as they were in the ancient past. Indian philosophy will become contemporarily relevant only when it is conceived as philosophy proper."[1]

Rajendra Prasad, likewise, says :

> "It is my feeling that the emphasis on the practical character of Indian philosophy has been overdone and it has caused more harm than good to its proper study... It has also resulted in the impression in the minds of many that Indian philosophy is philosophy in a sense different from the one in which Western philosophy is philosophy. This is noticeable from the fact that most of the Western scholars who have taken interest in Indian philosophy are not professional philosophers but orientalists or theologians."[2]

Second, there is no denying the fact that Indian philosophical heritage is long and continuous. "The first fact to be noted about Indian philosophy," says Debiprasad Chattopadhyaya, "is the accumulation of an enormous amount of philosophical material in its general fund resulting from a more or less continuous philosophical activity of two thousand five hundred years, if not more."[3] The question which arises in this context is the encounter between traditional Indian philosophy and modern philosophy, Indian as well as Western. Arnold Toynbee, for example, points out that of all the Asian civilizations, "personal contacts between Indians and Westerners have been more numerous and our Western iron has probably entered deeper into

1. Daya Krishna, "Three Myths About Indian Philosophy," *Quest*, Vol. 53 (1967), 16.

2. R. Prasad, "The Concept of Moksa," *Philosophy and Phenomenological Research*, Vol. XXI, No. 3 (1971), 382-83.

3. Debiprasad Chattopadhyaya, *What is Living and What is Dead in Indian Philosophy* (New Delhi : People's Publishing House, 1976), p. 1.

India's soul."[1] At the same time, Toynbee complains that the Hindu culture is the least understood culture in the West. If we put Toynbee's remark in a philosophical context, it would seem that India has understood and absorbed most of the Western philosophical thinking—ancient and recent—but the West did not understand and absorb India to the same extent. Some contemporary Indian philosophers, especially those associated with traditional institutions of higher learning, like the Sanskrit universities, think and write without knowing Western philosophy; others who were primarily trained in Anglo-American analytical philosophy or Continental Existentialism and Phenomenology conveniently ignore the Indian philosophical tradition altogether; still others who were trained in both the traditions sometimes think and write in comparative terms and, in their creative moments, synthesize the best of India and the West. This raises certain problems concerning the role of tradition in modernity : Can Indian philosophy continue to be 'Indian' in utter disregard to this ancient tradition ? What is living and what is dead in traditional Indian philosophy ? Should we modernize the tradition or traditionalize the modernity or neither ?

Third, since philosophy in traditional India is conceived as a means for attaining liberation (*mokṣa*, *nirvāṇa*, etc.), the role of the philosopher was to impart to the student the kind of wisdom that liberates the student from the mundane and earthly existence. And the quest for liberation is naturally bound up with a system of discipline—physical, intellectual, moral and spiritual. It is axiomatic that the best teacher is one who teaches through example. A philosophy teacher in ancient India was, therefore, the one who had himself attained *mokṣa*. From the description of a philosopher as a *jñāni* (a wise man), an *uttama-puruṣa* (the perfect man), a *yogi*, a *ṛṣi* (seer), an *ācārya* (a leader) and so on, the role of the philosopher in India is not difficult to comprehend. In traditional India, the philosopher is the paradigmatic individual who has not merely learned the *parā-vidyā* but also the *aparā-vidyā*.

Though the above conception of the role of the philosopher as the "spectator of all time and existence" is paid lip-sympathy

1. Arnold Toynbee, *The World and the West* (New York : Oxford University Press, 1953), p. 34 and Chapter III.

in contemporary India, it is not clear whether academic philosophers would consider themselves liberated individuals or whether they consider their role to impart wisdom to the students. What, if anything, should we expect from the contemporary Indian academic philosophers ? Should they cloister themselves in the academic ivory-towers contemplating the truth or should they get involved in social transformation and the liberation of humanity around them ? Should they take to the *pravṛtti-mārga* (activism) or *nivṛtti-mārga* (the path of quietism); the *karma-yoga* or the *jñāna-yoga* ?

Last but not least, there is the question of the future of Indian philosophy. Until recently, traditional cultures like India did not self-consciously raise the questions of the future. This is not because Indians tend to think in a temporal categories, but because their goals, ideals and aspirations are already contained in their rich, variegated cultural past. For the Indians, historically, the future, in a sense, is an unfolding of the past. The traditional Indian attitude to read the future in the past has changed somewhat during the past two centuries, due to India's exposure to the Western cultures, to the industrial, technological and political revolutions around the world and to the revolution of rising expectations among the Indian people themselves.

A typical question posed to the twentieth century Indian philosophy is : Where do we go from here ? "Today," says Jawaharlal Nehru, "India swings between the blind adherence to her old customs and a slavish imitation of foreign ways. In neither of these can she find relief or life or growth... True culture derives its inspiration from every corner of the world, but it is home-grown."[1]

I

More specifically, in our letter inviting the contributors to participate in this symposium, we have divided the problems into four categories: (I) What is Indian about Indian philosophy ? (II) What is the goal of Indian philosophy ? (III) What is the responsibility of the Indian philosopher ? and (IV) What is the

1. Jawaharlal Nehru, *The Discovery of India* (New York : Doubleday, 1946), p. 414.

future of Indian philosophy? We raised the following issues under each of the above categories:

"I. *What is Indian about Indian philosophy*? What do you consider to be the unique and distinguishing features of Indian philosophy? Is there a 'spirit' of Indian philosophy? Do you consider Vedānta or some form of transcendentalism to be the true spirit of Indian philosophy? Is the expression 'Indian philosophy' a contradiction, because true philosophy is neither Indian nor Western? Does Indian philosophy mean nothing more than the geographical reference to the kind of activity that took place (or is taking place) in the Indian sub-continent?

"II. *What is the goal of Indian philosophy*? As an Indian philosopher, what do you consider to be the goal(s) of Indian philosophy? Do you consider *mokṣa* to be the legitimate *summum bonum* of Indian philosophy? To what kinds of questions and what kinds of concerns are you most compellingly drawn? How do you identify your concerns as Indian and not Western? What is the role of Indian philosophical tradition as represented by the "schools" in the contemporary context? Do these schools of Indian philosophy have merely a historical interest or do they have relevance to the present-day philosophy? To what extent, if any, do you consider your conception of Indian philosophy and your philosophical thinking in general, are affected by Western philosophy and Western modes of thought?

"III. *What is the responsibility of the Indian philosopher*? What do you consider to be the responsibility of the Indian philosopher? Do you agree with the traditional conception of Indian philosopher as a 'realized' individual? Is the Indian philosopher in possession of a 'higher knowledge' which is denied to others? What, if anything, should be his social concerns?

"IV. *What is the future of Indian philosophy*? How do you conceive of the future of Indian philosophy? Does the Indian philosophical scene in the past one hundred years give you the impression that we are making 'progress' or 'regress'? What should be the role of Indian philosophy in the context of global philosophy—i.e. Indian philosophy *vis-à-vis* Western philosophy, Chinese philosophy, Latin

American philosophy, etc.? Should Indian philosophy imitate the styles of contemporary Western philosophy? Or should progress in Indian philosophy be native to the soil? What should be the relation between traditional Indian philosophy and the 'progress' of Indian philosophy? Can Indian philosophy break its connections with traditional schools and still remain Indian?"

II

Our invitees have responded to our challenge excellently. We have no intention of summarizing or paraphrasing the contributors' views, since everyone can speak for himself or herself without the editors' help ! The issues we have posed under the four categories delineated above are not exclusive of each other. Each category criss-crosses into the other. Consequently, the title of each essay should only be understood as the emphasis its author is placing without necessarily restricting himself or herself to the issue alone. Thus, a writer writing on the Indianness of Indian philosophy is merely placing a heavy emphasis on this subject but spills his or her writing into the future of Indian philosophy also.

Likewise our division of the essays into the three parts, viz. (I) The Indian Philosophical Tradition, (II) Tradition and Modernity, and (III) The Future of Indian Philosophy, is based on the emphasis each essay places in one of the three topics but each chapter necessarily spills into the other.

PART I

THE TRADITION OF INDIAN PHILOSOPHY

1

WHAT IS INDIAN ABOUT INDIAN PHILOSOPHY?

PRATIMA BOWES*

THE term 'philosophy' can be used at least in two different senses. Hence, its meaning needs a little discussion before we can begin to tackle the question this paper asks. One of these meanings, still current in non-academic circles, is 'love of wisdom' and wisdom consists in knowing how to live. This wisdom can be found in the realm of what is generally classified as 'religious thought', especially, the kind of thought that is concerned with man's self-understanding of himself as a spiritual being—an understanding that enables him to weather the storms of life with a certain calm mastery. This thought, even when systematically presented in a logical sequence, often does not qualify as philosophy in the academic circles of the Western world, where philosophy means rational analysis of concepts, especially those which act as presuppositions in our thoughts about things. Both kinds of philosophy do, as a matter of fact, exist in India but, traditionally, it has been the custom in the West to insist that only philosophy of the wisdom sort is to be found there; the other sort, like science, is exclusively Western. Hence the fashionable opinion that Indian philosophy is transcendental in

*Pratima Bowes is Reader in Religious Studies, University of Sussex, England. She is the author of several books, including *The Concept of Morality*, *Is Metaphysics Possible?*, *Consciousness and Freedom*, *The Hindu Religious Tradition*, *The Hindu Intellectual Tradition*.

character, something that is not a matter of rational discussion. And, of course, transcendental philosophy does exist in India in a form that can be said to be characteristically Indian and it is present in all the three Indian religions of antiquity, the Hinduism, the Buddhism and the Jainism. This thought is somewhat different from the kind of religious thought that characterizes Theism because it is more concerned with self-knowledge than with faith in God. This characteristic Indian spiritual thought envisages the highest possibility of man as a spiritual being to lie in the overcoming of his particularity, not just in the sense of being unselfish and full of loving concern for others, but through literally realizing himself as the one participating in an unconditioned and infinite dimension of being. This particularity is tied up with one's being a finite personality limited by a particular physical and psychic constitution that is private and peculiar to oneself. One transcends this in realizing infinite being and one's identity with all existence. This transcendental enterprise has been organized as a systematic school of philosophy in India, besides being present in the Indian culture as intuitive insight.

But all that is known as philosophy in India does not consist of this transcendental enterprise. However, except for one particular school called *Lokāyata* or *Cārvāka*, all Indian schools of philosophy, even those that are persistently realistic, empiricist and pragmatic in their outlook insofar as the world of ordinary experience is concerned, do recognize that a transcendental dimension does exist. And the reason for this is to be found in a cultural fact, something that makes for the Indianness of Indian philosophy, even of the non-transcendental sort (meaning not that it denies that a transcendental dimension of experience exists but that its immediate concern may be with something else). Anyway, the thinking that I shall look into here does consist of systematic, logical and reasoned pursuit of issues (it may even be a transcendental one) that need clarification when we think of what there is in the world and how we come to know what there is. What comes out as peculiar to India is not so much the doctrines—we get roughly the same kind of philosophical doctrines like realism, idealism, criticism, etc. in India as we get in the West—as the style and manner in which philosophical thinking was conducted in India. This I believe is to be understood as a feature that philosophy inherits from Indian culture and its world view.

All human activity, intellectual or otherwise, takes its distinctive shape within a culture that develops certain presuppositions as regards the nature of reality, that is to say, a world view. These presuppositions themselves no doubt grow out of human response to facts of experience, but they in their turn powerfully influence as to how men of a certain culture view their experience. (Incidentally the literal meaning of the Sanskrit term for philosophy is 'viewing'.) The important thing about the Indian 'world view', as I look at it, is not that it is a form of transcendentalism in which it is fashionable to find what is characteristically Indian. No human culture can be transcendental in the sense that its sole or primary concern can be transcendental values—values which are related not to the everyday business of life, its economic, social, political and such other activities which determine the day to day living of men as a group, but what transcends them, even if it is true that a particular culture can give transcendental values their due importance in the total business of living, such that they are accepted by most as a normal element in the organization of life. The Indian world view is organic as opposed to a world view that I call 'architectonic' and it is this world view that produced the peculiar brand of Indian transcendental thought rather than it being the case that Indian culture was a product of Indian transcendentalism. (However, the influence is, as always, both ways.) An organic world view should not be confused with the organic view of society or state which is supposed to exalt the society or state above the individual. A world view is about the nature of a whole and the relationship of this whole to the parts which constitute it, but it is concerned with the understanding of reality rather than the state or society. What I call the architectonic view—the typical Western world view—considers that a whole can be deliberately created according to a plan or purpose by bringing together parts which exist or can exist independently of the whole and the unity of the thing or the relationship of the parts to this unity is not something that belongs to the very nature of the thing, considered as a whole or as parts. It is acquired through the purpose that is given to it from the outside and what this purpose is can thus be clearly discerned. Furthermore, the purpose of the whole is not reproduced in the parts which, as parts, remain separable. This model of what being a whole means can then be used as a screen through which the nature of all things (all things are wholes made up of parts) are understood. An example of this model would be a house. The model of an organic world view would be a tree where the relationship between the whole and the parts is understood to be inherent in the structure itself which has an inner dynamics of its own—the seed being already programmed to grow into the trunk, branches, leaves and so on—it is not something that is given to it from the outside. The parts have their distinctive and plural functions and relative to these functions they have distinctive realities of their own, and these cannot be confused with one another. On one level of consideration, the whole is one because the parts have their being only within the unity of the total structure and not outside of it. On the other level of consideration, because the unity exists in and through the parts which have not come from outside but which express the detailed working out at different levels of functioning (roots do one thing, trunk another, branches yet another) of an inherent programme, so to say, the whole has, relatively speaking, many different expressions, or a plural being as well. Again this model can be used as a screen through which realities of all kinds, even ultimate reality, can be viewed. And it is my contention that Indian transcendentalism is one of the intellectual expressions of this organic world view. For it says that reality is non-dual, the same reality which is one at the ultimate level is plural at the phenomenal level. The man, therefore, (insofar as he is *Ātman*) is identical with Brahman. The *Bṛhadāraṇyaka Upaniṣad* shapes this idea on a mythical plane: Brahman, the ultimate reality, was one, but he/it wanted to be many so it became the many through different names, shapes, and functions. The many, therefore, are an expression of the being of the one. The organic world view thus allows that there can be many different expressions of the same thing and these expressions have their truth relatively to their name, shape and function. It thus combines the idea of unity (non-dualism) at one level with pluralism at a relative level of being where contradictory (better, opposite) characteristics can appear and equally claim to be true, relative to different viewpoints.

The Indian culture shows the influence of the organic world view in many of its characteristic expressions, and this is true of philosophy as well. Herein lies both the strength and the weakness of Indian philosophical thought. Its weakness lies in its lack of social criticism in the form of social, moral and political philosophy. (There is social, moral and political thought but no social, moral, political *philosophy*.) And this is a result of the organic world view. According to this view the world was not created once and for all at a particular moment in time by God to fulfil a particular purpose, God having given to things the laws according to which they function. Rather ultimate reality itself becomes it all (and this includes many different world systems, an infinite number, according to the *Viṣṇupurāṇa*) for no other purpose than to enjoy being many, and all things function according to the inner law of their being (*dharma*) which belong to the very nature of reality itself, being its expression. After a cycle of four ages lasting over millions and millions of years, the world is destroyed and all manifestations go back to Brahman from whence they came. But Brahman expresses itself again and thus it goes on without beginning or end. (The organic analogy is the seed which comes from the tree and gives rise to a tree in its turn in a never-ending cycle.)

Now, whatever exists, does exist according to a law, which is the law of its being and as such implicit in the thing itself, and it exists both as a unity and a plurality. Society too exists in this manner and its division into four *varṇas*,[1] carrying on the four kinds of essential functions in society on the basis of quality and competence, are also expressions of this unity. And this manner of its unity being maintained by a plurality of functions is, according to the organic view, the very law of being of society. The society exists for the well-being of all, but the well-being of one person is not a carbon copy of the well-being of another, for all do not have the same temperaments, aptitudes, needs, nor can they all perform the same functions. The well-being of an individual can be pursued through four goals, *dharma* (rightful

1. I consider that the *varṇa* conception is different from that of *jāti* (caste). There are four *varṇas* only and a *varṇa* can be determined on the basis of quality and function. There are thousands of castes and they are determined solely by birth, irrespective of quality and, these days, of function.

living), *artha* (material possession and prosperity), *kāma* (pleasure) and *mokṣa* (liberation) at different times and stages of one's life (*āśrama*). Society functions at its optimum if each human being acts according to his *dharma* (duties and obligations of his *varṇa*, also one's obligations just as a human being) as required at different times by the different stages of one's life. Once these ideas about the law of being of a society were arrived at, the organic world view—which takes it that if each thing exists according to the law of its being it follows that the law according to which it is existing is the law of its being—did not consider it necessary any more to raise *philosophical* questions about society or about moral or political issues. So these problems left to the various compilers of law books (*dharmaśāstras*, *arthaśāstras*, etc.) who worked out in detail who should do what, when and how but were either unaware of the presuppositions of these prescriptions or were not interested in being aware. Because of a lack of philosophical perspective on social questions, it was hardly noticed that the idea of *varṇa* which probably did not have a hereditary connotation to begin with, being capable of interpretation on the same lines as the divisions of philosophers, soldiers and common men in Plato's *Republic*, was being used as the justification for *jāti* (caste), something that is not only hereditary and divided into hundreds of exclusive groups but is in some way a denial of organic relationship in its ban on inter-dining and inter-marriage. Nobody puzzled over the explanation that these hundreds of exclusive castes have arisen out of the inter-marriage of the four *varṇas*. If such inter-marriages took place, the *varṇas* were obviously not exclusive, and if so what reason can there be for making castes exclusive? But these questions were not asked by philosophers, who did not treat social problems as philosophical issues probably because of their organic presuppositions. If society is functioning, it is functioning according to the law of its being and this makes the continued existence of a thing a sufficient justification for its acceptance. This, of course, does not follow even if all things do have a law of their being (poison has this too, but we are not obliged to drink it because of it). So I think that the philosophers in India failed in their task inasmuch as they did nothing towards developing political, social or moral philosophy in India. One reason for this non-development may be that philosophical thought was a monopoly of the Brahmin caste, whose privileges would have been under attack if questions were to be asked about the social system.

The organic world view was important in a positive way in the philosophy that did develop, as it was in a negative way in the philosophy that did not develop. Now I must make it clear that I am myself doing philosophy in talking about Indian philosophy and as such interpreting what is obtained from a particular framework of enquiry and not simply reporting facts. So what I am going to say may not be directly corroborated by any statement made by Indian philosophers—they certainly did not talk of the organic world view—but in my judgment the interpretative framework that I am using makes us understand better the philosophical activity of the Indians and particularly the way this activity was carried on. And this interpretation has direct bearing on the question of the Indianness of Indian philosophy. Having said this I shall now proceed to look at the activity itself.

One of the noticeable things about philosophy in India is that it is known not so much by the name of individual philosophers (as is the practice in the West) who did the philosophizing, as by a particular school of thought—a particular viewing platform—to one or the other to which every philosopher belonged. This is a significant fact, symptomatic of the culture in which this activity was carried on. Philosophy called itself 'viewing' *darśana*, and all schools of philosophy whether orthodox or heterodox were like platforms from which to view reality in a particular way—a way that is often set forth in the form of a few aphorisms, to be subsequently elaborated by other thinkers who wished to use the same platform. The schools did not historically develop in an evolutionary fashion, one replacing another and becoming more popular or fashionable than the other in the process. Although they were systematized at different periods yet once formulated they existed side by side throughout the formative period of Indian philosophy, that is to say, prior to the Islamic conquest of India, which gradually brought all indigenous Indian thinking to a halt. And it is one of the earliest to be systematized, *Nyāya*, which managed to survive, still as a developing thought pattern, in one corner of India right down to the seventeenth century when others had long before ceased to exist. Not only did philosophers put forward their thought not as their own thought but thought in elaboration of a viewpoint of a particular description, but there is even the spectacle of a particular philosopher, Vācaspati Miśra, who wrote commentaries on each of these viewpoints (to write a commentary means to elaborate the rationale of a system with a pro-attitude). He was able to do so despite being a Vedāntist himself because each viewpoint does have a rationale which can be justifiably advanced, as understood in its own terms, even if when it comes to adopting a viewpoint as one's own one can have a preference. The schools of thought were in fact particular points of view from which reality was looked at in characteristic ways, the ways providing a multiple number of perspectives relatively to which thinking about experience could be carried out by a number of people. As we shall see one of the most sophisticated logical doctrines developed in India by the Jain philosophers called *Syādvāda* (may-be-it-is doctrine), claims that there can be no thinking that is not relative to a standpoint and such a doctrine could develop only because all philosophical thinking was being carried out from one standpoint or another and some people who did the thinking were conscious of this fact (to a greater or lesser degree).

It was thought in India that a multitude of viewpoints can be legitimately advanced as valid points of departure in one's thinking about reality and they can be accepted as such, which explains the co-existence of all schools of thought despite debates and arguments between them on specific points or issues. This is not usual in the Western tradition where a particular type of philosophy becomes fashionable at a particular time when it practically replaces others and where two contrasting types of philosophy like Realism and Idealism are not pursued equally vigorously at the same time. The co-existence of all schools of thought does not, of course, mean that philosophers did not have their preferences, nor does it mean that they never found the reasonings of other schools of thought faulty in some particular or other. In fact vigorous arguments between the various schools did take place, which enabled each school to define its position on particular points with greater clarity and precision. However, with the solitary exception of *Cārvāka* (which is contrary to the presuppositions of Indian culture and did as a matter of fact disappear) the argument was that this or that school has got this or that point wrong and not that the whole school should altogether cease to exist in the way a Realist philosopher in the West may declare that the whole enterprise of Idealism is misguided. All that I have said so far about the practice of philosophy in India accords well with the organic world view and its relativism/pluralism in practice which accepts that the same reality may exist in many different forms at one and the same time, and thinking about each of these can have its truth relatively to its own point of view. I am not saying that each philosopher clearly understood the implications of the philosophical scene in India but some did, like Vācaspati Miśra, mentioned earlier, and there were others who tried to put the schools in some kind of hierarchical order of greater and lesser truth, and the Jains even developed a doctrine about it. I shall first give a brief account of this Jain doctrine before I go on to consider what other schools of thought were about. Naturally, I shall be selective as it is impossible to present the whole of the rich and sophisticated philosophical tradition of India in these few pages.

There are two Jain doctrines, one ontological and the other logical-epistemological, which together may be said to be the perfect intellectual (as against a mythical one found in Hinduism) expression of the organic world view. These are: *anekāntavāda*, the many-faceted character of what may be said to be the same reality—and *syādvāda*, may-be-it-is character of all predication in regard to this reality. Since the universe (or all reality) is complex it can be looked at *only* from some point of view (*naya*) or other—that is to say, there is no way of sizing this reality up by means of one descriptive statement—and there are many such different points of view. None of these points of view taken singly *completely* expresses *the* nature of reality but each can express *a* truth about it which is conditional on the point of view involved. So although it is not possible to know reality in its complex richness by means of one statement or doctrine, it is possible for us to continue to know it (as far as the intellect is concerned, that is), by means of a series of statements each of which will only be a partial truth as far as the whole of reality is concerned. Absolute affirmation and absolute negation of any statement are thus both inadmissible, for they must be understood relatively to a standpoint (*naya*). That is to say, we cannot say that reality is X or it is not X categorically, without any qualification, and a statement that is false if advanced absolutely may turn out to be true when suitably qualified by reference to the particular standpoint into which it fits.

Because of the importance of this doctrine for the understanding of Indian philosophy (in my opinion, that is) I shall permit myself a few quotes from *Sanmati Tarka* by Siddhasena Divākara.

> "All the *nayas*, therefore, in their exclusively individual standpoints are absolutely faulty. If, however, they consider themselves as supplementary to each other, they are right in their viewpoints."[1]

That is to say, every *naya* has its own justification and truth (because reality is complex), but if it arrogates to itself the whole truth and disregards the view of rival *nayas* it does not attain the status of a right view. Again, "if all the *nayas*," (there can be an infinite number of them) "arrange themselves in a proper way and supplement each other then alone they are worthy of being termed as 'the whole truth' or the right view in its entirety. But in this case they merge their individuality in the collective whole."[2] That is, they are then seen as aspects of something bigger than themselves and thus their normal aggressive and exclusive individuality as an assertion about reality is lost. So a man who knows about the many-sided character of reality and the conditional nature of truth never says that a particular view is right or that a particular view is wrong. He will try to find out in what way it is right or in what way it is wrong.

The Jains offer a schema, that of seven-fold formula of predication, to cover all possible kinds of statements that can truly be made of anything (as regards something is or is not the case) from different points of view, of which there are an infinite number. The seven stands involved here thus involve a schematic representation of the various kinds of statements that can all be truly asserted of the same thing at the same time if made from different points of view and it is not intended to limit the points of view one can adopt to seven. To show that every statement explores only one of several possibilities the statement is qualified by 'may be'.

1. S. Radhakrishnan and C. A. Moore (ed): *A Source Book in Indian Philosophy* (Princeton, N. J. : Princeton University Press, 1957), p. 270.

2. *Ibid.*

(1) May be X is
(2) May be X is not
(3) May be X is and is not (1 and 2 combined but looked at successively)
(4) May be X is inexpressible (1 and 2 combined but looked at simultaneously, which makes predicate either way impossible)
(5) May be X is and it is inexpressible (1 combined with 4)
(6) May be X is not and it is inexpressible (2 combined with 4)
(7) May be X is and it is not and it is inexpressible (3 combined with 4).

To assert any one of these statements and say that this is the only way in which the existence or non-existence of X can be understood is a dogmatic procedure and it makes us unable to see the many-sided nature of reality.

Another thing to notice about the Jain doctrine is that its relativism is perfectly compatible with choice and preference and the adoption of a particular point of view as one's own. The Jains themselves had a particular understanding of reality from which they advocated non-violence as a mode of practice and the liberation of the soul from all finite and limiting circumstances as the ultimate aim of life.

Jainism, as considered by the Hindus, is a heterodox school. That is to say, it did not recognize the Vedas (the sacred literature of the Hindus) as the foundation of all its thinking. There were two other heterodox schools of philosophy, *Cārvāka* and Buddhism. *Cārvāka* denied not only the authority of the Vedas but it pretty well denied most things dear to Indian culture, God, soul, (consciousness is a function of material elements, and this is contrary to all other opinions), rebirth, liberation and indeed the organic outlook itself. No wonder it eventually disappeared from the philosophical scene. The other heterodox school, Buddhism, I shall talk about later. But the fact that Jainism did not accept the Vedas does not mean that it rejected, like *Cārvāka*, the world view of Indian culture, and it was perfectly possible for this school to have developed a philosophical doctrine to express this world view.

Orthodox schools of Indian philosophy are those which accepted the authority of the Vedas as the basis of one's philosophical thinking and there are six such schools: Nyāya, Vaiśeṣika, Sāṁkhya, Yoga, Mīmāṁsā and Vedānta. But each of these schools went its own way (or one paired with another) in exploring the nature of reality that the Vedas affirm and each exploration was done from a specific standpoint of inquiry. The Vedas are versatile (being the repository of the organic view as far as the Hindu tradition is concerned) and they affirm the reality of all things, both material and spiritual. It was thus perfectly possible for the schools to affirm the authority of the Vedas and then adopt a particular standpoint in investigating the nature of reality. The standpoints varied from that of commonsense to transcendentalism but even a commonsensical standpoint accepted the reality of self and a transcendent (transcendent to space-time-causal categories) dimension of reality, both affirmed by the Vedas. But the acceptance of the transcendent dimension by all does not mean that all philosophy was transcendental philosophy, for this acceptance was perfectly compatible with realist, empiricist and pragmatist approaches to reality. Besides this side of transcendence, a mixture of commonsensical and transcendental concern, held together, is a perfect example of what I call the organic world view. What follows below is a brief account of the six orthodox schools and of the Buddhist philosophy.

Nyāya is primarily concerned with logical and epistemological questions, which takes for granted the reality of the world that figures in commonsense and we may say that the Nyāya standpoint of inquiry is commonsensical—the nature of knowledge and its validity, the instruments of knowledge (the various means by which we come to know what there is), the nature of truth and error and the like. (Contrary to Śaṁkara, the commonsense world has nowhere been denied in the Vedic literature and the Upaniṣads even declared that Brahman became food, air, water etc.) Nyāya as befits commonsense takes the world as talked about in language to be in its own nature, exactly as language suggests it is like and this is in sharp contrast with the Buddhist view of language and reality where language creates the reality it talks about (the Buddhist standpoint is one which wishes to destroy our commonsense understanding of things, as such understanding stands in the way of the realization of the Buddhist truth). Language is thus for Nyāya, a sort of copy of reality on the symbolic level and knowledge has no form of its own to give to things; on the contrary it assumes, on the mental plane, the form things have. In other words, the function of knowledge is to duplicate in our understanding the form of the various contents of this world that are there independently of us, and it is done through the use of various instruments of knowledge; its role is not to create the world as idealism supposes. Its epistemological stance is thus empirical, or better, experiential for it takes words like 'self' and 'God' to have real referents as well as words that denote sensory properties. And these words belong to the world of commonsense (it is philosophers who deny that they have applicability, not the average man) besides being sanctioned by the Vedas. The purpose of an investigation into knowledge is to gain a clear, consistent and detailed picture of the world as reflected in language and 'self' and 'God' are a normal part of our commonsense vocabulary. By 'self' is understood the subject of experience, the knowledge of which arises through direct self-consciousness in the wake of object knowledge or on reflection on such knowledge and the existence of God known either through direct experience (intuitive) as by the seers or through verbal testimony (a valid instrument of knowledge). Both the existence of 'self' and 'God' can be subsequently established through a process of inference (*sāmānyatodṛṣṭa* = analogical reasoning). As far as the objects with which sense contact can be made are concerned they are known, and must be so known if our understanding is to be called knowledge, through perception and inference based upon perception, and detailed discussion takes place in extensive Nyāya literature on both these instruments of knowledge.

Now there is another orthodox school, the Vaiśeṣika, which also investigates the world from the standpoint of commonsense but with a different stance to it. That is, its purpose is ontological rather than epistemological and it proposes that all that there is can be understood under the heading of seven categories. The *Vaiśeṣika Sūtras* of Kaṇāda does not mention God but because of the amalgamation of Nyāya with Vaiśeṣika—this happened because of their common standpoint—the system called 'Nyāya-Vaiśeṣika' is taken to be theistic. The seven categories (adopted by Nyāya) are substance (of which there are nine varieties including mind and self but not God), quality, action, universality, particularity, a relation called 'inherence' (as of quality in a substance), and non-existence. It is insisted that a description of experience needs the category of absence as well as of presence, to notice the absence of X in room Y is not quite the same thing as to notice room Y where X is not present without anyone noticing that this is so. Nyāya introduces another relation, that of causality. The Nyāya-Vaiśeṣika school comes upon the concept of atoms in course of reflection on 'substance'. These are imperceptible, of the smallest possible dimension or of no measurable dimension and it is out of the combinations of these, first in twos and then in three of these twos, that perceptible elements like earth, water, air, fire and ether arise. According to this notion of atoms, they differ according to their potentiality to give rise to different qualities. (The atoms of earth possess the potentiality of the quality of smell as different from atoms of fire which have the potentiality for colour and so on.) So qualities are not simply the result of different quantities of the same thing, as was thought in Greece.

The attitude in Nyāya-Vaiśeṣika remains commonsensical throughout. Space and time, for instance, are taken as objective realities in commonsense, so they are in the school, only they become infinite and pointless, points and instants representing conventional divisions of these realities. Self as in commonsense is taken to be the subject of experience because of which it is said to possess the attribute of consciousness rather than being of the very nature of consciousness (as in Sāṁkhya and Vedānta). God is taken to be a person; this as well as the idea that he is the author of the Vedas are commonsensical positions (as against philosophical positions that the ultimate reality is supra-personal and the Vedas have no author). The commonsensical orientation of Nyāya-Vaiśeṣika is shown in its discussion of both perception and inference. Objects do not produce an impression in the mind via the sense organs, (incidentally the mind is conceived as an organ of knowledge like eyes and ears, but an internal one), the sensory properties of the organs themselves take the form of the objects because of which the danger of representationalism, the doctrine that we only know mental images of things, not the things directly, is avoided. Because the sense organs are composed of the same atomic properties which go into the constitution of objects they take the form of—the eye is composed of atoms of fire, the same atoms give rise to colour—there is felt no difficulty in the matter of direct revelation of objects to the senses. Perception which is eligible to be called knowledge (that is determinate perception as opposed to indeterminate) issues in a judgment the business of which is to clearly set forth the complex content of what is being perceived as an entity qualified in a certain way, a simple example of which is 'the pot is blue'. Both the entity and the quality may themselves be complex and this can be comprehended through further qualification like 'the Chinese vase is peacock blue' and so on. The qualities inhere in objects and they are understood to be what they are through the apprehension of universals like blueness which is a real entity and which resides in blue objects, the reason why it has to be called blue rather than, say, green.

The Nyāya understanding of inference too is a refinement of commonsense reasoning which does not proceed by dividing itself up into inductive and deductive but rather incorporates both elements in a complex procedure. It goes like this: 'There is fire in the mountain' (conclusion stated first just as we often do in commonsense argument) 'because there is smoke' (reason). 'And whenever there is smoke there is fire' (this gives the ground on which the reason is advanced, the ground itself being based on inductive generalization), 'As in the kitchen' (this gives an example of the kind of instances on which the generalization is based). So the conclusion 'there is fire in the mountain' stated at the very beginning of the reasoning process is thought to be established on a valid process of inference involving both deductive and inductive procedures (that is, an understanding of invariable concomitance between fire and smoke, itself based on experience).

According to Nyāya whether a piece of knowledge is true or false can be determined by verification by the test of practice. If something we say is water actually quenches our thirst, the statement, 'it is water' is true. The definition of knowledge however is not that it works, this only provides a *test* of the validity of a piece of knowledge. Validity itself lies in correspondence with reality, a thoroughly commonsensical notion. Nyāya as distinct from Vaiśeṣika accepts two more instruments of knowledge. One is *upamāna* (similarity). There is an object B which we do not know and it resembles A which we do know. We are told B resembles A in such and such a way, then we come across B, notice the similarity and identify it as B. The common-sense slant of this particular instrument of knowledge is evident. The remaining instrument is verbal testimony. Nyāya was one of the most influential schools of philosophy that developed in India and it provided other schools with many of their basic tools of analysis. It also had the longest life.

The next school of philosophy is Sāṁkhya, the most misunderstood school. Its point of view is exploration of that particular element in man's being that is called *Puruṣa* or self and it does this by isolating it analytically from the rest of man's being, his psycho-physical system. This is often misinterpreted as a programme of man's isolation from the world, thought to be necessary for liberation. The word *prakṛti* (nature) means both man's psycho-biological system and the world in which this system operates and when Sāṁkhya talks about the isolation of *Puruṣa* from *prakṛti* it means *prakṛti* as present in man's being, because only by doing this man can come to know his *Puruṣa* nature, face to face. Sāṁkhya is not mysticism, although often mistakenly treated as such by many; and since knowledge about man's nature as Self is here pursued in a logical, rational manner, Sāṃkhya calls itself philosophy. And although man's knowledge of his nature as Self means liberation, the philosophy is pursued as a quest for knowledge of the Self rather than as a quest for liberation.

Sāṁkhya starts with the idea that there are two entirely distinct kinds of realities in the world, *Puruṣa* and *prakṛti*, both eternal and independent of one another but one is often confused with the other, when it comes to man's own reality, and herein lies the cause of man's suffering. Because the enterprise is concerned with man's nature Sāṁkhya leaves aside the question of God as irrelevant to its purposes, saying that as His existence cannot be proved we shall not be concerned with this question here. The two realities both lie within the realm of experience. *Puruṣa* often means in Indian thought consciousness as such, meaning the very principle of consciousness referred to as pure consciousness (and not a subject who enjoys conscious states of mind), and this is self-evident or better auto-transparent so that its presence cannot be denied. Nature too exists in such a manner that no question about its existence arises. (All orthodox schools are realistic in the sense that the existence of what we know independently of the act of knowledge is never questioned.)

According to Sāṁkhya there can be no interaction between these two realities so utterly distinct from each other, one the nature of pure consciousness, the other the source of rest of the universe, including physical elements, man's physiological and mental attributes and so on. Sāṁkhya dualism is thus distinct from what is known as mind-body dualism in the Western tradition. For according to Sāṁkhya mind and body both belong to the side of nature and the divide is between pure consciousness and mind-body, not between mind and body. Mental activities, including thinking, are not auto-transparent and they acquire this quality only when the light of pure consciousness also present in man is reflected in mental states, whereby they become present to themselves and consciousness itself is confused as a mental state rather than as a pure function of awareness that is present to itself. Mental activities are a part of the natural constitution of man and although much more subtle than the physical they belong along with the physical to *prakṛti*. Now in order to make discrimination between the two realities evident, Sāṁkhya goes in detail into the constitution of *prakṛti* and its manifestations showing how everything else in man but pure consciousness arises out of it. Then it argues that as there can be no interaction between pure consciousness and *prakṛtic* states, a man is nothing but pure consciousness and his identification of himself as *prakṛtic* states—this identification cannot happen unless he is conscious of mental states and he is conscious of them only because of the reflection of pure consciousness in them—is a result of confusion between the two realities. This I think is the real weakness of Sāṁkhya. In order to make clear the distinction between the two realities it makes them utterly independent of each other, so that man's understanding of himself as Self requires the rejection of the psycho-biological system as part of man's reality. This extreme step is not strictly necessary for achieving Sāṁkhya's objectives and Sāṁkhya is forced to contradict itself as a result of this step. Self or pure consciousness can have no individuality. *Puruṣa* is identified with Self and yet Sāṁkhya says that there is a plurality of *Puruṣas* because one man's liberation is not that of another. Surely these men cannot be just pure consciousness, if they were, the question of their liberating themselves from the psycho-biological system would not have arisen. So I believe that Sāṁkhya is taken in by its own strategy and an analytical distinction is hypostatised as a result into an absolute fact. However, to proceed with Sāṁkhya's explanation of how things arise out of *Prakṛti*.

Prakṛti (nature) accounts for everything in the universe except for pure consciousness. It has a manifest and an unmanifest being; it is unmanifest when the three strands of energy of which it is composed are in equilibrium and when all change or activity is of like kind. Manifestation, and this means evolution of *prakṛti's* potentiality for being, starts when disequilibrium happens among the three strands of energy which are subtle and can be conceived both in physical and psychic terms—*sattva* signifies physical manifestation like that of light and calm, poise and purity when applied to mental states, *rajas* signifies drive and expenditure of energy in the physical world as well as mental restlessness and *tamas* signifies inertia (physical), dullness and stupidity (mental). Evolution takes place from the subtle to the gross, *prakṛti* herself being nothing other than a system of subtle energies. The first to appear in the sphere of manifestation is cosmic intelligence which sets the stage, as it were, for all happenings (all happenings are law-governed). Then arises an I-making tendency, the tendency for individuation of what is so far undifferentiated being. Then arise the mind and the senses on one line of development, sensory qualities, subtle essence of the five elements to which these qualities belong, the five elements themselves and finally gross objects (in that order) on another line of development. A human being complete with body, the senses and the mind (that is, mental activities of thinking, feeling and willing) is an evolute of the natural order and he differs from other natural evolutes only in degree of subtlety of energy manifestation. Sāṁkhya, therefore, will accept all behaviourist and positivistic evaluations of man, including that of computer science which claims that there is no essential difference between human and computer intelligence, with one reservation. Besides the body and the mind the human being in his constitution shows the presence of something else, pure consciousness, an auto-transparent function of awareness (this is not to be confused with intelligent functioning), which is not an evolute of *prakṛti* and which has an independent being of its own. Indeed Sāṁkhya goes to the extent of saying that man is to be identified with this reality and his identification of himself with his mental happenings results from a reflection of this auto-transparent function of awareness in his mental continuum which becomes illumined as a result. That is to say, mental states become conscious because of the reflection of the light of consciousness in them and then man takes these states to be himself while, as a matter of fact, he is nothing but pure consciousness. Sāṁkhya's difficulty in saying that man is both mind-body, a natural system governed by nature's law, and a function of pure consciousness lies in the fact that according to it these two opposite kinds of realities cannot interact and man cannot therefore be a composite being. It does not use the more usual non-dualistic picture of Indian thought that all energy, spiritual to physical, belong to one continuum although differing in 'name, shape and function' at different levels of manifestation as that would not have served its purpose, of isolating the element of pure consciousness from everything else in man, his psycho-biological being, a technique whereby man can come face to face with that element of his being which makes his mental states conscious but which he takes (mistakenly) to be an attribute of his mind. This eventually means the denial of man's spiritual being, for mind can be explained in purely physical terms. It also means man's subjection of himself to suffering which arises out of the natural order.

The language of *Sāṁkhya Kārikā* is bound to sound very archaic to modern ideas, but the system is surprisingly "modern" in some of its implications. The school believes itself to be engaged in a 'rational' pursuit—*Puruṣa* is postulated on the basis of direct experience and subtle *prakṛti* on the basis of rational reflection. Nothing can come out of nothing, so the effect can only be a redistribution of the potentialities that are inherent in its cause. Things of this universe thus presuppose an infinite potentiality for being, and this is *prakṛti*. Intelligence is present in the functioning of nature, of animals and human beings, indeed in all law-governed activity, so this is the first evolute of *prakṛti* and not one of its later stages. Thought, feeling and action all take place without the aid of the auto-transparency of consciousness (although they may be illumined by this auto-transparent function and as a result become conscious of themselves as thought, feeling and action), so they too belong to nature's potentiality for being. But as the effect cannot be something that is not inherently present in the cause auto-transparency of consciousness cannot be the effect of intelligence or any other physical cause which is not in its own nature auto-transparent (as intelligence present in nature or the animal world is not). It is therefore not something produced, it is eternally there, just as *prakṛti* is. The system does not deny the existence of God, but considers the issue not to be relevant to man's recognition of his own nature as *Puruṣa* (Self). Man is not defined in this school (the same with most other Indian schools of philosophy) as a rational animal, or as a being capable of thought, but as pure consciousness. This consciousness is not to be understood just as awareness, something that is present in all intelligent functioning. Awareness is present in the plant and the animal world. What is extra in man is something else, the essential nature of which is to be aware of itself as present, being self-illumined (as intelligence is not, except when the light of consciousness falls on it—intelligence by itself means awareness of something given to it as an object, not awareness of itself as itself). What ordinarily passes as consciousness is consciousness of something or other and this could be profitably distinguished from pure consciousness by labelling it 'modal consciousness' which is a mental state illumined by the light of consciousness. Pure consciousness is just the auto-transparent function, considered by itself, without any association with a mental state. This dimension of reality can actually be experienced and how to experience it is the subject of the next school of philosophy, Yoga.

Yoga is usually paired with Sāṁkhya as Sāṁkhya-Yoga, for it accepts the philosophy of Sāṁkhya and then develops a technique of how actually to isolate the *Puruṣa* element of man's nature from the *prakṛtic* element. However, although the aim of Yoga is isolation of *Puruṣa,* the same as in Sāṁkhya, the tech niques used are such that they do not imply that man is just *Puruṣa.* (Actually Sāṁkhya itself may be so interpreted that what it says is not that man is *Puruṣa* and that his identification of himself with his psycho-biological system is a result of confusion but that *Puruṣa* is *Puruṣa* and it mistakenly identifies itself with *prakṛti,* the psycho-biological system that man also is.) For it is man as a psycho-biological system that has to make the effort to create a condition such that *Puruṣa* can come to see itself as *Puruṣa*. And this means that man is both *Puruṣa* and *prakṛti* (the psycho-biological system). But, obviously according to this school of thought, man's higher nature (that which is immortal) is *Puruṣa*, and man can get at it, initially at any rate, by stilling the *prakṛtic* element in him, because *prakṛti* occupies the whole of the stage and man fails to realize his *Puruṣa* nature without getting it out of the way. Once this happens man can continue to be *prakṛti* but as its master, not its slave, as the man unenlightened about his 'real' nature tends to be. And there is a hint of this in the *Yoga Sūtras* when it says that man must not only transcend *prakṛti*, having realized himself as *Puruṣa* in a state of *samādhi* (enstasis according to Eliade's translation but there is no English equivalent) he must transcend that state as well. And I take this to mean that an enlightened man is not only not a slave of *prakṛti*, he is not a slave of his enlightenment either and only if he is a slave of enlightenment need he cut himself off from *prakṛti* (this can be done only to a degree at any rate, as the *Gītā* says a man has to acknowledge his *prakṛti* nature even to continue to remain alive).

We need not go into detail about the techniques recommended by the Yoga school. They are partly ethical, partly physical, and partly mental. The aim is to make the mental continuum empty of all states and this needs ethical purification (this is needed even to start the process) and physical fitness (because the path is hard and it needs a great deal of striving). One of the mental techniques consists of withdrawal of the mind so that neither external nor internal stimuli can disturb its equanimity. And the application of this technique contributes enormously to our understanding of ourselves even as *prakṛti*. Like psychoanalysis, Yoga considers that the main motivations and drives behind our activities, (intellectual included) lie in the unconscious mind—this is a normal way of functioning of *prakṛti* and it is not constituted out of repressed material—as latencies. A conscious effort on our part to control the mind such that no stimuli can get in brings these latencies out in the open because of the drive on their part to get control. We thus come face to face with our *prakṛtic* constitution as well, especially those tendencies like lust, anger, jealousy, fear and so on, which constitute our primordial nature. Control of the mind, without any knowledge of what goes on there is impossible and what goes on there is normally below the conscious level, the reason why a special technique is necessary. With some control of the mind, concentration on one thing only to the exclusion of all else becomes possible and this leads to meditation and finally *samādhi*, a state in which the stage is completely empty of all *prakṛtic* elements and so *Puruṣa* shining by its own light can be realized as such. This is because there is no state of mind with which it can be confused and thereby get reduced to the status of a conscious state of the mind.

This self-understanding of man is considered philosophy rather than religion for its aim is knowledge and not faith or devotion. And as non-sensory apprehension or comprehension is considered to qualify as knowledge, in the Indian context, the fact that the knowledge involved is gained neither through sense perception nor through ratiocination—although ratiocination is certainly involved in Sāṁkhya deliberations—does not mean that it is to be labelled as mysticism (no Sanskrit term exists for "mysticism").

The contribution of Sāṁkhya-Yoga as regards the concept of "knowledge" is concerned is that although it agrees with Nyāya that in knowing the mind takes the form of the object the bias of the individual knower can enter into the knowing process and as a result, one and the same damsel can appear differently to different persons. It is thus in accordance with the relativism/pluralism of the organic world view despite the fact that it has its own philosophical position. It is not relativism in the sense that you can say what you like, for it suggests that we know things truly when we supplement our own view by all other possible views of it. Such a comprehensive knowledge is rare (if at all possible), so what we actually know is partial truth and so two people holding two different views may both be right in their own ways. In accordance with Sāṁkhya's own dictum we can say that its view (if indeed it holds this view) that man is nothing but *Puruṣa* has to be supplemented by the view that man is *prakṛti*, if we want a fuller understanding of man.

Sāṁkhya is dualistic, apparently at any rate, while the Vedas are non-dualistic, which may create some difficulty in our understanding how it can be said to be exploring Vedic reality. It does this exploration, of course, from its own point of view, that is, self-exploration, and the idea of Self is one of the dominant ideas in the Vedic literature. Since Sāṁkhya accepts Vedic testimony as a source of knowledge, I have come to think of Sāṁkhya dualism as an analytical device, contrary to what I have held in my previous writings on Sāṁkhya, and this device is necessary, for unless a complete separation is effected between consciousness and the mind so that consciousness remains but without the benefit of a mental state one takes it as an attribute of the mind. Consciousness then becomes consciousness of somebody (a psycho-biological organism) which must at the same time be consciousness of something, while pure consciousness as conceived by Sāṁkhya and realized by Yoga is not tied up with a particular psycho-biological organism nor need it be directed towards anything. It is a self-existent auto-transparent reality which may come to be qualified through the reducing mechanism of the limited mind-body system in the context of which it functions.

Mīmāṁsā, the next orthodox system to be considered, not only accepts the authority of the Vedas but its point of view is itself the establishment of this authority on what it believes to be 'rational' grounds. The Vedas have authority because man's transcendental goal, achievement of heaven or *mokṣa*, being beyond the scope of empirical knowledge, can be secured only by following the injunctions and prohibitions prescribed therein and the Vedas are to be taken as a compendium of just those injunctions and prohibitions, with a view to helping man to his transcendental goal. They are not about gods who figure there purely for the sake of imaginative appeal. And Mīmāṁsā does not accept the idea of God as the author of the Vedas either. The Vedas are eternal and they have no author, human or divine. The world too exists eternally, undergoing constant change, and it is a pluralistic world of a variety of things and selves. Selves create their own fortunes by their own actions. Apart from actions enjoined by the Vedas there are moral actions—these have instrumental value for religious life with its transcendent goal—which are based on considerations of human interest and happiness and they are of importance from an empirical, and also social point of view. Indeed Mīmāṁsā combines orthodoxy in the matter of Vedic authority over man's religious life with a mainly pragmatic attitude to values (non-religious), an empiricist epistemology and a realist ontology with regard to this-worldly affairs. The aim of all knowledge is action which is absolutely central to human existence. There are five instruments of knowledge: perception, inference, comparison, postulation and non-cognition (a special way of knowing by which the absence of things is discerned). All empirical matters are to be ascertained by these means which are actually used in the field of empirical knowledge.

The authority of the Vedas is sought by Mīmāṁsā to be established on the basis of certain theories of knowledge and language. Knowledge is valid by its own nature (this doctrine is called self-validity of knowledge) and it can go wrong only because of imperfections of human beings and defects in the instruments they use. In the case of the Vedas nothing can go wrong as no authors are involved, Vedic knowledge being self-generated and eternally existent. As for language (this is important because the Vedas exist in and through language) this is not a human creation either, it too exists as a natural phenomenon, formed as it is of sounds which are eternal. A certain combination of these sounds makes a word and the relationship between the word and its meaning is a natural and necessary one; it is not conventional, fixed by society. Meanings and things do not exist prior to and independently of words, words and things (or rather the universals which things manifest) are two sides of the same coin, so to say. (As we shall see the Buddhists too contend that things do not exist independently of language but for them language creates the thing whereas for Mīmāṁsā language expresses the essence of the thing and although this essence does not exist prior to language, language does not create it either.) Language and the reality it refers to exist together, as the same reality viewed in different ways. To be sure, there is no conventional element in language, since it has to be learnt, but Mīmāṁsā gives a most unsatisfactory answer as to where this element lies. I think that despite Mīmāṁsā's hunch that there is something "necessary", even "natural" about the use of human language and about some of the elements that go into the constitution of a language which cannot be explained as a fortuitous human creation—without language the specifically human world does not exist—or a pragmatic human convenience, the issue got bogged down by the need to establish the infallibility and the eternality of the Vedas. Since the absolute validity of the Vedas was supposed to lie in the particular order in which words are organized in the Vedic sentences, it appears that the conventional element in human language too lies in the particular order (different from the Vedic one) in which words are organized in ordinary sentences. This is a poor outcome of an important direction of enquiry about language but this was decided by the particular point of view from which Mīmāṁsā asked questions about it.

It appears to me that what Mīmāṁsā is doing is to uphold the ritualistic structure of the mainstream of Indian culture. It is possible to do so without God or gods but not religious ritual or performance of conventional duties as enjoined by tradition. Brahmin-dominated Hindu culture was heavily ritualistic, to question which so often appears questioning the Hinduism itself, as in the case of Buddha. But once ritual is taken care of, human understanding of other matters of importance could be realistic, empiricist and pragmatic. So we get here what some modern interpreters consider to be a peculiar mixture of orthodoxy and pragmatism-realism. But it is characteristic of the Hindu culture that no difficulty was felt over the fact that the philosophical attitudes one takes towards "matters of fact" should be so radically different from the ones one takes towards religion, because even the philosophers accepted that transcendent goals and their requirements cannot be judged in terms of empirical instruments of knowledge. However, with everything in its proper place, the empirical approach retains its importance in its own sphere which is far from illusory. And it goes further than most systems in recognizing commonsense ways of knowing such as comparison, postulation and non-cognition. (We say things like 'I see that X is not here.')

The next orthodox system is Vedānta, of which I shall consider only Advaita Vedānta of Śaṁkara which is given more attention than any other system of Vedānta by investigators, both Indian and western, because it fits in with the stereotype that has been built in recent centuries about Indian thought—its transcendental or spiritual character that rejects the world as illusory. The characteristic thing about Śaṁkara is not non-dualism—one can be a non-dualist after the fashion of the *Upaniṣads*, or even as a theist as are some people following the philosophy of Tantra, Vaiṣṇavism and Śaivism. Anyone who believes that at the ultimate level of understanding the reality present in all things would be found to be one and the same as the transcendent reality (so-called) that is infinite in its being, sharing in its essence in different degrees at different levels of being, is a non-dualist. What marks Śaṁkara out as different from any other non-dualist in the orthodox tradition is the status that he gives to the phenomenal world.

The orthodox tradition is generally acknowledged to be the inheritor of the Vedic-Upaniṣadic thought, books in which the reality of all things is affirmed time and again, particularly through myths, one of which (to be found in more than one *Upaniṣad*) says that the world of plurality exists because that which is one wanted to be many and so it became the many through assuming different name, shape and work. The one is of course still the Real of the real, other things are real only as its expressions and not as independent things. Because of this affirmation all orthodox schools offer a realist ontology and as its complementary an empiricist epistemology. Even Sāṁkhya which says that the real man is just the Self and not the mind-body, nevertheless, gives an independent and real existence to the world of nature out of which mind-body arises, and there is besides a plurality of selves. But there was a very influential development of an unorthodox nature (not "derived" from the Vedas, that is) within the Indian culture, viz., the Buddhism, which took the opposite path and instead of affirming everything it negated it all, saying that there is nothing substantial in the world at all, all things being bundles of fleeting, changing states or moments with no 'core' which can give them identity. This is tied up with the Buddhist metaphysical doctrine, 'everything is suffering.' (In the Hindu tradition, pre-Buddhist that is, Sāṁkhya affirms that there are three kinds of suffering that man can overcome through knowledge, but not the metaphysical doctrine that everything is suffering.) It follows that the ordinary belief in enduring things and selves is an illusion in the sense in which seeing a snake in a rope is an illusion (this originally a Buddhist example is later borrowed by Śaṃkara) and it is first in the Buddhist thought that the Sanskrit term *māyā* acquires the connotation of illusion, its meaning in pre-Śaṁkarite, orthodox tradition being 'magic like power of creation that can bring forth many out of the one.' The Buddhism, in accordance with its own strategy and metaphysics, develops—contrary to orthodox schools—an idealist ontology and epistemology and it is here that we first encounter in India the thought that the external world is a projection of the human mind and that things as we know them have no reality outside the knowledge of them in a knowing mind.

As I have remarked earlier, the way of the Vedic wisdom is affirmation because here ultimate reality is conceived to be delight (*ānanda*) besides being pure being and consciousness. All things are, because they arise out of this pure joy and are sustained by it as their ground. This underlying affirmation of a reality positively conceived gives the orthodox schools a realist bent as opposed to the idealist bent of Buddhism which is in accordance with its negative strategy of denial rather than of affirmation. But with Śaṁkara the Buddhist influence enters the orthodox sphere in a big way and he develops the so-called Advaita doctrine of *māyā* (in the Buddhist sense of illusion that lacks ultimate substantiality) by interpreting the Upaniṣadic affirmation of non-duality as numerical oneness rather than as a reality that remains one while expressing itself as many in the phenomenal world of change and transience. However remaining firmly within the Hindu fold, Śaṁkara did not completely abandon the orthodox way of affirmation and even realism of a sort.

In Śaṁkara's thought the reality that we experience as the phenomenal world is not a projection of the individual human mind, as in the Buddhism. It is independent of man's knowing activity and it is really there as long as man lives in ignorance. (So Śaṁkara advocates a realist epistemology as far as our knowledge of the phenomenal world is concerned.) What projects it is a quasi-real force called *māyā* that imposes the world of plurality on to the oneness (numerically interpreted) of Brahman. *Māyā* is mysterious—said to be a mixture of being and non-being, and no explanation is given how it comes to be there. It does not belong to Brahman, and man being himself the product of *māyā* cannot create it. As *māyā* does not express the creative power of Brahman what it projects 'disappears' when one realizes Brahman. But the non-existence of the world holds good only from the ultimate point of view, where the sole reality of Brahman is revealed; at levels below this (said to be the sphere of ignorance) the world is real enough. A better example of Śaṁkara's sense of illusion than the snake in the rope, it seems to me, would be two equal straight lines with arrows at both ends, one pair of arrows pointing outwards and the other inwards, the line with outward-pointing arrows appearing bigger than the line with inward-pointing arrows. This illusion is not individual but is built into the perceptual process. Also, Śaṁkara would have done better had he said not that the very existence of the world is illusory but the structure of meaning and significance that we build into our experiences are illusory and as a result we get attached, for this is what we have to transcend in order to realize the level of non-duality.

Anyway, the difference between the non-dualism of the *Upaniṣad* and that of Śaṁkara, as I understand it, is that the former sees multiplicity to express the essence of Brahman as multiplicity that is changing and transient, without thereby causing any diminution in Brahman's being—because Brahman is all—while Śaṁkara sees it as superimposed on Brahman by some force which comes from somewhere else. (This is supposed, under cover of inconceivability, not to affect the sole reality of Brahman as the one Reality.) The important point about this philosophy, however, is that it treats the Vedic knowledge from the point of view of exploring what there is ultimately, and from that vantage point Brahman is the sole reality with or without expressing itself in multiplicity. Śaṁkara's denial of multiplicity seems to me a strategy, whereby this ultimate Reality is presented to us, neat, as it were, without the admixture of anything that can detract from our understanding of it as the One Reality. That this can have undesirable side effects, is unfortunate.

The Buddhism arose as an ethico-spiritual teaching, the aim of which was conceived as *nirvāṇa*, a negative term meaning the extinguishing of everything that is associated with ignorance and suffering. Suffering is caused by attachment to the world and its strategy was to preach that the world does not really exist in the shape which we apparently perceive it to have and which creates attachment. Hence the philosophical schools that arose out of this teaching have an idealist leaning in their epistemology—the human mind projects or creates the world it perceives via latent impressions and conceptual activity, either wholly or in part. It thus develops the idea of the element of subjectivity in all experience whereby the world becomes, partly at least, a construction. Being a transcendental enterprise, that of leading man beyond the state of suffering, the fact that the world of experience is a construction is not viewed neutrally, as by Kant (for whom this does not in any way detract from its importance,) but is thought to give the world of experience the status of illusory being. All schools of the Buddhism, thus, involve a distinction between appearance and reality and the Upaniṣadic idea of two kinds of knowledge, higher (about Brahman) and lower (about the world) here is presented as the distinction between knowledge and ignorance. (This Buddhist terminology too, whereby the knowledge about this world is presented as ignorance, enters the Hindu sphere of thought.) All schools of the Buddhist philosophy are not equally idealistic, of course; of the four schools, two (Vaibhāṣika and Sautrāntika) are looked upon as realistic because, although the world does not exist in reality in the shape of enduring objects and persons, according to them there are some real elements (*dharmas*) of matter, mind and forces—altogether seventy two in number. Every element is a separate entity, but elements 'co-operate' with one another according to the law of combined dependent origination (this being that happens). That is, elements appear accompanied by others that arise in close contiguity. A moment of colour, a moment of visual sense and a moment of consciousness arising in close contiguity together represent a sensation of colour, but the colour itself is not an enduring quality that belongs to an enduring object. The idea of identity, endurance, etc. whereby the world becomes a stable world of things and beings in place of an everchanging scene of transitory events is contributed by the mind. And the subject of experience does not exist as a self, soul or ego either, he too is an aggregate of changing states of sensation, perception, feeling, inner drives and consciousness.

The Sautrāntika develops the idea of the unique particular as being the reality behind appearances by producing various intricate logical arguments (which are its own contribution as distinct from those of the Vaibhāṣika). The criterion of reality must be efficiency, efficiency must mean change and change must mean change at every moment. So there is no such thing as an object that remains the same for two consecutive moments. The argument against the idea of the whole as distinct from parts goes like this. Does the whole reside wholly in each part or only partially ? If the former, it would be exhausted in one part and if partially then we still need something else to produce wholeness, and so on. Likewise universals are unacceptable being only a thought construct, by means of which the world of appearance and ignorance is built up along with other concepts like substance, relation, etc. This view thus makes the Kantian distinction thing-in-itself and thing-as-it appears with this difference that for the Buddhist the thing-in-itself can be directly known in some special types of experience.

The Mâdhyamika school of Buddhist philosophy develops a critical attitude to the very use of concepts only by applying which human experience can be understood to have a certain nature. Here it is recognized that all concepts are relative to their opposites, so that, if there is no such thing as the 'same' object appearing at successive moments, there are neither wholly different particulars, as the concept 'different' has no meaning apart from the concept 'same'. Furthermore when we try to give a precise meaning either to the concept 'different' or to the concept 'same' we find that they are full of contradictions. It cannot, therefore, be said that reality is of the nature of discrete and unique particulars as distinct from universals or wholes. All concepts being of this contradictory character, there is no such thing as a true description of reality which, in its own nature, is void of all descriptive contents and cannot be known by intellectual means. So there can be no doctrine about the nature of reality, as doctrines have to use concepts and all concepts are essentially relative to their opposites. Insofar as all experience is dependent on a thought category it must be understood to be misleading as far as the true nature of reality is concerned. This as the Absolute is beyond thought.

This critical attitude which resulted in the denial of all metaphysics was followed by a school of pure idealism (Yogācāra). It rejects the Sautrāntika distinction between the thing-in-itself, the unique particular objectively given and subjective categories contributed by the mind by using a Berkeleyan type of argument to show that what we call the 'object' is the idea itself. So it holds that the whole of experience is a mental construction and is unreal through and through, but it differs from Mādhyamika in accepting one category, that of the mind, as real. Consciousness is the only reality according to this school, only its projections falsely believed to be objectively given are unreal or illusory. However, mind or consciousness that projects the phenomenal world of experience is not an enduring entity, it is still a matter of fleeting moments and ultimate reality is not to be understood as the mind that functions by splitting its contents into the subject-object distinction, whereby the world of phenomenal experience is created. It is of the nature of pure will beyond all distinctions and as such is the Absolute.

The fact is that whether or not the world is created by the mind for most of us it is there and our activities must take note of it. So every philosophy that considers the world to be an illusion is obliged to give some 'truth' to this illusion. Hence, develops the doctrine of degrees or levels of reality. The truth about the phenomenal level of reality is relative to our purposes of living and it is called 'ignorance' when seen in the perspective of absolute truth which is independent of our purposes. As the Buddhists look at it, language belongs to the phenomenal world and serves our purpose of making certain distinctions that have to be made in aid of living. To call something a tree is to say that it is to be distinguished from everything else which is a not-tree. As absolute reality is above such distinctions the only term that can be applied to it is 'nothing', meaning no-thing; and this negative description fits in with the Buddhist *via negativa*—trying to understand something in terms of what it is not rather than what it is. However, the organic view of Indian culture seems to have influenced the Mahāyāna schools of Buddhism, for although the Absolute is nothing, all things arise out of it, are sustained by it and go back to it. In fact, everything is non-dual with it as with Brahman of the orthodox tradition. In Theravāda Buddhism there is no thought of an Absolute, here the preoccupation is with the no-self nature of things. Yet, even when everything is said to be a fleeting process, the interdependent nature of things as appropriate to an organic world view is retained, so is the concept of rebirth (basic to the organic view) despite the fact that there is no identical entity moving from one life to another. Everything is dependently originating and the "nature" of all things is to be understood in terms of this relationship with other things. Nothing is on its own.

The organic complexity of things is also shown in the Buddhist doctrine of predication. The Buddhists reject the idea that one must say that A is either B or it is not B. The possibilities are four-fold. A is B, A is not B, A is both B and not-B, A is neither B nor not-B. This is not the same as the Jain theory of predication, the purpose of which is to tie every assertion with a particular standpoint from which it holds. Both are based on the recognition of the complex nature of experience but the Buddhists do not talk about standpoints. Their four-fold predication is based on the idea that in real experience qualities, relations, etc. that we wish to assert on things do not neatly arrange themselves as logical contradictions like A and not-A. (Not-A being a state of affairs that is created solely by a formal definition, it is not the name of any one thing in particular.) The qualities and relations that we happen to experience may be opposites like happiness and unhappiness but opposites can coexist and they do not, between themselves, cover the whole universe of discourse. One does not have to be either happy or unhappy, one may be both or neither with regard to the same thing.

I think that theories of this nature arise out of the background of an organic world view which holds that which is one at some ultimate level of considertion can also be many at levels below this and so many statements can be made about it, having truth-values of a relative nature. With this also goes the idea that Absolute truth is beyond language for language functions in the realm of relativities. Just to give another example of the influence of Indian culture on Indian philosophy. We have seen that there are six schools within the orthodox fold, and they explore reality from different points of view. If some particular issue had been thoroughly investigated by a particular school its procedures and conclusions with regard to this issue were often adopted with or without modification by other schools in their own investigation of the same thing. The nature of inference as developed by Nyāya for example, or reflections on Nature (*prakṛti*) as developed by Sāṁkhya were utilized by other schools and fitted into their own systems and everyone thought that this was a natural thing to do, for the culture itself did not insist on absolute and clear-cut distinctions and boundary lines between different things. Again, later commentators of Sāṁkhya and Mīmāṁsā, both originally non-theistic, imposed on these schools a theistic interpretation and this too was found to be a 'natural' thing to do. (Nobody was outraged by this treatment.)

It is in this particular area, the acceptance of a multiplicity of points of view with regard to the same thing and the relative nature of the truths thus arrived at that Indian philosophy can still contribute to philosophical thought. But this needs a good look at the old schools from the vantage point of our modern understanding of what the issues are with which philosophers are engaged.

2

IN SEARCH OF INDIAN PHILOSOPHY

SARASVATI CHENNAKESAVAN*

OFTEN the question is asked whether there can be different philosophies for different countries while there is only one science for all the world. Are the philosophies developed in different countries different from each other merely because of their geographical location, or are there fundamental differences? Western philosophic world has been in the habit of talking about Eastern philosophy and bringing under the pseudonym all brands of philosophic and religious thinking of the Asiatic countries. Similarly the philosophers in the Asiatic countries put together all philosophic thinking in the European countries and give them the name 'Western philosophy'. Even text books carry these names to indicate their contents. But is such a dichotomous division of philosophies into Eastern (or Oriental!) and Western possible? Are there not many different philosophical trends developed within Western fold itself which do not favour a common denomination? Similarly, there are many philosophical trends developed in Asia and for want of a better tag, they are usually denoted by the name of the country in which they had taken birth. Scientific thinking can be common to the whole world, for the natural and empirical world which they

*Sarasvati Chennakesavan is Professor and Head of the Department of Philosophy (Retired) Sri Venkateswara University, India. She is Fellow of the Royal Asiatic Society, and authored *The Concept of Mind in Indian Philosophy*, *Perception*, *A Critical Study of Hinduism*, *Concepts of Indian Philosophy*.

study is the same for all humanity. But it is not possible for philosophic thinking to be the same for the whole world. The methodology involved in philosophizing could be common, but the starting point, and consequently, the conclusions arrived at vary considerably. The fact that man started philosophizing because he was awed by nature seems to be an inescapable fact whether we consider Eastern or Western philosophies. But this led different people in different directions. The particular manner in which it developed in India is called 'Indian philosophy'.

There is yet another misconception about Indian philosophy which requires to be cleared. Indian philosophy is a variegated, multi-faceted tapestry and while it should not be identified with any one of the strands, it would miss its diversity and unity if it is not surveyed in the context of its multiplicity. But this all important truth has been forgotten and, more often than not, in Western Universities, Indian philosophy has come to be identified with a few philosophies of religion and the whole study has come to be tagged on to departments of religious studies. Perhaps the reason for this lies in the attitudes developed by the early twentieth century Indian philosophers who came into contact with the Western academic world. In their patriotic zeal to show off the specialities of Indian culture and Indian philosophy, they started emphasizing the religio-philosophic aspects of Indian philosophy, thus side-tracking world opinion into thinking that Indian philosophy is primarily religious philosophy.[1] This tradition has been built upon and enlarged by many Indologists in the West, with the result that today, the glory of Indian philosophy rests on the meagre support of its religiosity. It is time that these attitudes are changed and the many aspects of Indian philosophy are exposed to world opinion.

Recently, there has been a rebound to the above outlined situation. The latter part of the second half of the twentieth century gave rise to many young Indian philosophers trained in formal and analytical logic. These philosophers have tried to mould Indian logic into the forms of analytical and formal logic. This

1. Consider, for example, S. Radhakrishnan's *Indian Philosophy* where the emphasis is always on the spiritual nature of Indian philosophy. The Vedantic schools of Advaita, Viśiṣṭādvaita have always been emphasized as being representatives of Indian thought.

again is motivated by a patriotic fervour where the young philosopher, appreciating the keen analysis of Western logic, tries very hard to show off that Indian logic is equally, if not one better than Western, analytic, and attempts to mould the former into the forms of the latter. For these philosophers, it looks as though the specificity of Indian logical thinking has to be reformed, remoulded and cast in formal analytical forms to sustain its validity. This position is equally as difficult to accept as that of the earlier philosophers. The fact is that Indian philosophy is not merely a philosophy of religion nor can its validity and importance be sustained only if it were to ape analytical forms of thinking. As was said earlier, Indian philosophy is multi-faceted and gives many philosophical ideas.

When we talk of Indian philosophy, we should bear in mind that we talk of classical Indian philosophy which is usually the six orthodox systems and the three non-orthodox systems. The traditional etymological meaning of the word 'philosophy' as 'love of wisdom' may not hold good any more, just because it implies the presumptuous idea that philosophers, or to be explicit, those who profess philosophy are the only lovers of wisdom to the exclusion of all other disciplines. This definition would have been applicable when philosophy held under its sway all available knowledge. But today the world of knowledge is so vast and so impressive that philosophy has become only a critical analysis of the modes of thinking and thus has confined itself to be a part of the whole rather than the whole itself. However, we do mean by philosophy a particular kind of thinking and a particular manner of assessment. This is so basic that the word has come to be used as an adjective to other disciplines and we have today subjects like philosophy of history, philosophy of science, philosophy of aesthetics, and so on. All these mean a distinct attitude which underlies the thought and is so fundamental as to characterize the whole disciplinary development. Now the words "Indian Philosophy" are not used in this sense. For if the word 'philosophy' is understood in its adjectival capacity, then the word 'Indian' is also an adjective and the combination of these two adjectives conveys no meaning. Therefore, let us look elsewhere to find out what Indian philosophy is. That it was born and developed on the soil of India in ancient times takes care of the adjective 'Indian'. But the meaning goes deeper.

Like early Greek thought, Indian philosophy in the early days of its beginnings developed from a sense of wonder and awe inspired by nature. We have the early anthropomorphic attempts of deification of Nature and an effort to appease these deities by praises and offerings. The early portions of the Vedas consist of these efforts. But one important characteristic which surfaces from these early poetic praises of Nature-deities is that the Vedic Indian was conscious of what he was doing and was thus inhibited by taking his anthropomorphic deification to its fullest extent. It seems he was always aware that it was merely a device, an attempt, to bring into the daylight of human knowledge something deeper and greater. Man had no need to struggle for his existence for there was bountiful food and the seasons were kind. So he had started speculation on the various questions about nature which were plaguing his mind. The questions seem to be interminable and probing. His answers were directed by his instruments of inquiry which were poetical fancy and conceptual abstraction. His guides were the variegated processes of Nature. Seeing wonders all around him, he withdrew into himself to cogitate upon these and find some answer to them. This is the beginning of Indian philosophy and characterizes it throughout its development. This early speculation was religious in nature, but it gave room very early in its beginnings to a philosophic speculation. But this division is irrelevant as far as the Vedic thought is concerned for, at this stage, the Vedic Indian's religion was his philosophy. For example, look at this cry of the Vedic Indian :

> "What god with our oblations shall we worship"[1] and "They call him Indra, Mitra, Varuṇa, Agnī and he is heavenly, nobly winged garutmān. To what is one, sages give many titles, they call it Agni, Yama, Mātariśvan."[2]

It is this probing nature of the early Indian mind which led to the development of a variety of philosophies at a later stage. Even the Upaniṣadic thought shows this characteristic. But at this stage the early Vedic thought had already become a full-fledged philosophic inquiry. We find that both the methods adopted and the goals set for inquiry encourage philosophical aspirations. The method is one of discussion and dialectic. There is never any straight laying down of dogma. The teacher is one who is

1. *Ṛgveda*, 10, 121 (Griffith's translation).
2. *Ṛgveda*, 1, 164 (Griffith's translation).

fully qualified by his capacities for cogitation and self-inquiry to answer questions raised by the ardently inquiring pupils. The master used both the dialectic and the myth to expound his philosophy. Both the dialectic and the myth deal with the same subject matter but in different ways. In a dialectic, there is an investigation and a negation of the propounded hypotheses in order to construct a more profound hypothesis. In a myth, truth as seen by the seer, is woven into a story so as to make it more easy and contemporary for the aspirant to grasp. For example, the story of Naciketa who went to the Lord of Death because his father willed it so and after going there, started an argument with the Lord of Death about the truth that the soul is immortal is sought to be conveyed by a myth as well as a dialectical argument. All over the world cultures, we find that history has a beginning in myth. What happens in a myth, happens also in history. A myth symbolizes the fight and the triumph of the good over the evil and this is what people seek to bring about in history.

In classical Indian philosophy, the sense of chronology is absent. The Indian mind at that time was more concerned with the progress of concepts than with the personalities who are limited by time and space. Then again, denoting the disciples of a great sage by his own name to indicate the school of thought represented makes it difficult to fix a date for these schools even retrospectively. Thus, the development of the Upaniṣadic thought into systematized schools of thought must have spread over a long and amorphous period. As the thought was handed down orally from teacher to pupil and from father to son, it came to be designated as *śruti*, the heard truth. It was also the truth heard by the saints and seers by their inner ear during their profound cogitations and then passed on to their disciples.

The systems of Indian philosophy which emerged from the vast store of floating knowledge came to be known as a *darśana.* This is another word which characterizes Indian philosophy. While *śruti* is the heard truth, *darśana* is the seen truth. But 'seeing' here is not the ordinary seeing with the sense organ of eye. It is understanding 'seeing within'. Poincaré, the philosopher of science, maintains that seeing really means making what is seen a part of ourselves in the form of thoughts. Similarly the Indian *seer sees* the truth and makes it a part of his understanding and a manner of his life. Hence philosophy is not merely an intellectual exercise but a manner of regulating one's life in the light of known and understood truths. Thus philosophy, at least in olden times, formed a way of life, a world view which influenced their way of life.

What were these seen truths? Are they uniformly the same? If so, what makes for the differences in various philosophical systems? When we raise these questions we find that while all the systems claim to be accepting the authority of the Vedas, still many of them reinterpret the Vedic statements according to their own insights. In the non-orthodox systems of the Buddhism, the Jainism and *Cārvāka*, we find that the Vedas were rejected as an authority and man was encouraged to find answers and to use his reasoning power. In their early stages, the Buddhism and the Jainism were opposed to any authoritarianism in arriving at conclusions, even that of a God. Cārvāka system was a profound materialism which gave importance to man as a social being and emphasized this-worldly life rather than some unknown heaven or hell. This anti-Vedic attitude developed and gained momentum as the ages passed and their priests known as Śramaṇas came to be a force to be reckoned with by traditionalists. These people ridiculed all the Vedic concepts. Famous names like Sañjaya the sceptic, Ajita Kesakambali rejected knowledge by insight and maintained that man was nothing but merely the elements which disintegrate on death. Gośāla, being a fatalist, believed that man is a toy in the hands of nature. These were all great men associated with this stream of anti-Vedic thought. Hence, the systems of philosophy which were orthodox and believed in *śruti* and *darśana* had to have recourse to logical arguments to uphold their philosophical postures. Hence a very vigorous system of logic known as *pramāṇa śāstra* comprising of the system of Nyāya and to a lesser extent of the Vaiśeṣika system developed. Of these two, the Vaiśeṣika provided the ontic basis of a pluralistic realism for the epistemology of the Nyāya. The logical system of the Nyāya is accepted by almost all the orthodox systems with slight modifications and changes to suit each system's own ontology. Hence the Nyāya system is a very important system in Indian philosophy. It lays down the canons of reasoning and explores the means of knowledge. For example, we acquire knowledge not merely through sense organs but also by the activity of the mind. For all Indian philosophers, mind is not the same as the self or soul. Therefore, all the schools maintain that mind is a sort of lesion instrument which is neither similar to a sense organ nor identical with the self or soul. While the status of the mind is thus assured, its nature differs with different ontologies which is but natural. To the Nyāya philosophy, mind is material, though of a very fine matter, capable of enormous speeds. It is the internal organ which coordinates all sensory cognitions and gives them a meaning and purpose. But the validity of knowledge does not lie in mere sense-activity and the action of the mind. It lies in the suitability of such knowledge for procuring results. Such results must also be in conformity with the total knowledge available at any one time. Thus, the Nyāya and Vaiśeṣika systems are pluralistic, realistic and pragmatic in nature. Their pluralism and realism have a very stringent condition, namely, whatever is real must be perceivable. Even when conceptual entities like the atoms and the soul are postulated, they have to become perceptible at one stage or the other and to some sense organ or the other including the mind. The mind and the soul are knowable through inferential reasoning and they are to be found in constant conjunction. It is this conjunction coupled with the activity of the sense organs which gives rise to consciousness since the conjunction of the soul, mind and sense organs is present from birth to death as there is no time when consciousness is not present in man.

To the Nyāya and Vaiśeṣika systems there is no need for a creator God. The atoms are eternal and many in number and it is their combination that produces this world. Later commentators on these systems have given a number of arguments to show the need for a God. But the postulators of these systems were rigidly non-theistic, for they see no reason to call upon an alien principle like the deity to carry on the most natural of occurrences like the combination of atoms. Nor do the Naiyāyikas want a God for the purpose of attaining *mokṣa* through devotion to Him. On the other hand, *mokṣa* is to be attained according to the Vaiśeṣika by acquiring a true knowledge of what is real by distinguishing between that which is permanent and that which is not. So in what way are these two systems spiritual? Only to the extent that they postulate an *Ātman* which is atomic in nature but which is also superfine and invisible to the ordinary sense organs. Of course, as I have already stated, later commentators like the author of Kusumāñjali give a detailed set of arguments for the existence of a God. But the systems as propounded by their *darśanakāras* are non-theistic.

Let us now consider the next two groups of systems, the Yoga and the Sāṁkhya. The Sāṁkhya provides the ontological basis on which the Yoga with a slight difference builds up a physiological and psychological system of practical application which leads man to attain *mokṣa* by his own efforts. The Sāṁkhya is a dualistic evolutionary system postulating a material and a conscious entity as the primordial realities. It is the interaction of these two which evolves into this universe. The Yoga system is fundamentally an 'evolution' of consciousness. It is an evolution of consciousness from its hidden presence in matter to an independence from matter.

The law of contradiction says that a thing cannot be both 'A' and 'not-A' at the same time. But there can be no contradiction if it can be 'A' and 'not-A' successively. These are opposites. There are other types of opposites which are contraries and opposites which follow one another like night and day. There are also opposites which arise from the same source like matter and life. There are others which are neither contradictories nor contraries and they do not have the same source. But they are divergent like good and evil which coexist but have nothing in common. It is this type of opposites which are postulated by the Sāṁkhya as *prakṛti* and *puruṣa*. *Prakṛti* is primal nature, the four-dimensional continuum of space-time-matter-force. It is a symbol of that which is the formed and the un-formed substratum of the universe. *Puruṣa*, on the other hand, is the formless, pure, steady awareness manifested by all living beings. *Prakṛti* is both the invisible, subtle, unmanifested substratum, the *avyakta* and the formed, visible, physically manifested universe in the gross form, the *vyakta*. *Prakṛti* is a process, but not a process in the sense of spatio-temporal transition. It is a process of 'alternation' between its constituents which are the alternating alternatives. On the other hand, *puruṣa* is 'simple' for it has no constituents and hence has no change. By itself it is neither an evolute nor an evolvent. *Prakṛti* merely reflects the *puruṣa* who is in proximity. There is no other relation between these two, neither external nor internal. A man stands before a mirror hung on the wall. He is reflected only by the mirror and not by the wall. *Prakṛti* in its original state is like the mirror. This is given in a beautiful comparison in the *Praśna Upaniṣad* where matter is compared to moon and life to the sun. The evolution that follows is a psycho-physical evolution. That is, the external world and our consciousness of it is an experience in which both arise together.

It seems as if this evolutionary descent of the reflected-consciousness in Nature has gone wrong, because it has produced a divisive world of ego and non-ego, the 'I' and the 'other,' which has created all human problems. Here comes the Yoga system to teach us the method of getting rid of these problems. Yoga gives us a way to control in consciousness of this ego-principle, *ahaṁkāra*. This is its goal. By controlling the varieties in which *ahaṁkāra* manifests itself, the source of them is also controlled. Thus the goal of Yoga which is called *mokṣa* here is the 'return' of consciousness to its 'source' which is *puruṣa*. While the Sāṁkhya is frankly an atheistic school, the Yoga pays lip-service to the idea by postulating God as merely one of the alternatives for meditation and concentration.

The purpose of discussing the fundamentals of the above four schools is to bring to light the fact that they are different from the philosophies of religion which are intent on making Indian philosophy into a spiritual philosophy. However, even amongst the Vedantic schools, the Advaita system consists of the extreme point of view that everything other than Consciousness-Existence is not ultimately real. The school of Mīmāṁsā is a school which emphasizes the ritualistic aspects of the Veda while ontologically accepting a pluralism of reals.

Let us now consider critically some of the concepts fundamental to Indian philosophy so as to bring out the fact that there is no common connotation for these concepts. Let us discuss the concept of *mokṣa* which we have been discussing hitherto. *Mokṣa* has to be studied in two different contexts. One is the moral context and the other its metaphysical context. Let us take the latter first. Metaphysically all schools of orthodox Indian philosophy accept a soul. It is also conceived that such an *ātman* is bound by the dualities of pleasure and pain, sorrow and suffering, etc. The soul is all the time making efforts to get rid of such a state and attain freedom from these dualities. This original state of the soul is known as *mokṣa*. For each system of Indian thought, this original state of the soul is different. For the Nyāya-Vaiśeṣika Schools, the soul becomes without characteristics, like a stone, *pāṣāṇavat*, when it is released from the bondage. For the Sāṁkhya-Yoga, the soul becomes pure consciousness without any attachment or entanglement with matter (*prakṛti*). For the Vedāntic school, specially the Advaita school, the identity of the soul with Brahman is established when bondage due to ignorance is removed. Thus, different systems think of *mokṣa*, the final state of release, in different ways. But almost all schools believe that this *mokṣa* can be achieved and that there is a way to achieve this *mokṣa*. The nature of *mokṣa* might differ from school to school. But they all accept *mokṣa* is a goal which has to be attained.

But *mokṣa* is also considered as one of the *puruṣārthas* (worthwhile goals), which a man has to aspire for. The other three are *dharma*, *artha* and *kāma*. The fact that *dharma* is placed first and *mokṣa* last in naming these values does not mean anything else but that when a man acts according to *dharma* in his efforts to attain wealth and satisfy sensory pleasures, then he has taken a first step to attain *mokṣa*. Hence a man who desires to attain *mokṣa* has to act according to certain moral principles and disciplines. *Mokṣa* or salvation is the attainment of freedom from all evils, sorrow and suffering. This can be achieved in two ways. One is the way of complete withdrawal from all social and economic activities and becoming a *sannyāsin*. This is the way of negation, *nivṛtti mārga*. But all men cannot become *sannyāsins* or practise *nivṛtti mārga*. Hence, a positive way is also prescribed which requires man to participate in all activities of life with moderation and detachment. This is known as renunciation-in-action or the *karma mārga* of the *Bhagavad Gītā*. While man should not *shirk* his responsibilities as a member of a society, still he should not become attached to his role in the society and the fruits which result from it. Very often the question is asked if any man can act without a personal motive. To this the answer is provided in the *Gītā* where it is said that the lesser goal of individual benefit must be replaced by the larger goal of social benefit. When this happens, the individual also would benefit automatically. However, this transferring of a personal motive to a larger social motive is difficult. It is in this context that moral requisites for the attainment of *mokṣa* are insisted upon by all the systems. Although there is no actual mention of the scheme for moral activity in each of the systems, they all agree on the scheme given in the Yoga system for the control of the body and mind.

Attachment to the objects of this world which is the root cause for both pleasure and pain is due to wrong knowledge of the real nature of such objects. Attaining of discriminative knowledge, *yuktāyukta jñāna* is almost the first step in achieving detachment. Some practical suggestions are given for the attainment of this discriminative knowledge. These are known as *yamas* and *niyamas*. *Yama* means restraint. *Niyama* means daily obligatory observances which cleanse the body and mind.

Mokṣa has so far been described as a negative ideal involving the removal of sorrow and suffering. It is also a positive ideal. As a positive identity, it means a stage of ultimate bliss and happiness. Generally, for all the Vedāntins this stage is the original state of the soul before its entanglement with a body and mind. To the Advaitin this state of the soul as existence, consciousness and bliss (*sat*, *cit* and *ānanda*) is to be realized here and now and such an individual attains *jivanmukti*. For others, such as the Viśiṣṭādvaitins and the Dvaitins, the stage of *mokṣa* is only a post-mortem stage to be attained when the soul becomes free due to the divine grace of God.

Once the character of a person is modified by the constant performance of *yama* and *niyama*, then he must prepare himself to attain *mokṣa* by following the three lines of mental activity suggested here. The first is *śravaṇa*, hearing what is stated in the scriptures and learning about it from a competent teacher. Second, one has to cogitate upon what has been learnt to find out if it is satisfactory. This is known as *manana*. Third, there is *nididhyāsana* or contemplation on the truths so acquired. During the third stage, what was learnt intellectually, becomes part of one's experience and the person lives accordingly.

Who is this that seeks *mokṣa* ? It cannot be the body, for it by itself, has no desires. Hence, the idea of a soul comes into being. This idea of the soul is a very ancient one. We find the word in almost all ancient as well as modern languages which implies that the people who used these languages had some idea of a soul. This word 'soul' is used in many contexts and with many meanings. It is that which makes the body alive. It is that which is responsible for sensory perception. It is that which helps the human being in distinguishing good from bad. It is that which forms the thinking part of the human being It is the seat of emotions. It is the eternal something which resides in the physiological body of man and departs from the body at death. After death, according to some theologians, the soul gets reborn or attains *mokṣa* and stays at the feet of God. This theory is based on the traditional doctrine of *karma* in Indian philosophy.

In Western classical philosophy, the terms 'mind' and 'self' are used interchangeably. For the Indian philosopher, 'mind' (*manas*) and self (*ātman*) are different from each other. But nowhere in all the schools of Indian philosophy is it said that these two entities *exist* separately in the human body. They are always said to be acting as one thing, giving rise to the impression that they are one and the same. But they are not identical and empirically can be studied at a conceptual level as different things. The best way to study the nature of self is to quickly run through the history of the development of the concept.

The word *ātman* has three derivative meanings; 'to breathe,' 'to move,' and 'to blow.' But a progressive change in the meaning of the word took place as man's knowledge of himself increased. There is a story in the *Chāndogya Upaniṣad* which illustrates this point. Indra and Virocana, representatives of Devas and demons went to Lord Prajāpati and asked him to teach them about the nature of *ātman*. The first obvious answer is that the physical body is the *ātman*. But this was not satisfactory. For does this *ātman* become lame or deaf when these organs are not functioning in the body ? So the next answer is that the *ātman* is the dreamer of the dreams. But this also was not acceptable for the privileges of a dream body often are not real. Next the self is equated to the master who is enjoying deep sleep without dreams. Just like air, lightning and the sky which are by themselves formless, assume a form and a shape when associated with space, so also the *ātman* becomes the experiencer when associated with a body having a shape and a form. It is that which while not identifiable with the body can yet be known only through the body. It is the true subject which never becomes the object. In statements like 'I am writing now', the 'I' represents the *ātman* in the body.

There is yet another important way of arriving at the above truth by the Upaniṣads. There is the outer world of objects. There is the self or *ātman* in the body which gets a knowledge of this external world. The contact point of the *ātman* with the external world is the body. The physiological body is not the knower because very often we say "I am sorry I was not listening" even while we were apparently hearing the sounds. Hence, the self knows only that which it wants to know. Hence, this self or *ātman* is necessary for our day to day living.

The next proof we get in the Upaniṣads for the existence of the *ātman* is the analysis of the three states of experience. In the waking experiences, man's sense organs are awake and he has many experiences. In dream experiences, there is no contact with the sense organs as such, but the experiences are gathered through sensations and preserved. The dreamer lives through all such experiences sometimes magnified and sometimes distorted into associated experiences. Similarly, natural laws do not have their inhibiting force in the dream world. A man can fly or do unnatural wonders in dream life. Viewed together, the dream world and the waking world must have a connecting, continuous coordinator. An investigation for this coordinator leads the Upaniṣadic seer into analysis of the deep sleep state. Here the man is completely and totally unaware of anything while he is fast asleep. It might have rained, or thieves might have broken into his house, or anything could have happened. But he is dead to all such external happenings. When he wakes up, he says, "I slept so happily and soundly, that I was not aware of anything." Thus the person is saying that there is not only the non-existence of any dream states which are based upon physical states, but he is saying that there is also non-existence of the presence of the physical awareness of objects. This knower who knows he has no such knowledge is the self, or the soul or *ātman*. If the existence of such an *ātman* is not accepted, then each state of deep sleep would be a state of death. Since the soul exists and it knows it was not dead, but only happily and deeply asleep without any contact with the external sensory or dream worlds, the *Upaniṣads* claim that the nature of this soul is knowledge or conscious awareness and happiness or bliss and existence. That is, the *ātman* is *sat* (existence) *ānanda* (bliss or happiness) and *cit* (conscious awareness).

But the Vedic thought was beyond the reach of the common man for it involved the performance of *yajñas* and *yāgas* which were normally very expensive and involved the spending of much time and energy. For an agricultural community, this was not always possible. The concept of the *ātman* in the *Upaniṣads* was too intellectual for the common man either to understand or practise. Hence, there arose a systematic rebellion against Vedic thought which gave an entirely different version of *ātman*. The most rebellious of the group called the *Cārvāka* or the 'sweet-tongued' philosopher reduced all non-perceptibles to a state of non-existence. He argues that things like *ātman*, God, *dharma*, etc. are only names given to a certain physical and physiological experiences man has obtained through his sense experiences. The self or *ātman* is a name given to the individual's experiences which give rise to a sense of unitary personality. The body is a material substance made up of the four substances, earth, water, air and fire. Self or *ātman* is the result of the chemical combination of these elements. Just as the red colour of the mouth and lips results from chewing together nuts, leaves and calcium oxide, so also the *ātman* is an emergent quality of the combinations involved in the body.

The speculation of the Cārvāka gave rise in turn to two different concepts of the soul. In general, the Buddhist thought believes that there is no permanent existent, whether it be of the nature of matter or *ātman*. These are merely passing events which are bound together because of their similarity by name (*nāma*) and form (*rūpa*). The thing that is existent for only one moment gives rise in a causal manner to the next event in the series. The total series comes to be known as a *thing* having a name and a form. Since each momentary object is lost by the time our sensations reach it, what we perceive is a non-existent thing which continues to be known with a name and a form. Unfortunately, while early Buddhism applied this theory to all things, they do not categorically deny that, since this rule applies to the soul also, the soul is only merely a name and form. In early Buddhism as well as later developments of the schools, we deal only with *ātman* as an empirical concept and not as a transcendental existent. The Jain philosopher, being non-dogmatic, could not accept either the postulation of a self or its non-existence as the Upaniṣadic and the Buddhist philosophers have tried to do. So he maintains that the *ātman* is there, but it is something which pervades every minute part of the body. So it has got a size. The bigger the organism, the bigger the soul it has. The qualities of such a soul are dependent on the evolutionary developments and capacities of the body.

To the Nyāya and Vaiśeṣika systems, the *ātman* or self is a real substantive possessing qualities just like the element earth which possesses the quality of smell. As stated earlier, a general principle of this school is perceptibility as a sign of existence. Hence the *ātman* must be perceptible if it were to exist. But to be able to perceive, a thing must not only exist, but must also have some qualities. We can never perceive a colourless table. Hence the characteristics of the soul by means of which it becomes perceivable, are pleasure (*sukha*), pain (*duḥkka*), knowledge (*jñāna*) desire (*icchā*), aversion (*dveṣa*) and volition (*prayatna*). The Naiyāyika quotes the scriptures to maintain that the *ātman* exists. But he uses inference to prove its existence. Hence, the method of proving the existence of the soul is much more important to the Nyāya-Vaiśeṣika. The argument is as follows. A man sees an object, remembers having seen it before and recognizes it next when he sees and if he needs it, he desires and makes efforts to possess it. All this is possible only when there is a continuity underlying all these actions. Such a continuous thing is the *ātman* or soul. If this were not so, every cognition would be a new cognition and imagine the confusion of such a life ! The *ātman* itself is unconscious, but conscious knowledge arises in it when it comes into contact with the object as a result of the activity of the sensations. Such consciousness is fleeting and, hence, cannot be the essence of the soul. The knowledge of an object, whatever it may be, whether it be a fleeting sound or the more permanent substance, since it depends on the sensations, is momentary like the sensations. Consciousness which arises out of such a relation cannot constitute the essence of the soul, for then the soul also would become non-permanent. Hence the soul is not consciousness. There are a number of souls or *ātmans*. This is so because no man's feelings, emotions and knowledge are the same as the other man's. These souls are bound by body and mind. Each of the souls is unique and ultimate. But in their non-embodied state they do not have any characteristics and are like bare stones (*pāṣāṇavat*).

The Sāṁkhya-Yoga, in contrast to the Nyāya-Vaiśeṣika view, holds that the *ātman* or soul is of the essence of consciousness. It is eternal, immutable, and omnipresent. It is a passive and inactive entity for all activity belongs to *prakṛti*. The existence of this *ātman* or *puruṣa* is established by reason. Firstly, the body which is made up of matter, requires a sentient principle to make use of it. The conscious element which thus enjoys in the body is the *puruṣa* or soul. Secondly, *prakṛti* evolves, producing the various things of this world. These things are for the enjoyment not of *prakṛti* itself because that is impossible. They are for the enjoyment of the *puruṣa* who is the self. But the Sāṁkhya metaphysics maintains that there is only one *puruṣa*. While the *prakṛti* evolves itself into many bodies, it seems to be an impossibility for the *puruṣa* to remain as one. The only way out of this situation is to maintain that somehow the one *puruṣa* or supreme soul becomes or appears to be many.

We shall now proceed to discuss the notion of *ātman* according to Advaita Vedānta system. While giving an outline of the Upaniṣadic thought, we saw how they characterized the soul as that which is in the body and can be described as *sat*, *cit* and *ānanda*. In many *Upaniṣads* we find an identity established between the *ātman* which is the innermost reality of the human being and Brahman which is the ultimate reality of the whole universe. This identity is usually well-known. This *Brahman-ātman* identity, merely called Brahman usually is accepted as the only reality, one without a second, *Advaita* by Śaṁkara. While he accepts this indivisible, ultimate one as the reality, he is faced with the problem of how this One Reality is seen, known, and experienced as the many of this world. A form of this general problem is how this one Brahman is to be found not only as the *jīva*, the empirical self, but also as the body of the individual. This is a combination of a psycho-physical body and the 'conscious awareness' which is the self. This psycho-physical conscious organism is the empirical self. Śaṁkara accepts the individual, embodied empirical self, but accepts the self or *ātman* as eternal and one. It is here that the problem arises. Empirically, the *jīva* is to be described as the knower, enjoyer and the agent of conation and action. However, these properties belong to the self only when it is in association with the body. The soul by itself has no agency. The limiting adjuncts for the supreme *ātman* are the body and the mind. Just like the limiting conditions for water are the properties of the vessel in which it is found, so also the agency for the *ātman* is present due to the various combinations of the psycho-physical body. Hence, there are as many appearances of the self as there are limiting adjuncts.

In addition to saying that each empirical individual is only an appearance of the infinite self, the Advaitin also explains the nature of the self by adopting the doctrine of the *kośas* explained in the *Taittirīya Upaniṣad.* Normally, a person is recognized as a person only in his embodied stage. A disembodied person is not recognized and a dead body is not a person any more and we refer to it usually in the neuter gender as 'It'. Therefore the physical body is important for it is through the body that the *ātman* becomes an agent. This physical organism is a product of food that is eaten and digested. It is by this outermost covering that man comes into contact with the external world. This he considers other than himself as revealed by statements like 'my arm', 'my eyes' etc. This is called *annamaya kośa* or the 'sheath of food'. If Brahman and *ātman* are identical, then *annamaya kośa* should also be Brahman. This is matter or *anna*. It is not and cannot be opposed to Brahman which is the only real. If it is so opposed, then it becomes non-existent. This is not so, however, since the body exists. Hence, why and how the body restricts the *ātman* cannot be understood, while the fact of restriction cannot be denied. The next sheath is *prāṇamaya kośa* which is life. *Ātman* is associated actively as already stated with a body that is alive and not with a dead body. The next one is *manomaya kośa*, the sheath of intellect. The presence of *ātman* is more evident in a living body that has intelligence. Matter reaches out into life, which in its turn finds fulfilment in intelligence or consciousness. But mere consciousness is of no use if it is not conscious awareness. So in man this consciousness manifests itself as self-awareness or self-consciousness. This is the *vijñānamaya kośa.* The last sheath is that which inferentially proves the existence of *ātman* limited by the body, and which is experienced as pure unadulterated happiness in deep sleep. This is *ānandamaya kośa.* It is also a psychological fact that man seeks pleasure and happiness all his life while avoiding bitterness and unhappiness. At the same time there can be no unadulterated pleasure without pain. The pleasure enjoyed during deep sleep when man acknowledges that 'he slept happily' is an indication of the nature of *ātman* which is bliss.

There is yet another aspect of the self given in the *Upaniṣads* and accepted by the Advaitin. In every act of seeing, hearing and other sense activities, we are not only aware of the object that is sensed, but also of the fact that it is I who am sensing the object. That is, self-awareness is part of the knowledge of the object. This aspect of knowledge is called the *sākṣin* or the witness-self. The *jīva* is the subject which knows the object. Hence, it is the empirical self involved in acquiring knowledge. The *ātman* is *jīva* combined with self-awareness. That is, it is the knower who is aware that he is knowing. These are only two different names for the same *ātman* given for the sake of convenience.

Thus the *ātman* is not the mind which is the determining instrument; it is not the sensations obtained through sense organs, for these are only instruments working when directed to do so by an agent. The *ātman* is the knower, enjoyer and the agent. The Yoga system makes this very clear. The *ātman*, when it so wills, can control both the mind and the sensations.

From the above description, it should be clear that there are two possible types of theories accepted by Indian philosophy. As an immanent principle, the soul cannot be without the body and mind. At the same time, a meaningful experience for the body and the mind cannot arise if the self is not associated inseparably with it. On the other hand, there are theories which maintain that the self is not only immanent, but also transcendent. The argument is, if it is not transcendent, then there can be self-awareness or self-consciousness over and above the body and mind. Whether it is immanent or transcendent, it is not identical with either the body or the mind.

Such a soul is considered to be immortal by all schools except the non-orthodox schools. These schools deny any independent soul, hence the question of its immortality does not arise. What is immortality ? The idea of immortality arises out of the idea of imperishability discussed in the *Muṇḍaka Upaniṣad* in great detail. The question is asked: "By knowing what, Sir, is all this known ?"[1] The 'what' when used in any question always implies a 'that'. Here the question means that there is a universal behind all the particulars by knowing which all the particulars can be known. The implication of the question is that there is a something, a reality, which can be known and which is the primary Existence. This is the Imperishable. 'The Imperishable' means that which is neither born nor is destructible. According to science, matter is indestructible. What, then, is the difference between matter which is indestructible and the Imperishable implied in the Upaniṣadic question? Matter is indestructible, but it is not *aware* that it is indestructible. The character of indestructibility is one that has been found to belong to matter after empirical investigations and imposed on it from outside. That is, matter is not conscious of its own indestructibility, but it is we who know of it. The imperishable of the Upaniṣad is the Self which comprehends everything and is conscious that it is imperishable. This is what all the systems of Indian philosophy tend to establish.

What, then, is this imperishability that is a characteristic of the soul? The *Upaniṣads* say that the soul is that by knowing which everything else becomes known. It is imperishable for it does not arise from something and pass away after a period of existence. Its imperishability is the same as its indestructibility. That is, it is eternal. But does 'eternal' mean merely deathlessness in the sense that it is being born again and again? This would mean not *eternal* but *survival* meaning living again and again. Eternality does not mean mere survival in this sense. The eternal is that which has no death at all and it is also something which does not merely survive death. The Yoga system says it is *akṣara*, the Imperishable which is aware that it is imperishable. Although life is universal, it is only in man that life, in its evolutionary ascent becomes aware that it is imperishable. If, as is generally maintained, the soul were to cease its existence with the body, that is, if the hearing of the ear and the seeing of the eye and the speaking of speech and the thinking of the mind cease, then is there nothing left at all? The question involves a contradiction, because it asks "Is there non-being?" This is

1. *Kasmin nu bhagavö vijñnāte sarvamidaṁ vijñatam bhavatī*? *The Muṇḍaka Upaniṣad*, I.3.

not right, for we cannot predicate *is-ness* of something that *is-not*. Similarly, to predicate existence of what had never ceased to be is absurd. The *ātman* is an existent whose awareness has never ceased to be.

In Indian philosophy a general and subtle distinction is made between survival and imperishability. Survival conveys the idea that there is something which is existent at a particular time, ceases to be existent in that form for a period and again reappears in its original form. When this happens repeatedly, we say that that something has 'survived'. 'Survival' also hints at the possibility of that something perishing if it does not have the strength to overcome the obstacles. The whole idea of survival is time-bound with a possibility that at one time or other the soul might perish. The soul wears out many bodies even in one life and let us assume that in successive lives many more bodies are assumed and worn out. But just because there *are* many births and deaths for the soul how can we assume that there will not be a final death ? Hence a man who assumes that survival is immortality must be able to prove the interim life of the soul between death and birth, and secondly to prove that the soul can outlive the numberless births and deaths and that the very facts of births and deaths do not allow us to presume a final death without a consequent birth. Hence, it is not *sufficient* to maintain negatively that the soul does not die, but it has to be proved that it lives on forever, *śāsvataḥ*.

It is to accomplish this eternality of the soul that the Advaita system, basing its theory on the *Upaniṣads*, gives us the three states of consciousness we have already discussed earlier. The empirical evidence for this are the three states of consciousness, waking, dream and sleep. In the waking state, there is an assurance of the reality of the external world because the senses through which we perceive are all outgoing. But then we have to be sure that the *externality* of the external world is due to the fact that the external world is perceived, and perceived by the senses. The senses form part of the body which is also perceived and hence they are themselves external. Hence the question: "by what does the eye see ?" Late Professor N. A. Nikam makes a very interesting statement about this in his book *The Principal Upaniṣads*. His argument is here outlined. Unless *prajñā* or consciousness is already disposed to be outward-looking, it is impossible, by any means, to achieve any external knowledge. Hence, the outward biased consciousness makes use of the senses and the mind to achieve a knowledge of the external world. Even when the senses are inactive and cannot be the instruments for the outward consciousness, the very nature of the outwardness of the consciousness would still be functioning through the mind. Perhaps this is what happens in extra-sensory perceptions which the *Yoga Sūtras* so vividly describe.

In the dream state, it is said that consciousness is 'inward-looking'. This is only symbolical language. For in the *seeing* of the external world, the soul makes use of both the external sense organs and the mind which is considered internal in the sense of not being seen by the other sense organs. What is seen in the dreams are still external objects, but without the limitations of time, space and the relation of causality. The objects are mere images without any binding factors. But it is not merely a carbon copy of the external world, for the conditioning aids presented by the sense-perceptions are absent. However, it is 'external' in the sense that it is now the mind which provides the matter for the dreams. In deep sleep this polarity between the 'outer' and 'inner' vanishes. Consciousness is neither outward nor inward here. It is purely neutral. Here there is neither awareness of the external world nor even of the body and consequently of mind and sensations. It is a state of unqualified consciousness. How do we know this—for even in such a sleep there is someone who observes that which is asleep? Does this mean there are two souls? Indeed not. It only means that the self which is outward-bound withdraws itself from all outward activities and witnesses the sleeping body. These three states—waking, dream and sleep—constitute a stream of consciousness. But the ground for such a stream must be something which is distinguishable from the three though not different from them. This ground state is not any other than the three stages mentioned, nor is it a resultant of all of them. If this were so, then we should find some traces of all the three in it. As the *Katha Upaniṣad* says, it is that which is forever awake, does not come and go in terms of time like the other three states, but it is pre-existent and in a sense independent of the body and hence must survive the death of the body.

Having thus explored the possibility of establishing the eternality of the soul, we have now to deal with the doctrine of *karma* which forms an essential part of theologico-philosophical systems of Indian philosophy which accept the doctrine of *karma* and rebirth as an essential and integral part of its philosophy and religion. The word *karma* has many meanings. In our context, we have to take it as a causal theory which is effective over different births. This involves not only the metaphysical belief about the eternality of a soul, but that such a soul is involved in a causal chain of birth and death. The basic aspect of the theory is that the law of causation is applicable in both the empirical and transcendental realms. This means that in the moral realm every action, whether good or bad, must give rise to a reaction or result. Some actions produce their result immediately following the performance of the action and such results are facts of experience here and now. But many such actions have delayed reactions. The question is : what happens in the interim period to these results ? Sometimes the time lag seems to be quite a long period. To get over this problem, the ancient Hindu postulated the principle of *adṛṣṭa*, a sort of storehouse where, the unseen and yet potent repository, providing a bridge to cover the time lag. This automatically leads to the better known aspect of the *karma* theory, namely, the theory of reincarnation of the same soul in differing bodies till the *karma-phala* is exhausted. The nature of the embodiment depends on the nature of the fruits of the actions performed in a previous birth. But this theory, on the face of it, provides a deterministic explanation for the evils and sufferings of man. The contradictions of life are puzzling. A man who is continuously doing good according to his lights and capacities suffers a great deal even in this very life whereas the evil and the corrupt always flourish and prosper. A learned man begets an idiot and an illiterate one a genius. One may call it the environment, training and other circumstances. But all these are due to the fact of that particular birth in that particular situation. Hence the accumulated *karma* of past lives is now bearing fruits. As was sown earlier, the harvest is reaped later.

While many people satisfy themselves by this apparently strict application of the causal law, they fail to appreciate the lacunae that are involved. The law of causality is an empirical law. And it can be effective only within the parameters of empirical experiences. If the effect is empirical, the cause cannot be transcendental. Things belonging to one category cannot be explained by referring them to another category. Suppose, for the sake of argument, this is possible and we can argue from effect to cause. It becomes difficult to fix which empirical effect is the effect of which transcendental cause. Then we have also to think of the problem of plurality of causes, contingent and necessary causes, implicative causes, etc. All these logical problems have to be solved before we can link up rebirth as an effect with the fruits of *karma* as a cause.

There is still another difficulty to be faced and solved. Normally, economic well-being, a comfortable and affluent life, are attributed to good things done in the past and the opposite are said to be the result of evil deeds. Somewhere in this process, there seems to have occurred a link up between affluence and goodness, poverty and evil. This is least justified by any moral standards. Yet it is the accepted thing according to the *karma* doctrine. Then again, a whole family suffers for the misdeeds of one man in this very life. Whose *karma-phala* is active then? So the doctrine of *karma* and rebirth which gives an appearance of a well-adjusted theory, does still have many loopholes which have to be explored and the theory must then be either established more firmly or rejected.

All that I have stated so far is but merely an outline picture of the salient views normally attributed to Indian philosophy. A more detailed account or a more critical or evaluatory account is not possible here. However, the most important point to note is that, as far as the *darśanas* are concerned, they always start with given premises and then justify their assumptions from epistemological and logical arguments. Thus we will always find a continuity from philosopher to philosopher. Any treatise on Indian philosophy provides a more logical ground and critical analysis of its immediate predecessor's views with a view to either reinforce them or destroy them. Such a logical approach appearing continuously system after system is a peculiarity of Indian thought. But such development came to a halt abruptly a few centuries ago. From then on, all Indian philosophers of the modern day, except a few giants like Sri Aurobindo, have all been expanding or supporting the ancient systems, always ignoring that which for them was not convenient to reckon with. Perhaps it is this modern attitude which makes one wonder if there is anything specific about Indian philosophy. The philosophy in India in the past is much the same as all ancient philosophies, interspersed with a concern for right knowledge on the one hand and for a safe and happy life hereafter. There is this added characteristic that the postulators of Indian philosophy, that is the *darśanakāras*, and their commentators followed the inferential and dialectical method of establishing their premises. They have paid lip-service to authority and relied heavily on their logical acumen for the protection of their theories.

Indian philosophy in general has suffered much in the hands of its votaries, both Eastern and Western. Each has taken that part of it which would either enhance his personal image as a philosopher or give support to his particular brand of philosophical thought. Some have said it is purely other-world oriented, others that it is based completely on renunciation or *sannyāsa*, yet others that all Indian philosophy is absolutistic and non-dualistic, and still others that true Indian philosophy is only the theologically oriented. But all these attitudes omit to take into consideration the vast majority of other philosophical ideas developed through the ages which are devoted to rationalism, logical epistemology, materialism, dualism and other *isms* of the kind. Many Indian philosophers maintain that these are not presently current philosophies, the common man does not know anything of these things, and so we can only think in terms of philosophies which are acceptable to the general Indian man and which he thinks would provide salvation for him. As a result, departments of philosophy have started wearing *āśramite* garbs of one type or other. Recently, due to the political set up in the country, linguistic chauvinism has entered this field of personality cult. All this makes the reader and student puzzled and confused about the nature of Indian philosophy. In this late twentieth century, when the complexion of man's knowledge changes even as he walks on the ground, it is absolutely necessary for Indian philosophers to take up the challenge, give up their particular predilections, examine the ancient philosophical concepts for their adequacy to satisfy the quest of modern youth. Merely asserting repeatedly that Indian philosophy is great, that it is spiritual, is not going to make Indian philosophy great. Indian philosophy is as much a philosophy as other world philosophies. It possesses all the necessary ingredients to provide a rational full-fledged world philosophy. Only all the original treatises must be read with a new outlook, the mental cobwebs dusted, and the bright old philosophy must be presented as a young and disciplined one.

3

THE WESTERN AND THE INDIAN PHILOSOPHICAL TRADITIONS†

P. T. Raju*

IT is indeed difficult to discuss satisfactorily the similarities and differences between two philosophical traditions, which are some twenty-five centuries old, in an article however long. But many comparisons have of late appeared, some maintaining that there is absolute disparity between Eastern and Western cultures, some saying that they are the same in different garbs, and the rest holding positions somewhere between the two extremes and advocating reconciliation. True, some of the comparisons made by Western writers are sympathetic. Yet it seems necessary that the true perspectives of the traditions be understood in bare outlines, so that the spirit of either may not be missed in detailed comparisons.

Moreover, though it was long believed by some that "East is East, and West is West, and never the twain shall meet," the two *have* met, and after World War II little doubt is left of their having met. Men of thought are expressing their feeling that it is time for the two cultures and outlooks to be brought together

†Reprinted from *The Philosophical Review* Vol. LVI, No. 2, March 1947, pp. 127-55.

*P. T. Raju is Professor Emeritus, College of Wooster, Wooster, Ohio, U.S.A. He has published over one hundred research papers and several books. His main books include *Thought and Reality, The Idealistic Thought of India, The Concept of Man, The Philosophical Traditions of India, Introduction to Comparative Philosophy*.

into a higher synthesis, so that life may be livable on earth. Observed in their individual natures, the two outlooks appear now to be one-sided. The misery of Mankind seems to be on the increase, in spite of the comforts which science professes to bring and the consolations which religions offer. The two philosophies seem to be occupied with two different realms of being, each overlooking the fact that man on earth belongs to the other realm also. The need is now greater, therefore, and is more sharply felt, for combining the two philosophies into a higher synthesis, so that we can have a world philosophy, not only of the East or the West, not merely of this or that religion, or of this or that nation, but of the whole world, which can explain to man his true place in reality and can enable him to develop a balanced outlook on life. It is a duty incumbent on all great nations to encourage the development of such philosophy. And one expects that America will take a lead in this venture, which requires not only a sympathetic but a deeper and a more detailed understanding and appreciation of the perspectives.[1]

I

In evaluating the two traditions, it has been customary to rely upon philological and etymological interpretations. Such interpretations have been helpful in understanding Indian thought at some of its stages. But the natural limitations imposed upon this method are so great that even long ago Plato disapproved of such attempts.[2] Interpretations of philosophy from the side of the sciences of language result generally in strange and fanciful conclusions.[3] *Philology and etymology, along with comparative grammar and mythology, can be of help in understanding the meanings of words and concepts, only so long as systematic thinking does not develop; and their value varies, we may say, in inverse*

1. There are men both in India and the West who would not like to pollute their philosophies by widening their scope and including whatever might have been excluded and thereby introducing important ideas from outside. For a survey of contemporary philosophical activity in India, see the author's article, "Research in Indian Philosophy : A Review" (*Journal of the Ganganatha Jha Oriental Research Institute* [Allahabad], Nos. 2, 3 and 4, 1945), and also *Progress of Indic Studies* (Bhandarkar Oriental Research Institute, Poona).

2. Zeller, *Plato and the Older Academy*, p. 212.

3. See the author's article referred to above.

ratio with the development of systematic thought. This may be laid down as one of the important principles of comparative philosophy. It assigns the maximum possible value to the method. For often words acquire new and more meaning and significance, not only when the concepts are thought out in a system, but also when there is change of geographical and other conditions, which have little to do with the logic of systematic thinking. Mere philology or etymology cannot determine for us the meaning of words or concepts.

Without entering further into the principles of comparative philosophy, we may adopt, as a *modus operandi* for the comparison of the two traditions the comparisons of their origins, of their developments, and of their endings. Their origins are of the past and can no longer change. The endings, so far as we are concerned, are what they are in the present. In the future, the two traditions may blend; and the future historian of philosophy may trace two origins for the philosophy of his time, just as European culture of the present traces its birth to both Greece and Rome. Or possibly the two traditions may continue without regard for each other, which is certainly not to be desired. And as the endings for us are what they are now, the modes of their respective developments are also of the past. A careful understanding of the two traditions in these three aspects should enable us to determine the individuality of each with respect to the other.

II

That philosophy develops out of religion is a generally accepted theory. But some thinkers wonder why early Greek philosophy had so little to do with early Greek religion. Max Müller wonders why early Greece, with her great intellectual culture, could tolerate such religion[1]. The Dionysiac and the Orphic religions were the ruling religions of ancient Greece. But Gomperz writes that both of them "were moved by the heightened interest in the future of the soul, based in the first instance on their disdain for earthly life, and resting ultimately on the

1. *Science of Language,* II, 487. Cf. also his view of the difference between Greek and Indian philosophy in his *Theosophy or Psychological Religion,* p. 330 (in *Collected Works*).

gloomy view which they took of it."[1] But these features are not characteristic of the general European philosophical tradition and, though found to a certain extent in Socrates and Plato, are not the centre of their philosophical interest. Socrates used to be absorbed for hours in a trance. But his philosophical discussions were not chiefly aimed at describing the realities therein experienced. Both Socrates and Plato, as philosophers, are remembered mainly for their treatment of concepts or ideas and for their social theories. Hegel regards Socrates as the liberator of the concept from Being, in which, he says, oriental philosophy remained absorbed. Neoplatonism, which made soul the basis of its theories, appears in European philosophy, when it is considered as a whole, as a deviation that ends in a *cul-de-sac*. Dean Inge writes : "The great constructive effort of Neo-Platonism, in which the speculations of seven hundred years are summed up, and after which the longest period of unimpeded thinking which the human race has yet been permitted to enjoy soon reached its end, is of very great importance in the history both of philosophy and theology. Historically this is what Platonism came to be; this is the point at which it reached its full growth—its *τέλος* or *φύσις*, as Aristotle would say, and then stopped."[2] It then passed over into Christian theology and ceased to be of purely philosophical or metaphysical interest. Marvin also says: "Here unite Oriental thought and the religion of the Orphic worked out completely as a philosophy. Indeed, one may say that Greek philosophy ended, as it began in the West, an Orphic religion, and thus that this ancient Orphic conception of the world was never outgrown and discarded by the Mediterranean civilization. Briefly put, Neoplatonism as such contributed nothing to the scientific development of Europe, though it did carry within it to later generations some older Greek learning and traditions. Neoplatonism belongs rather to the history of European religion."[3] As part of pure philosophy, it had no progress.

But Marvin writes that Greek religion and philosophy are inseparable : "One of the most important aspects of Greek

1. *Greek Thinkers*, I, 84.
2. *The Philosophy of Plotinus*, I, 10.
3. *The History of European Philosophy*, p. 204.

philosophy is that it began and remained to the end a *religious philosophy*. It was always a *theory or way of life* as well as a theory of nature and of man; and it endeavoured to do for the cultured man in a nobler way what religion was doing in a less noble way for the people."[1] But he adds that two distinct currents run through the entire development of Greek philosophy, the Olympic and the Orphic, and that "Greek philosophy never completely breaks away from the early religious influence, but remains in the end two philosophies."[2] The Olympic religion, which encouraged a fearless scientific conception of nature, retained its distinctness up to the end and developed into the purely scientific philosophical tradition, while the Orphic trend ceased to exercise any influence on this tradition from the time of Plotinus onwards.[3] In Hegelian language, it is the Socratic emancipation of the concept from Being that forms the foundation of science and metaphysics. The original religious interest gradually got detached from this tradition. Socrates, Plato, and Aristotle, with whom Greek philosophy is generally identified, showed greater interest in nature and in man as part of nature than in questions of the inner world. Hence also the impression that Greek philosophy had so little to do with Greek religion. The first important work in European philosophy, Plato's *Republic*, deals primarily with man and society, and the book begins with the question about justice and not about the soul.

III

No scholar doubts that Indian philosophy originated in religion. But its origination is unique. Indian religion and civilization are now traced back historically to about 4000 B.C. Excavations at Mohenjo-Daro and Harappa disclose to us the existence of a peaceful folk, among whom the practice of yoga or meditation and the cults of Śiva and Śakti seem to be prevalent. The civilization is accepted by many to be pre-Aryan. The prevalence of yoga shows that the people of the time came to know of certain inner realities, for the discovery and

1. *The History of European Philosophy*, p. 75.
2. *Loc. cit.*
3. This is, however, a general estimate.

experience of which they began the practice of turning the mind and the senses inward. The Aryans began entering India from about 2000 B.C., to which age the Ṛgveda is assigned. The early Aryans were nature-worshippers, and it is still a disputed question[1] whether they brought with them the cult of yoga, or whether they did not find it prevalent in the country to which they migrated. They were worshippers of nature and her forces; and so their senses must have been directed towards things outside and not towards things within. Hence it is less likely that they brought the cult of yoga with them than that they found it being practised by the earlier settlers and adopted it. Some scholars believe that the ideas of *saṁsāra* and transmigration, that the world is a flow of misery from birth to death and death to birth, were alien to the early Vedic Aryans, and that they were incorporated into the Aryan ideas from some Malayo-Polynesian or Sumero-Dravidian myth.[2] Even Keith writes: "It is the conviction of the Brahmanas [some of the earliest parts of the Veda] that life on the earth is on the whole a good thing; for a man to live out his length of days is the ideal, and such traces of discontent as appear are mainly in regard to the doubt that man must feel whether he has a year more to live."[3] No theory of *Karma* which produces births and deaths has yet been elaborated, except the one that sacrifices and gifts bear fruit in the world to come.[4]

But by the time of the *Upaniṣads*, all these ideas were blended into a somewhat connected thought. The early *Upaniṣads*, which are generally accepted as pre-Buddhistic and pre-Jaina, are placed between 900 and 600 B.C. They contain discussions on *saṁsāra*, transmigration, the law of *Karma*, the immortality of the soul, higher and lower knowledge (intuition and intellect), the supremacy of the Absolute Spirit and its identity with the knowledge of it, along with discourses on sacrifices and forms of meditation. By the time of the *Upaniṣads*, the emphasis has already shifted from sacrifices to meditation upon and realization of the Brahman. The peculiarly Upaniṣadic doctrine of the four states of the Atman—the waking state, dream, deep

1. Keith, *Religion and Philosophy of the Veda*, II, 632.
2. Masson-Oursel, *Ancient India*, p. 139.
3. *Religion and Philosophy of the Veda*, II, 488.
4. *Ibid.*, p. 478.

sleep, and the original pure state—which supplies the psychological and the metaphysical basis for the philosophy of the *Upaniṣads*, has already been developed fully. By this time, the outlook of the Indian Aryans is saturated with the sense of the inwardness of reality, from whatever source this idea might have been borrowed. It is not merely taken in and added to the existing stock of ideas but made the basic principle. Reality is to be found, if at all, only in the innermost depths of our being: it is the Self or the *Ātman*. Hence psychology and metaphysics are the same.

Mahavira and Gautama, the celebrated founders of Jainism and Buddhism, were born in the sixth century B.C. The fact that they felt the need for starting religious schools laying so much stress upon *ahiṁsā* or non-injury makes one think that, in spite of the gradual shift of emphasis, in the *Upaniṣads*, from sacrifices to the realization of the Brahman through penance and yoga, people of the time were still performing sacrifices involving much shedding of blood and were thereby hoping to propitiate gods and to obtain merit irrespective of the purity or impurity of their lives. Both religions disbelieved in the authority of the Vedas, which preached sacrifices. Mahavira taught the reality of the *Ātman* but dispensed with God, while Buddha kept silent over questions concerning both and, like the other, laid chief stress upon ethical discipline. It should not be understood that either developed any system of ethical principles or prepared a code of morals directly concerned with social activity. Their ethics is individualistic; or to be more precise, it was concerned only with the conduct of the individual seeking to attain salvation by realizing the reality within him. It answered the question: What should a man do if he is to realize his innermost reality ?

The older Brāhmaṇic religion grew gradually and had its roots well struck in society, which cared not only for the other world but also for itself and its members. Hence the balance between interest in inward reality and interest in external reality was fairly well maintained. Society was divided into four castes—Brāhmaṇa, Kṣatriya, Vaiśya, and Śūdra. The life of the first three was ordered into four stages—*brahmacarya* or student life, *gṛhastha* or householder's life, *vānaprastha* or forest-dweller's life, and *sannyāsa* or monk's life. Every man was to pass through the first three stages, and renunciation of the external reality and acceptance of the inner was to be complete only in the fourth. Interest in the values of the external world was kept up by injunctions about duties pertaining to the first three stages and about sacrifices for obtaining greater comforts and pleasures. But Buddhism and Jainism contained little to keep alive interest in the values of this world. The sense of the misery of this world was intensified. Sacrifices were disallowed, not only because they involved destruction of life, but also because the pleasures of earth and heaven, both of which formed part of external reality, entailed rebirth, which was misery. Their philosophy had a strong pessimistic tone. Man was taught that he had to turn his mind and senses inwards, but he was not shown by what stages of life that inwardness was to be achieved. Man's position in nature and society was ignored, so that man lost his moorings in this world before establishing any in the other. But both Buddhism and Jainism had an immense appeal to the people in whom some of the bloody sacrifices advocated by Brahmanism must have produced intense disgust. Besides, what the new religions were preaching was nothing strange to the *Upaniṣads*. These themselves were teaching the inward nature of reality, though this teaching was one among many. What Jainism and Buddhism did was to take up the teaching and propagation of this truth alone. They had one advantage. As they severed all connection with the Brāhmaṇic religion, of which caste system was made an important part, they could teach the truth in its purity to the Śūdras also. But they worried themselves little with social organization. And what social organization laymen should have was practically left to the Brāhmaṇic religion to decide; so that real Buddhism and Jainism were actually confined to monasteries. When the Muslims destroyed the monasteries and orthodoxy revolted, Buddhism disappeared from India, and Jainism could survive only by some imitation of the orthodox caste system. The principles of *ahiṁsā* and vegetarianism were adopted by the orthodoxy, Buddha was made one of the *avatāras* or incarnations of Viṣṇu, and Buddhism could not justify independent existence. Even the Jainas do not care even now to call themselves non-Hindus.

After the advent of these two religions, more and more *Upaniṣads* appeared which, in one form or another, devoted themselves exclusively to questions of inward reality and show traces of Buddhist and Jaina influence.[1] Everything that appeared new in these religions and that had a special appeal to the people, not only practices but also thoughts, were absorbed and assimilated; and Hindu philosophy grew richer in content.

If we now compare the origins of western and Indian philosophy, we see the difference between the tendencies quite clearly. It is admitted that the languages, Greek and Sanskrit, originated in a common source, and that the peoples who at first spoke them belonged to a common stock. But the philosophical interests of the two, after the branches separated and settled down in different countries, became different.[2] In Greek philosophy as a whole, the feeling that there is an inner world and interest in it are not totally lost. But interest in man as such and in society is stronger; it is scientific and ethical.[3] Greek philosophy is concerned more with the question of how to lead a good life on earth than with the question of how man can realize the inner reality. The first great philosophical work of the West is Plato's *Republic*, while that of India is the *Bṛhadāraṇyaka Upaniṣad*. The chief aim of the former is the study of society and man's place in it, while that of the latter is the study of the *Ātman* and the methods of realizing it. The method adopted by the former is the Socratic dialectic, which aims at

1. See Keith, *Religion and Philosophy of the Veda*, II, 503. The *Muṇḍaka Upaniṣad* is regarded by Hertel as being particularly influenced by Jainism.

2. Max Müller says that "the Greek and Indian streams of thought became completely separated before there was any attempt at forming definite half-philosophical, half-religious concepts" (*Theosophy or Psychological Religion*, p. 65). Often the inwardness of Indian philosophy is equated to the negative attitude to the world and is attributed to political disasters, etc. But Schweitzer has rightly seen that it is not due to them, though he does not give any explanation. (See his *Indian Thought and its Development*, pp. 19 ff.) Only in the West did philosophy turn inward whenever there were such disasters. For instance, for the Jews conquered by Nebuchadnezzar, the Kingdom of God became inner. Similarly for the Greeks conquered by Macedonia, happiness became inner, as it was no longer found in the life of the city state. We see the inner Kingdom of God emerging as the outer kingdom in the organization of the Church, the moment an opportunity was given. (See Erdmann: *History of Philosophy*, I, p. 253.) But in India, this has never been the case. See the author's article, "Indian Philosophy : Its Attitude to the World" (*The Vedanta Kesari*, XXI, 169).

3. See Max Müller : *Theosophy or Psychological Religion*, p. 330.

the formation of concepts necessary for the understanding of outer reality, while that of the latter is the denial of one entity after another until we come upon a reality that cannot be denied. There is little endeavour to frame a concept of this reality, and all importance is attached to its realization. To sum up the difference: Greek philosophy attempted to understand the ways of outer life and Indian philosophy the way to inner life, and both were thinking that they were in search of ultimate reality.

The view that the Socratic detachment of the concept from Being rendered European philosophy scientific and made scientific thought possible is not without justification, though it would be wrong to think that Indian philosophy had no theory of concepts. The nature of concepts or universals was discussed, not in the *Upaniṣads* themselves but by Kanada and Gautama, the founders of the Vaiśeṣika and the Nyāya philosophies; and they belonged to about the second century A.D. Both accepted the universal (*jāti* or *sāmānya*) and the particular (*viśeṣa*) as two of the fundamental categories of reality. But this acceptance did not lead them to a philosophy like Platonic idealism but to a pronounced pluralistic realism. The question, What is it that is most common to the things of the world? was also raised but raised in the peculiarly Indian form, What is it by knowing which everything else is known, or what is it without which nothing can exist? Just as, for instance, many Western idealists asked for a natural universal or a universal that is concrete and real and not merely conceptual, artificial, and abstract, so the Upaniṣadic seers wanted to know the real and ultimate universal; and this they found to be the *Ātman* or the Brahman. But this inquiry of theirs has the appearance also of the search for a being in which everything else is merged and as such seems to be open to Hegel's criticism. Indian thought, particularly of the *Upaniṣads*, was not so much interested in a conceptual construction of the world as in pointing to the reality, which, it thought, was identical with our innermost reality.[1]

1. It is unfortunate that some Indian enthusiasts make this difference in emphasis a reason for condemning Western philosophical tradition as a whole. As this paper shows, it is the opinion of the author that, in spite of the deep spiritual interest of the Upaniṣadic tradition, it is one-sided as much as the European tradition is but for a different reason. Modern western

It is not to be understood that thereby either tradition is superior to the other, but that each tradition is laying special emphasis on one part of man's life, though not completely ignoring the other. The truth preached by religion that ultimate reality is our innermost reality was seriously accepted by the *Upaniṣads* and made the foundation of their metaphysics; so that it was felt that if the Upaniṣadic philosophy of the *Ātman* was disproved, this religious truth would be disproved, and no religion could have a real foundation. Greek philosophy, on the contrary, though not uninterested in this religious truth, was more interested in the life man had to live on earth; accordingly it had to determine man's place in nature and society, for which purpose it had to build up a conceptual framework of nature, society, and man. Hence the importance for the Greek of the method of discovering and framing concepts; whereas for the Indian, the reality in which he was interested being inner and a matter of experience, the formation of concepts was of secondary importance. Hence the Upaniṣadic tradition could not promote science in the sense of the study of the facts of outer experience. But it did promote the study of the facts of inner reality, a study which unfortunately is dismissed by some Western scholars as a study of mystic experience.[1]

philosophy is tending to be more and more a system of scientific thought, the aim of which is rather the presentation of the view of the world as a whole than a search for ultimate reality. To say that the scientific concepts which this philosophy handles are mere concepts and not ways of practice (praxis) is to ignore what philosophers of science say. But as these concepts belong to external reality only, any world view that claims to be complete, based on them alone, appears to be a mere conceptual construction, as it cannot touch inner reality. Further, experiments with inner reality and search for it involve a mode of life, whereas experiments with the outer reality and search for it need not involve a mode of life. For instance, both a liar and a truth-speaker can be scientists, but the former will in vain search for inner reality. Probably it will be less misunderstood if it is said that western thought deals with external reality and the Indian with the inner rather than that one is a way of thought and the other a mode of life, that one is only theoretical and the other practical, and so forth. The Western man may say that the very fact that he is more practical than the Indian implies that his outlook and philosophy are more practical than the latter's. He may also point to the different philosophical systems of India and say that they are conceptual constructions and differ from one another.

1. One recent misleading evaluation of Indian philosophy is calling this inwardness by the name of introversion after Jung. It should never be

IV

If we now compare the development and the present conditions, the individualities of the two traditions become still more clear. There is a general opinion among the historians of western philosophy that the Middle Ages contributed nothing to the growth of philosophical thought. It is said that modern philosophy from Descartes onwards took up the thread where Greek philosophy left it, so that the Middle Ages formed a pure blank. Medieval philosophy was only theology based upon faith, to support which was the main function of reason. Modern philosophy detached reason from faith and continued the Greek tradition of pure scientific thinking. But the opinion that the Middle Ages had no philosophy is controverted by some. De Wulf thinks that those ages did possess philosophical systems as distinct from theology.[1] The Middle Ages produced not only scholastics but also anti-scholastics. St. Augustine, St. Anselm, and Thomas Aquinas were the leading thinkers of scholasticism; John Scotus Eriugena and Nicholas of Cusa of anti-scholasticism. "Pluralism, spiritualism, liberty, personal survival characterise scholasticism on the one hand; monism, materialism, moral determinism, and impersonal immortality are found in anti-scholasticism on the other."[2] Gilson maintains that the Middle Ages had a distinct philosophy of their own, which was Christian philosophy. This was not merely applied Platonism or Aristotelianism. Those times made their own contribution to the growth of Western thought, by continuing the ancient tradition and developing it in their own way. Christian philosophy was unique in making God the fundamental philosophical principle. "Now we know of no system of Greek philosophy which reserved the name of God for a unique being, and made the whole system of the universe revolve round this single idea."[3] ". . .the

forgotten that the introversion spoken of by Jung in its extreme form is abnormality and lunacy, whereas the deeper the inwardness which Indian philosophy advocates, the saner becomes the individual. It is safer not to use the words introversion and extroversion in this connection. If religion preaches introversion, in the sense in which Jung understands the term, then it could never have effected mental cure.

1. *History of Mediaeval Philosophy*, I, vii.
2. *Ibid.*, p. 15.
3. *The Spirit of Mediaeval Philosophy*, p. 43.

primacy of the Good, as Greek thought conceived it, compels the subordination of existence to the Good, while on the other hand the primacy of being, as Christian thought under the inspiration of the Exodus conceived it, compels the subordination of good to existence."[1] All Christian and medieval philosophy asserts the identity of essence and existence in God,[2] who is just the pure act of existing.[3]

Another great master of the medieval mind, Henry Osborn Taylor, holds a different opinion about it. It was more or less a transmitter of Greek thought and Neoplatonism, and had itself little original to contribute to philosophy. "It was not its destiny to produce an extension of knowledge or originate substantial novelties either of thought or imaginative conception. Its energies were rather to expend themselves in the creation of new forms—forms of apprehending and presenting what was (or might be) known from the old books, and all that from century to century was ever more plastically felt."[4] The structure of Neoplatonic thought was such as to fit every form of worship.[5] "Christianity and Neo-Platonism were an expression of the principle that life's primordial reality is spirit. And likewise with Christians as with Neo-Platonists, phases of irrationality may be observed in ascending and descending order. At the summit the sublimest supra-rationality, the love of God, uplifts itself. From that height the irrational conviction grades down to credulity preoccupied with the demoniacal and the miraculous."[6] St. Augustine was a Platonist; but his understanding of Plato was appreciably coloured by Neoplatonism.[7] And through Augustine, Neoplatonism influenced the whole of medieval philosophy. "For all the Middle Ages the master in theology was Augustine."[8]

One doubts whether the general estimate of medieval thought as given by Taylor is not after all true. The age may possess a

1. *The Spirit of Mediaeval Philosophy*, p. 55.
2. *Ibid.*, p. 61.
3. *Ibid.*, p. 52.
4. *The Mediaeval Mind*, I, p. 13.
5. *Ibid.*, p. 49.
6. *Ibid.*, p. 51.
7. De Wulf also says so. See his *History of Mediaeval Philosophy*, I, p. 127.
8. *The Mediaeval Mind*, II, p. 433.

few original thinkers. But the impression which an Indian student of medieval philosophy gets is that it is the application of Greek thought as developed in Neoplatonism, with of course certain modifications. Both Neoplatonism and Christianity made Being the fundamental principle, whether it is called by the name of God or by any other name. And this Being is beyond reason. What Gilson says about the difference between the idea of the Good and that of Being is equally applicable to Christianity and to Neoplatonism, which is a blend of Platonism and oriental thought. That Being is the fundamental principle of metaphysics. It is also a distinctly Upaniṣadic idea. The idea of the Good is arrived at by Plato from the side of concepts as such, while God or Brahman is arrived at from the side of Being. Plato conferred Being upon Ideas. But the Indian philosophers, not even excluding the Naiyāyikas and the Vaiśeṣikas, for whom universals and particulars are some of the fundamental categories of reality, denied Being to them. This is a very significant difference, the importance of which does not yet seem to have been noticed. Why do the Upaniṣadic thinkers refuse to speak of the concept of the *Ātman*, and why do they say that thought and concepts cannot reach it? Why do even the Mahāyāna Buddhists do the same? Because the Being or reality to which the concept is to be applied is within the applier, including and transcending him. This does not mean that a synoptic view of the universe is not attempted by the *Upaniṣads*. They do speak of the *Ātman* and the Brahman, and we get an idea of both. But this idea itself can never be their Being. When we apply the idea of chair to a physical chair in the judgment, "This is a chair," the idea or predicate reaches the Being of the physical chair. Yet the ideality or conceptuality of the predicate chair is not thereby lost; the predicate is still capable of being applied to other physical chairs. Even in the judgment, "This is the centre of the earth," which involves uniqueness, and in which the predicate and its ideality are entirely limited to the This, the predicate is still ideal. The distinction between the subject that makes the judgment and the object about which the judgment is made still persists. But it is impossible to make the judgment, "This is the Brahman," for the Brahman is the core of our Being and cannot be pointed to by the demonstrative This, as we point to the physical chair or to the centre of the earth; for if we are able to experience it, we lose our distinctness as subjects from the objects, which is a necessary precondition of every judgment. This is what the *Upaniṣads* mean when they say that language and concepts do not reach the Brahman. It is obviously false to say that they do not speak of it, or that they do not give us a synoptic view of the universe with the help of its idea. In any case, ideas or concepts as such have no being.

Though Plato attributes Being to ideas and says that particulars possess Being only so far as they partake of the ideas, the Socratic method by which these ideas are arrived at—which is the method of the formation of concepts or universals—and the forms which the controversy about the universals took in medieval thought, combined with the common opinion that Being is experienced here and now as the Being of the things around us, and that pure Being, whether treated as a universal or not, would be the barest abstraction from concrete things,[1] make the general reader think that Plato could attribute Being to his ideas only by some logical legerdemain, and that in his ideas essence and existence are difficult to identify. Their identification in God is not new to Neoplatonism,[2] by whatever name it calls its original principle. For Neoplatonism, the idea of Being is more fundamental than the idea of the good. Plotinus, unlike Plato, was little interested in the social life of man. "God has no need, says Plotinus, of the virtues of the citizen."[3] And on the whole, Christian philosophy also showed little interest in social thought, except so far as it concerned Christian preachings and institutions. All this shows that Christianity, as Taylor says, did not originate novel thoughts or concepts. In an important sense, Plato, Aristotle, and Plotinus were the standards of Christian philosophical truth.

Further, Christian philosophy, as philosophy, suffered from one disadvantage, its insistence on faith. This is not merely faith in God, though even that will not be admitted into philosophy by many. It is faith in the revelation of a particular

1. It is very strange that Christian critics of the Upaniṣadic idea of the Brahman as the ultimate reality, which is existence, forget that according to leading interpreters of medieval thought, their God Himself is such existence.
2. R. B. Tollinton, *Alexandrine Teaching of the Universe*, pp. 21 and 23.
3. *Ibid.*, p. 19.

historical person, Jesus—which suggests that other mortals cannot have that revelation and realization. Jesus may be the Logos, the mediator between man and God. But can there not be such mediating principle in each man ? Neoplatonism could give an affirmative answer and could thereby give man a nobler status in the world. Besides, by treating the mediators between man and God as principles, it was more philosophical than Christian philosophy, which is rather the application of philosophical principles to certain historical persons in order to understand the role which they play in religion.[1]

But it need not be thought that Christian philosophy had no influence on modern European thought. True, the Orphic element of Platonism, which reached the high watermark of its development in Neoplatonism by blending with oriental thought, was recast and refashioned by Christianity according to its own needs. But this process had its own effect on philosophy. It resulted in making Self (as the primary principle of reason) the basic philosophical principle. This was not a deliberate achievement of Christian thought. Modern philosophy wished to liberate reason from faith; and this it thought it could accomplish by separating the object from the subject, matter from mind, taking the object for itself and leaving the subject for faith and religion. This was really the adoption of the objective or scientific attitude by modern philosophy, which belonged to and was fostered by the Olympic element of ancient thought—an attitude which receded to the background in Neoplatonism and was condemned throughout the Middle Ages. The new attitude, resulting from the Renaissance, tried to make terms with Christianity by leaving out the subject. It thought that reason could deal with the object in isolation from the subject. Both rationalism and empiricism took up this attitude, though they studied the object in different ways, one by reasoning as in mathematics and the other by observation as in the natural sciences. But the epistemological and the body-mind problems to which such procedure gave rise, demonstrated the futility of it; and the objective attitude itself, which became conspicuous in British empiricism, betrayed its inherent self-contradiction,

1. Cf. the so-called *ādhyātmika* interpretation of the *Rāmāyaṇa*, according to which the characters of the story are philosophical and psychological principles.

when one of its advocates, Berkeley, said that the so-called objects could have no reality apart from mind. In Spinoza's philosophy, subject and object were again unified into the pure Being of substance, called God. Neoplatonism and Christianity thereby reasserted themselves. The idea of pure Being as the first principle of philosophy may be traced to the Eleatics; but it was a very crude concept in their philosophy. It did not constitute the primary principle of Plato or Aristotle. The disparity between the subject and object was not felt at that time, and the idea of pure Being was not attained by the unification of the two. By Spinoza subject and object were treated as attributes of Being. Hegel found fault with this method and turned this ultimate principle of substance into spirit or self-consciousness. That is, the ultimate principle is not only substance but also subject. In self-consciousness, the self is both subject and object. The Christian God and the Neoplatonic One now become spirit or self. This development of thought in European philosophy is due to the influence of Neoplatonism through Christianity. Plato does not seem to have called the ultimate principle of philosophy by the name of self, though Aristotle called it thought of thought. Aristotle treats God as the prime mover; but it is difficult to understand how thought of thought can be the prime mover. In the Hegelian idea of spirit, all these ideas find their unification.

But the introduction of the idea of self as the first principle, it was thought, introduced subjectivism into philosophy and brought ruin to the objective attitude, which alone could be rational and scientific. Hence arose the reaction against idealism of all types, the Platonic, the Berkeleian, and the Hegelian. Whether we treat ideas as values, mental states, or categories, it is said, we give preferential treatment to the subject as opposed to the object, which is harmful to all scientific philosophy, which permits only an objective attitude. The subject is only an object among objects. This new philosophical attitude can hardly deal with inner reality, for inwardness refuses to be explained in terms of outwardness, and outwardness can never be turned into inwardness. Whitehead and all schools of realists, Alexander, and Russell now adopt this attitude. The pragmatists also take to it. This is inevitable, because of the separation of subject and object at the beginning of modern philosophy, which implicitly treats the subject as one of two entities. The Hegelian development of it through Spinoza is understood as exalting one over the other and as even neglecting the second but not as bringing to the forefront a reality that is deeper than the two. For this attitude, that there is inwardness at all in our experience, becomes an ultimate philosophical mystery. Whitehead treats it thus. The subject, for him, is a "superject,"[1] which is the emergent actual occasion due to the realized togetherness of the individual essences of eternal objects. It is to be found not only in conscious beings but also at the inorganic level. It is again a concretion of a number of occasions. And this concretion remains a mystery, to solve which God is postulated. Evidently reason cannot solve it. The Hegelian principle of self, which was a principle of reason or thought, now becomes the principle of irrationality. Consequently, our inner life must lie outside the range of philosophy.

Such on the whole is the atmosphere of contemporary Western philosophy. It is unnecessary to refer to other philosophical trends like positivism, agnosticism, phenomenalism, naturalism, materialism, etc., which are more avowedly objectivistic. Whitehead is undoubtedly one of the foremost leaders of Anglo-American thought. In him many modern philosophical tendencies seem to have converged, and his ideas may be taken as representative. For him, philosophy is not so much a search for ultimate reality, inner or outer, as it is the working conception of the world as a whole. He claims to be a follower of the Platonic tradition. But in his philosophy is to be found only one of the strands we have noticed in Plato, namely, the intellectualistic, conceptual, or scientific. Further, even in Hegel we shall not be far wrong if we say that the inwardness of reality is not as such recognized. Both Hegel and his followers made self so formal a thought-product as to derive from it only a method for the explanation of reality. The Being of self was practically overlooked; and self was treated as reason in its highest activity and not as transcending reason, so that it lost the true inwardness of ultimate being. True inwardness is religious inwardness. But Hegel places philosophy above religion. There is practically no Christian philosopher of the Middle

1. *Process and Reality*, p. 39. See also *Science and the Modern World*, p. 230.

Ages who would accept the notion that reason can comprehend God and can be more than God. "As with Neoplatonism, there was in Christianity a principle of supra-rational belief in all these matters. At the top the revelation of Christ, and the high love of God which He inspired. This was not set on reason, but above it."[1] The setting of the philosophical consciousness, by Hegel, over the religious shows that the inwardness of reality, which religious consciousness alone can give, is not treated as ultimate. The philosopher, as the spectator of all existence including the inner, is detached from it; and his philosophy has turned out to be that of one who is external to reality and for whom reality is external.[2]

Modern western philosophy may therefore be taken as the triumph of the objective, or to be more exact, of the outward attitude over the inward. The word objective may be taken as opposed to the subjective. But true religious consciousness is not subjective consciousness but the deeper inner consciousness, which is the ground of both the subjective and the objective. What is meant is that man now looks for reality not within himself but outside himself. Almost all the tendencies of modern western philosophy are examples. Even humanism adopts this attitude. Man is the physical being as we see him. Whatever lies deep within him does not concern philosophy. Certainly, this attitude has its advantages. Because of the growth and spread of interest in things mundane, the lot of human beings has improved. Man is not comforted with the promise of happiness in heaven but is made comfortable and happy here and now. Intellectual and scientific progress could not have been what it is but for this attitude. Moral, political, and social institutions are being given new forms through its influence, and superstitious elements are being eradicated. We are having new systems of moral, political, and social thought, and the philosophy that strengthens and propagates this attitude should by all means be encouraged. India badly needs it and is now becoming increasingly conscious of the need. But to

1. *The Mediaeval Mind*, I, p. 60.

2. Probably Christianity by its insistence on the historical revelation of Christ and faith in His mediation is also responsible for creating an external attitude to religion. Christ (as a historical person) being external to us, our religious consciousness naturally adopts outward reference.

keep the attitude within bounds, it is essential to note that the adoption of that attitude alone leads to an unbalanced life.

V

The development of Indian philosophy has its own peculiarity, though its growth is of a less complex nature. The deep inwardness reached in the *Upaniṣads* and intensified after the rise of Buddhism and Jainism has never been lost. The *Jīva* of the Jainas, the *Nirvāṇa* of the Buddhists, the *Ātman* of Nyaya and Vaiśeṣika, Sāṁkhya and Yoga, the Brahman of the *Upaniṣads* as understood by every Vedāntic system are inner realities. Not even the Viṣṇu of the Vaiṣṇavas and the Śiva of the Śaivas and the Śakti of the Śāktas were left out as realities to be realized outside man. It made no difference whether the system was monistic or pluralistic, realistic or idealistic. Further, philosophy in India is just the exposition of this inwardness. The absence of the dogma that it is absolutely necessary to believe in a historical person as the mediator between God and man rendered the speculations purely philosophical. Many of the schools—Jainism, Buddhism, and even Vedāntism in its highest developments—dispensed with the personal God. Indian thought was thereby freed from any subservience to theology. In fact, for the Indians there is no separate system of thinking called theology. Christian theology, whatever may be its contribution to philosophy, started as the application of the pure philosophical thought of Greece, which it derived through Neoplatonism. But in India, such a procedure was never adopted. Even if we take the local religions like the Pancarātra and the Pāśupata into consideration, it is the Upaniṣadic philosophical tradition that absorbed them rather than vice versa. Their Gods, Viṣṇu and Śiva, got identified with the Brahman, and their highest developments became systems of the Vedānta.

As the Upaniṣadic religion had no dogmas and did not grow around a particular historical person, wherever it spread it did not destroy. It spread by incorporating every local religion, be that the worship of a benevolent god or a barbarous deity. The process of incorporation lay in conferring its own inwardness upon every cult, even though barbarous, of external worship. The forms of worship were given a new meaning; their aim was explained to be the creation of inwardness, which was ultimately to dispense with all forms of external worship. Every god was a form of the Brahman, and every goddess a form of the energy of the Brahman. The truth of both was inward; the figures in temples were only symbols.

It may be said that the relation between Neoplatonism and Christianity is just the same as that between the Upaniṣadic philosophy and the local cults of India. Just as Christianity assimilated Neoplatonic philosophy, the local cults assimilated the Upaniṣadic. But what happened was precisely the reverse. It is the Upaniṣadic tradition that absorbed the local cults. Christianity, whatever use it might have made of Neoplatonism, treated it as pagan, oriental, and un-Christian. On the other hand, the local cults of India are proud of being called Upaniṣadic. Rāmānuja, Mādhva, Śrīkaṇṭha, Śrīpati, and many other Vaiṣṇava and Śaiva teachers wrote commentaries on the *Upaniṣads*, or the *Brahmasūtras*, or both; and each contended that his philosophy alone was the Upaniṣadic philosophy. But none of the Christian fathers was correspondingly enthusiastic about Neoplatonism. Among the Indians, only the Jainas and the Buddhists did not care to trace their philosophy to the *Upaniṣads*, though as a matter of fact they were developing the Upaniṣadic philosophy of inwardness in their own way.

The development of the Upaniṣadic tradition is therefore a development of the philosophy of inwardness. The *Upaniṣads* themselves do not contain systematic expositions of inwardness. They contain statements of several truths or experiences, sometimes with some exposition and proof but often without them, of different persons belonging to different times and places. The *Bṛhadāraṇyaka* and the *Chāndogya Upaniṣads* were composed about the seventh and the sixth century B.C. Mahavira and Buddha belonged to about the sixth. Till then there were no systems of thought, though there were already germs of different schools,[1] and there were controversies between their exponents. Towards the beginning of the second century B.C., a schism arose within Buddhism, and during the discussions between the rival sects speculations about both logic and religion

1. See B. M. Barua, *A History of Pre-Buddhistic Indian Philosophy*.

started. About the beginning of the Christian era, the Buddhist *Prajñāpāramitās*, with their stress upon knowledge, were composed; and they mark the beginnings of the Mahāyāna as different from the Hīnayāna. This was the time when serious system building started. A number of schools began vigorous thinking. The Pāśupata (Śaiva) and the Pancarātra (Vaiṣṇava) schools also entered the philosophical stage at this time.[1] The formation of philosophical concepts seems to have been taken up in earnest from about the first century B.C., and continued up to about the seventh A.D., in all schools. The Buddhists excelled both the Jainas and the orthodox schools in system building. The great Mādhyamika and the Vijñānavāda systems of the Mahāyāna are much earlier than the Vedāntic systems, though the ideas of the Vedāntic systems are earlier than those of the others.[2] In the orthodox fold the first attempts at system building were made by a series of aphorisms or *sūtras* called the *Vaiśeṣikasūtras* (second century A.D.) of Kaṇāda, the *Nyāyasūtras* (second century A.D.) of Gautama, the *Mīmāṁsāsūtras* (second century A.D.) of Jaimini, the *Yogasūtras* (third century A.D.) of Patañjali, and the *Brahmasūtras* (fourth century A.D.) of Bādarāyaṇa.[3] The *Sāṁkhyasūtras* belong to as late as the fifteenth century A.D. By about the seventh century, commentaries on most of the *sūtras* were composed, though those on the *Brahmasūtras* are not available before Śaṁkara. Gauḍapāda is the first great Vedāntic advaitin whose writings are extant. He belonged to the seventh or the sixth century. Śaṁkara belonged to the eighth, and his is the first great available commentary on the *Brahmasūtras*. Other commentaries belong to later periods. Then followed the Śaivaite systems of thought in the ninth century, the most important of which is the *Spanda* (*Pratyabhijñā*) system of Vasugupta. Abhinavagupta is the greatest exponent of this school, which came to acquire the

1. It is said that these may be earlier, and the germs of their ideas can be traced to the Ṛgveda.

2. None of the works of Kāśakṛtsna and other Vedāntins referred to by Bādarāyaṇa in his *Brahmasūtras* is available, and we cannot say whether those works were detailed expositions or short discourses and utterances as in the *Upaniṣads*.

3. There is no unanimity about these dates.

name of Pratyabhijñā in his time. The great scholar king, Bhoja, belonged to this school.

Both Śaiva and Vaiṣṇava religions contain pluralism and monism, realism and idealism, and systems holding some middle positions. And yet the view of the inwardness of reality is constantly maintained. After all it is the *Ātman* that is to be meditated upon by all.[1] For monism, it is the same as the Brahman or ultimate reality; and for systems which admit some difference between the two, it is akin to the Brahman, and the Brahman is to be realized within it. Controversies between the schools led to elaboration of logical principles, theories of knowledge, psychological and metaphysical speculations, and theories of conduct. But generally these subjects are not discussed in separate treatises. As Taylor says of the philosophers of the Middle Ages,[2] the ancient Indians were not interested in knowledge for the sake of knowledge, but in knowledge for the sake of salvation, and the subjects were discussed in the same book as necessity for such discussion arose. But a few separate books, called *prakaraṇa granthas* (treatises on subjects), were written, especially on theories of knowledge. But these separate treatises on different subjects are not as many as one would wish.

One important phenomenon that happened in India is the disappearance of Buddhism from its native land. The Mohammadan invasions, the revolt of Brahmanism under Kumārila, the absorption of the highest phases of Buddhist philosophy by the Upaniṣadic through the efforts of Gauḍapāda and Śaṁkara, and the growth of Śaivism contributed to its disappearance. It has already been observed that Buddhism is the religion of inwardness par excellence, and its sole concern was inwardness. Its organization in India was practically confined to the monasteries; and when the Mohammadans destroyed them, Buddhism disappeared. Besides, there was the revolt of Kumārila on behalf of Brahmanism. And there was no occasion for the revival of even Buddhist philosophy; for the Vijñānavāda of the Mahāyāna, according to which Vijñāna or consciousness was the nature of ultimate reality, and the Śūnyavāda, according to which the Śūnya or the Void or Emptiness of all determinations

1. *Brahmasūtras,* IV, 1, 3.
2. *The Mediaeval Mind,* II, p. 62.

occupies that high place, were absorbed by the Vedānta of Gauḍapāda and the Śaivism of Kashmir.[1] The latter incorporated both. Between the third and the fourth states of the *Māṇḍukyakārikās*, which is a Vedāntic work, is placed a fifth state called the Śūnya, by the *Spandakārikās* of Śaivism. Thus the *Ātman* is said to have five states, wakefulness, dream, deep sleep, Śūnya, and the fifth which is the highest, identical with Śiva himself, and is pure *vijñāna*. In other words, the orthodox schools, while incorporating the philosophical concepts of the heterodox schools and of each other, generally assimilated their spiritual experiences also, so much so that, when Buddhism disappeared, no spiritual need was felt in India to revive it. Kashmir Śaivism, it is generally believed, developed under the influence of the Vedāntic Advaita, which contains both the ideas of *spanda* (vibration) and *pratyabhijñā* (recognition). Gauḍapāda himself regards the world as the *spanda* of *chitta* (mind).[2] And the view that our realization of the Brahman is not a becoming something other than ourselves, but is the recognition of our identity with it as eternally accomplished, belongs to Śaṁkara's Advaita as well.

The development of the philosophy of inwardness into full-grown systems took, we may say roughly, twenty centuries—from about the tenth century B.C. to about the tenth A.D. The wonder of it is, as the Western writers point out, that no thinker in these twenty centuries cared to give us a book like Plato's *Republic* or Augustine's *Civitas Dei*. Western thinkers generally remark that Indian religion is unethical. If the statement means that Hinduism permits immorality, there cannot be a greater untruth. Hinduism has as stringent moral codes as any other. But if the statement means that ancient Indian philosophy has not handed down to us any system of ethical thought, it is mostly true. But it should not mean that Indian philosophy did not insist upon what we generally regard as moral principles as absolutely necessary for religious progress. There cannot be a greater falsity than to say that Buddha's religion was unethical But he never discussed ethical principles

1. See the author's article, "An Unnoticed Aspect of Gaudapada's *Mandukya Karikas*," *Annals of the Bhandarkar Oriental Research Institute*, XXVI, Part I.

2. See the same.

relating to social structure. His ethics, like any other Indian teacher's ethics, was the ethics of inwardness. There is a very important sense in which it is more ethical than the ethics of the West. Western ethics loses its meaning except in society : a Robinson Crusoe has no ethics. But Indian ethics has its importance even for a Robinson Crusoe. It is meant to fit into any social structure and laws. It is chiefly concerned with the discipline of the individual and is the fulfilment of social ethics.[1]

If the word ethics is understood as principles of discipline governing conduct irrespective of society, then Indian philosophy contains as much ethics as the western. There is systematic thinking about this discipline, so far as it concerns the path of inwardness. Even Christian philosophy could not have given a profounder ethical thought, so far as the aim of life is taken to be inner realization, than Buddhism.[2] If Christianity, like Buddhism, is a religion of intense inwardness, its ethics must indeed be capable of being fitted into any system of social ethics. God and man do not change; but our social ideas and rules of conduct change from place to place and time to time; and this change does not preclude the duty of man's realizing the inner truth. Somehow this supreme duty must make other duties subserve itself, without coming into conflict with them and without hindering social progress. That is why Buddhist religious ethics could accord with the social ethics of quite different countries, India, China, Japan, Burma, Annam, etc. Its ethics was the completion of the social ethics of these countries; and it did not oppose its own ethics to theirs.

The western criticism of Indian thought is based on an ambiguity in the meaning of the term ethics. The word is derived from ethos, which means customs, manners, etc., of communities. Indian philosophy has no system of thinking about such manners and customs. But the word ethics means also good conduct;

1. Attempts are made to interpret Hindu society according to the principle of *Dharma* (Law, Norm, Reality). But it cannot be proved that the philosophical meaning of *Dharma* was ever applied to the formation of society, and that its philosophy was first thought out and then an application made of it.

2. See Mrs. Rhys Davids, *Buddhist Psychological Ethics*; A. V. Govinda, *Psychological Attitude of Early Buddhist Philosophy*; and Tachibana, *The Ethics of Buddhism.*

and the conclusion is falsely derived that Indian religion does not insist on good conduct. But no other religion insists upon stricter morality than the Indian. The defect of Indian ethics, which we now feel, is that it in its turn is incomplete so far as the life of action concerns this world.

Like ethics, Indian psychology also was occupied with the inward. To quote what was said elsewhere: "If such a philosophy [of inwardness] is consistently and systematically developed, its attitude will be reflected in its ethics, metaphysics, epistemology, psychology and so forth. Just as we denied that, for the ancient Indian, there was a philosophy separate from religion and a religion separate from philosophy, similarly we should deny that there was ethics, epistemology, or psychology separate from religion. Psychology gives us different levels of inwardness; epistemology and metaphysics describe how that innermost reality blossomed into the world of subject and object; and ethics prescribes the ways in which if our life is disciplined, we reach that innermost reality.[1]

The advent of Islam did not contribute much to Indian philosophical thought as such; for its own philosophical developments were meagre, when compared to those already existing in India. Whatever it itself incorporated from Greece and Alexandria had little novelty for the Indian. Like Christianity, it could not be grafted on another religion. Developed round a historical person and with many dogmas, it had to destroy wherever it went; and unlike Buddhism outside India, it could not complete whatever was found incomplete. But it did give rise to some reformed religions like the Vīraśaivism (Militant Śaivism) of South India, the non-idolatrous Sthānakavāsī sect of the Jainas in Gujarat, and Sikhism in the Punjab. To philosophy, its contribution is negligible. The advent of Christianity also has only similar effects.

The present condition of philosophy in India, if by it we mean original activity, may be described as stagnant. The Christian missionaries first took interest in it, not to encourage it but to find defects in it and thereby prove the superiority of Christianity. Meanwhile, Europe, in particular Germany, began studying it; and the discovery of Sanskrit learning was hailed by Schlegel

1. "Indian Philosophy : Its Attitude to the World" (*The Vedanta Kesari*, XXI, 169).

as next in importance to the Renaissance. Vast stores of Buddhist philosophy were discovered. Then Indians themselves began studying their ancient authors, using the same scientific methods as the Europeans. There were the Indian Renaissance and the creation of national feeling. Indians have now understood the comparative greatness of their ancient thought; and a few critical minds have noticed its comparative shortcomings also. They feel that one-sided inwardness is as harmful as one-sided outwardness. Reconciliation between the two is talked of. But it is not seen that true reconciliation is not possible without synthesis, and no attempt at a synthesis is made philosophically.

It has been remarked that, in ancient Indian philosophy, logic, ethics, epistemology, metaphysics, psychology, and religion are singularly mixed up. Modern scholarship, following western models, is trying to separate them and to bring the Indian speculations into life with the western. Yet comparatively little work is done in ethics and psychology.

VI

This brief delineation of the two philosophical traditions, it is believed, throws into relief the peculiarity of the two perspectives. The western tradition is essentially a philosophy of outwardness, and the Indian a philosophy of inwardness. It is not meant that in either tradition the other element is completely lacking. Its presence is felt only incidentally now and then; it is otherwise pushed to the background and even neglected. And the Indian tradition is more consistently inward than the western is outward. Now and then in the latter, inwardness comes to the top and stays there for a fairly long time, particularly in Neoplatonism and medieval thought. But if this inwardness is really due to oriental influence—even Orphism is said to be oriental—then Western thought as such may be treated as essentially outward in its attitude. Even the differences between empiricism and rationalism, realism and idealism, materialism and spiritualism, etc., in western thought, are differences within this attitude and belong to the tradition of outwardness. Similar differences are found in the Indian tradition. It is, however, not to be thought that every Indian is an ascetic, without any sense of enjoyment and any taste for pleasures.

What the ancient Indian felt was that no philosophy was required to justify pleasures and enjoyments, whatever be the forms prescribed for them. Probably he was mistaken here. An affirmative attitude to the world needs philosophical support, as life here has to be ordered according to ideals and principles. What the Indian thinkers accomplished, namely, the division of life into the four *āśramas* or stages, was not enough; and they accepted the caste system as it formed itself, without any endeavour to introduce a principle for recasting it whenever necessary. In short, the philosopher as such was indifferent to all. For instance, Buddha preached salvation to all; but he did not care to teach equal social status for all. It would be unfair to say that either he or Christ was a capitalist. Neither cared to think of economics or politics. Their only concern was with salvation.

Bearing these two main differences in view, a few contrasts in detail may be pointed out.

First, Indian philosophy is Ātman-centric. Both the starting point and end of philosophy are the *Ātman*. Everything originates from the *Ātman* and is dissolved in it. It is the centre of interest, the central principle in metaphysics, psychology, ethics, aesthetics, and religion. But western philosophy is society-conscious. Philosophy begins as a social adventure among the Sophists. Even modern science is said to be a social venture.[1] How to lead the best life on earth is the main concern and not infrequently the only concern. And life is social. Hence the peculiar outlook of western philosophy. Even the inwardness which Christianity endeavoured to foster was gradually changed into outwardness by the empirical or what Whitehead calls the historical revolt.[2] As Professor Radhakrishnan says in another connection: "It is not the pale Galilean that has conquered, but the spirit of the West."[3]

Secondly, for the Upaniṣadic tradition, man is part (*aṁśa*) of Īśvara or the Absolute, which is within him. For this theory, it is immaterial whether the individual retains his individuality or not in that reality. The highest aim in life is the realization of that reality. But for western philosophy, man is part of nature, which is to be controlled.

1. Levy, *The Universe of Science*, ch. iv.
2. *Science and the Modern World* (1926), 11.
3. *Eastern Religions and Western Thought*, p. 271.

Next, according to the *Upaniṣads,* for man to be happy he should control his mind and attain a state of desirelessness.[1] But the western tradition has gradually developed the idea that man should control nature and make it serve his needs.

In the fourth place, whether reality is immanent or transcendent, ultimate reality, according to Indian philosophy, is the other to everything conceivable.[2] But western thought, particularly the contemporary, is showing greater and greater dissatisfaction with such an idea. The neo-idealism of Croce has brought down the transcendent Absolute of Hegel, and Marx claims to have placed the Hegelian Absolute on its feet again. Russell, Whitehead, Dewey, Alexander, and many other contemporary great thinkers see reality here itself. Even immortality is interpreted as belonging to the life on earth.[3]

Fifthly, preoccupation of thought with pure inwardness and the consequent indifference to externals have produced in India a purely universalistic outlook, which is, for example, exhibited in the tolerance which Hinduism shows to Islam and Christianity. The value of social solidarity, much less that of nationhood, was not felt by the ancient Indians. The present national feeling is not due to Indian philosophy. It may be admitted that Christianity is universalistic. But western philosophy on the whole promoted thinking in terms of society. It is not meant that India had no tribes or tribal feelings and conflicts. But thinking was never encouraged in terms of them. And we should not overlook the fact that for more than half a century philosophers of the West are speaking of national philosophies. Political and social thought of the West is the contribution of philosophers. But India has no political and social thought which may be regarded as systematic.

It may again be repeated that this presentation of the two traditions, with a view to throwing their peculiarities into relief, is not meant to prove the superiority or inferiority of one to the other. Each tradition has a long history and can count very great names as its followers. The world can no longer be left a zoo of cultures and philosophical traditions. It has to become one, and reflectively one, though this oneness is already being

1. Some contemporary Indians are vigorously attacking this attitude.
2. Cf. *neti neti* of the Upaniṣads.
3. Cf. Alexander, *Moral Order and Progress,* p. 413.

felt, sometimes happily and other times painfully. It is time for the two philosophical traditions to become one, each acting as the fulfilment of the other.

In the end, one point may be brought to the notice of the reader. Indian philosophy has no important developments from about the fifteenth century A.D. It has produced no new system of thought and has created no new philosophical concept. Only very recently, after the advent of the British, have Indians begun taking serious interest in their ancient philosophy. But the interest is still antiquarian and not originative and creative. To compare western philosophy, which has up to date developments, with the Indian, which stopped progressing by about the fifteenth century, it may be thought, is unfair; for the richness and variety of modern western philosophy, its manifold development covering all spheres of life, is lacking in the Indian. There is a large amount of truth in this criticism. The efforts of leading Indian philosophers are now devoted to expositions and interpretations, though a few are aware of the need for creative work. But whatever forms creative work will take in the future, if the Indian universities encourage it, it will be a continuation and expansion of the Upaniṣadic tradition, by including whatever the tradition formerly excluded. It has to be a synthesis of Indian and western philosophical traditions. Similarly, however manifold its development has been, the western tradition will lack completion until synthesized with the Indian. The two traditions are really counterparts of each other; and that they are so must now be philosophically recognized—which necessitates a new synthetic activity that can demonstrate the truth.

Post Script

The editors of this book selected this paper of mine published long ago in *The Philosophical Review* (March, 1947)[1] for inclusion in the book. They have also invited me to add what I think

1. P. T. Raju, "The Western and the Indian Philosophical Traditions," *The Philosophical Review*, Vol. LVI, No. 2 (March 1947), 127-55.

today about the subject after over thirty years. But curiously enough, my own views have not changed very much, whatever my readers think about me. The purpose of the editors is to determine : (1) What is 'Indian' about Indian philosophy ?; (2) What is the goal of Indian philosophy ?; (3) What is the responsibility of the Indian philosopher ?; and (4) What is the function of Indian philosophy ? In my view, the answers to these questions were indicated by me in my Presidential Address, "Indian Thought : Past and Present" (All India Oriental Conference, 1948—Section on Indian Philosophy and Religion); my Presidential Address, "The Task of the Indian Philosopher: Present and Future" (All India Darsanik Parishad, 1958); my *Introduction to Comparative Philosophy*;[1] *The Concept of Man*;[2] and *Lectures on Comparative Philosophy*[3] and several other places in which I did comparative philosophy in depth and which have attempted to show in deep and basic details the peculiarities, advantages and disadvantages of what is generally called Indian philosophy.

Now, what is 'Indian' about Indian philosophy ? One may as well ask: What is Greek about Greek philosophy ? What is German about German philosophy ? and more importantly, what is Chinese about Chinese philosophy ? The questions can be answered by skimming the surface or by going deep into the theoretical structures of the traditions. Geographical and political causes prevented Chinese thought from being systematically absorbed by the Western; nor was it absorbed by the Indian. But has not what even the peculiarly Chinese philosopher, Confucius, said relevance for all times and chimes ? How much of what is called Chinese Wisdom is not found in the teachings of the Indian epics, *purāṇas*, *itihāsas*, and *mahākāvyas* ? These epics are full of practical wisdom and some philosophy for man and society. Some of what Confucius said may be outdated. But essentially, his social concern, his *Ausgangspunkt*, is not unimportant for any time. Has not the standpoint of Marx, who

1. P. T. Raju, *Introduction to Comparative Philosophy* (Carbondale, Ill: Southern Illinois University Press, 1970).

2. P. T. Raju and S. Radhakrishnan : *The Concept of Man* (London: George Allen and Unwin, 1966).

3. P. T. Raju, *Lectures on Comparative Philosophy* (Poona : University of Poona, 1969). Also A. J. Bahm's *Comparative Philosophy* (Albuquerque, N. M. World Books, 1977) is worth considering in this connection.

has supplanted Confucianism in China—is it not for a time?—the same concern ? If it is recognized that what is central to Chinese thought is present in Western thought—although not at the centre—what will be the residue in Chinese thought that can be called purely Chinese ? Yes, there will still be something. But that something will be outmoded, about which even the Chinese educated will be apologetic—which in practice amounts to disowning.

What should we say about Greek and German philosophies? They have become part of the current of Western philosophy. Have not Kant, Hegel and the German transcendentalism had much influence on the British, American, French, and Russian philosophies ? Have even the British stopped mentioning their names ? Where are we to draw the line between the so-called East and the so-called West ? Between materialism on the one side and spiritualism and humanism on the other ? Between modern science with its culture and the spiritual life with its human concern ? To do so will be absurd in view of what we observe over the whole world. Whatever the British say, British idealism, philosophies of history, and Scottish theology owe a great deal to German scholars and thinkers. But the post-Kantian idealism, which characterizes the Golden Age of Germany and its influence on the Romantic Movement and theologies, which were wafted over to the British Isles and even to America, imbibed quite profound elements from the *Upaniṣads* and the philosophies of the Vedānta. Yes, just as Chinese scholars differentiate between Buddhism in China and Chinese Buddhism, one may differentiate between the Vedānta in Germany, which we may say is confined to German Indologists, and the German Vedānta, which is the work of German philosophers who were idealists, romanticists, salvationists (*nirvāṇists*) and similar thinkers. But such differentiations are not significant when we consider global thought currents. (It may be useful here to read the Introduction to my book, *The Problem of the Self*.[1]) Now, when particular traditions are absorbed in the universal thought current, will the traditions retain their peculiarities in any concrete form, except in the minds and works of cultural analysts, who separate strands constituting the unity

1. P. T. Raju, *The Problem of Self* (The Hague : Martinus Nijjhoff, 1968).

of the rope? Furthermore, if philosophy gains, in the near or distant future, a common aim as the characteristic by which it will be called philosophy, how much of these isolated characteristics of the philosophical nationalists and provincialists will remain intact? The same questions can be asked about religions. In their case, the tendency to defend their peculiarities, either by discovering them or inventing them, and to emphasize their superiority, is stronger than in philosophy, although it is often found in philosophy also as philosophy makes inroads into religion. Once recently I had the experience of a Christian pastor who retorted: "Do you want me to believe that Christianity is derived from the Vedas?" when I had remarked that, according to many scholars, the Vedas and the Avesta were the oldest literature of the Aryan race. Has he drawn a rational or sentimental conclusion? In Canada also I had the same experience, and I suspected some vested interests and motives also. Not only comparative religion but also comparative philosophy is considered to be the Devil's Work, just as Śaṁkara was called in India a Buddhist in disguise (*pracchanna-bauddha*). Friedrich Max Müller had the worst reaction of the type in the nineteenth century. Is Bradley right in saying that philosophy is the discovery of reasons for what we believe on sentiment (I substitute 'sentiment' for 'instinct') and are the anti-religious thinkers right in saying that religion is the acceptance of the superstitions of our ancients? What are we talking about when we are talking about religion and philosophy? Are we talking about the same subjects? There is now greater confusion in understanding these terms than ever before. For even philosophy in the important universities of the English-speaking countries is not what it has been, viz., the philosophy of the Grand Tradition.[1] Philosophy is defined as philosophizing, which has resulted in dilettantism, even frivolity, lack of earnestness and of universal guidelines; it is said that philosophy is the throwing overboard of metaphysical statements, all of which are said to be meaningless, as though these statements are floating in a vacuum ready to be picked up.

1. Bertrand Russell's view that pure, logical rationality has to be the guide to life (cp. the Greek view) is absurd. How can logic, which has been turned into a hypothetico-deductive science, be a guide to life, as such logic can have no moorings?

But what is metaphysics ? Indian philosophy is still studied in many places as though it is some antiquarian material or some primitive thought. It is against the attitude of such study that I have been insisting upon studying it as metaphysics—unfortunately, metaphysics also has been in bad repute now—with the same humility and earnestness as that shown towards Plato, Aristotle, Kant, Hegel and other great Western philosophers. For me, the word 'metaphysics' means what it meant for Aristotle—for which he does not seem to have cared very much and about which the Hellenistic philosophers were earnestly concerned—namely, what is beyond physics (*physis*, *bhāva*, what is beyond Becoming including psychology and sociology). It is, therefore, ontology, the study of Being, which I showed in my recent studies[1] to be identical with the I-am (I-consciousness, *ahaṁdhī*) and by reaching which, as one scholar says, cognition, knowledge and faith (*śraddhā*) take rest and settle down. He means that mind reaches unagitated Being from Becoming (agitation and uncertainty, compare Descarte's *cogito*). This is not speculative metaphysics, for speculation lacks restfulness and stands suspended as the construction of a possible hypothesis. In the *sum* or the I-am of the Cartesian principle, there is the conscious self-certainty of one's Being, not a blind, irrational leap into something. This is what Buddha practically taught, and Heidegger and some others like him intended to teach theoretically or rather by existential analysis. Even Kierkegaard's leap into something unknown is not a leap into something absolutely unknown; for how does he know that there is something, which is not intellectually or in some other way grasped, into which man has to leap ? If that something is so absolutely unknown as Kierkegaardians seem to say, even its existence must be unknown. But Kierkegaard knows that it exists. Then the right interpretation of his position is that the leap is a leap into something which is the reality of one's own transcendental existence or Being. Unless a deeper level, a transcendental level of the Being of one's I-am is accepted, Kierkegaard's position will lose its value. And if accepted, the shipwrecks and the inevitable failures of life taught by Jaspers and Sartre

1. P. T. Raju, "Being : How Known and How Expressed," *International Philosophical Quarterly*, XV, No. 2 (June 1975), 161-79.

will lose their tragic sting, as the self-transcending nature of the I-am is recognized both in theory and experience. We may say that Becoming is Being in vibration (*spanda*) and Being is Becoming without the process of vibration; and for every moment of Becoming, Being stands in its transcendence. As one Sanskrit savant said: What is metaphysics for, if not as a theoretical guide for spiritual realization? Otherwise, it will be disconnected experiments in theorizing, defining each experiment as the true philosophy at the whim of the thinker. Such activity turns philosophy into some amorphous intellectual speculations about proximate and ultimate problems of the universe, which can at the most be speculations about cosmology. That is why metaphysics lost its distinctive meaning and prestige, and philosophy is equated to the activity of philosophizing, whatever that be according to the person philosophizing.

One distinctive character of Indian philosophy is that, in spite of many cosmological theories and speculations which even ontology cannot completely avoid, it on the whole stuck to the main view of metaphysics as the theory of what lies beyond Becoming and, in addition, as leading to practical ways of reaching the goal. (Of course, many contemporary philosophers in Indian universities are exceptions.) If Western philosophy, deliberately or by accident, adopts the same attitude to the subject, it will meet Indian philosophy; and the stream of both endeavours will flow as one, joined also by the Chinese and the Jewish streams. Even then, the question, "What is 'Indian' about Indian philosophy", will have the same significance as the question, What is Greek about Greek philosophy?, and neither question will cease to have meaning.

II

For the question's meaning can still be significant in spite of all the streams joining and flowing together. It is unfortunate that Paul Deussen's volumes on *The History of Philosophy* are not available in English translation from German. His work, of course not up to date, is really the first great attempt to make history of philosophy a history of philosophy of the whole world. Bertrand Russell recognized that unfortunately histories of philosophy, including his own, were only history of Western philosophy. Perhaps nobody brought the importance of

Deussen's work to his notice. Deussen gave great, if not equal importance, to the Chinese and the Indian philosophies. We can see in his work the specific importance of the contributions which each tradition could make to philosophy. Before him, the tendency was to dismiss the Chinese and the Indian contributions as of little or no significance, and to treat those thinkers who attached any importance to them as eccentrics. This tendency is still prevalent, having been, for a long time, strengthened by the phenomenon of colonialism, and any admiration of foreign outlooks and religions is now called a "craze"—which is unfortunately substantiated by persons who take advantage of it. A craze is a false and temporary earnestness, a temporary groping for something lacking in the prevalent culture and religion and tolerated by them and their pressures. But if there is really some essential, undeniable value for man in the life and culture admired, the earnestness cannot remain temporary, but lasting and eternal, at least as long as humanity lasts.

We should ask a deeper question about philosophy being peculiarly Chinese or Indian. Is a philosophy Chinese because it was born in China? Gunpowder was born in China, but it is no longer Chinese and nobody calls it "Chinese powder." Indeed, the simple way of understanding a term like "Indian philosophy" is to think of it as what was born and developed in isolation in the geographical area now called India. But if all essential thought is universal or has universal applicability, and if essential human nature is universal—which we do and have to assume them to be—then the irreducible and non-universalizable peculiarities will be accidents of geography; and all that is generalizable and assimilable by other cultures is important for man in all the lands. It is this generalization and assimilation, not merely in thought but also in practice, that can reduce conflicts and make world peace possible. If, for instance, Christianity maintains that Christ is the only Son of God and all men not believing in him are beyond God's realm and protection; and if likewise Islam declares that Christ is only a prophet, not certainly the greatest, and Mohammad only is the greatest and the last of the prophets, the way is open to conflict, when their followers fanatically cling to such beliefs. There is also another trend which thinkers read in international relationships: The Israel-born religions are true religions, superior to the India-born and China-born and that the followers of the Israel-born religions are close brothers as against the followers of the other two. I have not noticed this attitude among the Jews. However, the particularistic attitudes are not conducive to world peace, although every religion claims that its aim is world peace (but unfortunately on its own terms).

Another mistaken or half-mistaken procedure in evaluating philosophies is to deduce the structure of the philosophical outlook of a people from the structure of their language. This practice became a fashion after the great German scholar and thinker Alexander von Humboldt. But what are we to do if there are thinkers in that language who developed more than one philosophy of their language? They indeed studied the structure of their language as well as any outsider. This is particularly so of Sanskrit, in which there are at least a dozen philosophies of language, of which those of Bhartṛhari, of the Mīmāṁsā, and of the Nyāya-Vaiśeṣika are typically important. The first is the most profound I have known; and all the three can be generalized and made applicable to many languages other than Sanskrit, including the non-Aryan. What von Humboldt said is very helpful—upto a degree only—in studying the general outlook of primitive people who do not have a philosophy of language of their own. Even then the philosophy of their language has to be substantiated by deductions from observable ways of their life, by somewhat the kind of philosophy (*Lebensphilosophie*) associated with the name Wilhelm Dilthey. But even this helpfulness may not remain valid after those people become educated and philosophically self-conscious. In view of this phenomenon, what is peculiar to Indian philosophy has to be told also by Indians themselves, as they were for millenniums before B.C. and have been philosophically self-conscious, in the light of comparisons with other philosophical traditions. In fact, it is the Indians who first developed the philosophy of linguistics, and Pāṇini wrote the first philosophical grammar of any language. However, the comparisons of the different philosophies of grammar should not be superficial, and should be controlled by guidelines supplied by the principle that all earnest philosophies are plans for the search of Being within Becoming, of peace within the turmoil and struggle for existence.

III

My experience both in India and outside shows that one is generally apologetic and has to be so, if one is earnestly religious and aims at one's spiritual uplift. This is a common trend particularly in academic circles, the members of which generally say : "Oh no, my interest in religion is only academical." I heard it even of and from persons who led celebate lives all their life in the name of the God and the Supreme Spirit. But with my meaning of metaphysics, I do not wish to be apologetic. The result may be that I shall not be regarded as a true academician. This attitude toward me does not bother me. But I can affirm that I am academical. "Academical" does not and should not mean lack of earnestness and conviction about what one is led to by his research—either practical, theoretical or experiential. It is a great Upaniṣadic truth, viz., the person (the I-am) is made up of faith. (*Sraddhāmayo ayaṁ puruṣah*). This statement is wrongly understood often as "man is full of convictions." But it is more in line with the Cartesian principle, "I think, therefore I am"—but deeper than it. It is faith—undoubtable conviction—of one's own (of one's I-am's) existence. Otherwise, why should not man doubt that he exists ? And why is one who entertains such a doubt regarded as being out of mind ? Is this conviction peculiar to Indian philosophy and enough to make it peculiarly Indian ? In any case, Indian philosophy—particularly the Upaniṣadic tradition and its branches—is essentially ontological and existential, not only in theory but also in practical life. It touches, and is not satisfied until it touches the roots of Being; and culturally, it is not content until its cultural forms like music and language are traced to their roots in Being. It is not satisfied with mere forms of Becoming.

Finally, I have to add that I do not stand by the dates given in the main essay. It looks that the early historical periods in the development of the constructive stage of Indian philosophy belong to about the fifth and the fourth centuries B.C. The tendency of many Western Indologists to place them much later in the A.D. is regarded generally as prejudiced. In matters of ancient history like that of India, there seems to be evidence almost for and against many views. Some contemporary historical scholars say that even the Mohenjo-Daro civilization was not pre-Aryan, but Aryan. If this theory is strongly substantiated, some of the dates have to be pushed further back.

IV

Two questions remain to be answered: (1) What is the responsibility of the Indian philosopher? and (2) What is the future of Indian philosophy? I think that the answers have already been suggested. Taking the second question first, I think that the future of Indian philosophy will be what the future of German philosophy, French philosophy, Greek philosophy, and Russian dhilosophy will be, assuming of course that philosophers of the future will not be mere dilettantes, arm-chair philosophers, light-heartedly and even frivolously talking, hair-splitting, arguing for and against problems and their solutions, but earnest thinkers about life, its problems and solutions, its aims and ways of achievement. It seems to me that it is this attitude which some of the contemporary existentialists like Karl Jaspers have in mind when they say that the philosopher ought to get involved in his philosophy, not merely in the success or failure of an intellectual game.[1] This is again what the ancient sages of both the East and the West wanted philosophy for. Even Plato's philosophy would not have had that appeal and applicability which it has to even our times, had he not fled for life from Syracuse and earnestly delved into the political and social problems of life. The world is becoming one and the earth may even send out colonies to outer space. In that event, provincialism and nationalism will be matters of the past, and man will speak of his American, European or Asian origins, as he speaks of his British, French, or German origins in the United States. Yet, the spiritual and intellectual quest about life and its purpose will be everlasting; and into it the Indian, Greek, Chinese and German philosophies will enter as contributions to solutions of ever-recurring and newly shaping problems of human existence. They will not be dead, but will become part and parcel of the general push forward of the spiritual and intellectual quest.

Regarding the responsibility of the Indian philosopher—I mean here by "Indian philosopher" not one who is confined to studying and teaching ancient and classical Indian schools, but one who belongs to India—I have already said something in my papers referred to above. Provided he is earnest about

1. Compare the Indian ideas of *Kathā* and *vāda*.

philosophy—provided, as it is said, he lives to do philosophy, but not merely does philosophy to live (to obtain a livelihood)—he, and in my opinion, every earnest philosopher, has to be spiritually oriented, whether or not he is able to reach great spiritual heights. From that spiritual standpoint, he has to take into consideration the human problems which other cultures, particularly the highly advanced ones, have created; and he has to make every attempt to assimilate and absorb whatever is essential and true wherever it is found. Just as no nation can afford to exist now in isolation, no philosophy can be living if it does not try to comprehend other philosophies and incorporate their truths. It is a vain attempt to exclude even the so-called irrationalisms from philosophy; for they represent an essential aspect of human life. Spirituality and rationality are omnivorous; they absorb, swallow, everything that is real and true, even irrationalisms. Not only nations but also philosophies tend to become extinct, if they cannot absorb what lies outside them. Here lies the meaning of the Spirit of the universe, including all living beings, being one. It remains one by absorbing everything. It is this absorption that is the main aspect of comparative philosophy in depth; otherwise, it will be shallow. The aim and responsibility of the Indian philosopher has to be such absorption.

4

THE QUESTION OF INDIANNESS OF INDIAN PHILOSOPHY

K. B. RAMAKRISHNA RAO*

THE question of Indianness of Indian philosophy has two implications: (a) that there is something unique or typical which makes Indian philosophy 'Indian', and (b) that there is nothing special about it to earn a designation of its own.

Ever since comparative studies in philosophy and religion were undertaken, there has been a continuous dialogue on particular problems and unique distinctions of Eastern and Western philosophies. Eminent thinkers and scholars have devoted their energies in maintaining one side or the other, and some have even tried to find a synthesis of the points of view to arrive at a 'World Philosophy'. Significant reflections of these attempts are found in independent works, and sometimes brought to focus on platforms of International Conferences and Congresses.[1] Mention must be made of the participants who have done a lot in this direction, the notable amongst them being Charles A. Moore, E. A. Burtt, F. C. S. Northrop, W. E. Hocking, S. Radhakrishnan, P. T. Raju, Ananda Coomaraswamy, W. T.

*K. B. Ramakrishna Rao is Professor of Indian Philosophy and Head of the Department of Philosophy, University of Mysore, Mysore, India. He is the author of *Ontology of Advaita with Special Reference to Maya, Theism of Preclassical Sāṁkhya, Advaita as Philosophy and Religion, Problems and Perspectives of Advaita,* etc.

1. See, for example the proceedings of the three World Conferences of Philosophy organized at University of Hawaii under the stewardship of Professor Charles A. Moore.

Chan, H. Nakamura, etc. Discussions on the problem have been lively, sometimes undertaken on sincere academic grounds, and sometimes sliding into passionate expressions. Contents, methodology and goals have been discussed for establishing differences or identities of philosophies Eastern and Western. Though no consensus has been arrived at regarding the problem, counselling on any hasty generalization in favour of any one point has also been expressed by Charles Moore thus: "that any simplification is an oversimplification when we are speaking or thinking in terms of entire cultures or philosophical traditions or geographical areas."[1]

If philosophy is understood to be an intelligent intellectual response to situations of life, or is taken as an attempt to understand problems of reality or existence and value, the possibility of common or diverse approaches cannot be denied or avoided —common between unconnected peoples and times, diverse between the same cultural or historical groups at simultaneous or different times. Agnosticism, atheism, idealism, realism, monism, pluralism, empiricism, transcendentalism, positivism or even existentialism are features of philosophy the world over. Plato and Kant, Hegel and Bradley are as much reflected in India, as the Buddha, Śaṁkara and Rāmānuja are reflected in the West. Indian thinking is as much Indian as it could be Western, or vice versa, from many points. For a sane estimate, labels such as *Indian* or *English*, *Greek* or *American* are just conventional. Comparative studies have introduced a mellowing effect on estimates of exclusive nature by saying that philosophies are, to a large extent, complementary. The most unique attempt at discovering the typological distinctions of Indian (or broadly, Eastern) and Western by Northrop (viz., that the former is philosophy by intuition i.e. understanding things by their aesthetic component, and the latter is philosophy by postulation, i.e. understanding things in their theoretic component) did not prevent him from concluding that they are mutually complementaries.[2] Burtt is another writer, whose investigations have led him to the same position. He says: ". . .at their heart the

1. C. A. Moore (ed), *Philosophy and Culture : East and West* (Honolulu : University of Hawaii Press, 1962), p. 701.

2. F. C. S. Northrop, *Meeting of East and West* (New York : Macmillan, 1950).

two (East and West) attitudes do not contradict each other, they can be viewed as mutually complementary. Not only do they agree on a high valuation of man in his distinctive potentialities."[1] In his 'discovery', as he wishes to be understood, he says: "the cause for treating philosophies as different is an underlying philosophical presupposition," which each philosopher carries with him. He says, "it is vital to remind ourselves that there are presuppositions we think *with* so naturally and constantly that it requires a severe wrench for us to free ourselves from their clutches sufficiently to think *about* them. . .that is why the issues. . .are often hard to resolve."[2] In his analysis, specially, of some of the most important concepts that occur in Indian philosophy (such as 'experience,' 'truth,' 'liberation,' '*karma*,' 'causality,' etc.) and the Western approach to them, Burtt has shown that it is one's natural *presupposition* which has stood in the way of useful dialogue or mutual understanding. He writes: "Most Westerners who have seriously inquired into Oriental thought have the puzzling experience of discovering that while there appears to be essential equivalence of meaning between certain of their traditional categories and corresponding Indian or Chinese concepts, in the presence of others they seem to confront something alien and opaque."[3] But, he points out that if one were to overcome or wrench out from one's presupposition and discover the *context* and the genius out of which concepts and philosophies have grown, it would become evident to him that what appeared alien and opaque would not remain so. The position of Radhakrishnan is clear regarding the issue: "There are no reasons to believe that there are fundamental differences between the East and the West. Human beings are everywhere human and hold the same deepest values. The differences which are no doubt significant are related to external, temporary social condition and are alterable with them."[4] The significant instance of C. A. Moore pointing to the meaningless way in which claims are made about 'spirits' of Western or Eastern

1. E. A. Burtt, "A Basic Problem in the Quest for Understanding," in C. A. Moore (ed), *Philosophy and Culture : East and West*, p. 689.
2. *Ibid.*, p. 674.
3. E. A. Burtt, "How can the Philosophies of East and West Meet ?" *Philosophical Review*, Vol. LVII, No. 6 (1948), 590.
4. S. Radhakrishnan, "The Indian Approach to the Religious Problem," in C. A. Moore (ed), *Philosophy and Culture : East and West*, p. 255.

philosophies, will have to be mentioned here. In a thorough assessment of the matter, Moore has tried to establish that the West has no 'spirit' to it, that it could set itself against the claim of a 'spirit' of the East.[1] More examples of thinkers who speak of the problem in this strain can be brought in here, but this much may be sufficient.

If scientific, positive, logical or pragmatic characteristics are claimed for the West, they are, in no less degree, available in Eastern thinking. If transcendental, intuitive and ascetic features are associated with the Indian or Eastern thinking, they are no strangers in the West. Summing up the deliberations of the Third East-West Philosophers Conference held at the University of Hawaii, in 1959, Professor Charles Moore has, with emphasis and confidence, said :

> "We have learnt to overcome the routine and tragic cliches which have in the minds of many isolated East from West...*the* East and *the* West."[2]
>
> "Mutual understanding is made easier and alleged mutual inscrutability proved false by the discovered fact that 'we have everything in both.' That is, we find in both East and West representatives of and concern with and knowledge of practically all types and colours of philosophy, despite differing emphases."[3]

II

The tenor of the argument or position indicated above helps very much to remove the rancour that was behind Rudyard Kipling's statement that East is East, and West is West, and never the twain shall meet, and to minimize the inaccurate judgment of Schweitzer about Indian philosophy. But that does not put a stop to the dialogue nor solve all problems of understanding between the Eastern and Western philosophies. Finding of wide ranging similarities are, no doubt, necessary for formulating bases for 'world philosophy', but it would not be justifiable to equate them for reasons of their similarities, or underestimate the distinctive perspectives and modes which philosophies of the world take. In these are to be seen the distinctive contributions that philosophies make to the world of philosophy. A *synthetic*

1. C. A. Moore, "The Spirit of Western Philosophy," in W. R. Inge, et. al. (ed). *Radhakrishnan : Comparative Studies in Philosophy* (London : George Allen & Unwin, 1951), pp. 43-85.
2. C. A. Moore (ed), *Philosophy and Culture : East and West*, p. 701.
3. *Ibid.*, p. 703.

'world philosophy' defeats its own purpose, vitiates its own judgment, for it annuls the creative and native response of the minds to the problems of life and reality. The importance of this aspect is, however, not forgotten, happily, by those who have argued for similarities and correspondences. It would be true to the historical growth of different philosophies projecting unique perspectives or responses from existential situations to philosophical problems to say that they constitute the very dynamics of philosophic activity. Burtt seems to have caught the spirit of this, when he writes :

> "The contrasting convictions that have guided them [East and West] can thus reveal the full force of their challenge to our quest for mutual understanding. As these convictions now interact with increasing vigour, it is possible to see the decisive virtues and defects of each more clearly than would be the case, if in the past each had been confused by the provocative presence of the other."[1]

This highlights the importance of reckoning the typological distinctions of philosophies and the necessity to consider their individuality on its own merit. However, whether types of philosophies are necessarily related to regional or natural ecology is also a question which cannot easily be solved. There have been attempts in that direction, but to make that a point of departure may not be correct in view of similar philosophical activity and response at dissimilar regional or ecological circumstances.[2] National denominations also may not be correct, for the nations besides developing a 'typical' philosophy also harbour alternative perspectives and modes of philosophies, as is fully evident in the history of philosophy of East and West. For instance, considered as a nation, India has produced Buddhism and Jainism, besides Vedic philosophy (which may be designated as 'Hinduism' in contrast). In such cases of nations giving birth to alternative systems of thought, the task would be to determine the 'typical'. It is also true that philosophies arise out of and as 'time-spirits'. There are estimates of Modern

1. C. A. Moore (ed), *Philosophy and Culture : East and West*, p. 689. See also W. E. Hocking's contribution in C. A. Moore (ed), *Philosophy East and West* (Princeton : Princeton University Press, 1946), p. 11.

2. See, for example, Huston Smith, "Accents of the World Philosophies," *Philosophy East and West*, Vol. VII (1957), 7-20.

Existentialism which proclaim it as 'a philosophy of crisis' and not having any roots in the otherwise general cultural pattern of a society or community. And so, Existentialism of 'a time' or 'epoch' would have to be distinguished from Existentialism of a 'transcendent' nature, not only going beyond the crisis of an age, but also referring to being in its primordial, pre-logical or pre-psychological nature or state. To this category belongs the Vedic (Hindu) Indian philosophy. Thus, even if we admit of the reasonableness of differences in philosophies, fast and hard denominational associations may be ultimately wrong, and may, at best be taken as just conventional.

With this, as background, we may ask the question 'What is *Indian* about Indian philosophy ?' As a sort of preliminary discussion, which forms the subject matter of the present paper, we may note two significant attempts at enumerating the 'characteristics' of Indian philosophy, one of Professor Charles Moore and another of Professor Hajime Nakamura.

In an interesting contribution to *Philosophy East and West*, Moore summarizes, as it were, the consensus of thinkers and writers in their attempt to characterize Indian philosophy and presents them thus[1]: Indian philosophy (1) is motivated practically, i.e. with an objective of overcoming grief or suffering, as against the Western attitude of treating philosophy as a disinterested love for truth; (2) makes use of intuition but not reason, and is interested in 'realization' of truth, in contrast with Western dependence on reason with a marked unconcern for 'realization'; (3) accepts the authority of the Vedas, and is unable to seek truth freely and openly as evidence dictates, in contrast with the Western view which calls for complete freedom of investigation depending on factual evidence, and drawing conclusions supported by factual evidence, examined and interpreted by reason; (4) is mere 'rationalization' but not a reasoned free search for truth. It *makes reasonable* the arguments and conclusions; (5) has a goal in '*mokṣa*' or '*nirvāṇa*' which is 'otherworldly', is an 'escapism' or points to 'denial of life;' (6) is predominantly 'pessimistic;' (7) has an exclusive concern with the 'spiritual,' as opposed to the Western attitude of open-

1. C. A. Moore, "Philosophy as Distinct from Religion in India," *Philosophy East and West*, Vol. XI (1961), 3-26.

mindedness; (8) is a philosophy of values, in contrast with the Western, which is concerned with facts; (9) is inclined towards 'inwardness' in contrast with the Western preference to the outer and the physical; and lastly, (10) is absolutistic and mystical.

Delineating the *Ways of Thinking of Eastern Peoples*,[1] Professor Nakamura offers the following analysis of the Indian way of thinking: (1) Stress on the universal, (2) preference for the negative, (3) minimizing individuality and specific particulars, (4) the concept of the unity of all things, (5) the static quality of universality, (6) subjective comprehension of personality, (7) primacy of universal self, (8) subservience to universals, alienation from the objective natural world, (10) introspectivity, (11) metaphysical bias, and (12) the spirit of tolerance and conciliation.

Though overlapping, this is a fairly exhaustive commentary in the form of characterization of Indian philosophy, and the unwary may be satisfied with it. But to stop with this would be unjust. For one thing, the observed characteristics may just be phenomenological descriptions; and for another, may fail to answer the primary question: 'why' the Indian mind chose this way of thinking than any other, or what rationale lies hidden in the perspective Indian philosophy has taken to view the problems of life and nature. This touches the problem of understanding the proper springs of action which produced the type of thinking called *Indian*.

Though it is not intended to pass a judgment on Moore's contrasting Indian with the Western stand on each of the items, the immediate impression that anyone forms would be anything but appreciative of the Indian spirit, even leading to declaring the Indian position to be medieval, scholastic, pre-scientific, if not unscientific. That is why, one should be wary with regard to any *skeletal attempts* at 'enumeration'. It would be a tragic irony, if one were to accept the 'characteristics' at their face value, but not go into the conceptual analysis and understanding of them, which alone would go a long way in avoiding misconstruing of genuine Indian spirit. Even to raise the question of the 'Indianness' of Indian philosophy may not be academic

1. Hajime Nakamura, *Ways of Thinking of Eastern Peoples* (Honolulu : University of Hawaii Press, 1964), pp. 41-168.

in intent, as such doubts, instead of being innocent, may conceal an attitude of arrogance. And so, to be really academic, it should *arise out of actual contact and working with the ways of life and culture* that have stood the test of times. This warning is made in the light of an assertion of Professor Moore himself, who debars intermixing cultural history and religion of a people with considerations of their philosophy ![1] Moore's position stems from a strange treatment of philosophy, as if it could/should be treated in isolation, like studying an object placed on the laboratory table of a scientist. Where such a method has its own merit in science, it may not be true in philosophy, for the *nature* of the subject matter is different. In its original sense of 'love of wisdom,' philosophy means something more than a cold intellectual curiosity, and takes the whole range of experience in and through/beyond the historical processes involving incessant interaction of thought and life, in their deep sense. While this *gestaltian* character of Indian philosophy should not be missed, is it not surprising, that it is being sabotaged, at the preliminary stage itself, by Professor Moore in his paper "Philosophy as distinct from Religion in India ?"[2] For what reason the attempt is made, one cannot say, except that a false sense of being true to the *philosophy* of India ! The whole tenor of Indian philosophy is to be as comprehensive as it is deep, as analytical as it is synthetic, as much fact finding as it is evaluative. And so, philosophy in India involves the whole of experience, where, religion and social culture are strong elements, making and being made by philosophy.

Looked at it in this way, and with reference to Moore's listing, it would be a travesty of truth to say that the 'evidences' of Indian philosophy (viz. the Vedas) are unquestioned or dogmatic authorities, and that for an Indian thinker reasoned evidences are unwanted, or at best reason is only made use of to defend *a priori* presuppositions, the Vedic intuitions. He warns us not to mistake rationalization for reasoning, for the former is not a philosophical method. Whoever has said that the Vedic 'evidence' is to be dogmatically accepted? Literally translating, is 'veda' a 'sound' or a 'word' ? How much do we mistake the

1. C. A. Moore, "The Spirit of Western Philosophy," in W. R. Inge, et. al. (ed), *Radhakrishnan : Comparative Studies in Philosophy*, p. 47.
2. *Philosophy East and West*, Vol. XI (1961).

outward sense of the term '*śabda*', when applied to '*veda*' ?" The philosophy of *śabda* or '*śabda-brahman*' goes beyond any physical or phonetical sense, and the '*sphoṭa*-theory' of the Veda is not to be halted at the surface level. Does the Western mind know of an '*anāhata śabda*' (un-uttered or unstruck sound?), which is as much a component of a still deeper truth, as it is the foundation of the spoken or the heard sound? The word we utter, the sound we make, does not originate at the 'throat' or the 'larynx'. It is only '*vaikharī*', as Indian philosophy would say, and which is traced to subtler roots through '*madhyamā*,' '*paśyantī*' to '*parā*', from which everything originates. Whoever has said the Veda is just a *book* ? Has not the great exponent of Indian thought, Śaṁkarācārya, said that '*Upaniṣads* (meaning Veda) do not constitute an agglomeration of words ?'[1] Does not the Indian philosopher know that the 'nature of an object of an inquiry determines not only the type of knowledge, but also the means of knowledge ?' A clear perception of the distinct natures of objects of knowing demanded distinct approaches, and where observation and reasoning are needed, they have amply been used and factually based. Development of Indian logic and epistemology, which forms a significant part of Indian philosophical thinking, should inspire awe, even if one is blind towards other branches of it.

If 'denial of life' has been the creed of India, its message of good life, a peaceful and harmonious life, and 'living upto a hundred years' (a benediction, which is even now repeated), would not have been looked upon with respect.

If '*mokṣa*' ultimately does not mean freedom from necessity and contingency, no philosophy of freedom can offer us a better deal or ideal.

If truth and value, which are interchangeable, are not the arbiters in life, science and practical needs would have left life monstrous and meaningless, and even dry.

If 'inwardness' in Indian philosophy is meant simple 'subjectivism,' a great part of it would have been obsolete, and just because it means the search for the 'essence' of things, its 'objectivity' is easily discernible.

1. '*nopaniṣad śabda rāśiḥ*'—Śaṁkara, *Commentary on Muṇḍaka Upaniṣad*, I,1,5.

If 'absolutism' does mean rejection or annihilation of the relative and the empirical, much of India's culture including the ethical, religious and other positive aspects of life would have been not intelligible. The 'absolute' is a standard of perfection and fullness, in the light of which everything, including action, are assessed for their meaning and value.

Lastly, if 'mysticism' stands for inexplicability and obscurantism, much of life's intimate, non-verbal, non-logical experiences would have been thrown away as worthless fantasies. Whereas, 'mysticism' is a super-normal method of feeling the pulse of the real in its pure state, free from all conditionings and inhibitions that a divided existence presses on authentic experience. Is it not true, then, that an assessment of Indian philosophy *demands an intimate understanding of the life and vision of the people who have built it up through centuries of self-criticism and self-evaluation*? Indian philosophy is 'holistic,' if we may call it so, and presents a wholesome commentary on life and reality, and will have to be taken thus.

III

Perhaps, for understanding the typological distinction of Indian philosophy, as is suggested above, one should start looking into the type of wisdom expressed in the basic texts of Indian philosophy and culture, viz., the *Upaniṣads* and the *Gītā*, which would give the needed perspective for such an inquiry. They put us straight on the 'ontological platform,' as it were, of our belonging to a *continuum* described as 'unity of being,' which alone holds and fashions all aspects of our life and thinking—the social, ethical, religious, philosophic and even the aesthetic. One need not feel shy of calling it a 'metaphysical' or 'transcendental' stand of existence, drawing into its vortex all that has being, but without itself being overrun or outworn. F. C. S. Northrop, in a meaningful way, has described it as the most fundamental characteristic of the Eastern thought (which specially applies to India), viz., a belief in an 'undifferentiated aesthetic continuum.'[1] It is 'undifferentiated,' for it is unaffected by the differentiations characterizing the particular and the

1. F. C. S. Northrop, "Complementary Emphases of Eastern Intuition and Western Scientific philosophy," in C. A. Moore (ed), *Philosophy East and West*, pp. 186-87.

individual, and so, is the unbroken universal. It is a 'continuum,' for it is beyond the divisive mechanism of time and space, and is the beingness of all existents. It is 'aesthetic,' for it is directly available as self-evident in everybody's experience. *It is either linking oneself with such a continuum, or not, that distinguishes Indian philosophy from the rest.* It is only as an explanation of this truth, that all 'characteristics,' listed either by Moore or Nakamura, follow as corollaries. The linking renders all the change in outlook and life, since it is an act of discovering the being of oneself, or finding one's ontological position in the scheme of existence. This is the same as saying that a being is not complete in and by himself and reaches beyond into others for his own fulfilment. This is awakening into a situation of 'ideals' being 'actualized.' The term 'realization' (a much maligned and misunderstood concept, referring to an unpredictable, hypothetical futurity), is to be understood in this sense where potentiality and actuality, essence and existence, existence and value, get identified. In the modern usage of humanistic philosophy or psychology, we have a term 'self-actualization,' which may be taken as a near approximation to the Indian conception of 'self-realization,' where one's whole personality is involved in the making of man, when the ideal of fulfilment is reached. It is such a natural and free state, where one is in harmony with one's self, and so, is in harmony with the rest of the universe. Rising above from all empirical necessity, and the limitations of relative wants, such a state exudes peace and contentment, which would even pervade and beneficially affect all forms of beings around. It becomes a state of *absolute standard* or reference, helping us to sort out, judge and evaluate all the relative, practical, empirical, and even the scientific facts. The orientation arising out of this ontological discovery is virtually a rediscovery, and is possible in each man's life. It is a restoration of what one really is, but forgotten in the rabble of the relative. A contentment, which is not simply psychological, but as one arising out of an awareness of the fullness of being, needing nothing in itself, naturally is *ascetic* in character, not in the sense of a repulsing renunciation, but in the sense of a discriminating restorative reception. All things get corrected and illumined here, by the act of 'self-discovery,' which says nothing, and is not in need of anything bereft of its value. Instead of being 'negative,' as is mistakenly taken, the orientation, thus coming about, is so refreshing and adds dynamism to an otherwise cold and mechanical process of the world order. Under its illumination, life is looked at with a freshness, that social laws, ethical principles, political organizations, economic pursuits, scientific understanding and technology, are all seen from a perspective of creativity, adding vitality and lustre of satisfaction to life. Under its inspiration, the human society would be so much transformed, that a social culture which manifests these within its ambit would be vibrant with life, and peaceful in itself. Such a picture of a creative and self-balancing society, where values guide thought, and wisdom controls adventurism, must be distinct and different from the rest. Such is the Indian way of philosophy, understood as a *way of life*, and reflected in its culture. Taken in this proper sense, it points to a balance of mind and heart, wherein the usual antithesis obtaining between different ideologies creating conflicts and tensions in life, is assimilated by a synthesis of light and illumination rendering life more livable than not, more beautiful than ugly. The much maligned 'spiritual,' under the context, means *human* in the humane sense, and demands an expansion of vision, ensuring in its wake, freedom, harmony and understanding amongst the existents held within a scheme of 'fellowship' and within the context of an unexpendable biological or natural ecology.

This is an 'essentialist' philosophy of Self, which Indian philosophy calls '*ātmanism*,' whose dimension being infinite, is all inclusive on a *unified plane of self-being*. Every element or thing counts here, for, in this unified field theory any point could be the centre of the universe, and the universe itself having no circumference or boundaries, the centre extends all over, being one with the universe which is itself boundless. It is free from all sorts of alienation, as there is nothing alien to it. If any mark or characteristic impulse is to be detected in the course of Indian philosophy, which has run for more than five thousand years, it is to be seen in this adventure of 'actualization of the Self' (i.e. '*ātmanisation*'—as it is said, '*sarvam ātmaivābhūt*').[1] This is not rendering philosophy into mentalism or psychologism or subjectivism, but pointing to a *real normal* attitude of experiencing

1. Śaṁkara, *Commentary on Bṛhadāraṇyaka Upaniṣad*, IV,6,15.

inter-subjectivity, wherein the object is penetrated and lived-in as the self. It points to infinite comprehensiveness, where the 'I' is not the small ego, but 'we'; the 'now' is not the present moment, but the divisionless '*simul*' or 'eternal simultaneity.' As the basic ground is the principle of the Self, the modicum of transformation happens through consciousness, i.e. through and by consciousness, which, being identical with essence, is as comprehensive as existence itself and all its modifications or appearances. It is only against the background of this truth, that Indian philosophy is: (a) *intuitive*, over and above the ordinary reason and logic, (b) *universal*, over and above the casual particular, (c) *impersonal*, over and above the ordinary and egoistic individual, (d) *inward*, over and above the alienating external, (e) *practical*, over and above the expedient factual, natural and scientific, (f) *inclusive*, over and above the life-killing or devitalizing exclusion, and (g) *transcending*, over and above the dispiriting negation.

It is evident, from the above, that the whole perspective is evaluational, and takes a transcending dimension, and, therefore, estimates 'objects' in space, and 'events' in time, in the light of a far-fetching experience, adding significance and value to any individual occurrence.

Thus, Indian philosophy may seem to the outsider as having no interest in the immediate and the empirical. It may, likewise, seem that it is disinclined to view the physical phenomena as having any importance, either in their creative aspect or in their scientific worth. But, it is only to be understood, that the Indian mind is not interested in taking the physical and the scientific as *isolated or isolable facts from the rest of existence or experience*. Being engrossed in the discovery of 'essence,' whose expressions are the things in existence, in a unified field of being and value, Indian philosophy tries to restore the worth of the things, against the wider background of life, and by the method of balancing between creativity and restraint. The world of facts and science are not simply dismissed, but restored of their true value to life and thought. In this way, under its illumination a greater, nobler and wholesome response to them may be forthcoming, and even offered, so that they be lived with greater emotional satisfaction of a homely belonging adding a dimension of warmth, which may be lacking in a pure, cold and frigid objectivity of alienation.

To know the perspective of Indian philosophy towards physical and positive sciences, and their subjects, may not be out of place here. Indian philosophy has no quarrel with the objective treatment of nature by the sciences, biological and physical; nor does it entertain doubts with regard to the veracity of scientific truths about nature, i.e. laws of its working, how things come about and pass off, and so on. In fact, it even warns against any ambition of philosophy to look scientific, in its technical sense. Philosophy can only be interpretative of both the scientific object and scientific truth, in terms of life and value for life. Philosophy, which discriminates, does not claim for its cosmology a scientific certificate, and Indian philosophy does not. The great Śaṁkara has said that both 'creation' and 'dissolution' of the cosmos are not to be understood in the mythological (*purāṇic*) sense. Creation is not like begetting a child, he avers. Assign the world a value and place in and for life, it is 'created'; sunder it from the same, it is 'destroyed.'[1] This is a valuational outlook, and the scientific viability is not contended nor debated. From the Indian sense, thus, God being 'antecedent' or being 'consequent', as A. N. Whitehead enunciates, is ridiculous. But, for a scientifically oriented philosopher like Whitehead, the working together of theology and science was felt a rational necessity, and he put it forth as a brilliant piece of genius, in his *Process and Reality*. But how much he offends the basic conception of theism (or theology) by his theory, is so very clear. Indian philosophy keeps clear of this misjudgment. Its perspective deserves respect and attention. Indian philosophy does not deny the reality of physical nature, but only warns against delinking it from its ground or 'essence' or 'cause' of it, call it *elan vital*, God, *Īśvara*, Brahman, Absolute, it is just the same. This essence is equally shared by the living and the non-living, and is necessarily related with value in the sphere of the living. We are to measure the glory and worth of the physical nature in terms of its being an expression of the essence, and not as being different from it. Those who have perceived this inner connection of things rejoice at the beauty of the expression we call 'the world,' and are blissfully at home with all creation.[2] This is an aesthetic approach to reality,

1. Śaṁkara, *Commentary on Bṛhadāraṇyaka Upaniṣad*, II,4,12.
2. '*tuṣyanti ca ramanti ca*' as the Gītā says, X.9.

as well, of the Indian mind, so conspicuously found in the arts of the country. Where the whole culture of the Indian society is inspired by this intuition and has expressed itself in its realistic involvement with the world by beautifying it with its poetry, music, sculpture, painting, dance and drama, it would be nothing but an insipid reaction to isolate Indian life and culture from its philosophy. This phase of India's life is full of its message, viz., the world of objects has life, insofar as it is an expression of an inner essence, which not only gives birth but also gives it an absorbing and captivating creative lustre.

Indian philosophy maintains the identity of essence and expression or cause and effect, or of the inalienable dependence of the effect on the cause. If this relationship is broken, or at any time forgotten, the objective physical reality may continue, but in terms of meaning and value for life, it will have ceased to exist. It is only the undiscerning who would mistake the dead for the living, and that is here, mistaking physical reality for all reality. This mistake is 'illusion' or *māyā* (which term, again, is a much mistaken one). Not that the world of objects are taken to be physically non-existing, but will have lost its meaning for life. If value-reality is not, thus, distinguished from physical reality, we are entrenched in an error of judgment (not of perception), leading us to create imbalances in life's ecology, not in the biological sense, but in the ethical and social senses. Much of the social agony arises thereby. It is here, philosophy has a warning for all the behavioural as well as all physical sciences, and their technology that their progress should have a built-in valuational-eye to control themselves in handling society and nature. The instituting of checks and balances in the use of atomic energy is in point. How much life is linked with nature, and how things get their meaning in association with life, can be sorted out in man's reaction to a dead person. While the living body is adorned and loved, the corpse is committed to flames or buried. The one had value, the other has nothing. Indian culture is, in principle, averse to mummifying the dead. The whole philosophy of existence is so well reflected in this cultural trait, whose message cannot be missed by one working on Indian philosophy. To get into the 'essence' (i.e. virtually '*ātman*') of a thing so that the thing could be lived in full which is the purport of the endeavour is what Indian philosophy simply means by 'spiritual'. The term itself may not be smeared with any sort of esoterism or obscurity, but only to be taken in its dimension of inclusiveness within one's own authentic living and nothing more.

It is to this end Indian philosophy has evolved a rigorous course of training aiming to perfect each and every faculty of man, so that in one sweep, the whole is grasped in its purity and plenitude. It formulates a fuller discipline, which is not pinned down to a form of mere intellectual reaction, in the form of an 'inquiry'. The knowledge aimed at in this scheme of training may not be forthcoming at all, if inquiry is not aided or not prefaced by a thorough moral purity and spiritual/religious zest. The discipline is significantly termed '*adhyātma yoga*',[1] which is not simply '*yoga*', a commonly understood method of controlling mind or breath. It is a life-long process, and is undertaken as a proper education for knowledge and experience of the philosophical truth,[2] i.e. where knowledge and being are authentically realized as identical.[3] The *sine qua non* of a philosopher, thus trained, is *absolute certainty*, born out of a full participation in a basic, universal and necessary truth. That is to say, the 'truth' Indian philosophy is interested in is not simply logical and circumstantial, but experiential, and so takes the form of an identity of knowing and being. As any split between knowing and being may harbour within it the possibility of doubt, due to the difference in being between the subject and object, indubitability is assured in a direct intuition of the infinity of the knowing subject (or the Self), whose state itself is a resolution of all dichotomies of 'I' and 'Thou' or 'It' available in the ordinary dialectics or logic. A truth that is self-certified by the identity of the subject and object is one that is established prior to the logical development of thought into the knower and the known. In the same breath, it points to an identity of being and value. For, in all seekings, it is only the self that is sought, as even the realist's predicament of the impossibility of directly knowing another mind or object proves; but also,

1. *Kaṭha Upaniṣad*, II.12.

2. The Indian sense of a life-long training is indicated in the scheme of *Āśrama Dharma*, where no stage of life is ignored, or underestimated for preparing one to the highest realization.

3. *brahma veda brahmaiva bhavati—Muṇḍaka Upaniṣad*, III,2,9.

in seeking the self, the highest value is sought, as no higher value exists than being one's self. Thus arises, in Indian thought, the ultimate dictum, "That Thou Art".[1] This is reached in the 'silence' of a non-logical intuitive state of being the self, whose plenitude overwhelms all expression in a verbal fashion, but fills one's being and captures others too. The immensity of an ocean is not expressed in any further act, but in its being the ocean. That is how all ordinary subject-object epistemology loses ground in the plenitude of self-being. This is the meaning of transcending thought. It is a felt fullness and lived authentically, not requiring a logical proof. The truth, that is spoken of this state, is not of/by correspondence nor consistency, but *is* existential veracity, whose self-evidence is manifest in all revelations of knowing and intimations of feeling and willing. This characteristic explanation of the identity of knowing and being on the one hand, and of being and value, on the other, is alien to Western epistemology and axiology.

To this end, a training of a single life may not be sufficient and so, Indian philosophy accepts the reasonableness of a continuous probation or preparation through births, if need be. A single individual's experience and verification may not be sufficient, and so, invites the experience of an ethos, or generations of evaluation. A single or partial adventure of reason may not be authentic, and so strives for a vantage mystic experience, when the whole field of existence stands revealed to consciousness, when not only the conflicting particularities and individualities are resolved against the wider canvas of being but also their values determined.

The persistence of Indian culture and philosophy beyond the frequent affectations of historical, political, religious and cultural onslaughts is a proof, if proof is needed, for its invulnerability, which is entirely due to the perspective of transcendence and openness of mind, and of an utter respect for any worthy experience, from wherever it may come. There is thus absent, in Indian philosophy, compulsory conversions in matters philosophical or religious. It is a perspective which has helped India see beyond the momentary judgments of people or groups of them. Indian philosophy arises as a *total response to a total life*

1. '*Tat tvam asi*' : *Chāndogya Upaniṣad*, VI,8,7.

and is interested in a total training of man, so that particular successes or disappointments do not affect the composure of the mind, which is geared *to envision a total light and meaning*. This vision effects a two-fold elevation, both of matter and spirit. They are elevated to the status of the divine, either as being identical with the divine or as participants in the being of the divine. That is, an individual person, instead of being dismissed as a physiological or as a social entity, is considered a *value*, an *end in himself*. Physical nature is treated not as a mute matter, but as a purposive entity in the scheme of reality. This understanding of both man and nature is hardly available to one who does not have the type of intellectual or moral training. Indian philosophy, therefore, arises as a 'vision' (*darśana*) of a *ṛṣi* (seer) who has the whole of existence, ini ts depth and width, available to him at any moment, not only to fix the position and value of things, but to receive them with an open-heartedness as of no inconsequence totally. No effort in the direction of a total experience and comprehension is in vain, says Krishna, who gave such 'total' and, therefore, a 'divine vision' to Arjuna.

If one were to be properly introduced to this tenet or the spirit, structured within the philosophical thinking of India, it is possible to look at it with a more congenial appreciation than is presently available. Any alien to the spirit of Indian philosophy is only to be treated in a way which gives him an intimate opportunity to know the broadside of our perspective and understanding of life and reality, where reason is not discriminated against, where empirical reality is not rejected but is properly shown its value for life, where scientific pursuits and gains are given the dignity of culture under the aegis of value orientation. It is a manifest truth that Indian philosophy offers not a lopsided view of the world or of reality, but a fully mature vision, coordinating in its method all the ingenuities of man, so that man and his civilization may live. It is a cosmic approach and a cosmic vision. Any limiting characterization of it as belonging to any geographical region, to a particular people, or as being simply conceptual or ideal, or as extra-empirical and mystical, etc., would be hardly doing justice to the spirit of Indian philosophy which harbours no such limitations, either in its theory or practice.

5

THE QUEST FOR AN ONTOLOGY OF HUMAN SELF

RAMAKANT SINARI*

I

THE most unique feature of human reality, somewhat ambiguously expressed but acutely felt, extraordinarily, by the founders of Indian philosophy, is its refusal to remain totally immersed in the realm of empirical experience. Indian philosophers, like phenomenologists and existentialists in our own time, have shown most intense awareness of the fact that human consciousness is a perpetually self-surpassing process, a state of being and non-being, a constant oscillating movement between the worldly and the other-worldly.

Nothing can posit itself as permanent and rigid on the field of man's conscious self. We "jump" over every given spatio-temporal point, over every state of realized freedom, over every fulfilment, and over all that we are *here* and *now*. The paradox of *ātman* (the self)—one of the key concepts in Indian philosophy—consists in its being actually anchored in the world and yet not being exhausted by it.

*Ramakant Sinari is Professor of Philosophy and Head of the Department of Humanities and Social Sciences, Indian Institute of Technology, Bombay, India. He was a Fulbright Scholar at the University of Pennsylvania. He did his graduate work in the State University of New York, Buffalo. His major publications include : *Reason in Existentialism* and *The Structure of Indian Thought*.

The history of Indian philosophy is a narrative of how the Indian *cogito* has in different periods of time translated into thought, language, and action, and even into religion and art, the singular experience of its living through phenomenal and transcendental levels. Since the Vedic-Upaniṣadic times when the ontological basis of man's empirical existence was named as *Brahman* (or *ātman*), the uncharacterizable abyss or vastness, or as the most elusive *sat-cit-ānanda* (being-consciousness-ecstasy), Indian thinkers have invariably looked upon man's worldly being not only as a bondage but also as a superimposition—a kind of veil of ignorance—on self's potentially self-luminous being.

The pre-eminent concern of Indian philosophers through ages has been to break through what is regarded as obvious by the "surface" consciousness, i.e., through the domain of appearances contained in the everyday and natural world, and reach the primordial, essential ground from where the very act of experiencing seems to flow.

II

To be in the world is to experience that apodeictic sense of being a conscious subject (an "I" locus as it were) in and around which events are felt to occur. There is a certain naturalness and continuity-through-change about this experience, whose exact width and depth have not been and indeed cannot fully be verbally captured. Something ineffable, slippery, and enigmatic lies spread out before one's attention when one turns it onto one's own sense of being. The most immediate impression a person has about his own existence is that he is there as a centre of the entire world-experience, a canvas of sensations, perceptions, ideas, meanings, feelings, desires, mental fluctuations, judgments, and so on. In fact, if there is any problem in philosophy which could be called the most basic problem of all, it is that human subjectivity (i.e. that to which we refer as the ego) behaves as a kind of two-pronged act—on the one hand it is the consciousness of its being present *in* the world and, on the other hand, it is the consciousness of its being present *to* itself.

The fact of presence—of ourselves as consciousness-in-the-world and of ourselves to ourselves—is the greatest mystery about our humanness. Why are we *present* in the world rather than not being there at all? Why are we present *to* ourselves as world-experiencers rather than being simply there as perhaps animals are? Why are we as egos or subjectivities, both empirically based and "open" consciousnesses?

It is now increasingly accepted that the ancient Indian mind possessed a remarkable disposition to see through the phenomenal and overt side of human life in order to reach its indisputable *raison d'être*. The basic preoccupation of this mind was with capturing the total meaning of the very emergence of our world-awareness. The highly profound ontology of the self Indians constructed does not have the virtue of being conducive to the material or world-based welfare; but it has a power to indicate a perennial solution to the problem of existence an individual would some time or other face during the most intimate dialogue with his own being. The search of ancient India was for the infallible way by which one could possess one's own total self.

III

In the history of philosophy in the early West, the interests of the seekers of the ultimate origin of the universe have been both objectivity-rooted and subjectivity-rooted. The ancient Greek thinkers (Thales being a typical example of these) accounted for the source of the universe by trying to define the substratum of physical objects. The various theories regarding the foundation of the universe they constructed are objectivity-rooted, i.e., they broadly assume the basic physical autonomy of all that exists.

However, in this initial phase of Western philosophy the aeriform nature of man's soul, and for that matter of the whole cosmos, was suggested by Anaximenes. He says: "As our soul which is air holds us together, so do breath and air encompass the whole world."[1] He spoke of this aeriform soul as boundless and pregnant with an infinite number of creations. Like Heraclitus some time later, he almost equated the act of breathing with the act of living, and popularized a kind of biological idiom for the description of our abstract experiences. Perhaps Anaximenes's attempt to bridge the individual consciousness and the cosmic boundlessness by introducing the element "air"

1. John Burnet, *Greek Philosophy* (London : Macmillan, 1961), p. 25.

is the first subjectivity-rooted theory in Western philosophy. His philosophical fragments represent a mind clearly turning inward and stretching to touch its own boundaries. Heraclitus was more poignantly aware of the expansive inner reality of man than any other ancient Greek philosopher. "You cannot find out the boundaries of soul; so deep a measure hath it,"[1] he remarks. He found that the most spirited element in nature is fire and used it as a symbol for the effervescent and fleeting act of consciousness. He displays an extraordinary sense of inwardness when he writes on the place of the human soul in the universe. Clearly, the analogy between the living being and the fire, which Heraclitus set forth, can be easily seen to have a bearing on the subjectivity-rooted explorations of later philosophers, such as Parmenides, Empedocles, and Anaxagoras. By his unique insight, Heraclitus tried to map out what is today called the "inner space" of human existence. The phenomenon of combustion is aesthetically most vigorous and ever insatiable among natural phenomena and signified for Heraclitus the total absence of steadfastness which man's act of living, in its essence, is.

The objectivity-rooted interests in the early Greek thought are the forerunner of the later development of Western science. To look upon the universe as the "outside" pole of knowledge is an essential part of the conduct of science. So far as Greek philosophy is concerned, it is with Plato that the objectivity-rooted thinking of the Thales type gave way to the strongest emphasis on subjectivity, the investigation of the objects of sense-perception to the intuition of the transcendental "Forms" or "Ideas," the natural or ordinary standpoint to the ontological standpoint. Philosophy for Plato was the search for "reality" behind "appearances," for the essences behind objects, for the universals at the root of particulars.

In fact, Socrates and Plato are the first subjectivity philosophers in the West to discredit systematically the explanation of the universe from an exclusively objective point of view. They were not concerned so much with the question what the ultimate ground of the physical world is as with determining the nature of that agency in man through which truth or the meaning of existence could be comprehended.

1. John Burnet, *Greek Philosophy* (London: Macmillan, 1961), p. 59.

The progress of philosophy through Descartes exhibits two main tendencies: one which is true to the objectivity-rooted interests of the pre-Socratics like Thales, and the other reflecting the subjectivity-rooted interests and concentrating on the structure of the knowing mind. The first tendency finds its complete embodiment in science and technology—the spheres in which the constitution of the universe and the natural laws governing it are taken as objectively real and are explored. Descartes himself was a mild subscriber to this tendency, for he referred to the *Cogito* as a sort of mirror placed vis-à-vis the physical world. One of the claims of rationalism since Descartes, and of science of all times, is that the riddle of existence can be solved by means of the study of the object as it is. Basically, any objectivity philosophy results from an exclusive stress on the outer-directed, impersonal, and logical activity of the human mind.

The objectivity-rooted philosophy, however, leaves behind what Husserl has called the greatest wonder of all wonders, viz., the subjectivity of the knower. Every system of knowledge that accounts for what is *given* to consciousness by presuming it to be objectively there, overlooks essences that form the governing principles of the knowing mind.

It is true that the objectivity-rooted inquiries are natural to the entire make-up of the human mind. Since we are beings in an embodied state which is responsive to the world outside, our curiosity to know the world in its objective state is intrinsic to our station as mind-poles in the world. This is the reason why human thought in its primal anthropological stage could not but be objectivity-rooted, and thus was indistinguishable from some form of naturalism. In the history of Western philosophy, first Aristotle and then Kant, have figured as the bridge-throwers between the objectivity-rooted and the subjectivity-rooted trends that prevailed almost in a sporadic fashion since the time of the pre-Socrates.

The principal tenor of philosophy in ancient India was clearly subjectivity-rooted. Preoccupation with the investigation of the human self dominated the Indian seers' mind from the days of the *Upaniṣads*, both as a programme in what could be called the ontology of human reality and as a way of life. To work out an ethics of salvation or *mokṣa* was indeed the final motive of this ontology.

Apart from the sparsely spread traits of naturalism (or, more appropriately, pantheism) in the Vedic-Upaniṣadic literature and rather a well-organized materialism of the *Cārvāka* school later on, idealism bordering on the most unrestrained subjectivism pervades the whole history of Indian *Weltanschauung*. The philosophical movements in India, such as, Sāṁkhya, Yoga, Advaita Vedānta, Buddhism, Jainism, are an expression of the subjectivity-oriented ontology of the ancient Indians.

There was no time in India's history when an ontological quest for the meaning of man's existence in the world could give way to the objectivity-centred research. The ultimate goal of human life, his transcendental destination, his urge for self-fulfilment through self-realization never ceased to be the *leitmotif* of Indians' philosophical enterprise. The story of Indian philosophy from Yājñavalkya to Sri Aurobindo represents the subjectivity-rooted, ontological interests, the uniquely enunciated ego-exploring sensibility, which would repudiate all objectivity-directed tendencies whenever they arose out of a kind of antithesis to the main stream of India's thought.

It is not easy to determine the exact reason why the early Indian thinkers turned away from an empirical study of objects. The approach to reality they had was essentially metaphysical and ethical. Even the epistemological and logical investigations they made were not for their own sake but as a way of finally conducive to showing that they have in-built limitations and, therefore, must not be allowed to contain our fundamental search for a comprehensive ontology of human self. Thus, probably, while in the process of living and experiencing a life environed by ups and downs and purposefully withdrawing from the external, physical world to enjoy a few moments of spiritual silence, they might have been enticed into the undeniable mysteries of inwardness and pure subjectivity.

IV

To investigate the world of objects is undoubtedly a rationally controlled endeavour. At every stage in this endeavour, it is assumed that mind, through its categories and principles, has a capacity to mirror reality. Any doubt with regard to the extent of this capacity is generally repudiated because it is argued that science, where the rational method of explaining phenomena finds its fullest expression, has given out numerous admirably accurate readings about the universe. The main presupposition of science that it is by means of a system of logico-mathematical relations that the complete comprehension of the constituents of the universe could be fixed has thus remained the sole guiding principle of scientists. Indeed, whether in science or in scientific philosophy, the objectivity-rooted research has its own advantages: its findings are empirically definitive, most accurately expressible, many a time reducible to mathematical models, and least ambiguous when put in language.

But the objectivity-rooted theories or systems, without any extension into the ontology of human self, appear to hang in vacuum. Actually the questions, such as "How does knowledge take place?", "What is the role of the subject-pole, or subjectivity, in knowledge?", "What is *really* known *outside* the knowing subject, or does subjectivity *somehow* posit whatever that is known by it, outside itself?" cannot be answered if one's inquiry confines itself strictly to the domain of empirical objects. All objectivity-rooted knowledge has for its ontological foundation the "dark" and unknown dimensions of man's subjectivity. Unless we are able to map out these dimensions phenomenologically, as it were, knowledge cannot be said to be apodeictic.

The principal design of the ontology of the knowing subject should be to comprehend the ever-changing field of his inner space by some kind of intuitive perception and to articulate what *happens* in it. Unlike the objectivity-rooted studies, therefore, the ontology of the human self has to proceed in a certain "unnatural" direction: it involves introspection, a rigorous self-searching, what I have elsewhere called an inward-seeing sensibility,[1] and a thorough and critical probe into the very genesis of the process of world-experiencing. It pertains to the conduct of this ontology to dig deep so to say in our *inside* in order to find out its structure and meaning. Again, by the very logic of its method its operation would be so sweeping that it may restrain itself (whenever it does so) only arbitrarily, that is, by some kind of a call for action in the empirically given situation. A certain attitude has to be consistently present in one who explores

1. For a pointed treatment of this concept see my book *The Structure of Indian Thought* [Springfield (Illinois): Charles C. Thomas, 1970], pp. 184 ff.

the field ofs ubjectivity ontologically: one has to let his consciousness expand and motion his inquiring mind to race with it. The inquiring mind is unable to outrun the underlying subjectivity whose sweep is greater than that of the inquiring mind itself.

Although the subjectivity-oriented approach has now and then figured as very significant in the history of Western philosophy —for instance, in Descartes, Berkeley, Kant, Fichte, Wundt, William James—the thought whose ethos it has dominated in toto is that of India. It built up a profound self-exploring ontological system which has pervaded through the whole Indian culture as an ideology and as an ultimate science of life. Elsewhere I have characterized this system as *ātmalogy*.[1] The only philosophical movements in the West today which have mirrored the subjectivity-studying reflection similar to ātmalogy are psychoanalysis, phenomenology, existentialism, and humanistic psychology.

The aim of ātmalogy is to encompass through transcendental insights, or *dṛṣṭi*, the whole meaning of one's own existence. Such an encompassing constitutes, according to Indian metaphysics, the highest wisdom, an enlightenment, since it awakens in one the overwhelming comprehension of the essential, pre-verbal foundation of one's ego and world-experience.

Different facets of consciousness—such as, its emergence from almost a void at its inner core to the worldly state, its positing itself as an "I," its manifestation as a thinking, discriminating, logical, linguistic, and social individual, its psycho-physical location *here* and *now*—could be studied by a method not bound by rules but by spontaneous, presuppositionless, and creative intuition. Such an intuition was called by Indian metaphysicians *darśana* or vision.

In Indian philosophy, no inquiry has been regarded as more radical than the inquiry into the mystery of human reality—its phenomenal and transcendental horizons, its worldly (*vyāvahārika*) anchorage and its flight to the other-worldly (*pāramārthika*),

1. The function of ātmalogy is to direct consciousness toward itself, to intensify its self-transcending process, and to put it in a position from where it can observe its own roots as it were. Ātmalogy is an extremely ego-splitting discipline which the metaphysics of the Orient is known for. For my introduction to ātmalogy as an epistemological method see my book *The Structure of Indian Thought* [Springfield (Illinois): Charles C. Thomas, 1970], pp. 77 ff.

its outward and inward dispositions. The dissolution of the mystery is something each person has to realize within himself. It is every person's business to find a solution to the problems, *Who am I*? and *What is the foundation of my world-awareness*?

The most penetrating insight with which Indian ontologists saw and unravelled the riddle of human existence is bound to remain a force challenging the purely world-anchored paradigm of welfare and development current in our own time and of the future. The conviction embodied in Indian ontology undoubtedly arose from a certain abiding faith in the ethics of "Work your own solution." Although seemingly solipsistic, this ontology is pregnant with a vision of far-reaching importance for the building up of a social order where every individual's conduct would be governed by a transcendental outlook.

V

The vision embodied in Indian ontology could be clothed in a current idiom. For the sake of convenience, we will call the phenomenal horizon of our subjectivity (that is, what Indian philosophers named as *jīva*) "Existence 1" and its transcendental horizon (that is, the *ātman*) "Existence 2". By naming them this way it is not suggested that they are two autonomous domains of our being: they are rather two strata of experience within the same psychic structure. Existence 1 and Existence 2 are orders of consciousness—the former being immersed in the data derived from the environment (the world and the people) and in the ordinary epistemic modes of our being, and the latter is a sort of standing spectator, a supra-conscious eye, uninvolved in anything that constitutes these data and modes. In other words, Existence 1 is world-based and, as such, denotes our ego-consciousness but Existence 2 is the "inner man," the unfathomable hollow as it were over which the "I" sense floats.

Most of us in our routine, everyday life, operate as Existence 1. That is, Existence 1 is our ordinary in-the-world existence. It manifests certain principles (those that organize its experience)—assumptive, categorical, logical, grammatical, contextual, linguistic, and so on. It is along this existence that thinking, calculating, perceiving and knowing the world, decision-making, comparing, and several other intellectual processes take place. In introspection and self-analysis, however, Existence 1 steps behind and doubts, interrogates, shuffles and reshuffles its position as an introspector, plays the language games, robes meanings in linguistic expressions and unrobes them. Existence 1 is the cogitating consciousness that we at any given moment during our wakeful life find ourselves to be.

Existence 1 is "outside" Existence 2, whose main characteristic is "open awareness." Existence 2 presents itself as pure reflection, as a field against which Existence 1 appears as a figure. Existence 1 is double-edged (in fact, that is the nature of human subjectivity that comes within the grasp of our mind when we even slightly concentrate on it) in the sense that it has a background thinning into Existence 2 and a foreground receptive to and delimited by the hard reality of the physical world. The phenomenologists' description of consciousness that it is intentional should thus be understood as referring to Existence 1 vis-à-vis the impressions (the sense-data, percepts, ideas, images, etc.) *given* to it. Existence 1 signifies the "directedness of mind toward its objects." It constantly runs toward something or other, has a "solid" base in the spatio-temporal, and is always intertwined with the body. It is only in the region of Existence 1 that science has originated and functions, and it is only to this region that its reach is confined.

When one considers its background, Existence 1 seems to dissolve in Existence 2. The latter is a vast expanse of Being, a sea of *śūnya* or Nothing, an unverbalizable but very real experience of trans-mental awareness. Originally, logic and epistemology, unless they investigate the anthropological roots of human thought itself, are attempts for defining the geometry of Existence 1, which, for all that we know, one can hope to completely decipher in terms of scientific propositions and an all-inclusive formal system. Language being at the very centre of its activity, Existence 1, as the nominalists have suggested, manipulates objects, percepts, ideas, universals, and judgments as if they were all linguistic entities. However, what is enigmatic as regards its very act of being-in-the-world is that it is never without a sense (whatever its intensity) and its background extends into an elusive Existence 2.

Existence 2 represents man's inner space, the amorphous and pre-reflective "inside" within us, the transcendental foundation of all our attitudes, thought patterns, and meanings. If we approach Existence 2 from a commonsense point of view, it would be difficult to distinguish it from Existence 1 or its fringe. For in most of us, most of the time, Existence 1 imposes on Existence 2. Minds given to predominantly object-directed thinking are only casually aware of Existence 2's transcendental presence. The "play" of attention—that is, the shifts of attention from object to object, the attention's range, its condensation and rarefaction—is watched by Existence 2. Although it is not accessible to any precise description (for no description reaches beyond Existence 1) Existence 2's presence and activity could be confirmed on the ground of its undeniable manoeuvering in relation to Existence 1. It has the power to determine the course of Existence 1 by injecting into it, in the most unforeseeable manner, an idea, a view, a flash of genius, a mood, or even a suicidal seed. Existence 1 obeys, totally unawares, the momentum that is given to it by Existence 2. It is perhaps by referring to this Existence 2, Existence 1 nexus by the term "Substance" that Spinoza, like Indian ontologists, held that human self's freedom and inner necessity are one and the same thing.

In different metaphysical traditions, different expressions have been used to allude to Existence 2. The expressions, *puruṣa*, *śūnya*, *Existenz*, Being-for-itself, the Pure Ego, *Dasein*, Nous, in Eastern and Western philosophies speak of an awareness that transcends Existence 1. The most direct expression of Existence 2 is its role of witnessing and reflecting on Existence 1. To Existence 2, Existence 1 is present, active, and engaged in and affected by situations and worldly affair. Existence 2 cannot encompass itself fully, since it is an area of awareness where most primal meaning-forms seem to telescope into a rich scenario of essences, universals, intuitions, memory, and above all into the unique abyss of trans-mental Nothing. If we become introspective and direct our mind onto the fringe of Existence 1, we realize that here our sense of presence slowly fades out into a background of esoteric and undecipherable absence, i.e., a sheer qualitiless Non-being from where all "presences" might have emerged.

An interesting echo of this remarkable theory of the emergence of the human self from almost a total vacuity at its point of origin (in other words, the emergence of *jīva* from *ātman*) can be found in the philosophy of Jean-Paul Sartre. Sartre's theory of consciousness, like that of the self in Indian ontology, centres on the problem how from the transcendental, spectator-like awareness in the background (that is, Existence 2) the world-experiencing ego (Existence 1) posits itself.

In his brief but highly metaphysical work, *The Transcendence of the Ego*, Sartre shows that consciousness itself is freedom, a spontaneity, a stream, a "Nothing" in the sense that it has the basic creative quality of positing its experience-contents outside itself. The ego and the world are not extraneous to consciousness. They are already there for consciousness, whose primary function is to put them together in a subject-object relationship. For Sartre pure consciousness (that is, Existence 2) does not create the world but finds it already constituted by the ego, which springs up from pure consciousness itself. There is the objective world, the "in-itself," but there is *this* consciousness, *this* living reality that witnesses the world being experienced. Consciousness is slippery, "self-nihilating," and yet truly existent as the transcendental ground of the whole ego-world nexus. Sartre describes it through the words of Antoine Roquentin :

> A pale reflection of myself wavers in my consciousness. . .Consciousness exists as a tree, as a blade of grass. It slumbers, it grows bored. Small fugitive presences populate it like birds in the branches. Populate it and disappear. Consciousness forgotten, forsaken between these walls, under this grey sky. And here is the sense of its existence: it is conscious of being superfluous. It dilutes, scatters itself, tries to lose itself on the brown wall, along the lamp-post or down there in the evening mist. But it *never* forgets itself (italics original).[1]

Sartre uses the word "consciousness" to indicate that fully unmappable psychic space in us on which the ego-experience somehow condenses. Incidentally, the relation between the pre-conscious and the ego he conceives has an admirable similarity with the *puruṣa-ahaṁkāra* (or the pure-self-cogito relation in the oldest Sāṁkhya school in India). Although, by the very nature of its unity with the world-experiencing ego, consciousness is always the consciousness *of* something, in itself it is Nothing. In any given situation, therefore, it is consciousness that introduces negativity, either actual or possible. In fact for Sartre, all

1. Jean-Paul Sartre, *Nausea*, Robert Baldick (Trans.) (Middlesex : Penguin Books, 1965), pp. 241-42.

instances of negation have their origin in the ontological Nothingness at the centre of human reality. He writes :

> "Man is the being through whom nothing comes to the world. . .Nothingness is the ground of the negation because it conceals the negation within itself, because it is the negation as being."[1]

Now one could maintain that Sartre's endeavour to show, by referring to what he regards as the expressions of nullity in man's day to day life, that consciousness (Existence 2) is basically a flow of blanks is an answer to the age-old problem why in the midst of positive situations there are often fillips of negativity. There are, for instance, bursts of unexplainable destruction, ruin, collapse, failure, fall, disaster, defeat threatening almost every apparently sound and wholesome state of being. The sight of suffering that shocked the well-cared-for psyche of the royal Gautama and put him on the path toward Buddha-hood lies underneath every overt plus-experience man is capable of.[2]

On the face of it, Existence 1 appears to be firmly planted in the world of reason, clear and logical thought. It is able to construct systems for producing marvels. In this sense it was qualified in Indian ontology as *vyāvahārika* or practical. However, something continuously holds it under its shadow so to say, with a readiness to suck it into total oblivion. This shadow is the shadow of Nothingness—the total oblivion. This shadow is the shadow of Nothingness—the transcendental or *pāramārthika* Reality—under which Existence 1 operates.

VI

Actually there is no definite way in which the field of Existence 2 can be fully delineated. Any discussion, therefore, pertaining to the structure and contents of Existence 2—its anthropological heritage as it were—vis-à-vis Existence 1 is bound to remain blocked by the problem whether there could be any intellectual model by which we are able to picture the entire subjectivity of man.

1. Jean-Paul Sartre, *Being and Nothingness,* Hazel E. Barnes (Trans.) (New York : Philosophical Library, 1956), pp. 24-28.

2. Suffering is one of the expressions of Nothing hidden at the basis of human reality. See my "The Experience of Nothingness in Buddhism and Existentialism" in Margaret Chatterjee (ed.) *Contemporary Indian Philosophy* (London : George Allen & Unwin, 1974), pp. 273-93.

Incidentally what J. N. Findlay[1] has called the transcendental spelaeology is in itsexplorative aims similar to ātmalogy. For Findlay it could be made to function like an archaeological inquiry into meanings, essences, forms, and into the whole world archetypes, images, and "seeings" in the subterranean layers of the self. Indeed such a spelaeology, unlike ātmalogy, would bear no ethical objectives.

It is significant that some of the highly metaphorical epithets, current in the history of metaphysics, for the ontological stratum of the human self—for instance, "stream," "breath," "flow," "light," "*nirvāṇa*," "Tao"—point to the unascertainability of its contents. This ontological stratum (that is, Existence 2) is man's innermost being. It is an act and not a state; it is open-ended and not closed. Indian ontologists have constantly referred to its total apprehension of itself as *mokṣa* or absolute freedom.

Suppose I am shaken out of deep and restful sleep suddenly. The environment (to which my Existence 1 is receptive) gushes forth into me and makes me awake. Now perceptions begin to touch my attention, which cognizes and lingers around some of them. A dialogue appears to go on between Existence 1 and these attended-to perceptions. Every one of them is a "meant" something: it springs up and creeps on the canvas of consciousness, and vanishes. Where did it come from ? And where did it vanish into ? Why did *that* particular perception or impression touch Existence 1 ? Why did it throw *this* particular meaning in me and not some other meaning ?

For Existence 2 there is hardly any respite. It is a continuous undercurrent of my ego-consciousness, the movement of a reality (in itself empty) that uninterruptedly radiates its presence onto Existence 1. Whatever happens in Existence 1 lies registered on it. Nothing in Existence 1 is seen by it as standing still in the present, or being self-contained in its meaning, in its associations, its knowability. Existence 2 represents spontaneity, creativity, and freedom. It "feels" that things and events occur in Existence 1, that these have a connection with the world outside. One runs into a vacuum if one attempts to capture

1. See J. N. Findlay, *The Discipline of the Cave* (London: George Allen & Unwin, 1966), pp. 24-26.

Existence 2. It is a kind of "absent" witness of the train of meanings passing *there* outside it through Existence 1. To guide Existence 1 toward Existence 2 so that it can apprehend it in its entirety is like boring holes in the sea.

By any standard the most outstanding inquiry into the field of Existence 2 and its role in relation to Existence 1 is found in the Advaita Vedānta of Śaṁkara, who sees Existence 2 as a principle of truth, that is, that innermost being (*ātman*) in us which throws its beam on the activity of our empirical consciousness or *Jīva*. To use Śaṁkara's findings, Existence 2 could be regarded as the subtlest inward sense, the *antaḥkaraṇa*, constantly operating through its modes (*vṛttis*): the mind (*manas*), the intellect (*buddhi*), the ego-sense (*ahaṁkāra*), and the memory (*citta*). When we know something, Existence 2 witnesses the act of knowing by focusing its light on it and illuminating it in the entire expanse of darkness and Nothingness. Although Śaṁkara did not regard the transcendental horizon of man's existence as essentially Nothing he posited it as the primordial qualitiless background of all positivity.[1] For him Existence 2 as *anubhava* (the highest experience) is absolute inwardness, pure self-luminosity, unqualified freedom.

For Śaṁkara human reality is worldly and other-worldly, *saguṇa* (having qualities) and *nirguṇa* (qualitiless), or Existence 1 and Existence 2 at the same time. Understood as the innermost depth of our being perceived from within, the *ātman*-experience forms a domain about which scientific statements would always remain sterile. The indubitable truth, Śaṁkara says, is that the "pure" and "self-luminous" *ātman* is not grasped by the rational thought but by a super-rational insight inherent in us.[2]

VII

The single difficult problem which the ontology of human self is unable to evade concerns the verbalization of self's transcendental probe into Existence 2. Existence 2 behaves as the

1. Śaṁkarāchārya, *Vivekachudamani*, Swami Madhavananda (ed.) (Calcutta : Advaita Ashrama, 1966), pp. 102-06.

2. For this characterization of *ātman* see George Thibaut (Trans.), *Sankarāchārya : Commentary on the Vedānta-Sūtras* (Sacred Books of the East, Vol. xxxiv) (Delhi : Motilal Banarsidass, 1962), p. 243.

indeterminable and mysterious foundation of the phenomenal reality of our life. We are *in* the body ("We are our bodies," Gabriel Marcel tells us) and in the world. There is nothing in our ordinary experience about which we can be so certain as about the fact that our life is practically world-anchored. Unless by means of a special psychic discipline one were to disconnect oneself from everything that makes one worldly, one's being given to oneself as Existence 1 would remain the obvious truth of one's existence. Man's "natural" existence is Existence 1—it comprises his immediate awareness of being amidst objects and persons, his constant discovery that he is a "presence" amidst presences. And yet Existence 1 is not self-contained: its roots go deep into the transcendental vacuity of Existence 2.

Neither our ordinary language nor the formalized, scientific language governed by the fixed rules of grammar, logic, syntax, and lexicon can claim an access to the entire territory of Existence 2. For the sphere of operation of these languages is Existence 1. Being a social product, a tool of inter-subjective communication, the human language, both ordinary and formalized, can successfully capture the domain of Existence 1. What descends in this language, in its pattern of sentences and propositions, is the impressions and their interrelations as they arise in Existence 1. To Existence 1, Indian ontologists maintained, Existence 2 stays forever indescribable (*anirvacanīya*).

Language has shown tremendous efficacy in expressing man's interaction with the world, in man's understanding and control in respect of things and persons around him, in the shaping of science and technology. However, between the oceanic expanse of Existence 2 and Existence 1's efforts to grasp it there prevails a gulf. This gulf is actually between meaning-intuiting and meaning-articulating. Attempts have been made by metaphysicians and mystics to narrow down this gulf. However, the gulf cannot be completely bridged.

In fact, one of the activities of ontologists of our time is to mould the existing idiom and to bring about linguistic innovations with a view to capturing inside linguistic settings the constitution of Existence 2. If one considers some of their inevitable ontological searches into the hidden ravines of the human mind, psychoanalysis, phenomenology, existentialism, and humanistic psychology could be pointed out as systematic endeavours to develop methods by which the structures in Existence 2 could be brought up and interpreted on the level of Existence 1. In traditional Indian ontology, *Upaniṣads*, the *Brahma-Sūtras* and its commentaries, and the *Bhagavad-Gītā* have been the most outstanding linguistic feats of saying through the word the unsayable roots of the *Brahman-ātman*-experience—that is, the experience of Existence 2.

What is incumbent on the practice of language for the verbalization of the ontological is the preservation within the linguistic units the authenticity of Existence 2. Such linguistic units have to have the flexibility for seizing the basic flashes of creativity in Existence 2—Existence 2's trans-phenomenal insights, the spontaneity and freedom of its acts, and also the esoteric and gnostic dimensions originating from and extending into Nothing.

VIII

Subjectivity continuously breaks the dividing line between the positivity of Existence 1 and the negativity of Existence 2. To a self-exploring design directed toward ascertaining from what ontological basis (*Brahman*, *ātman*, Being, God, or Nothing) we emerge as real and human, what agencies in us shape the width, the breadth, and the meaning of our experience, how we are "thrown" in the universe as self-conscious beings, there is no phenomenon more bewildering than the gradual fading-out of our sense of being *present* as Existence 1 into the seminal void of Existence 2. The aim of the language of Indian ontology was to picture that transcendental region by referring to which the language of Existence 1 has to resort to a kind of silence.

In fact the confessions of the mystics world over, like the free verse of poets, are attempts to throw out their innermost experiences, their meaning-intuitions—which invariably contain a certain intensity of emotion—into a fluid, unconventional language.[1] Obscurity and ambiguity, the overflow of meaning, multiple dimensions of the sense of being-in-the-world and of transcending the world are invariably present in his linguistic constructions when a philosopher leaves his anchorage in the world of empirical facts and sees inward. Such linguistic

1. For a pointed discussion on the relation between the feeling of self-identity and the luminosity of mind see Anne Bancroft, *Twentieth Century Mystics and Sages* (London: Heinemann, 1976), pp. 329-36.

constructions struggling to capture the elusive foundation of the self, the self's possibilities so to say, are amply evident in the writings of modern existentialists (particularly of Kierkegaard, Heidegger, and Sartre) as they undoubtedly form the very spirit of the ontological literature of ancient India.

Since most of the time our sense-organs give us the knowledge of the physical world alone, our linguistic constructions necessarily refer to this world. Such linguistic constructions picture the world and are largely free from ambiguity and nebulousness. However, as we transcend empirical experience consisting of worldly references and think in terms of subterranean structures and nuances, the ordinary linguistic act becomes self-defeating. This is why in metaphysical discussions, as in the most intimate conversations among people subscribing to more or less the same concerns, ratiocination and verbalization constantly endeavour to contain what is *felt* by the individual as obvious, self-evident, indubitably true. Philosophy cannot afford to underestimate the importance of this endeavour.

There is no substitute for the passion of a philosophy to strive to bring down to the level of intellect and language the primordial meaning of man's being in the world. Nowhere has this passion been more crystallized than in ancient Indian philosophy. Indeed, ātmalogy in which the ontological quest of Indians is best embodied cannot be said to be a complete science of the self. But the originality of outlook it entails in the world of self-exploration techniques has something perennially inviting about it.

Ātmalogy is the unique tenor of the Oriental culture—its theories of reality, mysticisms, religions, arts. It is without any fetters. Unlike the totally logic-bound positivist-mechanistic-behaviourist cult for which the philosophical temperament of the West is known, ātmalogy would declare how limited the reach of logic and reason to the mystery of the human self is. After all, it is not that we are intrinsically incapable of capturing the unfathomable depth of our consciousness. The fact is that we have not made a sufficient effort in that direction.

In the intellectual climate of the future where science and technology might reduce man to a function, a manipulable object, ātmalogy might have something abiding to teach. It will teach us that our inside reality is the main source of most of our problematic situations.

6

SOME REFLECTIONS ON THE INDIAN VIEW OF PHILOSOPHY

K. N. Upadhyaya*

INDIA has perhaps the longest continuous history of philosophy, over five thousand years, and yet it is generally ignored by Western philosophers as well as by some contemporary philosophers of India trained almost exclusively in recent movements of Western philosophy. Most of the Western writers of the History of Philosophy make no mention of Indian or Eastern philosophy and yet justify the title of their work as History of Philosophy. They usually presume that there has never been a genuine philosophy in the East. Oriental philosophy is simply a misnomer. It is only a few careful philosophers, such as Bertrand Russell, who use such titles as *A History of Western Philosophy*. Despite the publication of a number of works on the history of Indian philosophy by S. Radhakrishnan, S. N. Dasgupta, J. N. Sinha, M. Hiriyanna, C. D. Sharma, S. C. Chatterjee and D. M. Datta, P. T. Raju and others, some serious doubts and reservations about the nature of Indian philosophy still prevail concerning the question whether Indian philosophy is worthy of philosophic consideration or is merely a subject of antiquarian interest. On the one hand, there are some who consider Indian philosophy as the cradle of the philosophic wisdom known to man and on the other, there are critics who reject its very claim to bona fide philosophy.

*K. N. Upadhyaya is Professor of Philosophy in the University of Hawaii. He has authored several scholarly articles and a book *Early Buddhism and the Bhagavad Gita*.

This ambivalence is mainly on account of the fact that firstly, there is some ambiguity about the use of the term "philosophy" and secondly, there are some serious misunderstandings about what is called Indian philosophy. In order, therefore, to determine whether Indian philosophy is a genuine philosophy we have first to clarify (at least tentatively) what is meant by philosophy and then to see whether in the light of the general character of philosophy, Indian philosophy qualifies for this title. We shall critically examine the reasons owing to which Indian thought is said not to deserve the title of philosophy. If we find that Indian thought satisfies the generic features of philosophy as much as its Western counterpart, we can discuss whether there are some distinctive features of Indian philosophy over and above the generic ones which legitimize its title as Indian philosophy along with some other philosophies under the rubric of global philosophy. In the light of the general trend of Indian philosophy, we shall then make some brief remarks concerning its possible future prospects.

Do we have a definition of philosophy which is universally accepted ? The answer is no. If we follow the lead of etymology, and take philosophy to mean "love of knowledge", it does not seem to solve our problem. Many questions pertaining to the nature, method and object of this knowledge remain unanswered. Perhaps the safest way to answer it is to follow established usage and admit that kind of pursuit as philosophical which is so recognized by usage. But there is not just one kind of usage even in the West. One may say that Plato and Plotinus, Bradley and G. E. Moore, Thomas Aquinas and A. J. Ayer cannot all be put under any one philosophic umbrella. Often when we try to decide what philosophy is, we actually prescribe what philosophy should be. In other words, the question of the nature, method and aim of philosophy is itself a philosophical question and the answer varies with one's philosophic standpoint. It seems, therefore, difficult (even prejudicial) to spell out the specifics of philosophy in a neutral way which would be acceptable to philosophers of all persuasions. But since we want to have some ground to stand on, we may proceed with a working definition of "philosophy" which should be broad enough to encompass all varieties of Western philosophy and yet it should be distinguishable from science and religion with which it sometimes tends to be confused. Shall we then, staying close to its etymology, simply say that it is mainly a rational attempt to know the reality as a whole? Probably this would work, because being "mainly a rational search for knowledge", it can be easily distinguished from religion which is said to be mainly based on faith rather than on reason and chiefly concerned with the practical application of, rather than the theoretical search for, knowledge. At the same time, being concerned with the knowledge of reality "as a whole" it can be easily distinguished from science, which aims at compartmentalized knowledge.

Now, does Indian philosophy readily fit into the above general framework or working definition of "philosophy", or is it reducible to religion, as its critics allege? Before answering this question it may be borne in mind that firstly, Indian philosophy, like Western philosophy, is not of any single kind. It is well-known for its richness and variety. In the course of its long history, it has produced many diverse philosophies, such as, materialism and spiritualism, theism and absolutism, pluralism and monism, realism and idealism, with many subdivisions. Secondly, the problem becomes more complicated because we find no terms in the Indian tradition exactly corresponding to the Western terms "philosophy" and "religion". The terms "*darśana*" and "*dharma*" commonly used in the Indian tradition for "philosophy" and "religion" respectively are merely the closest approximations, and they are broad enough to lend themselves to meanings which are not connoted by their Western counterparts.[1]

This should make it clear that we cannot and must not expect to see one-to-one correspondence between the thoughts of the two different cultural milieus. But if the two thoughts exhibit substantial affinity for one another and fit into the same general framework, there is no reason why the two should not be given the same title, provided of course, that none of them makes a radical deviation dangerously approaching the camp of a distinctively different discipline. Allowing thus for individualistic differences, it can easily be shown that what we call Indian philosophy

1. K. Satchidananda Murty observes: "It is a curious thing that Sanskrit contains no word "philosophy". In Arabic also this seems to be the case, and owing to the influence of Greek civilization, the Greek word itself seems to be accepted by the Arabs, and "philosophia" is now an Arabic term." *The Indian Spirit*, p. 132.

justifies itself fully for the title of philosophy. As is at once evident from the opening aphorisms of the basic texts of some of the major Indian systems, such as, Vedānta, Mīmāṁsā, Nyāya and Vaiśeṣika, Indian philosophy is mainly a search for the knowledge (*jijñāsā*)[1] of ultimate reality as well as a rational critique and explication (*anvīkṣā*[2] and *vyākhyā*[3]) of the given facts and their underlying ground. Critics of Indian philosophy may, however, call attention to some other features of Indian thought and in the light of them may try to unseat it from the pedestal of philosophy. It is, therefore, vitally important to examine their charges before making a final verdict on the status of Indian thought.

It is alleged that in view of its general nature as well as in terms of some of its specific attitudes, doctrines, methods and purpose, the so-called Indian philosophy is indistinguishable from religion. Some of the major charges may be listed as follows :

1. *Indian philosophy is spiritual* :

This fact is clearly and sometimes over-enthusiastically stated by many Indian philosophers themselves. In the words of Radhakrishnan : "Philosophy in India is essentially spiritual . . . The spiritual motive dominates life in India . . . The dominant character of the Indian mind which has coloured all its culture and moulded all its thoughts is the spiritual tendency."[4] According to S. C. Chatterjee and D. M. Datta "the common stamp of an Indian culture" consists in "the unity of moral and spiritual outlook".[5] This is regarded as an out and out religious approach opposed to the purely intellectual concern of Western philosophy.

2. *Indian philosophy is intuitive and mystical* :

Truth in Indian thought is said to be realized through intuition rather than by reason. Critics, therefore, point out that Indian

1. *Athāto Brahma-jijñāsā*, *Brahma Sūtra* I.I.1; *Athāto dharma-jijñāsā*, *Mīmāṁsā Sūtra* I.I.1.

2. The etymological meaning of Nyāya or Ānvīkiṣiki school given in *Nyāya Bhāṣya* is as follows : *Pratyakṣāgamābhyām ākṣiptasya anvīkṣā tayā vartata ity ānvīkṣikī*, *Nyāya Bhāṣya*.

3. *Athāto dharmaṁ vyākhyāsyāmaḥ*, *Vaiśeṣika Sūtra* I.I.1.

4. S. Radhakrishnan, *Indian Philosophy*, Vol. I (London: George Allen & Unwin, 1923), pp. 24, 25, 41.

5. S. C. Chatterjee and D. M. Datta, *An Introduction to Indian Philosophy*, 6th ed. (Calcutta: University of Calcutta, 1960), p. 12.

philosophy is mystical, basing its doctrines on mystical experience rather than on reason, which, they claim, is the sole tool of any legitimate philosophy.

3. *Indian philosophy is authoritative* :

Of the two main branches of Indian thought, one branch consisting of six major systems, called the orthodox systems, clearly recognizes authority as a source of knowledge and accepts the validity of the Vedic authority. Even in the other branch which includes the Buddhism and the Jainism, although the Vedic authority is rejected, the authority of the founders is not challenged. The Buddhists and the Jainas pay allegiance to their own scriptures. Thus, barring the solitary exception of Indian materialism, authority almost reigns supreme in the whole of Indian philosophy, leaving little room for the free rational search which is considered indispensable in Western philosophy. The scarce use of reason that can be seen in Indian thought is hardly more than a mere rationalization.

4. *Indian philosophy is motivated by a practical concern* :

As against Western philosophy, which seeks knowledge for its own sake and considers disinterested search for knowledge as the distinctive feature of philosophy, Indian philosophy proceeds to seek knowledge with the avowed purpose of terminating suffering.

5. *Indian philosophy is pessimistic* :

It is again and again emphasized in Indian philosophy that life is full of suffering and a man must find an escape from it. This, the critics contend, is a typical mark of religion. Distinguishing philosophy from religion, C. F. Lavell observes: "There is a type of mind to which the confusions and maladjustments of the world are a distress and a fear—flight from them to some refuge of faith a necessity. Religion, not wholly but quite largely, springs from this distress and fear . . . There is another type of mind [the scientific-philosophic] to which no refuge is needed because there is no distress, to which confusion is not a horror but a fascination, a summons to investigation and action."[1]

1. *A Biography of the Greek People* (Boston and New York: Houghton Mifflin, 1934), pp. 132-33.

6. *Indian philosophy is other-worldly* :

Life being branded as a vale of misery, the interest of Indian philosophers shifts from this life and world to some other life and world. Belief in transmigration, speculation about heaven and hell and the doctrine of *karma* and rebirth are various expressions of this mentality.

7. *Indian philosophy is concerned with salvation (mokṣa)* :

It is claimed that no Western philosopher is concerned with *mokṣa* or *nirvāṇa* which may be a goal of religion, but surely not of philosophy.

8. *Indian philosophy is subjective* :

Its chief objective is the realization of the Self by controlling the senses and the mind with little concern for the reform of the world and control of outer nature. This self-centred attitude, practically disregarding the outer world, appears as a religious mentality.

9. *Indian philosophy is static and unprogressive*:

Because of its fascination for self-centred religious concerns, its beliefs in a static Brahman and the doctrine of *karma* leading to fatalism, Indian thought has ended in stagnation and unprogressiveness.

If what has been stated above is the whole truth of Indian philosophy, its claim for the title of philosophy surely stands defeated. But, as we shall show in the sequel, many of these summary pronouncements are based upon superficial grounds, some of them involve serious distortions and misrepresentations and, quite often, they mistake a half-truth for the whole truth. Thus, we can easily show that they represent a partial, one-sided, grossly exaggerated and hence misleading position.

During the long course of the development of a culture, many diverse ideas are produced and, hence, it is not difficult to show some such elements in almost any philosophic tradition. In order, therefore, to have a judicious view, one must go by predominant trends and features of the thought process. It is very important to remember in this connection that the concept of philosophy (*darśana*) in the Indian context is somewhat wider and more comprehensive than its Western counterpart, and the

Indian notion of religion (*dharma*) is also very much free from its usually loaded and perjorative sense in the West. Indian philosophy, thus, can have a close relation (although not one of identity) with religion in the Indian sense of the term without being adversely and perniciously affected by religion in the Western sense. The untenability of the above charges can at once be shown if we indicate briefly the import of the Indian view of philosophy and religion and their reciprocal relation. We can then adduce some additional evidence to demonstrate the faulty character of these allegations.

Two words, *ānvīkṣikī* and *darśana*, used in the Indian tradition for philosophy, reflect the nature of Indian philosophy quite well. *Ānvīkṣikī* literally means "review" or "critical examination". Vātsyāyana, the author of *Nyāya Bhāṣya*, defines *ānvīkṣikī* as "a critical examination of the data provided by perception and scripture."[1] The Nyāya school of Indian philosophy, which is noted for its rigorous logical and epistemological concerns, fully expresses this notion of philosophy. The other word, *darśana*, means "seeing" or "insight" which, evidently, emphasizes clear vision or direct realization of the truth. Very early in the Indian tradition it was realized that some deeper aspects of reality cannot adequately be grasped merely by the senses and the intellect. Indian philosophers in their serious quest for truth, however, would not admit easy defeat and would explore other and more potent means of uncovering the truth. This has led serious-minded inquirers to develop higher faculties of knowing which, for the lack of better words, are called intuition. This view of philosophy is exemplified by the Yoga system of Indian philosophy. The word *darśana* may also be taken to mean a "standpoint". It was in this sense that Indians admitted the possibility of more than one *darśana*. It may be noted here that the logical and epistemological methods of Nyāya and the techniques of higher insight discovered by Yoga are, with more or less emphasis and with some modifications, common possessions of almost all systems of Indian philosophy. They are, as it were, two poles of Indian philosophy—the intellectual and the spiritual. One cannot, therefore, have a balanced view of Indian philosophy without taking into consideration these dual elements.

1. See note 2 on p. 140 for its original Sanskrit version.

If philosophy is concerned with the total view of reality, it must take into consideration the various modes of our experiences, viz. sensory, mental, as well as intuitional. The world of waking, dream, dreamless sleep and transcendental experiences cannot all be duly comprehended and assessed by the exclusive use of either the senses or the mind. It is unphilosophical to assume, without proper scrutiny and examination, that supra-sensory intuition is not a genuine and valid experience, as sense experience and intellectual experience are. The fact that the former is rare and hard to attain, while the latter are more common and easily accessible is no ground to discredit the former. The faculty of fine aesthetic discernment of an artist cannot be ignored, because it is a rare possession of some highly cultivated persons.

It may also be pointed out here that some Indian philosophers notwithstanding their full realization of the importance and use of reason, do not recognize it as the sole distinguishing feature of man. The *differentia* of man, according to them, is *dharma*, the power that enables man to discern what is morally right or wrong (which, of course, includes the rational power). As it is said :

> "Men and beasts are alike in matters of eating, sleeping, fearing and sexual activities. *Dharma* alone is the additional prerogative of men, and those who are devoid of *dharma* are like beasts."[1]

Dharma is the power which "supports or upholds."[2] It sustains man and the universe, and brings about social cohesion. If, therefore, *dharma* ceases to be observed properly, then the binding ropes of society are loosened, as it were, and in that case society would be in the same state as the planetary system would be in the event of the dwindling of the gravitational force.

Dharma expresses itself in the form of such practice (*sādhanā*) as is in accordance with the fundamental truth and the cosmic moral order. In its genuine form, it is thus a necessary practical side of philosophy. As Sri Aurobindo points out : "Religion

1. For detailed discussion of *dharma*, see author's paper, "Dharma as a Regulative Principle" in K. K. Mittal (ed.) *Quest for Truth* (Delhi: Professor S. P. Kanal Abhinandan Samiti, 1976), pp. 546-53.

2. *Dhāraṇād dharmam ity āhuḥ . . .*, *Mahābhārata*, Śānti Parva, 109.12 and Karṇa Parva, 69.59.

imparts a dynamic, active, and practica lorientation to philosophy."[1] He further amplifies :

> "Philosophy is the intellectual search for the fundamental truth of things, religion is the attempt to make the truth dynamic in the soul of man. They are essential to each other; a religion that is not the expression of philosophical truth degenerates into superstition and obscurantism, and a philosophy which does not dynamise itself with the religious spirit is a barren light, for it cannot get itself practised."[2]

Affiliation of a serious philosophy with a genuine religion, then, instead of being considered undesirable, should be regarded as highly desirable for an integrated life. One can rightly say that philosophy without religion is empty and religion without philosophy is blind. Hence, the view of some scholars that the "time ... has come when students of philosophy all over the world, particularly in India, should think afresh and separate Indian philosophy from Indian religion",[3] is unwarranted, being based upon mistaken notions of Indian philosophy as well as Indian religion.

In the light of this clarification, it should not be difficult to see that the charges levelled against Indian philosophy emerge from either misconceived notions of Indian philosophy and religion or they mistake what is only a part for the whole of Indian philosophy. In the latter case, some charges levelled against Indian philosophy will fall upon Western philosophy as well.

Let us now examine the first charge of spirituality. If some undaunted seekers of truth in the course of their resolute search came to discover some spiritual reality underlying variegated phenomena of the world, should they have shown intellectual dishonesty or cowardice by refraining from bringing it to light ? In fact, they should be admired for sharing their hard-earned discovery with others, and for encouraging others to verify it through their own experience. In any case, it is only one aspect of Indian philosophy and is not applicable to some materialistic

1. Sri Aurobindo, *Heraclitus* (Calcutta : Arya Publishing House, 1947), pp. 46-47.

2. Quoted by Adhar Das, *Sri Aurobindo and the Future of Mankind* (Calcutta: University of Calcutta, 1934), p. 53.

3. S. K. Saksena, "Basic Tenets of Indian Philosophy" in his book, *Essays on Indian Philosophy* (Honolulu : University of Hawaii Press), p. 23.

and naturalistic philosophies of India.[1] Also, as Constantin Regamey has shown, there is no dearth of spiritualist philosophers even in the West.[2]

So far as intuitive and mystic experiences are concerned, we have already pointed out that they have a rightful place in the comprehensive scheme of philosophy, and they are not necessarily matters of religion. If the rational method was to be regarded as the exclusive method of philosophy, many important philosophers of the West such as Socrates, Plato, Aristotle, Plotinus, all Christian mystics, all rationalists, the entire Moral Sense School, the Natural Law intuitionists of the eighteenth century and Bergson, who make use of intuition (without knowing its full implications) cannot be considered philosophers. We have already indicated that we cannot arbitrarily restrict the definition of philosophy.

Much confusion is created by calling Indian philosophy authoritative. One tends to read into this appellation a sort of dogmatic unquestionable acceptance of some truth arbitrarily handed down from some inexplicable source above. This, however, is not true in the case of Indian philosophy. Firstly, if by "authority" we mean the Vedic authority, then there are only two major schools of orthodox Indian thought, namely, Mīmāṁsā and Vedānta, which are directly based upon the Vedic authority. The remaining four Orthodox systems developed their philosophy on independent grounds, giving only a superficial acceptance to the Vedic authority, and Heterodox systems completely reject it. But, on epistemological grounds all Orthodox schools, except Vaiśeṣika and the Jainas among the Heterodox schools, clearly recognize authority as a separate and independent source of knowledge, specially in regard to such objects as are not amenable to other ordinary sources of knowledge. In the words of S. Suryanarayana Sastri,

1. Numerous books dealing with materialistic and naturalistic thoughts of India have been referred to by Dale Riepe in his paper, "Recent Assessments and Misconceptions of Indian Philosophy" in K. K. Mittal (ed.) *Quest for Truth*, p. 79.

2. Constantin Regamey, "The Meaning and Significance of Spirituality in Europe and in India" *Philosophy East and West*, Vol. X, Nos. 3 & 4 (October 1960 & January 1961), 105-34.

> "If philosophy is really an attempt to obtain the view of the whole, it ought to embrace the whole; our perceptive powers are limited to the *here and now* of experience, and reasoning proceeds only with the help of characteristic marks and examples from the world of perception."[1]

That which is beyond perception and inference, he points out, "requires to be intuited; it has been so intuited in the past and the result is the knowledge contained in Scriptures."[2] Not to avail oneself of hard-earned rare wisdom of competent authorities (who have learned the truth for themselves, and are, thereby, in a position to speak with authority) is to deprive oneself of a valuable treasure and rare opportunity. And surely, what is thus professed is claimed to be verifiable. It is interesting to note that the three steps to truth which are normally mentioned in the Orthodox tradition, namely, (1) *śravaṇa* (listening to the truth), (2) *manana* (rational reflection), and (3) *nididhyāsana* (absorption), explicitly emphasize that the truth learned through authority has to be rationally examined and then finally experienced for oneself. Śaṁkara, the noted champion of the Vedānta, makes it clear that the purpose of the Scripture is to enhance our knowledge of the unknown and not to distort or contradict what is already known through other valid means. As he observes: "Even if a hundred texts declare fire to be cold or without light, they would not acquire validity."[3] The existence of an amazingly large variety of systems within the same so-called authoritative tradition is a positive proof that reason is allowed full play in Indian philosophy and authority is open to rational examination and criticism. It is not infrequent that the Scriptures were openly challenged and undermined even within the same Orthodox tradition.[4]

The fact that Indian philosophy is dominated by a practical outlook, that it calls attention to the suffering of the world and that it advocates *mokṣa* as a state free from suffering cannot but be regarded as symptoms of its realistic and experiential

1. S. Suryanarayana Sastri, "On the Study of Indian Philosophy" in *Collected Papers of Professor S. Suryanarayana Sastri* (Madras : University of Madras, 1961), p. 7.

2. *Ibid.*

3. *Gītā Bhāṣya* XVIII.66.

4. *Muṇḍaka* I.2.7-10 and the *Bhagavad Gītā* II.46 & III.11-12, for example, make disparaging remarks about the Vedas and their rituals.

character. The difficulty raised on the grounds of practical outlook is very flimsy. "Not even a fool undertakes some work without a purpose,"[1] observes Śaṁkara. Why should a philosopher engage himself in the most challenging task of philosophy without a clear and practical knowledge of his purpose ? This purpose, however, does not vitiate the objective character of philosophical knowledge. It is made clear that the purpose of terminating suffering can be fulfilled only by pure, objective or unbiased knowledge. Thus, this purpose cannot militate against what is called in the West "a purely disinterested search for knowledge." Besides, we must not lose sight of the fact that a genuine desire or love for knowledge (*jijñāsā*) is basic to the Indian philosophic quest, and doubt, rational nature of man, as well as criticism and defence of different philosophic positions also play significant parts in the motivation behind Indian philosophy. In the Nyāya school, for example, doubt is said to provide the chief incentive for philosophic speculation. It may also be pointed out that despite the claim of disinterested theoretical knowledge in the West, many practical political or ethical concerns are evident in the philosophic pursuits of at least some of the Western philosophies. The Socratic view that virtue is knowledge points in the same direction. In the Pragmatic philosophy of William James, truth is said to be determined in terms of utility.

Regarding the Indian concept of *mokṣa*, it may be noted that it is directly linked with the highest knowledge, and, thus, it is more a matter of epistemology than of religion. It is not an imaginary escape, but a verifiable realization of truth. Cases of a somewhat similar ideal can be pointed out even in certain forms of Western philosophy, such as Stoicism, original Epicureanism, and Neo-platonism. Schopenhauer and possibly Spinoza also seem to entertain a similar ideal.

The charge of subjectivism is based on the lack of proper understanding of the glory and grandeur of the immortal soul, by meditating upon which the mystery of the entire universe is said to be revealed. It is, indeed, a remarkable contribution of Indian philosophers, as we shall shortly explain. Likewise, the Indian concept of eternal Brahman and doctrine of *karma*,

1. *Brahma-Sūtra Bhāṣya*, Introduction.

if wrongly interpreted, may give rise to a static view of reality and create the impression of a fatalistic and unprogressive society. Their full philosophical implications cannot, however, be discussed within the limited space of this paper. We can only say that these concepts are said to be based upon experiential claims of Indian philosophers and cannot simply be dispensed with by branding them as mere matters of faith.

After having demonstrated the truly philosophical nature of Indian philosophy and having indicated in a general way some of the peculiarities of its nature and approach, we may now point out some of its other distinctive features in more specific terms. But the question may be raised at this point as to why Indian philosophy should be any different from Western or any other philosophy. Is not the expression "Indian philosophy" an oddity, because true philosophy is neither Indian nor Western? If we do not speak of, say, Indian mathematics (despite there having been great Indian mathematicians), what justification is there to speak of "Indian philosophy" in addition to just philosophy?

Without trying to be elaborate, attention may at once be drawn to the fact that no sound analogy holds between mathematics and metaphysics. The former, though applicable to experiential contents or entities, deals mainly with abstract forms and cannot itself be considered as one of these contents or entities, whereas the latter is supposed to be concerned with experiential (in a comprehensive sense) contents or entities, and not merely with abstract forms. Mathematical calculations and geometrical theorems hold good universally in all cultures and countries, but such is not the case with philosophical doctrines and theories. In other words, the former is not culture-bound, while the latter is. Therefore, despite accepting some broad general features and frameworks of the subject, it may not be incorrect to make distinctions between Greek philosophy and Indian philosophy or between Western philosophy and Eastern philosophy. Since the philosophical activity takes place within a certain cultural setting, it tends to bear the mark of that culture. Culture is shaped by the history and history in its turn is influenced by geographical and other conditions. Therefore, somewhat analogous to the distinctions made between Indian and European history or geography, one can within the general framework of philosophy make a meaningful distinction between Indian and Western philosophy.

We may now point to some of the more important distinctive features of Indian philosophy. They are to be called distinctive in the sense that they are either completely absent or are not found in any dominant form in Western philosophy. In view of the limited space, no detailed explanation of them will be offered here. Among these distinctive features mentioned below, some are reflective of the basic attitudes and perspectives of the Indian tradition, while others are the results or achievements of its philosophic pursuit. Most of the features are held in common by all systems of Indian philosophy, while the others are applicable to them with some exceptions or limitations:

1. *Philosophy as the highest branch of knowledge* :

Unlike other disciplines dealing with ordinary (lower) knowledge, philosophy according to the general traditions of India is supposed to deal with higher wisdom (*parā vidyā*). It is, therefore, to be taken most seriously and cherished as the most valuable possession. This knowledge is said to be cultivated after thorough preparation and with unshakable determination. Śvetaketu finished all his education before he received instruction in philosophy from his father. Nārada had to work for long years before he went to Sanatkumar for the philosophic wisdom. Śaṁkara and Rāmānuja both lay down intellectual and moral pre-requisites for the study of the Vedānta. It may sound incredible to most of the people in contemporary settings, but the life and teachings of the propounders of the different systems of Indian thought clearly bear witness to the fact that they dedicated their entire life to the cause of philosophy. Their daring spirit, boldness and depth of thought can hardly be overstated.

2. *Synthetic approach*:

Indian philosophy deals with this subject in an integrated way. Unlike Western philosophers, who treat separately the different branches of philosophy, such as epistemology, metaphysics, ethics, etc., traditional Indian philosophers treat them integrally and discuss them accordingly. Unlike such Western schools as rationalism and empiricism which lay exclusive emphasis on reason and experience, respectively, Indian philosophy generally (though there are a few exceptions) explains experience in such a way that both outer (sensory) and inner (rational or intuitive) experiences are included in it, and thus Western opposition is reconciled. Even while recognizing the supremacy of *mokṣa* as the highest goal, Indian philosophy integrates other objectives of life, viz., happiness, wealth and moral virtues with it.

3. *Cycle of the world process and the notion of infinity* :

All Indian systems except *Cārvāka* have the bold vision of the infinity of the world process. The supreme reality is infinite and the world is without beginning. The process of evolution and dissolution of the world continues indefinitely in cycles. India's mathematical invention of zero may probably be linked with this cyclic approach.

4. *Majesty of man* :

Human life is invaluable because human beings alone have the potential to realize the supreme goal. "There is nothing higher than the human being,"[1] declares the *Mahābhārata*. The soul is uncreated and eternal, however low it may have sunk in this creation. When, through the process of evolution, it reaches the human level, it can then, by utilizing the opportunity offered by human life, realize the highest goal.

5. *Introspective approach* :

Since the soul is the eternal inmost essence of man and it contains within itself the clue to the mystery of the whole universe, meditation on it becomes the most vital concern of man. That the macrocosm is contained within the microcosm is the essential secret of Indian wisdom.

6. *Karma and rebirth* :

Indian philosophy offers an important solution to the problem of evil, suffering and inequality. In the limitless world, souls without beginning are going through the consequences of good and bad actions which they themselves chose to perform in the past. While reaping the results of their actions, they are simultaneously utilizing their limited freedom (with the load of

1. *Na hi manuṣyāt śreṣṭhataraṃ hi kiñcit*, Mahābhārata Śānti Parva, 180.12.

karmas increasing, the freedom is correspondingly curtailed) to perform new actions. The world is, thus, a moral stage where we play our respective roles and, in accordance with our performance, make our future. It also provides an opportunity to learn our lessons and even reach the stage of enlightenment.

7. *Unique combination of love for tradition and freedom of thought* :

Indian philosophers have generally been conscious of tradition and, out of respect for the past, they seldom claim originality in their thought. Even while propounding astoundingly new theories, they generally submit with humility that they are simply reformulating ancient wisdom. Most of the great names in Indian philosophy, such as, Śaṁkara, Vācaspati, Rāmānuja, Vātsyāyana and many others, claim only the modest title of commentator. This approach seems quite consistent with the theory of *Satkārya-vāda* (according to which what is produced is said to be already contained in its material cause). But this attitude is so widespread that even the famous logician Jayanta, an upholder of the opposite theory, *Asatkārya-vāda*, declares that nothing absolutely original can ever be said.[1] What is ingenious to see is the remarkably varied interpretations that they make while demonstrating their allegiance to the past. Reverence for authority, thus, does not militate against progress. It must not, however, be forgotten that authoritative texts which they try to comment upon are usually the works of highly talented philosophers. In any case, it is interesting to note that unlike their Western counterparts who, even while working under the influence of their predecessors and borrowing much from them, erect the edifice of their philosophy on the old debris, Indian philosophers tend to highlight the old texts and try to speak through them.

8. *Respect for life and thought* :

As a result of the mixing and mingling of so many races and tribes at a very early stage of the development of Indian thought, India developed a composite culture and learned to live with mutual tolerance. This eventually contributed to the development of great respect for life as well as for the opinion of others.

1. *Kuto vā nūtanaṁ vastu vayam nūtprekṣituṁ kṣamāḥ*; *Vaco-vinyāsa-vaicitrya-mātram atra vicāryatām*. *Nyāyamañjarī* (Introduction).

The former in the form of avoidance of all injury to life (*ahiṁsā*) constituted the greatest moral virtue of India. The latter in the form of freedom of thought paved the way for philosophy of standpoints which expressed in the Buddhism and the Advaita Vedānta as lower and higher (Vyāvahārika and Pārmārthika) standpoints and in the Jainism as the judgment of relativity (Syādavāda). It also promoted an atmosphere of healthy and constructive debates which became a great tradition in India and added to the development of philosophical knowledge.

9. *Disinterested approach to empirical science* :

Indian philosophy, as already pointed out, has been closely associated with religion and has developed an introspective approach. This might have been responsible for its lack of fructifying contact with the natural sciences. In this respect the Indian and Western approach by and large seem to be mutually opposed to one another. It is well-known that ancient Indian and Greek cultures made great advancement in mathematics, astronomy and medical science. The Indian astronomer Āryabhaṭa made the discovery of the rotation of the earth and the actual cause of the eclipses, and medical researches done by physicians showed the correct anatomy of man. But these researches, unlike those of Bruno and Galileo, did not create any stir in India and Indian philosophy remained almost unconcerned. In this particular case, though, the reason might have been that Indian philosophy and religion never had geocentric views, but even otherwise Indian philosophy has been largely unconcerned with scientific development. This attitude of indifference to science by philosophy, a highly respected discipline of India, may have adversely affected the growth of the Indian sciences.

10. *Harmony between man and nature* :

At the early Vedic stage, Indian philosophy uncovered an eternal cosmic order (*ṛta*) running through the whole universe. Its doctrine of *karma* emphasized that man is the maker of his own destiny. Nature is considered subservient to the purpose of man and it provides the field for his action. In Indian metaphysics, soul and nature form an organic whole under God and are thus harmoniously related. Thus, there is no inherent antagonism between man and nature. Although nature is finally to be transcended, this transcendence is made possible through a balanced and harmonious response to it. An Indian philosopher does not pronounce the universe to be absurd, as Sartre does.

11. *Emphasis on experiential approach* :

Despite the dominant idealistic trend of Indian philosophy, the attitude of Indian Idealism towards experience is very different from that of Western Idealism or Rationalism. Knowledge according to Indian philosophy originates from and culminates in experience (*anubhava*).[1] This experience may be outer sensory, inner mental, or the highest intuitive experience. Direct experience or intuitive knowledge is the only way to remove ignorance, the root-cause of suffering, and thereby to secure the absolute freedom (salvation). Only that knowledge which emancipates or brings about immortality is the true knowledge, declare the *Upaniṣads*,[2] and that is none other than the direct experience.

In closing we would like to say a few words concerning the possible future prospect of Indian philosophy. During its long history, Indian philosophy has gone through many rough weathers and, in moments when it was found languishing, it received a new lease of life on account of its synthetic or assimilative character. As noted above, Indian philosophy developed this trait very early in its history. The Upaniṣadic thought which is considered a peak point in the pre-system-building period of Indian philosophy was a result of the confluence of Aryan and pre-Vedic non-Aryan thought.[3] Even in the recent past when Indian philosophy was dwindling under the yoke of British rule, and English missionaries, with a view to exposing weaknesses of Indian thought and culture and establishing superiority of their own, were studying Indian languages, writing books and translating a number of religious and philosophic works from Sanskrit, a new wave of consciousness was created

1. *Anubhavāvāsanatyay. . .ca. Brahmajiñāsā* Śaṁkara's Commentary on *Brahma-Sūtra* I.2.

2. *Sā vidyā yā vimuktaye*; *Vidyayā amṛtam aśnute.*

3. K. N. Upadhyaya, *Early Buddhism and the Bhagavad Gītā* (Delhi: Motilal Banarsidass, 1971), pp. 75-87, 91.

in India. There emerged a new class of intellectuals in India who eagerly absorbed the essentials of Western thought and utilized them for the advancement of their own religio-philosophic culture. Although some of them, such as Dayanand Saraswati and a few others, were revivalists who emphasized going back to the ancient ideals, the movement which vitalized Indian spirit and brought triumph for India was guided by such reformists and syncretists as Raja Ram Mohun Roy, Ranade and others. This historical pattern brings the message home to us that the future of Indian philosophy depends on the synthetic and assimilative approach of Indian philosophers towards contemporary Western philosophy. We must not lose sight of the fact that all that is old is not necessarily good, and all that is new is not despicable. The Indian philosopher of today must, therefore, widen his perspective and sharpen his philosophic tools through a thorough and careful study and a balanced assimilation of the movements of contemporary Western philosophy. That has been the typical Indian way to encounter other thoughts and cultures. That is how Indian philosophy has enriched itself and survived in the past and will continue to do so in the future.

7

TOWARDS A BETTER UNDERSTANDING OF INDIAN ETHICS

DIPANKAR CHATTERJEE*

I. *Ethics of Virtue and Ethics of Duty*

IN commenting on a footnote in Prichard's now famous "Does Moral Philosophy Rest On a Mistake?" Frankena points out that even though Prichard rightly noted the distinction between virtue and moral goodness and even though he observed that "the remoteness of (modern moral philosophy) from the facts of actual life" is due to its neglect of the ethics of virtue, still, interestingly, "Prichard ... insists that 'moral philosophy has, quite rightly, concentrated its attention on the fact of obligation' ... rather than on virtue."[1] Frankena concludes his essay: "It (modern moral philosophy) must fully explore the possibility of a satisfactory ethics of virtue as an alternative or supplement to one of obligation ... It may even find, if it does so, that it has been based on a mistake Prichard did not recognize, one he himself made."[2]

Central to this controversy is the distinction, often drawn by many moral philosophers, between the rule-oriented modern

*Dipankar Chatterjee is Assistant Professor of Philosophy, University of Utah. He studied at Visva Bharati University, India, and the University of Washington, U.S.A. and has published his researches in *Philosophy East : West* and other philosophy journals and books.

1. W. K. Frankena, "Prichard and the Ethics of Virtue: Notes on a Footnote," *The Monist*, 54, No. 1 (1970), 4.

2. Frankena, p. 17.

moral philosophy with its almost exclusive concern with obligation and rightness of action and the virtue-oriented ethics of, say, Plato and Aristotle where life's overall goal as to what *to be*, as determined by some ideal theory of human nature, takes precedence over the rules regarding what *to do*. McDowell puts the distinction thus :

> On (one) view, the primary topic of ethics is the concept of right conduct, and the nature and justification of principles of behaviour. If there is a place for an interest in the concept of virtue, it is a secondary place. Virtue is a disposition ... to behave rightly; the nature of virtue is explained, as it were, from the outside in ... (On) a different view, to be found in the philosophical tradition which flowers in Aristotle's ethics ... (the) question ("How should one live?") is necessarily approached *via* the notion of a virtuous person. A conception of right conduct is grasped, as it were, from the inside out.[1]

My aim in this essay is to show that we can get a better perspective of Indian ethics if we view it as a type of virtue ethics. Surely, there are some obvious differences between the Platonic-Aristotelian ethics and the ethical systems which developed in India: most notably, they differ with regard to their notions of life's *summum bonum*. If the Platonic-Aristotelian ethics is called "virtue ethics" because it derives rules of conduct from life's ultimate goal, which is conceived as cultivation of virtue, then Indian ethics ought to be called "liberation ethics" because of its similar emphasis on liberation from "bondage". A liberated state of existence manifests virtue, but it would be wrong to characterize such a state as a virtuous state from a Platonic-Aristotelian point of view. However, notwithstanding this and other differences, there are remarkable overall similarities between these two systems of ethics; hence it is helpful to group

1. John McDowell, "Virtue and Reason," *The Monist*, 62, No. 3 (1979), 331. Frankena speculates that today's Western emphasis on rule ethics is "possibly inherited from the theological legalism and voluntarism of medieval Christianity." (Frankena, p. 16) According to Anscombe: "The answer is in history: between Aristotle and us came Christianity, with its *law* conception of ethics... In consequence of the dominance of Christianity for many centuries, the concepts of being bound, permitted, or excused became deeply embedded in our language and thought... But if such a conception is dominant for many centuries, and then is given up, it is a natural result that the concepts of 'obligation', of being bound or required by law, should remain though they had lost their root." [G. E. M. Anscombe, "Modern Moral Philosophy," *Philosophy*, 33, No. 124 (1958), 5-6].

them together and contrast them with the rule-oriented ethics of modern moral philosophy.

Accordingly, for the sake of convenience, I propose to characterize both the Greek and the Indian ideals of life as types of virtuous existence. In fact, the liberated man in the Indian system is a paradigm of virtue: he manifests such cardinal Indian virtues as detachment, compassion, and wisdom. The fact that such a man does not conform to the Platonic-Aristotelian model of a virtuous life should not distract us here.

II. *Obligation and Motivation in Ethics of Virtue*

Frankena examines the idea that an ethics of virtue has to be "mixed" with an ethics of duty to be plausible; he concludes that it *is* possible, conceptually at least, to live entirely by ideals of virtue without resorting, at some stage, to rules.[1] But, we should note that even though it is possible to have a "pure" ethics of virtue, historically all systems of virtue ethics have been mixed with rules of obligation. However, these rules are not necessarily moral rules, given the way morality is understood in modern moral philosophy, but are rules of obligation which are based primarily on prudence and propriety. These rules are set, unlike those in ethics of duty, in the overall context of life's overriding goals, such as liberation in Indian philosophy or the virtuous life of contemplation in the Platonic-Aristotelian ethics.

In any virtue ethics, people surely feel that there are things a person *ought to do*, but often this feeling translates into exhortations rather than rules. And in those occasions where the feeling is expressed as rules, the motivation is quite different from the ones which, according to modern moral philosophy, make a rule uniquely moral. In an ethics of virtue, a person is supposed to do something because doing it is in his enlightened self-interest and, therefore, should appear to him to be proper and motivating. Such propriety should be evident to anybody who is mature, cultivated, and reflective (i.e., anybody who believes in the overall goal of the system !).

In most virtue ethics there is a built-in motivation for doing the right thing (i.e., the proper thing), and this is because it is

1. Frankena, pp. 6-10.

believed that to recognize some act or character trait as virtuous requires knowing that it is best for one ("virtue is knowledge"), and such knowledge is motivating. In other words, to recognize something as virtuous is to be motivated towards it *ipso facto.* Hence it seems that most virtue ethics have held an "internalist" point of view where motivation is said to be internal to obligation. The "externalists", on the other hand, claim that a reason for action need not be a motive; for them, obligation is at most a justifying reason for doing an act, but, they point out, justification and motivation are two separate issues.[1]

In most ethics of virtue, however, justification and motivation are not separate: to know that one should do something is to be motivated to do it. In the Platonic-Aristotelian ethics, one cannot go against one's best judgment: Socrates denied the possibility of weakness of will (*akrasia*) and Aristotle, in his attempt to compromise, held that even though the incontinent man has the right knowledge, he does not act *against* his knowledge.[2] In Indian philosophy, too, it is generally held that virtue requires the knowledge that virtue is best, and this knowledge is motivating. Śaṁkara, a leading exponent of this view which emphasizes knowledge, held that there are two ways in which people give in to passion. There are some men who welcome the opportunity to surrender and do not regret it later on unless some misery results from it; Śaṁkara described them as ignorant fools (*mūrkha*), whereas there are men who succumb to the force of passion, but instead of feeling good about it they feel miserable afterwards, *even before* suffering results from their actions.[3] This shows, according to Śaṁkara, that these men in

1. I borrow the terms 'internalist' and 'externalist' from W. D. Falk, "'Ought' and Motivation" in W. S. Sellers and J. Hospers (ed.) *Readings in Ethical Theory,* (New York : Appleton-Century-Crofts, 1952), and from W. K. Frankena, "Obligation and Motivation in Recent Moral Philosophy," in A. I. Melden (ed.) *Essays in Moral Philosophy* (Seattle: University of Washington Press, 1958). Although these two terms are used by Falk and Frankena in the context of *moral* obligation, it has been pointed out to me by my colleague Bruce Landesman that these terms are equally applicable in the case of virtue ethics. There is no internalist-externalist dispute in virtue ethics, not because it is conceptually inappropriate, but because virtue ethics already comes down on one side of the issue, the internalist.

2. *Nicomachean Ethics,* 1146 b10-1147 b15.

3. *The Bhagavad Gītā : With the Commentary of Śrī Śaṁkarāchārya,* ed A. Mahadeva Sastry (Madras: V. Ramaswami Sastrulu, 1947), 115 (III. 39ff.).

the latter category are otherwise knowledgeable about their own good, but somehow this knowledge is temporarily clouder by passion, so much so that afterwards they feel as if they were forced to act by passion.[1] Consequently, Śaṁkara held that a man under passion does not act against, but in the absence of, his best judgment; thus Śaṁkara also denied the possibility of *akrasia*.

However, virtue is too perfect a state for many people to attain; given that people usually are motivated to act more from prudential interest in non-virtuous things than from any virtuous ideal, it is a task in any virtue ethics to see that people are made to realize the supreme worth of a virtuous life. However, because a virtue ethics determines what is in one's interest from what one should aim at in life, and not the other way around, it believes that virtue is its own reward and should by of intrinsic interest to everybody. Accordingly, because everybody is not virtuously inclined, a virtue ethics usually calls for some sort of "moral" education to make people see that virtue is in their best interest. It is believed that such realization would automatically motivate them to be virtuous. Moral education in such a system, then, consists of making people realize the difference between what they take to be in their interest and what is really in their interest.

This is especially true of Plato and Aristotle. Plato's *Republic* is primarily a book on such an education. Aristotle's suggestion that moral teaching should consist of instructing us to do what a virtuous man would do is another example of such an idea. It was believed that such "imitation" over time would produce the virtuous disposition and understanding and would in turn make a person spontaneously motivated to undertake virtuous acts and develop virtuous character traits.

In the Indian context, a man of virtue who is liberated from the psycho-social bondage of a routine existence is not led to action on the basis of any principle or rule as a man would be if he were to perform his actions from a moral sense. However, Indian philosophers realized that most people are far from being liberated and would, therefore, require rules and constraints to be able to lead good lives. According to the Indians, these

1. Sastry, p. 114 (III.37ff.).

people are in need of *dharma*, which is the Indian equivalent of the Platonic-Aristotelian moral education.

III. *Dharma and Prudence*

Before I proceed further, I must note that my exploration of Indian ethics will be highly selective. The scope of my essay would not allow me to go beyond the Hindu tradition to other Indian systems, such as the Buddhist and the Jaina, nor would I be able to cite all ethical schools even within Hinduism itself. Nonetheless, I believe that much of what I shall have to say in the remainder of the essay will be generally true of most of the schools in the Indian tradition. The vastness and diversity of the Indian thought makes it almost impossible for any investigator to examine all aspects of the tradition within the scope of a short essay, and without some qualification as noted above, it is not advisable to generalize about Indian ethics as such because it is not a homogeneous body of thought.

It is almost customary for scholars to hold that the ideals of *dharma* and *mokṣa* are not on the same plane of value: the *mokṣa* experience has intrinsic worth whereas the empirical experiences of a *dharma* life have at most an instrumental value, i.e., they have value to the extent they are conducive to the attainment of *mokṣa*. Franklin Edgerton's distinction between the "ordinary norms" (*artha*, *kāma*, and *dharma*) and the "extraordinary norm" (*mokṣa*) is an example of this perceived value-dichotomy.[1] Goodwin argues that because *mokṣa* is said to be of sole intrinsic worth, and because of the "unworldliness of (this) Indian ideal"[2]. . ."value for the Indian is conceived in such fashion that *nothing* can be of intrinsic worth."[3] He cites several Indian scholars such as Radhakrishnan, Maitra, Swami Nikhilananda, Mahadevan, Aiyer, and Hiriyanna to prove his point.

Whether there is indeed an "absolute value-dichotomy"[4] in Indian ethics between the empirical and the transcendental and whether the ultimate Indian ideal manifests an "unworldliness"

1. Franklin Edgerton, "Dominant Ideas in the Formation of Indian Culture," *Journal of the American Oriental Society*, 62 (1942), 151-52.

2. William F. Goodwin, "Ethics and Value in Indian Philosophy," *Philosophy East and West*, 4 (1955), 343.

3. Goodwin, p. 331.

4. Goodwin, p. 342.

are questions which, important and interesting as they are, I do not want to get into here. Rather, what interests me more, for my purpose in this essay, is the claim by numerous writers, mostly Western, that not only is there a value-dichotomy between *dharma* and *mokṣa*, but that the two ideals are not mutually compatible. Van Buitenen writes :

> In other words, *dharma* is all that activity that a man, if he is to live fittingly, is required to contribute to the fixed order of things, to the norm of the universe, which is good and should not be altered. . .*Mokṣa*, "release," is release from the entire realm which is governed by *dharma*. . .It stands, therefore, in opposition to *dharma*. . .*Dharma* upholds the established order. . . *Mokṣa*, however, is the abandonment of the established order, not in favor of anarchy, but in favor of a self-realization which is precluded in the realm of *dharma*.[1]

The reason for this "opposition" is traced back to the historical origin of the two concepts. Ingalls points out that the "notion of *mokṣa* is a much later one in the history of Indian thought than the notion of *dharma*."[2] The latter notion occupied a central part in the literature of the Vedas and other early texts which were exclusively concerned with the maintenance and well-being of the world order. The term '*dharma*' was understood either as a cosmic rule giving things their essence or nature, or, in the human context, as the most important goal of life to be pursued. In the latter sense, the term implied moral concepts which "were fully as anthropocentric as the Greek concepts."[3] The terms '*mokṣa*' or '*apavarga*' did not appear in the literature "until the late Upaniṣads. . .and the second layer of the epic. What is more, there were orthodox schools which refused to recognize *mokṣa* for many centuries."[4]

Ingalls thinks that in the epic texts, as well as in most orthodox literatures, *mokṣa* was recognized as a state of being which lies beyond the discipline of *dharma* but was thought to be achievable by means not radically different from the one needed to conform to *dharma*. He cites the *Bhagavad Gītā* as the culminating instance of this trend, but also notes some exceptions, such as Śaṁkara's Advaita Vedānta, where this attempted harmonization

1. J. A. B. van Buitenen, "Dharma and Moksa," *Philosophy East and West*, 7 (1957), 36-37.
2. Daniel H. H. Ingalls, "Dharma and Moksa," *Philosophy East and West*, 7 (1957), 45.
3. Ingalls, p. 43.
4. Ingalls, p. 45.

of the two goals within a single path was seriously challenged.[1] Other writers, however, point out that even though *mokṣa* quickly gained respectability in the *dharma* oriented literatures of the early period, and eventually became the highest goal of life, it still somehow retained its original antinomy to *dharma* and hence the path prescribed for the attainment of *mokṣa* was usually thought to be radically different from the one meant for *dharma*. These writers cite the *Gītā* more as an exception to the trend than as the epitome.[2]

This alleged incompatibility between *dharma* and *mokṣa* is forcefully stated by Goodwin in the form of an indictment of the Indian idea of empirical life in general and *dharma* in particular. He writes: "If empirical existence be non-value as such, the distinction between value and disvalue does not fall within the empirical, i.e., between pleasure and pain, but between the experience of liberation and *any* empirical experience, whether pleasurable or painful."[3] Given that, according to Goodwin, "there is no basis for choice among 'natural values'. . . The only moral question is a choice among intrinsically worthless means... (The Indians believe that it is) possible to give man guidance as to the relative *intrinsic* values of things. It is not."[4] Albert Schweitzer, in his *Indian Thought and Its Development* made the famous observation that the Indian quest for liberation is essentially life negating. Goodwin cites Schweitzer to support his contention that *dharma* and *mokṣa* are incompatible ends: ". . .'ethical world and life negation is in itself a contradictory and non-realisable idea. For ethics comprise world and life affirmation.' "[5]

It seems to me that both Schweitzer and Goodwin showed a lack of understanding of one of the most fundamental ideas in Indian philosophy, which is that *dharma* and *mokṣa* operate on two different levels, and even though the former is of less value (or, perhaps, *dis*value, if Goodwin and others are right) from

1. Ingalls, pp. 45-46.
2. cf. van Buitenen, pp. 37, 38, 39-40; Austin B. Creel, "Dharma as an Ethical Category Relating to Freedom and Responsibility," *Philosophy East and West*, 22 (1972), 163, note 34.
3. Goodwin, pp. 342-43.
4. Goodwin, pp. 341-42.
5. Goodwin, p. 342.

the liberated point of view, it nonetheless has its own intrinsic worth in the empirical realm. Goodwin believes that it is not possible to give man guidance in the matters of empirical import where all things are equally worthless. The idea of guiding a man to his highest good is interesting in Hinduism but could easily be misunderstood. It is not that the masses are to be guided by a liberated man who imposes his own standard of value on people; nor is it that such a man attempts to guide them with the disquieting knowledge that there is really no basis for choice among things which are all non-value. In Hinduism, people are not meant to be guided by any other standard than that which is understandable by them from *their* point of view. This is where *dharma* comes in as a form of "moral education" which is meant to lead people, at their own natural pace, to an understanding of their highest good.[1] The basis of choice among values in the life of *dharma* is prudence: this idea is often overlooked by the Indian scholars themselves when they characterize practice of *dharma* as *moral* pursuit. The operating principle in *dharma* is not morality as it is understood in modern Western philosophy, because *dharma* is set in the context of an ethics of virtue which is different from modern rule-oriented morality.

The Hindu *dharma* involves a complicated set of rules and regulations which are designed to set one on to the eventual course leading to liberation through rigidly controlled life-style and social role. It is believed that to follow one's set duties is the right thing (in a non-moral sense) to do, because, due to the emphasis placed on discipline, self-control, and fellow-feeling, it is expected that such a scheme, along with proper guidance and right examples, is eventually conducive to a virtuous life and consequent liberation from bondage.

However, the rules to be followed in Hindu *dharma* are not rules of *moral* obligation but mostly of prudence and propriety. But, again, a *dharma* life is a prudent and proper thing to pursue *not* because it is in one's enlightened self-interest (because of its being conducive to *mokṣa*), but because such a life-style promotes most of one's *everyday* interests. That is, even though

1. Thus, the Indian idea of ethical guidance is different from the Platonic-Aristotelian idea of moral education which has a built-in impatience for people's natural pace and inclinations.

people are usually self-interested, they are mostly not "enlightened"; hence, if people are to be motivated to pursue a life of *dharma* on prudence, then something other than enlighted self-interest is to be brought in. It must be shown to them that to be a man of *dharma* is in (what *they* take to be) their interest. (A *dharma* life is also meant to be in one's *ultimate* interest, which is its primary justification, even though one may not know it at the time or may not find much interest in the prospect.) In such a framework, then, the Indians would not have to justify virtue in terms of its being conducive to anything other than virtue itself, nor would they have to subordinate life's overall goal, which is liberation, to rules of conduct. These points are required if Indian ethics is to remain primarily an ethics of virtue.

To understand the Indian rationale that it is indeed prudent for a common man, from his point of view, to follow his *dharma*, it is necessary to understand two other Hindu objectives of life: *kāma* and *artha*. I propose to analyze the notions of *kāma* and *artha* in the manner in which Feinberg analyzes "ulterior" and "welfare" goals, because I believe that *kāma* and *artha*, as goals, *are* Feinberg's ulterior and welfare goals respectively.[1] Feinberg holds that a man has interest in something when he has a stake in it.[2] This is also how a Hindu argues when he claims that a man's being interested in something is due to his having a *svārtha* (stake) in it. However, according to Feinberg, a man's fleeting desires or wants for objects do not constitute his having a stake in them. For the Hindus, too, one can have interest only in *objectives* or goals (*puruṣārthas*) rather than in mere objects of desire, and this can happen, in the realm of "self-interested" existence (as opposed to the non-self-interested realm of a liberated existence), in two ways: (a) one takes interest in something in an involved and passionate manner, at least partly for its own sake (the *kāma* way), and (b) one is also interested in things in an objective and manipulative manner (the *artha* way), valuing their achievement as means to the attainment of the *kāma* interests. Objectives under (a) are called *kāma* (meaning, passionately desired) objectives because their being objects of

1. Joel Feinberg, "Harm and Self-Interest," in P. M. S. Hacker and J. Raz (ed.) *Law, Morality, and Society : Essays in Honour of H. L. A. Hart* (Oxford : Clarendon Press, 1979,) 285-308.

2. Feinberg, pp. 285-86.

interest is due to their being *desired* by one (but not in a fleeting or idle manner), whereas *artha* (meaning, instrumental) objectives are to be desired *because* they are of interest to one insofar as they lead to the attainment of the *kāma* interests.[1]

An *artha* interest could turn into a *kāma* one if one gets too involved in its quest in a misdirected way, i.e., if one ends up desiring it for its own sake, at least partly as when, e.g., one "worships" money. A *kāma* interest, on the other hand, may either cease to be in one's interest altogether when one stops desiring it—at one time, say, it really mattered to one if one could be a lawyer, but no more—or it could turn into an *artha* interest if one now desires it merely to attain some *kāma* objective. One's desire now to be a lawyer to please one's parents is such an example.

Now, implied in the Indian perception is the belief that the mark of a prudent life is to entertain just a selected number of *kāma* type desires for a few socially approved ends. The presence of a limited number of *kāma* desires would mean a limited range of interests, *both kāma* and *artha* types (because *artha* interests are there due to the presence of *kāma* ones); hence, the chances are greater of promoting most of one's interests. A *dharma* life, unlike the one in a modern consumer society, rigidly controls the possibility of entertaining unnecessarily fanciful or transitory desires and appetites; the desires allowed in such a context are few and are supposed to be of a stable type, thus being conducive to goals like *kāma* and *artha*, and are said to be in accordance with a man's social role and inclination.[2] A man of *dharma*, then, plays it safe,[3] and thereby ensures the chances of maximum

1. See Feinberg, p. 286, for an account of how ulterior and welfare interests are related to wants and desires.

2. Such a scheme of creating and pursuing one's interests obviously involves indoctrination and social conditioning, which are admittedly a big part of a *dharma* life. However, it is to be noted that this is how most of one's fields of interests are created and sustained in *any* society.

3. To show that the intrinsic value for the Indian philosopher is identified with the unchanging and the perfect, Goodwin quotes Radhakrishnan : "We long for a good which is never left behind and never superseded." [*Eastern Religions and Western Thought* (Oxford : Oxford University Press, 1940), p. 81, quoted by Goodwin, p. 331]. In a footnote to the above quotation Goodwin rightly comments: "Dewey finds Western thought to have been plagued by a 'quest for certainty'; it would seem that Indian philosophy

harmonious fulfilment of his desires and of consequent promotion of his interests. It is from this point of view, the Indian philosopher would contend, that to follow a life of *dharma* is a mark of prudence. Śaṁkara, for example, echoed the Indian view when he claimed, following the *Bhagavad Gītā*, that the performance of somebody else's *dharma*, by neglecting one's own, is fraught with fear and danger, and ultimately leads one to hell (i.e., to one's ruin), whereas one's own duty, properly performed, leads one to heaven.[1]

The overall idea in Indian ethics is that the pursuit of one's *dharma* makes one self-interested in an unselfish way, i.e., in a way which is not at the expense of, or in disregard of, the interests or wants of other people where it is avoidable.[2] After a man is well-grounded in his *dharma*, being disciplined, self-controlled, and unselfish, he perhaps someday sees, given the presence of some other factors such as proper guidance and right examples, that his greatest good lies in developing his highest potentials, i.e., in cultivating self-knowledge, compassion, and other virtues. Then he would not try to find out if being liberated would lead him to any good that he valued as a man of "worldly" prudence; rather he would realize that being a man of such sublime virtues is itself the highest good.

After pursuing a course leading to the ultimate good, such a man might end up being liberated, and at that stage his actions would no longer be self-interested. They would flow from his intrinsically good desires which can neither promote nor go against his interests, for, being settled in wisdom and giving up his ego, he does not have a stake in anything any more. According to the Indians, a liberated man does not stand to gain or lose depending on the outcome of his act;[3] if he did, then he would have been still in "bondage." Admittedly, the

has been plagued by a 'quest for security'. " (p. 331, note 49) In Indian philosophy, a man of worldly prudence plays it safe by conforming to his own *dharma*, whereas a man with enlightened self-interest longs for the security of a blissful existence in liberation. The basis for such a "quest for security" in both cases is prudence.

1. Sastry, p. 113 (III.35 ff.); also, p. 477 (XVIII.48 ff.).

2. This is how Feinberg characterizes a self-interested person who is unselfish. See Feinberg, pp. 294-96.

3. This is Feinberg's idea of somebody's having a stake in something. See Feinberg, p. 285.

progress from a selfish existence to an exalted virtuous life, *via dharma* and beyond, is a very slow one, especially when people are left to their own inclinations and natural pace; but, then, the Indians are in no hurry. They believe in reincarnation !

Because Indian ethics has no place for moral obligation and moral goodness as they are understood in modern Western moral philosophy, the Indians would not find it downright immoral that a man of *dharma* lives mostly by prudence or that a liberated man is oblivious to moral rules and principles.

PART II

TRADITION AND MODERNITY

8

TRADITIONAL INDIAN PHILOSOPHY AS A MODERN INDIAN THINKER VIEWS IT

KALIDAS BHATTACHARYYA*

A. *Problems in the Right Perspective*

WHAT we mean here by 'traditional Indian philosophy' is the corpus of philosophical doctrines and dissertations that have been current in India for at least two millenniums and communicated from generation to generation mainly through Sanskrit language and largely also through Pāli (as in the case of Hīnayāna Buddhism) and Prakrit (as in the case of Jainism). The beauty of the whole tradition is that it was a perfectly living widespread study among Indian philosophers till only the other day—till, one may say, a hundred and twenty-five years back—though growing some time in one direction and some time in another, emphasizing now one group of problems and now another and not unoften passing through periods of stagnation and decay. Perhaps, as all living organisms do, it absorbed sometimes some alien doctrines and, might be, at times changed drastically. But it was always after all the *Indian* mind, remaining Indian all through, that changed that way, softly or drastically. This was

*Kalidas Bhattacharyya is (Retired) Professor of Philosophy, Visvabharati University, India. He was Director, Center for Advanced Study in Philosophy and Vice-Chancellor (1966-70) of Visvabharati University. Written a large number of articles and books. His most famous books include : *Alternative Standpoints in Philosophy*; *Object, Content and Relation*; *Philosophy, Logic and Language*; *Presuppositions of Science and Philosophy*.

the case even during the whole period of Muslim rule in India: the mainstream was the old traditional Hindu and Jaina philosophy, with whatever of Buddhism was till then extant.

The picture altered, however, with the Britishers consolidating their hold on this country. They somehow captured the Indian mind, primarily, through the display of their newly developed science (and technology) which appeared to be an unfailing source of ever-growing material well-being and, secondarily, through the loud announcement of the three human values—equality, fraternity and love—which, though originating in the West with another earlier movement known as Renaissance, not always consistent with the spirit of science and technology, came somehow to be associated with them. The Indian mind—at least the mind of the mainstream that was Hindu—being thus captured, Western learning found an easy access to this country. Another fifty years, and we find all original Indian learning—foremost among them, Indian philosophy and Indian medicine—pushed to the background. By the end of the nineteenth century it would have, practically, disappeared had it—particularly Indian philosophy—not been brought back to the fore by some orientalists and linguists (mostly historians) of the late nineteenth and early twentieth century, and, paradoxically enough, most of them were Europeans. In a way, thus, Indian philosophy was revived for those Indians who had been trained in Western learning.

This revival has passed under the name of (Indian) Renaissance, though—few have noticed this—with the meaning of the word 'renaissance' turned upside down. What happens in genuine renaissance is that under the impact of some powerful new ideas people with a *living tradition* adjust those ideas to that tradition: normally long-forgotten classical ideas come to be absorbed in the then current tradition. What happened, however, in India in those days was quite different. Forgotten by the English-educated Indians and only half forgotten (because only half noticed) by the vast mass of traditional Indians (who had till then no English education), the *so-called* 'newly found' Indian ideas could not possibly be freshly incorporated in an existing living tradition; for, even as unnoticed, they still informed the bulk of the day-to-day life of even the English-educated Indians, let alone the vast mass who had not that education till then. So if there was any question of adjustment, for the English-educated Indians, it was that of the traditionally Indian (though half forgotten) ideas with the English (in effect, Western) ideas that were newly acquired. Naturally, what these English-educated Indians did was to understand and interpret the traditional Indian ideas—Indian philosophy, for that—in terms of ideas that were Western. This is no renaissance. If there could be any such really in those days, it would have rather interpreted the Western ideas in terms of ideas that had been traditionally Indian.

Only a handful of original thinkers like B. G. Tilak, Sri Aurobindo, Gopinath Kaviraj and, among the constructive technical philosophers, K. C. Bhattacharyya and a few others have done this. Most of the others who have done philosophy in India since have more or less servilely accepted Western philosophy, and that too as it was understood by the British thinkers, and granted recognition to that much only of Indianism which was intelligible in terms of Western ideas. The rest was rejected as dogmatic, magical, tribal, romantic, speculative and what not?

Thus, on one side there have been these Western-educated philosophers who (i) are either much too Westernized as stated above or (ii) have authentically re-discovered traditional Indian ideas, so much so that practically what they have done has rather been to understand Western philosophy in terms of philosophy that is traditionally Indian, or (iii) have been just historians of (or linguistic scholars in) Indian philosophy, treating the different aspects of that philosophy more or less as museum pieces, not meant to be actively committed to. And there have always been, on the other side, old-type Indian thinkers, and some stalwarts even now, in the field, though their number has been fast declining. Most of the present-day old-type thinkers are, however, satisfied with a dictionary type of scholarship, content with knowing what the old-day stalwarts in their schools and their commentators had written, though for that reason they cannot be said to be treating that philosophy as just a museum piece, for they are still committed to their schools. A handful of these old-type scholars have also studied Western philosophy, though to what benefit it is difficult to assess.

The difficulty with these old-type scholars in Indian philosophy is that they live in a self-contained world of their own and do not care to communicate with others except in their own limited world. In the field of learning, on the other hand, people of the whole world form one community, learning from others and giving their own to them. This was the state of affairs even in the old-day India. Western education may have done us incalculable harm but it has after all restored us to that 'one world'. We cannot afford to alienate ourselves and engage in a sort of in-breeding in the field of ideas. That would only be false patriotism and harmful nostalgia.

There is, of course, a danger on the other side too. Western-educated scholars may too easily interpret Indian ideas just as they would like and, repelled by the methodological subtleties of the later-day (say, since the thirteenth century) Indian philosophy, may only be satisfied with rough and ready ideas which more often overshoot the mark than not. A true modern *Indian* thinker would be one who, conversant with as many details as possible, whether of methodology or of content, of the traditional Indian philosophy, is also versed in relevant branches of Western philosophy and its logic and epistemology.

There is no question, however, of his being bogged down in details. Every genuine philosopher is, first, a generalist, and then a specialist in one or two branches. It is not necessary, therefore, that a genuine modern Indian philosopher (or even an Indian scholar in philosophy) will have to master all the details and subtleties of both Indian and Western philosophy. It is enough that he is conversant with the basic ideas of these two philosophies. If he has to turn to Western philosophy, this is because he has to communicate with the people of the West.

There are people who hold that philosophy as a body of *truths* (true statements) like mathematics and sciences, ought not to differ from people to people. This is not, however, a correct view. Mathematics and sciences are not humanistic studies and may not, therefore, differ from people to people. But not so are studies that are humanistic. For any particular people, humanistic studies have perforce to be coloured, circumscribed and motivated by certain basic, though evidently local (because not common to all people of the world), ideas and attitudes and also by how the 'truths' so found have to be utilized in particular historico-geographical circumstances.

This is true, perhaps, of mathematics and physical sciences too. How otherwise could there be different schools regarding even the fundamental attitudes of mathematics as an intellectual pursuit? How, again, could there be so many types of physics? A later type of physics has not always developed (and superseded an earlier type) solely in deference to some recalcitrant (fact or) facts which, for their explanation, require some basic changes in the very fundamentals: new attitudes have often been formulated more or less *a priori* and then found suitable for dealing with some recalcitrant facts. Even if it be true that facts are the ultimate determinants of the type of science one has at a particular period, this very *attachment to facts* may itself be counted as one among several basic attitudes. Had it not been so there could not arise the present-day discipline called 'philosophy of science.' Kant accepted the attitudinal correctness of mathematics and physics of his days and offered a philosophy of mathematics and physics accordingly in his *Critique of Pure Reason*. But even in that *Critique* (in the part known as 'Transcendental Dialectic') he circumscribed all that he said about these two disciplines and in his *Critique of Practical Reason* established the basis for an alternative (if not a superseding) study, viz. metaphysics, though now from the point of view of 'practical reason'. Basic attitudes, thus, are what ultimately count in every field, and explicitly so in philosophy.

If, in spite of all modernization, three-fourths of the day-to-day life of a modern Indian is still lived in the old traditional Indian attitude, is it not incumbent on a present-day Indian scholar in philosophy and, more so, on an Indian philosopher of today, that he should be at home with his traditional philosophy, at least simultaneously with, if not earlier than, his study of Western philosophy? If a modern Greek whose mind is perfectly in tune with that of the rest of the Western world assiduously studies ancient Greek philosophy, if only as a matter of nostalgic love for his forgotten ancestors, how much more necessary is it for a modern Indian philosopher to be well at home with his own traditional wisdom?

One could deny all this, even after all that we have said, if only it could be shown that Western philosophy has *more efficiently* dealt with the problems raised in the traditional philosophy of India, either through working out better and more acceptable solutions to many of them or by rejecting the rest as gratuitous, unanswerable or illegitimate for some definite reasons. This could be said more forcefully if it could, in addition, be shown that Western philosophy since the Greek days down to the present-day linguistic analysis, phenomenology, existentialism, symbolic logic, philosophy of science, etc., has raised *a number* of other important issues undreamt of in traditional Indian philosophy and offered solutions that are very relevant to the present-day world culture.

We shall show, however, through the pages that follow, that most of these are unfounded claims. It is not true, we shall show, that Western philosophy has offered better solutions to the problems that are common to it and the traditional Indian philosophy. We shall further show

1. That practically none of the problems of Indian philosophy which Western philosophy, older or modern, propose to reject as gratuitous or, for whatever reasons, unanswerable are really so;
2. That when Western philosophers claim that some of the problems which are of far-reaching importance to them do not figure at all in Indian philosophy or figure there only occasionally or very cursorily, this is not always true (some of them have figured very prominently, though in different forms, and some in special systems, not in all);
3. That if some important problems of Western philosophy have not figured at all in Indian philosophy or figured only distantly and cursorily, the same is true of some very important problems of Indian philosophy not figuring at all in Western philosophy or treated there only distantly and cursorily (which only shows the difference in their fundamental attitudes, none of which can be condemned *a priori*); and
4. That if some of the problems, very important for Western philosophy, have been neglected or treated only cursorily, this is because to the traditional Indian mind they appeared to be gratuitous, or unanswerable because illegitimate or for whatever other reason.

All depends, we repeat, on the difference in the basic attitudes of the Western and the traditional Indian philosophies to life and the world. To this we shall turn later. We shall also see how far in the present-day 'one world' the differences could be smoothed out.

B. *Identical Problems in Western and Traditional Indian Philosophies*

Most of the problems dealt with in Indian philosophy are similar to those in Western philosophy and the solutions to each of them are almost as varied as in Western philosophy. Even the method of treatment is practically the same—punctilious observation, phenomenological analysis, theorization and systematization, verification with reference to actual facts, reasoned establishment, i.e. inference (not *anumāna* alone) from observed data (and from other truths already accepted) and linguistic analysis carried, in later days in India, almost to fantastic feats.

There is the problem, for example of the most general classification of all things of the world into 'categories' like substance, attribute, universal, particular, relation (mostly, inherence), negation (absence), etc. Each of these categories is thoroughly studied, analyzed and divided exhaustively into sub-categories. There is a thorough study, in each system, of what exactly the terms 'substance,' 'attribute,' 'universal,' etc. mean, whether the designation in each case is a reality *sui generis* or interpretable in terms of another and how exactly the categories are related to one another; and similarly with regard to the sub-categories. Much of the study of the sub-categories is on a par with the old-day science of any advanced people, though, for whatever reason, much more attention is paid to the consideration of self and whatever is directly connected with it, viz. knowledge with its subject-object distinction; involvement in 'nature', both physical and psychic; unconscious impressions and dispositions; freedom from such involvement and elimination (exhaustion where direct elimination is not possible) of these dispositions and impressions; relation between self and knowledge; whether the uninvolved (free) self is individual or cosmic—relation, in other words, between the individual and the Absolute; relation, in particular, between self and body (the latter with its senses and material constituents), etc. The question is particularly asked whether self, with or without knowledge (consciousness), can persist (or be even imagined to persist) apart from body with which it evidently stands involved and apart equally, from the objects known; whether such pure knowledge (consciousness) is still (or can be) an object, after all; if 'yes', whether or not there would be an unending series of introspection behind introspection, or whether self (=pure consciousness) would be altogether different from all 'objects' and, so far, called unintrospectable, self-evident pure subjectivity; whether, again, such subjectivity is still a substantive thing (reality, though not object) *sui generis* or just a function, an act, a power, and, if any of these latter, whether it is ontologically different or non-different from the substantive that is said to have that power and, if non-different, whether somehow we have still to admit both the substantive and the power or dispense with either (and, if we have to dispense with either, with which one), etc.

All these problems, and many more, have been thoroughly thrashed out in different systems of Indian philosophy; and exactly as in Western philosophy, if not more so, all sorts of solutions have been offered with exquisite analysis and argumentation and based on impartial observation of facts as far as possible. Exactly as in Western philosophy, if not more so, the answers that each system has given to these questions are so finely adjusted to one another to form a grand self-complete unity that they appear all to be of one piece. Within each system, different philosophers have often indeed differed on subtler details, but the general intertwining of basic solutions remains intact; and where a particular philosopher belonging to a particular school has differed on a number of details and yet connected with one another and with the basic doctrines of the school he is at once taken as the originator of a new sub-school. Discussions for millenniums by philosophers of different schools and sub-schools on these broad basic points and subtle sub-points regarding the problems of self and whatever else is connected with it have formed a vast and rich philosophical literature—certainly not speculative in any derogatory sense of the term but as analytical, perceptive and ratiocinative as any best mind of the modern age can imagine it to be.

On these issues the Nyāya-Vaiśeṣika philosophy would largely be the counterpart of the empiricism of the West except that this Indian counterpart has tackled, even in all possible details, many of the philosophical problems which no Western empiricist, be he of the old type or of the new, would care to touch. With his basic empirical attitude, the Nyāya-Vaiśeṣika thinker is still a metaphysician, and this is nothing paradoxical for the Indians. Nyāya-Vaiśeṣika would never fight shy of the supersensible, provided it is correctly inferred from observed data and other truths already confirmed; and in this they are no worse than even the modern scientists who allow so many super-sensible entities, their common defence being that these super-sensibles are still understood in the language of the sensible, only pushed a little beyond their normal empirical limits. Of this defence we shall speak later. Let us, in the meantime, see what are the super-sensible entities that Nyāya-Vaiśeṣika has admitted.

The foremost among them is *self*. Some of these thinkers admit indeed that self is directly perceived through 'inner sense' through which we perceive mental states like pleasure, pain, etc.[1] But others who do not admit this would yet not hesitate to *infer* it. Not only self, the empiricist Nyāya-Vaiśeṣika would even admit, on grounds of inference, atoms, binaries, persisting impressions (*saṁskāras, vāsanās*) and dispositions (*adṛṣṭas = karmas* resulting from good or bad deeds)—dispositions that tend, of themselves, to mature into new experiences with appropriate hedonic tones (if necessary, in a life after the end of the present life) and even God; and, over and above these—even among the day-to-day ways of perception—illusion, perception of any or all particulars as just instantiation of a genuine universal and the *yogin*'s perception of the future and the distant. In the case of the last two, viz., *any* instantiation of a universal, and the distant and the future for the *yogin*, they admit, indeed, that these are all *perceived*, but immediately add that these are no *normal* cases of perception, meaning, thereby, that if anyone denies perceptibility in these cases, this can be inferentially demonstrated to him. The Nyāya-Vaiśeṣika thinkers are thus prepared to admit anything that can be validly inferred, however *unverifiable* it may be through sense-perception. The only empirical criterion they still adhere to is that these super-sensibles are only extensions *of the sensible* beyond their normal limits, and thus are not what others call 'transcendental' which is qualitatively different from the empirical. The Mīmāṁsakas and the Jainas too are largely of this temperament. Some contemporary empiricists in the West, be it noted in this connection, have permitted this much extension of empiricism.

1. When one so perceives *knowledge* through inner sense, this latter is given a special name, viz. 'introspection', because, obviously, it is constitutionally *reflective*, in contrast to the perception of other mental states which, primarily, is unreflective.

Philosophers of other schools, however,[1] who have studied the varied problems enumerated above, have spoken of them, and also their solutions, as *transcendental*, i.e. beyond all conceivable extensions of the empirical. In other words, while according to Nyāya-Vaiśeṣika (and probably also according to Mīmāṁsā) everything whatsoever is in Nature, 'Nature', according to them, meaning *all* that there is, every other Indian system (barring, of course, *Lokāyata* of which we shall speak later) has understood *self* (and the Absolute where it is different from *self*), its original freedom, its free reference to Nature, its getting involved there, its effort to get away from that involvement and practically all that is directly connected with such involvement or dissociation, as every bit trans-natural, i.e. transcendental. According to all these transcendentalists—be they of the Sāṁkhya or Yoga or any of the Vedāntic, Śaiva, Śākta and Mahāyāna Buddhist schools[2]—self's free reference to Nature, and retrospectively, therefore, its progressive getting away from *involvement* in that Nature, is the same thing as Kant's 'transcendental anticipation' (construction) of Nature, which, again, is, in idea, little different from what Husserl calls 'intention'. As now, the 'intended', just so far as it is 'intended', is constituted entirely by 'intention'—nothing that is independent of it and stands on its own account—to understand Nature as an independent well-structured system of objects, having nothing to do with self except including and affecting it in order that it may know that Nature, would just be its basic involvement there, maturing later into all sorts of mundane activities. From the transcendental point of view of Kantian construction or Husserlian intention, this would be a *wrong* understanding, after all, though as born in this world we start our life that way. Kant and Husserl have not in so many words pointed to the wrongness of this understanding; they, like most of the transcendentalists in the West, were more interested in progressive dissociation and parallel free intentions. Indian transcendentalists, on the other hand, are very much alert about the error operating behind this involvement, though they differ substantially, as we shall see later, regarding its

1. As much in India as in the West. For the time being we are concerned with Indian systems.

2. The Jainas, it appears, belong half tot he transcendentalist camp and half to the empiricist one, even regarding these topics.

exact place and magnitude. Except, however, on this point, the Indian and Western transcendentalists have practically said the same things.

Regarding the exact place and magnitude of the transcendental error about the status of Nature, it all depends on how much, if at all, that Nature is understood as already over there, independently of any intention, construction or anticipation. Kant and Husserl have held that there is somehow an independent Nature, though not exactly in the form in which we have it in mundane life, for quite much of the latter is only 'intended' or 'constructed'. What is really independent stands as 'bracketed', as 'unknown', i.e. wholly as indefinite. So do Sāṁkhya and Yoga speak of *prakṛti* as wholly independent and over there, even transcendentally, though as wholly indefinite. A great merit of Sāṁkhya and Yoga is that they understand the process of dissociation (which is more primary, even in Kant and Husserl, than construction or intention) to be as much *puruṣa* (subjectivity) dissociating itself progressively as, at the last stage, *prakṛti* (the indefinite base of Nature) dissociating itself, thereby lending credence to Husserl's notion of 'bracketing'.[1] The result is the same in all the three cases, Sāṁkhya-Yoga, Kant and Husserl. The structured Nature is a real construction, a real intention, though the difference between Sāṁkhya and Yoga, on the one hand, and Kant and Husserl, on the other, regarding the place and magnitude of the transcendental error involved should not be overlooked.

Advaita Vedānta, however, as distinct from all these three, has been an extreme type of transcendentalism, holding that freedom as dissociation, being the most primary character of self, has to be pushed back to its optimum feasibility, i.e. to it being just itself, all forward-looking freedom—construction or intention—being itself at the root an error. Mahāyāna Buddhism, we shall see later, is just a variant of this extreme form of transcendentalism; and other schools of Vedānta have differed, as much from Advaita Vedānta as among themselves, regarding how much of the forward-looking freedom—'freedom to', i.e. intention or construction—has to be admitted as real movement.

1. Object's withdrawal from the involvement corresponds to Husserl's 'bracketing of Nature' and subject's withdrawal to his 'reduction'.

The Western parallel to the Mahāyāna form of extreme transcendentalism we find in all forms of Dynamism or Irrationalism, but it is difficult to find a parallel to Advaita Vedānta. Fichte and Scopenhauer come closest to it. More of these later.

The transcendental contents—the 'intended's—might also be considered real or quite another ground, viz. that 'intention' or 'construction' is after all a real power (function) of self, which self is considered real without any question. (Why exactly, we shall have occasion to see later.) This power is exactly what is called in the Upaniṣads '*māyā*', and in the Tāntrika scriptures '*śakti*'. While Advaita Vedānta would consider it as, in whatever way, outside (and to what extent appearing to be independent of) self, other Vedāntins and the Śaivas and Śāktas would call it a real power, a real function, of self, and in no way independent of self, being that self itself as functioning or, at the least, as capable of functioning. As this power is understood as different, in varying measures, from self or not, accordingly there are different schools of non-Advaita Vedānta, Śaivism and Śāktism. But for the fact that in all these transcendental Indian systems the *ultimate* is, after all, subjectivity *par excellence*, parallels to all these non-Advaitic systems may be found in Plato, Aristotle, Leibnitz and other Rationalist systems in the West.[1]

Buddhism, however, particularly of the Mahāyāna types, though belonging to the transcendental group, stands in a different class altogether. It does, indeed, admit of Nature as wholly constituted (intended) by the subject, speaks also of progressive withdrawal of subject, regards both intention and withdrawal as ultimately unreal and delineates the stages and sub-stages in all details, and appear that way to be very much in line with Advaita Vedānta; yet much like Kant in his *Critique of Pure Reason* and like Husserl through much of his 'intentional' adventure, it refuses to stop ultimately at a substantive (entitative) self (Husserl's 'ego') at the end. At different stages, indeed, of withdrawal there *appear* different pseudo-selves—partly bound and partly free—but they are all *pseudo*-substantive, i.e. only *pseudo*-selves, though, undoubtedly more and more purified forms of subjectivity. So, if there is no substantive self anywhere,

1. Aristotle differs, indeed, with Plato in not having understood the 'Ideas' (intended's) to be as transcendental as in Plato, i.e. transcendent. In this respect it is Nyāya-Vaiśeṣika, rather, which would parallel Aristotle.

particularly at the so-called end, what remains of the traditional self is only a subjective act, a function, process or dynamism—a power, one may say—but without any substantive entity that has that power, function, etc. This corresponds, again, to Kant's 'transcendental apperception' and the dynamism of all philosophies of 'change'.

So far with *self* and whatever is connected with it, viz. knowledge, etc. it is an extraordinarily rich philosophy—rich with diverse truths, diverse systems and details and subtleties of all sorts, and all substantiated to the utmost of human capacity!

Then comes Indian Logic—another impressive well-developed study, pursued from different angles by different schools of traditional Indian philosophy. In one important respect, indeed, it falls seriously short of the Logic that has developed in the West since the days of Aristotle: it lacks *formal* Logic. This lack we shall consider later. But in the meantime, and except for that lack, it is decidedly a classic achievement for any people. It is a Logic which is at the same time a full theory of knowledge. The problems it tackles are : (i) what is knowledge, (ii) what is its relation to object, (iii) types and sub-types of knowledge—perception, inference, etc., with subdivisions of each, (iv) 'sources of valid knowledge' (*pramāṇa*) in each such case, (v) the relation of knowledge to language, (vi) semantics and syntax, (vii) why and how far testimony is valid, (viii) elaborate theories of error, (ix) belief and (established) truth—what makes an awareness true, i.e. theories of validity (*prāmāṇya*), (x) indeterminate perception, judgmental perception and judgment, (xi) nature and types of fallacy, (xii) whether and how far memory is a source of valid knowledge, etc. The wealth of details and the subtleties of this Logic, developed through ages in different systems of Indian philosophy, make it much richer and more systematic and in many respects more advanced than what has till now been achieved in the West, except that the traditional Indian mind had, for reasons we shall soon discuss, little interest in formal Logic in which the Western mind has excelled beyond measure: the various systems of 'Symbolic Logic' developed in the West are, undoubtedly, phenomenal achievements, though never of any interest, as we shall soon see, to whatever is truly Indian.

For millenniums, Indians have studied the various categories with all their sub-types and always in their interrelation. They have thoroughly discussed the nature of each category and sub-category and discussed also whether all of them should be recognized or only some of them, the rest being interpreted in terms of those already recognized. For example, all the Indian systems, except most that are Buddhistic, have admitted substance as a legitimate category, and each side has defended its case to the utmost. Among the different sub-types of substance they have laid special emphasis on time, space, self and mind (the distinction between self and mind we shall study later), and the discussion on space and time, specially in Nyāya-Vaiśeṣika, Yoga, Buddhism and Jainism, is at least as thorough as any anywhere in Western philosophy (not in modern Western *science* where space and time are more or less postulates, working hypotheses, necessary symbols of a kind—nothing that are more significantly realities or genuine features of the real). The category of 'universal', too, has interested all the Indian systems. While Nyāya-Vaiśeṣika, Mīmāṁsā and Advaita Vedānta have insisted that it is a reality over there, though about its relation to the corresponding particulars they have offered different accounts, at least as detailed and thought-provoking as any in Western philosophy, the Buddhists—call them nominalists or conceptualists—have denied universals altogether. The Buddhist refutation of universals (as realities over there) and the Hindu and the Jaina rejoinders may, like many other studies in the traditional Indian philosophy, constitute a perfect example of genuine philosophical dispute, as much regarding content as regarding method. So is the case with the extensive philosophy of language developed on both the sides and disputations in this field between the Hindus and the Jainas and among the Hindus themselves. It is unfortunate that this rich philosophy (as modern as any modern discussion could be) is practically ignored by the present-day Indian scholars who count in the field, not to speak of the Western scholars in philosophy who cannot possibly have any idea of these unless we the Indians place these our treasures before them in a language they understand.

Self-identity is another interesting category, but more interesting are the categories of *negation* and *relation*. It is interesting to see how the traditional Indians have easily disposed of many situations that are called 'relation' by Western philosophers. These so-called relations are simply reduced to certain otherwise intelligible categories like some substance, attribute, etc., and, if necessary, covered by certain linguistic subterfuges (*vide* '*vikalpa*' of Yoga). The only genuine relation that some of them, particularly the Nyāya-Vaiśeṣika thinkers, recognize is inherence—inherence of attributes (including motions) in substances, of wholes in their parts and of universals in corresponding particulars. But, even then, they would never hold that this 'inherence of B' in A again *inheres* in A, that way (How exactly, we shall presently see.) disposing of the vexed problem whether A's relation to B has to get related again to B (or even to A), and, if so, how. Western thinkers have solved the problem a bit too easily either by postulating that 'relation' is an ambulatory, self-relating entity, requiring no further relation to get related to original relata, or by showing that it is a universal, intending thereby that a universal is no *entity* requiring to get related to the corresponding particulars almost as an adverb does not require to be related to the compounding verb. The idea behind both the alternatives is perhaps that the so-called relation between a relation and either of its relata is only a linguistic feat, though, maybe, one that is necessary.

Traditional Indian philosophers would not deny that in certain cases it undoubtedly is a mere linguistic feat, signifying nothing actual. But this is not the case everywhere. What oftener is the case, particularly with regard to the 'inherence of B' in A, is that this inherence, which, by definition, is a necessary (internal) relation belongs to A's very stuff, meaning probably that (i) it is the very nature of a substance to possess *some* attribute of motion or individuality (*viśeṣa*), (ii) of an attribute, motion or individuality to belong to some substance, (iii) of a whole to belong to *some* parts, and (iv) of parts to form *some* whole. [A schism between substance, on the one hand, and attributes, etc., on the other, or between a whole and parts, appears only when '*some* substance', '*some* attribute', '*some* whole' or '*some* part' is understood as a *definite* substance, a *definite* attribute, etc.] Regarding the relation between 'inherence of B' and 'A', this is the view of the Nyāya-Vaiśeṣika thinkers. The Advaita Vedāntins and the Buddhists, however, would cut at the root of the entire problem either (in the case of the Advaita Vedāntins) by drawing no philosophical distinction between 'some attribute' and 'this particular attribute' (and similarly between 'some substance' and 'this particular substance', etc.) or (as in the case of the Buddhists) by denying all talk of substance and standing receptacle and, regarding the inherence of a universal in relevant particulars, by denying universals altogether.

So much as regards the relation of inherence and of that between 'inherence of B' and 'A'. With regard to other relations, however, traditional Indian philosophers almost unanimously hold that quite many of them, like that between father and child, are only a series of facts between two facts at two extremes (in the present case, father and son)[1] and that a good number of others, like *on*, *before*, *after*, *right*, *left*, etc., are only attributes, these attributes being related to the corresponding substances exactly as attributes like colour, taste, etc. do. And, if there are some relation-like entities still unaccounted for, they are to be understood, as far as possible, in the language of the categories already admitted.

How far this view of relation is tenable is, of course, a different question. But so also is any Western idea of relation, older or modern. What we would like to point out here is that through ages, the Indians have worked out very systematically different theories of relation which should be thoroughly studied as much by the present-day Indians as by Western scholars. This is just a sample of how the Indians have treated the category of 'inherence' or, for that matter, 'relation'. There are many other subtle distinctions drawn—distinctions not merely for the sake of intellectual analysis but having far-reaching impact on their entire metaphysics.

Their treatment of negation is more exhaustive, subtler and more profound, and almost every system, except the earlier extant Sāṁkhya and Yoga, has dealt with this category. The nature, reality and kinds of negation; the import of negative judgments of different sorts—indeed, the entire metaphysical import of negation; the relation between a negation and the corresponding positive (particularly the positive locus of that negation) and, in that connection, the concepts of origination, continuance and destruction; possibility of absolute negation, i.e. whether all negation has to be or some may not be against

1. This reminds us of John Stuart Mill.

the background of something positive as not only presupposed but, maybe, even posited by it; and, in that connection, the problem whether the entire world can at all be negated—these are mainly the problems about *negation* in the traditional Indian philosophy.

If we exclude how relation and negation have been studied in modern Symbolic Logic, the treatment of these two categories by the traditional Indian philosophers has been more extensive, more detailed and more thought-provoking than that in the West. This, however, is not surprising. For, while in the West the problems of negation and relation have only been occasionally raised and systematically dealt with by a few only, in India they, particularly the problem of negation, have been of major importance for all systems of philosophy, except probably earlier Sāṁkhya and Yoga. The Indian treatment of relation and negation should not, however, be assessed against how these two notions have been developed in modern Symbolic Logic. Symbolic Logic, growing in the pattern of computers (though not so much knowingly in earlier days) has treated relation and negation as only useful instruments for computation (calculation). Necessarily, only that much of each has been taken into consideration which would help speedy and efficient calculation. Independent analysis of these concepts is, by profession, out of scope there. So with many other concepts there, like 'if,' 'all,' etc. Necessity of calculation has worked there as a steam-roller blunting all the subtle nuances of these concepts. Symbolic Logic, by pruning these concepts to their requirement, may have worked miracles in other directions and may have, because of those miracles, earned a right to assert whatever it has made of them. But philosophy is not Symbolic Logic. Because of success in technical skill, Symbolic Logic, preferring to side with science and technology, may have pushed all 'philosophical' logic to the background. But let not philosophical logic emulate, for that reason, its temporarily successful competitor.

Thus, by referring to certain philosophical topics, taken almost at random, we have shown how a great many of them, discussed in Western philosophy, right from the days of Thales, through the system-builders of the Middle Ages and early modern period, to the contemporary philosophers of various brands, have been studied in Indian philosophy at least as thoroughly, seriously and systematically as there, if not, at places, more so. What all this points to is that a modern Indian thinker ought not to ignore his traditional philosophy, for there is at least a likelihood that systematic treatment for millenniums may have thrown new light here and there. And, above all, there is the question of national prestige.

C. *Alleged and Genuine Lacunae in Indian Philosophy*

Sometimes we are told that many favourite topics of Western philosophy, very important in the context of modern times, have not been touched at all in Indian philosophy at any time of its long history, and some such problems have been touched only lightly and cursorily. The charge, however, is not true for all the cases they mention. Some of the said topics have been discussed in traditional Indian philosophy in just a different form and some, though discussed in many details, not all at one place and systematically. All depends on how precisely the traditional Indian mind has viewed the problems. Some of the issues, however, we admit, have not been studied at all or only lightly studied. Let us illustrate all the three types of cases.

Materialism, we are told, has been so systematically ignored that whatever of it has at all been discussed here and there in Indian philosophy is only some superficial aspect, its major commendable aspects, viz. its empiricism, naturalism and humanism (in human-social affairs) remaining completely unnoticed. True, in one or two texts there has been some systematic study of its methodology, its (negative) ontology and the ethical consequence; but it has all been extremely brief and the doctrines developed and formulated in a manner that they could be easily done away with.

The charge, we contend, is true in one respect but false in another. But before that let us see what exactly was the form of materialism that the traditional Indian mind had to counter. If in their logic (methodology) the materialists—popularly known as *Lokāyatas* or *Cārvākas*—have spoken so hard against *inference*, we should not miss their central motive. It was to deny—at least, discredit—all easy talk of the supernatural, whether transcendental or just supernormal. All the other systems, irrespective of whether they were Hindu, Buddhist or

Jaina, relied too much on the 'spiritual' side of man and all that was required for it in their epistemologies, ontologies, ethics and social philosophies. The *Lokāyatas* wanted to check all such excesses and insisted that the so-called 'spiritual' truths could neither be perceived nor inferred, and were certainly not to be accepted on the *ipse dixit* of scriptures or any authority whatsoever. That these are none of them undisputed *observed* phenomena has after all to be admitted, unless, of course, one insists on mystic intuition which, however, cannot thrust its truths on *others* except as demonstrated through inference. That is why these *Lokāyatas* were so keen to show the limitations of inference. That this is the correct history can be gathered from some extant ancient Buddhist and Jaina texts. The 'materialists' who were dominant in those days and whom the early Buddhists, Jainas and some Sāṁkhya-Yoga thinkers challenged were the *wise* (*suśikṣita*) *Cārvākas*, not the crass materialists against whom the later Hindus had an easy walk over. Nowhere in the world have crass materialists who want to reduce man to the status of lowest animals—perhaps lower down still—ever found any secure foothold. It is they, these crass materialists, who—if at all there has ever been any *serious* thinker of this brand—have argued against *all sorts* of inference; and later Hindu thinkers have found in *them* easy targets. The *wise Cārvākas*, against whom the early Buddhists and Jainas fought, were only against that type of inference which seeks to establish *unverifiable* supersensuous, i.e. trans-natural, truths. It is always easy to refute crass materialism and the corresponding denial of *all* inference. It is even easier to show that the denial of *all* inference, as much as crass materialism itself, is basically self-contradictory. But not so the *wise* form of (i.e. *suśikṣita*) *Cārvākism* with its attempt to limit inference to what much belongs to Nature (one may say, is 'verifiable'), including even man with all his special endowments, provided these endowments are not utilized by man to alienate himself from the rest of that Nature but for knowing it and bettering it (including himself). This is naturalism and humanism as we understand the doctrines today, and it must have dominated at least for some time in some parts of ancient India. How else could there be serious references to it in early Buddhist and Jaina literature and in the great Hindu epic, the *Mahābhārata*? These *wise Cārvākas* were held in some esteem even by their contemporary critics as, after all, good naturalists (might be, scientists too) and good humanists (might be, politicians too).

Naturalism (which one may call 'applied empiricism') and humanism could not, however, hold out in India, obviously because the Indian mind was constitutionally averse to these. It was constitutionally disposed toward things that were somehow, and to whatever extent, over-natural, though not necessarily anti-natural, for that. This explains the constitutional religious bent of the Indian mind, its adoration of those who had revelations of 'higher' truths and, therefore, for these truths themselves. A large section of the Indians have absolute faith in these truths, though these were revealed to others (whom they adore, paradoxically enough, mainly on the ground that they said these truths were revealed to them). This faith is, in essence, the much-maligned *śabda-pramāṇa* (testimony as a valid means of knowing) of the Indians, to which too the *Cārvākas*, both gross and wise, were as hostile as to inference of anything that is over-natural.

It does not follow, however, that all schools of Indian philosophy were as zealous about the over-natural as about testimony (as a valid proof). Buddhism, for example, was openly against testimony, though it never denied a sort of mystic intuition as ultimate realization, and this realization was after all of truth that was somehow trans-natural, though this trans-naturality could not be posited as a sort of Being beyond (outside) Nature, i.e. as over-natural, it being, according to the Buddhists, this Nature itself but viewed from the standpoint of trans-natural freedom. Three systems, again, all professedly Hindu, were unambiguously against all that is trans-natural, if by that is meant something that (i) does not belong to Nature and (ii) is qualitatively different from it, which both, however, were permitted by all other Hindu systems. These three systems were Nyāya, Vaiśeṣika and Mīmāṁsā (and probably also the Jainas would agree that far with them). The supernatural, in their view, is still a natural item, only pushed beyond its *normal* limits: it is only the super*normal* natural. Such, for example, we have already seen, are these philosophers' atoms, binaries, *adṛṣṭa*-s, selves, gods and even the omniscient, omnipotent God where He is admitted. As for their attitude to *testimony*, these philosophers are certainly not against it as a valid proof. But, somehow, for at least the Naiyāyikas, if not also for the Vaiśeṣikas, it *has also to be* rationally (inferentially) substantiated; and often indeed citations from scriptures are appended just for (additional) corroboration. The Mīmāṁsakas are indeed much more respectful to scriptures (we mean the Vedas): one may even say that they are almost entirely scripturalists. Yet, however, they confine scriptural credibility exclusively to those sentences the validity of which cannot be established otherwise, say inferentially, and these, according to them, are mostly, if not wholly, *injunctional* (prescriptive or prohibitory) sentences.

It follows that the Naiyāyikas, Vaiśeṣikas and Mīmāṁsakas are not far away from naturalism and humanism (i.e. from the higher form of materialism of the wise *Cārvākas*). They would only like to extend the boundary of materialism even beyond where these wise *Cārvākas* had pushed it to. We must, however, note one important point here : they could be called advanced materialists only so far as their philosophies are concerned; and philosophy means for them only systematic intellectual account. So far, on the other hand, as their life is concerned, i.e. with regard to their *activities*, whether for ultimate deliverance or for better happiness, they would categorically refuse to belong to any school of materialism, even to what is nowadays known as naturalism or humanism.

A second—and, for that, a futile—charge that is sometimes brought against traditional Indian philosophy is that it is not as systematic and thematic as Western philosophy is usually supposed to be. Those who bring this charge betray their colossal ignorance of Indian philosophical literature. The *Upaniṣads* which, compared with later philosophical literature, are considerably unsystematic constitute only the early phase of Indian philosophy much as pre-Platonic Greek philosophy does, compared to the whole story of Western philosophy. If, again, the *Puāṇas* and some other older literature are considered *philosophy*, that would be using the term 'philosophy' in a wide enough sense. Systematic Indian philosophy begins with *aphorisms* (*sūtra*-s) of each system and probably also with some earlier literature like *Sāṁkhyakārikā*, *Abhidharmakośa*, etc. Commentaries on these earlier texts, sub-commentaries on these commentaries, sub-sub-commentaries on the sub-commentaries and so on, on the one hand, and independent treatises (*prakaraṇa-grantha*-s) on the other, developing at least through a full millennium and a half till two hundred years back, constitute a vast, systematic and extraordinarily rich philosophical literature that can easily compete with, if not, in points of methodology, exceed what is best at any time in Western philosophy. So far as systematization and precision of statements are concerned, the Indian philosophical literature that has, since the thirteenth century, developed under the influence of neo-Nyāya technique has no competitor yet anywhere in the world. It involves at every step subtlest possible precision—an entire technology of precision, one might say, as much in discovery as in statement. The technique is baffling to anyone who has not got used to handling it for years together, more baffling than in the case of Symbolic Logics of the modern days (and, probably for that very reason, fast receding into oblivion). The complaint might, therefore, be quite the other way around, viz. that (at least the later-day) traditional Indian philosophy has been rather *over*-thorough, *over*-systematic and *over*-precise.

A third charge, often seriously brought against traditional Indian philosophy, is that it has nowhere studied systematically and in a sustained manner problems of ethics and social philosophy. The charge, however, is less than half true and false more than half. If by 'ethics' is meant study of fundamental concepts like *action*, *freedom*, *action with selfish motive*, *action without such motive*, i.e. altruistic action or action that is categorically imperative, *relation between action and its result*, *the ultimate aim of life*, and of topics like listing virtues—both primary and derivative—, how and why to practise virtues and avoid vicious acts, theories of punishment, rights and duties, which one of these is primary and which derived—if these are the major among the problems of ethics, then most of these have been studied as systematically and thoroughly as possible in Mīmāṁsā, a good number in older Nyāya and Vaiśeṣika, quite many in Buddhism and Jainism, and the concept of the ultimate aim of life in all Indian systems and often in minute details. It is a pity that these excellent discussions are often missed because they have been separately studied at separate places, and not all consolidated as one study, as in Western ethics. Even the scripture known as *The Gītā* has spoken a lot, and systematically enough, on many of these basic concepts, and the beauty of this scripture is that it is at the same time a more or less elaborate *philosophical* treatise on *social life*. Normally, however, in Indian literature social problems have been studied only in the context of prescribing social virtues,[1] as we find in treatises known as *Dharma-sāstra* which started in very early days with *Kalpa* and *Gṛhya sūtra*-s and contained in the ever-recurring literature known as *Smṛti* (sometimes also called *saṁhitā*). These latter literatures are mostly indeed prescriptive, but contextual theoretical discussions are often found in between. This has happened only because the traditional Indian mind has been constitutionally disposed toward practical life, and theories have largely been requisitioned for the solution of such practical problems. Even art and poetry in India have developed in practical contexts and Indian theories of art are more prescriptive than purely theoretical. One may even say—and this has been reiterated off and on by traditional Indian philosophers—that even the huge theoretical literature known as philosophy is basically prescriptive of how to attain the ultimate objective(s) of life, though here at least the Indian theoretical mind far outshoots the basic practical motive, much as it does, though in lesser measure, in Indian mathematics.

Western ethics has also studied, particularly in recent days, another set of problems involving the linguistic analysis of prescriptive (including prohibitory) propositions of various types *vis-à-vis* indicative propositions, equally of various types. Interestingly enough, Indian thinkers, ever since the earliest days and much more thoroughly in later days, have discussed these problems in all their nuances very systematically, particularly in Mīmāṁsā and Nyāya and to a good extent in Advaita Vedānta, Buddhism and Jainism. Linguistic study developed in strides not merely in the field of ethics but equally well in other departments of Indian philosophy, and all these mostly in connection with the study of *śabda-pramāṇa* (knowledge through testimony) and oftener, again, exactly as in contemporary Western philosophy, in the context of indicative *vs.* prescriptive propositions.

1. Called *dharma*. Ordinarily, except in Buddhism, the word '*dharma*' has this social import ingrained. Of course, it is used in other senses too, sometimes spiritual, sometimes secular.

Linguistic analysis and philosophy of language (one may call it as much a sort of grammar as philosophy) is a marvellous new development in the West. It has centred mainly round the Western languages, particularly English. A more developed, more systematic and far more wide-ranging study has been in vogue and in continuous development in the different traditional systems of Indian philosophy, centring, of course, round Sanskrit, and, in addition, and often in a more serious systematic attitude, in treatises on grammar, particularly on philosophies of grammar (and also in Śaiva, Śākta and Buddhist and Jaina Tāntrika literature). Sometimes we are told that philosophy of language is only a recent development in the West. Nothing would be a greater travesty of truth than this. The recent-day Westerners have certainly developed it independently. But could they have not worked out a greater miracle if only they had known what miracle had been already done in India ?

A fourth charge, equally serious, levelled against traditional Indian philosophy is that it has not developed any kind of *formal* logic. The charge is largely true. The traditional Indian mind is constitutionally impervious to any consideration of form for its own sake quite as much as it is to any theoretical study for its own sake. 'Impervious' does not mean that if necessary it cannot. It only means that it is not generally interested in form and theory for their own sake. Should, however, for any reason it gets interested, it can do miracles as it has done in philosophy and mathematics. Yet while in the theoretical study called philosophy it has said nothing systematic and elaborate on form (formal logic) it has done exactly that, and to the full extent it was possible in those days, in mathematics. This qualifying clause 'and to the full extent...' has been inserted deliberately : we mean that though it was never interested in forms as such, it could at times be interested in forms *of facts*, i.e. in forms insofar as in their study there was reference *pari passu* to the facts of which they were forms. The mathematics (particularly the algebra, geometry and trigonometry) that it developed was concerned with forms of 'facts and their actual relations with one another'. Indian mathematics was, in other words, not formalistic but intuitionistic, to use two terms designating two kinds of mathematics in the West. The traditional Indian mind found no interest in weaving all types of nets in empty space. It could not even get interested in such forms of facts (and of thoughts as facts) as Aristotle could be interested in and develop a full formal logic form. Probably, it sensed that it had had enough of the theoretical in its philosophy and naturally shrank from adding more.

One must not, however, miss the fact that something like formal logic was developed in neo-Nyāya. It was mainly a formal logic of *propositions* and *concepts*—a sort of symbolization in order to present them as precisely as possible. Undoubtedly, it has some similarity with the Aristotelian forms of terms and propositions, and they even combined these forms into more or more complex forms of propositions. Yet, however, they did not advance further to combine the already complex forms of propositions into those of inference. The reason is clear. While the forms of propositions that Aristotle studied were *sui generis*, not what resulted from combinations of forms of concepts —and similarly with the forms of syllogism *vis-à-vis* those of propositions—with the Indians, in either case the forms of propositions were mostly only summations of the forms of the corresponding concepts, and similarly with the forms of inference in relation to those of propositions. This is probably the reason why the Indians did not develop a complete or even a near-complete formal logic in the line of Western logicians.

Whatever formal logic the Indians may claim to have was developed only in a later period, say, from the thirteenth century onward till the other day. Earlier than that there was no formal *logic* anywhere, except in a distant way in Buddhism, particularly in Vijñānavāda, and, one might say, distantly also in the Jaina theory of *Anekānta*. The Buddhists' *vikalpa*-s (conceptual constructions) were thought-*forms* empiricalized in typical empirical contexts; and their *apohavāda* was the doctrine that X as X is conceptually just '*anything* that is not not-X'—or, briefer still, to be X is more fundamentally just not to be not-X, negation, for these Buddhists, being obviously more primitive than position.

These Buddhists could have developed an entire formal logic out of such negations, a logic which might have been a new addition to the many systems of the present-day Symbolic Logic in the West. But they did not develop it, even though they were more formal minded (though through negations so far) than other Indians. In their logic of inference, again, they spoke a lot about form and one of their three basic types of inference was candidly formal. (The other two were also formal, though not so obviously: their formal character was evident from the type of *necessity* they were said to involve.) Yet, however, they never proceeded further to develop a full or even a nearly full formal logic either of propositions or of inference. The reason, perhaps, was the same that worked in other Indian minds: there was no interest in mere (possible) forms unless they were definitely known as forms *of facts*.

Early Indian thought proceeded *formally* again whenever it offered an *a priori* classification of facts (what Alexander calls 'widest possible classification of facts') into different categories and sub-categories. Such classification is obviously a formal procedure: the different classes are the different forms (of facts). In a way, undoubtedly, such classification is mostly empirical too, because it is very often a classification of facts that are sense-experienceable; yet, however, it is not just an inductive procedure. A merely inductive classification can never claim the type of completeness that is claimed by any classification of things into different *categories*, and of things under one category into different sub-categories. Nobody would say that he has collected things *as far as possible*, meaning that certain things might have been left unconsidered. Wherefrom could this firm assurance come unless the whole procedure was fundamentally *formal* of a kind ? Lest this should be treated as a useless pastime with empty possibilities, later Indian thinkers, particularly the Naiyāyikas, have, in their excessive zeal for empiricism, said openly (i) that such classification is always empirical, (ii) that they have completed each such classification as far as it has been practicable for them, (iii) that there is no *absolute* certainty anywhere, any honest cognition being certain so long as it is not positively contradicted or doubted on some substantial ground, and (iv) that if anyone points out that some fact has not been considered they are prepared to consider it and change their classification accordingly (but most often they argue rather that, some way or other, the alleged unconsidered fact has already been considered). This, however, betrays an unnecessary sensitivity on the part of these later thinkers; for, elsewhere and for ages they had considered 'forms *of facts*' in various contexts, and they had found nothing wrong with them. (The two concepts 'form' and '*a priority*' are very close to each other.) What all the Indian thinkers have been consistently against is the consideration of forms *as such* and *a priori* computation of such mere forms without any consideration, simultaneously, of what obtains in the actual world.

As for the Jaina's *anekāntavāda*, if it is a sort of formal consideration, it too is definitely within such limits. Within such limits, again, formal consideration is loudly in prominence in what the Naiyāyikas and other Indian thinkers call *tarka* (*ūha*), i.e. corroborative justification or, negatively, *reductio ad absurdum.* This is entirely, and very obtrusively, a formal procedure, though the overall context here too is some empirical truth inferred according to the normal rules of what the Indians call *anumāna* which, at least in the case of what is known as *svārthānumāna* (inference for oneself only), is after all a self-conscious mode of associational passage from particulars to particulars, self-conscious in that whenever needed it can be assessed as to whether it is based on a (sufficiently) reliable ground of similarity. The ground of similarity has to be one that cannot be (easily) challenged (on different counts); and, desirably, one is required even to start with precautionary rules. These rules, however, have often been stated very formally so that one may proceed (almost) *mechanically* with these rules exactly as in any strictly formal procedure, the only difference being that the procedure here is not one of computation but just one of application. The overall context here too is material-empirical.

Formal procedure is more or less obtrusive again in what the Naiyāyikas have called *parārthānumāna*—inference which, over and above being the associational passage spoken of above, is also a *demonstration* to convince others. This *parārthānumāna* is unambiguously a formal application of an empirical rule (induction) to a given individual case, its last step being invariably prefaced by a clear formalistic 'therefore'.

Formal procedure is evident again in what the Mīmāṁsakas and Advaita Vedāntins have called *arthāpatti*—a way of knowing through the postulation of what precisely is formally needed to straighten an apparently paradoxical issue, i.e. to reconcile or tide over two conflicting claims. Formalism, however, goes that far only and works, as usual, in an overall empirical context.[1]

1. Traditional Indian philosophers sometimes mention *sambhava* as a

Traditional Indian philosophy, specially Nyāya, contains an extraordinarily elaborate chapter on 'fallacies', at least as elaborate as any that is Aristotelian, but none formal at all. While practically all the many fallacies elaborated in the traditional Aristotelian logic are *formal* ones, all the fallacies, elaborated at least in an equally detailed manner, in Indian logic are empirico-material. And yet, a little close study reveals a startling correspondence between them, showing that forms which have been extracted from matter and elaborated in their mutual relations into different formal systems in the West are always considered in India *qua* embedded in (material) experience and treated that way only. For both Platonists and Aristotelians forms are autonomous *a priorities* and treated autonomously in their own interrelations, the only difference between them being that while for the Platonists they do not remain all the while embracing the material empirical world, for Aristotle they always remain so, autonomous though they are for both of them. Indian philosophers would, however, consider them almost as empirical abstractions except that each of them can also be tackled by itself, though not necessarily in their interrelations; and even the Buddhists who are known as nominalists or conceptualists would grant this much of autonomy to them, almost as anyone would grant such autonomy to *language-forms*.

This peculiar attitude to forms has prevented the traditional Indian thinkers from attaching all the significance to the term 'reason' that has been attached to it by the Western Rationalists. Traditional Indians would normally identify reason with what they call *anumāna*, and sometimes with *arthāpatti* too. At the most, they would use the term to signify *yukti* (i.e. *tarka* or *ūha*, discussed above). But none of the Platonic and Kantian worlds of forms (*a priorities*), in their many levels and as interrelated, was ever even conceived of by the Indians except—and that too intelligibly enough—in their treatment of language, i.e. in their grammar and some philosophies of grammar, and, paradoxically enough, in their algebra, geometry and trigonometry. We say 'paradoxically' for two reasons. First, if they could treat forms so systematically and even *computatively* in these

valid 'method of knowing' (*pramāṇa*). The example, so often given is : a jar contains one hundred coins, therefore, it certainly contains eighty coins. The process is entirely a formal one.

mathematical studies, it is strange that they never even thought of it in their logic and philosophy : they never even thought of mentioning it as a kind of cognitive procedure (*pramāṇa*) in their logic even though on occasions they added so many to their usual three, four, five or six.[1] The whole thing is paradoxical for a second reason also. It is that the Indians who had developed these formal branches of mathematics were of the same race as those who had developed logic. The paradox does not lessen a bit even if it is held, as some 'historians' have claimed, that they learnt (at least these branches of) mathematics from others, say the Greeks. The only conceivable explanation, though we are never sure how far it is acceptable, is that astronomy, town-building and other projects, particularly astronomy, which required enormous tedious computations, whether arithmetical or geometrical, forced them to *formal* mathematics to simplify the matter. Mathematics was not all *empirical* in the old-day world, as the modern Westerners claim : some European geniuses had already formalized some of its branches; and if in India it was empirical like the traditional Indian logic, that empiricality, as we have already seen, was not of a shallow type, divorced altogether from *a priori* forms.

To the traditional Indian the word 'reason' (or its equivalent), as used in the West, is highly ambiguous. That aspect of it on which the Western Rationalists have built their transcendental metaphysics, or on which Kant built his *Critiques* and his immediate followers reconstructed metaphysics, is, however, highly prized in all *transcendental* schools of Indian philosophy, though, that way, it is never identified with inference, argumentation, logical procedure, etc. For the Indians it is, so far, only a sort of *phenomenology*, sort of immediate realization of overnatural subjectivity somehow 'intending' (constructing) objects at various levels, these objects being, *phenomenologically*, nondifferent from the intentions. It is a phenomenology, however, which, in every such transcendental system except Buddhism, particularly of the Mahāyāna type, and the corresponding Tantras, is transformed immediately into metaphysics, with pure ego (subjectivity) as much substantivized as also absolutized to

1. *Sambhava* as a *pramāṇa* comes, indeed, very near it, but there is nowhere any elaborate treatment of this *pramāṇa*.

the extent of transcending and yet covering, in whatever way, all pure egos so substantivized. 'Intention' is, in those systems, understood as a 'power', a 'function', a sort of dynamism, of that Absolute Ego, either really pertaining to it or only wrongly understood as so pertaining, (in the latter case) being in itself nothing coordinate with that Ego—even as its parts—and, therefore, nothing, in any sense, besides it and, therefore also, nothing of any ultimate being. The Buddhists, however, went the other way about : they regarded the 'dynamism' itself to be the ultimate; and as dynamism, power or function is nowhere any (substantive) *being*, nor also *nothing*, therefore, this ultimate 'dynamism' was to them wholly indeterminate, called '*śūnya*'—the whole system corresponding that way to Kant's *Critique of Pure Reason* very deliberately understood as a sort of *metaphysics*. One may also say that it is Fichteanism *minus* its Ego, or the philosophy of Schopenhauer, or, to whatever extent, that of Hegel but without his category of Being and any of its correspondent at any level, understanding 'being' of any sort, including 'Being,' un-Hegelianly enough, as a *false* negation of what is primarily 'non-being' (non-being, in other words, as the metaphysical starting point).

Thus, if modern scholars argue that some of the basic notions or attitudes of Western philosophy seem to be absent in the traditional Indian philosophy, this, we have shown, is either because sufficient attention has not been paid to this Indian philosophy or because these concepts and attitudes are present there only to the extent the traditional Indian mind has been interested in them; and there has always been some good reason why it has not been as interested in them as the Western mind.

D. *The So-Called 'Dogmas' in Indian Philosophy*

The last serious charge that is levelled against traditional Indian philosophy is that some doctrines which are ultimately of momentous importance for Indian philosophy and life have just been accepted without serious analysis and examination —accepted either because they have just been in vogue since the hoary past, or entirely on the *ipse dixit* of scriptures (not always the Vedas and often scriptures of lesser credibility). These, for example, are (i) the doctrine that everything of one's present cycle of life is a result of what he had done in the just previous cycle,[1] everything of that previous life is similarly the result of what he had done in a cycle of life still earlier, and so on, so that there is no freedom (free activity) anywhere in any life, (ii) the doctrine that yet this chain can be snapped, with the result that a particular cycle of life will not be followed any longer by another cycle (which means that the particular man has attained salvation), (iii) that because there is no freewill anywhere moral action is superficially understood as only what has been socially ordained either by tradition or in authoritative works of higher and higher statuses, ending with the Vedas, (iv) that the traditional Indian theory of punishment has, for this reason, been either preventive or just retributive, (v) that *traditions* and *schools* in Indian philosophy have overdone what was required of them : they have crippled originality and freedom of thought, (vi) that to include testimony as a source of valid knowledge has been an open, almost criminal, challenge to 'reason' which is so much adored today by 'scientific' minds, (vii) that yet at places and particularly in the entire body of the later-day Indian philosophy—notably in neo-Nyāya and, closely on its heels, in other systems of philosophy—there has been an unnecessary parade of linguistic and other subtleties rendering the whole study into a costly intellectual luxury, (viii) that the traditional Indian philosophy has unnecessarily, and even to the point of unintelligibility, distinguished between self and mind and distinguished concepts like *dik*, *deśa*, *ākāśa*, *parimāṇa*, *dūratva*, *antikatva*, etc. which could all pass under the blanket notion 'space', as in Western philosophy, (ix) that the 'science' it has offered under the head '*kṣiti*', '*ap*', '*tejas*', '*marut*' and '*vyoman*' is very primitive, (x) that Indian philosophy has nowhere developed a detailed psychology of wish, desire, will, impression, imagination, etc. and has unnecessarily, in some systems, elaborated at a great length the concept of 'self-illumination (self-evidence)' of knowledge, consciousness or self, etc. Let us see how far these charges can hold out.

I

In a sense, in traditional Indian philosophy there is, of course, no room for 'freedom of will' : every detail of man's life, includ-

1. We are considering '*prārabdha*' only, deliberately keeping out of account '*sañcita karma*.'

ing even his activities (that lead willy-nilly to some enjoyment or suffering) is determined. But is this, on any count, any novel doctrine unknown in the West ? Do not so many Western philosophers and scientists deny 'freedom of will' ?

'I *can* do this or that' is as empty an expression as 'I *could* do this or that' after something has been actually done. If possibilities, retrospectively, are so far all empty, so are the possibilities that are prospective, and whatever is actually done is determined wholly by circumstances—by given physical nature (including physiological factors), by social tradition, by heredity, by fear, allurement, etc.—and if also by one's 'choice', that 'choice' is just another name of predisposition, native liking, one's own response, etc. which, too, are all equally determined. This doctrine of determinism is nowadays regarded as even more *scientific* than the 'too easily spoken of' freedom of will. When the traditional Indian speaks in the same strain, he does not say anything else. Only, a genuine inquirer, he seeks to study the matter more closely. Why is it, he asks, that he is in a particular situation, has a particular body and a particular society with all their normal functionings and idiosyncrasies, a particular parentage and heredity, even particular likes and dislikes not explained by any known factor or factors, including heredity ? Are all these just accidents to be simply accepted as given ? If further explanation is possible why should we not go further and stop only where we are all compelled to stop ? Besides, even modern science holds, and insists so much on it, that the 'given' is not all neutrally there, that quite much of it, its major portion, is *said to be* there just so far as a mind chooses or even expects that, the 'choice' or the expectation too being equally determined by circumstances beyond one's present control. The approach to the whole problem is as much like that of the presentday phenomenologists as of the *scientists* of body and mind. The object one experiences is what one chooses to experience —in the language of phenomenology, what one 'intends.' Only, when the scientists and the phenomenologists still talk of a 'Nature' over there (from out of which the experiencer selects)— Nature that, in phenomenological language, stands 'bracketed' (in Kant's language, 'thing-in-itself')—Nyāya-Vaiśeṣika, Mīmāṁsā and probably also the Jainas would admit a whole host of atoms of various kinds and space, time, etc. out of which, they say, the experiencer constructs the variegated world and believes that it stands before him, some of the various constructions being peculiar to each particular experiencer, some common to a number of them and some, viz., those which are normally said to belong to the world as such, to all of them. Every special construction is determined by the special predilection of a particular experiencer and the common ones by their common predispositions. The common predispositions are in modern days regarded as family heritage, social heritage and world heritage—in each case, both physiological and cultural—and individual idiosyncrasies as wholly accidental. What, however, the traditional Indian insists is, first, that, in deference to the unfailing law of causation, even these idiosyncrasies have to be traced to earlier causes, but, then, since these idiosyncrasies are, in some form or other, evident since one's birth the causes will have to be traced to the *earlier cycle of life* : traces of happenings in that earlier cycle must have continued to the present life, and similarly with that earlier cycle, and so on. When, however, so much is granted it would only be a small step to admit further that there is a self (or something very near that) which, abiding through all the cycles of life, carries these traces. Not an illegitimate *further* step, and the traditional Indian would interpret the so-called 'common features' of the world, and even that world itself, as but the 'common *experience* (for all)' constructed because of common impressions and dispositions formed and accumulated in a previous cycle of life by people of a common group—large or small—the largest group being the people of the world as a whole—similarly with all special and common features in all previous cycles of life retrospectively *ad infinitum*. The only things that, according to these Nyāya-Vaiśeṣika, Mīmāṁsā and Jaina thinkers, are not constructed (intended) are those which, according to them, are eternal, viz. atoms, space, time, etc., and even pure selves (i.e. selves as distinguished from bodily *cum* psychological 'I's). (What exactly 'self' and 'psychological I' means, we shall see later.)

The *transcendental* Indian philosophers have advanced one step still further with the same logic. They have 'phenomenologically reduced,' in the same way, even these eternal entities, understanding them as just purest objects (objective *a priorities*) *most primarily* 'intended' (constructed) phenomenologically, even the pure self so far as it is objective being one such. This *objective* pure self is but the *prakṛti* (*pradhāna*) of Sāṁkhya-Yoga, *Māyā*, *Prajñā*, *Hiraṇyagarbha*, etc. of Advaita Vedānta and whatever corresponds to it in Buddhism. It is exactly the transcendental counterpart of the 'self' of Nyāya-Vaiśeṣika, Mīmāṁsā and Jainism—always an object, whether detectable by some introspection (which is a cognition other than that self) or as evidencing itself (though even then as an *object*).

Whatever we have said so far constitutes the basis of the traditional Indian doctrines of determinism, succeeding cycles of life, *karma*, *adṛṣṭa*, etc. We write 'etc.' because while *adṛṣṭa* is the unconscious trace of what one *does* in one life and continues till and passes over to the next life, there is another type of unconscious trace, called *vāsanā* which is the trace left by our *knowledge* of things in one life passing similarly into the next. The Indian doctrines of wholesale determinism, cycles of life, *karma*, *adṛṣṭa*, etc. are not as irrational as they are often depicted to be.

II

And yet it is a fact that traditional Indian philosophy (barring, of course, all forms of *Lokāyata*) believed that this chain of birth after birth could be snapped by cutting at the root of impressions and dispositions. This could be done, according to them by two methods, detachment and cognition proper, though, of course, even in this case detachment is a necessary prerequisite. What here appears paradoxical to the Western (and many *modern* Indian) thinkers is that if all the events and activities of any cycle of life are determined as already shown, it would be impossible, patently contradictory, to hold at the same time that the impressions and dispositions of a certain cycle of life could somehow be rendered ineffective. Really, however, there is no impossibility here, nothing that is contradictory, for this 'apparent' impossibility is accomplished primarily by *detachment* which as *freedom proper*, not the alleged psychological phenomenon of 'choice', belongs to the *transcendental* dimension of man and is not, therefore, a coplanar contradictory of determination. Like the 'transcendental freedom' of Kant's *Critique of Practical Reason* it cuts at the very root of all psychological (i.e. naturalistic) determination from a totally different plane. True, non-transcendentalist philosophies like Nyāya-Vaiśeṣika and Mīmāṁsā have also admitted (final) detachment as a *naturalistic* phenomenon caused by the merits accumulated at the fag-end of a progressive series of various acts through a series of cycles of life; but this is only a desperate attempt to translate what is inevitably a transcendental affair into the language of the empiricist (naturalist).

Detachment as freedom proper is primarily the refusal of man[1] to submit to the determinative forces of nature (including impressions and dispositions active as congenital compulsions), the power to dissociate himself, keep away, withdraw—this is negative freedom, 'freedom from'—and, in effect, to get installed in man's proper essence (the Absolute) either in the form of 'Self as Being' (called *Puruṣa*, *Ātman*, *Brahman*, etc.) or in the form of pure subjectivity as Act, Function, Dynamism, etc. (called *Nirvāṇa* or *Śūnyatā*). According to some of the traditional Indian systems, one so installed in Essence may, and, according to some, must, also review Nature exactly as it is metaphysically constituted, i.e. as maturations of private and 'common' impressions and dispositions acquired in the cycle of life preceding—in short, phenomenologically, i.e. as only 'intended,' 'constructed' (of course, with the additional perception as to which traces and dispositions are maturing into different items of experience). All this is positive freedom, i.e. 'freedom to'. Though for some Indian systems it is primarily *free cognition* (knowledge proper = metaphysical, *yogic*, intuition)—cognition as much of the essence of man as, in addition, of how items of experience are ultimately 'intended' (constructed)—it may also be *free action*, very like what Kant called pure morality = categorical imperative (with its various formulations) and what in Indian philosophy is known as *niṣkāma-karma*. Of the two aspects of 'freedom to' one which is just the realization of the essence of man is always free *cognition* and the other which either views the world (experience) metaphysically or acts accordingly is, obviously, either free *cognition* (as the first alternative) or free *action* (as the second). Many philosophers, mostly the Vaiṣṇavas, have added 'free emotion': and throughout the history

1. None but man has this prerogative, called freedom. This is exactly what distinguishes man from other creatures, even from gods (how from the latter we need not discuss here).

of Indian philosophy there has been an endless debate as to which of these three is primary and which only preparatory.

So, freedom as described above is not inconsistent with all-round determination. Rather, there would have been a huge inconsistency if freedom in some form or other were not admitted. For, if impressions and dispositions are to get exhausted, as they must, with maturation into actual experiences, there would possibly be no scope for another cycle of life; and if, for whatever reason, the experiences (including actions) at this next cycle can again generate impressions and dispositions, that would mean that there is no end to these cycles following one another. All these puzzles, however, get solved as soon as freedom in the sense described above is recognized. It will then be held (a) that mere mechanical movements—behaviours as different from actions—do not generate any abiding dispositions that tend to mature into some experience with appropriate hedonic tone [cf. the maxim '*moral* actions (alone) must have their appropriate rewards and punishments.'], the dispositions, if any, that it generates getting defunct just in course of time; (b) that some amount of freedom in the sense of resistance to force of nature is present in all human actions, even though in spite of that freedom man oftener submits to nature than not and sometimes does this very deliberately (in other words, chooses freely not to be free); (c) that it is only in these two cases that those human behaviours which are known as actions generate appropriate dispositions; (d) that impressions (*vāsanā*-s) only lend concrete shapes to the maturation of dispositions, so that, with the generation of dispositions controlled and ultimately rendered defunct by the exercise of 'freedom from,' these *vāsanā*-s also are rendered impotent, and, further, they can also be neutralized by the newly generated impressions of corresponding right cognitions; (e) that with progressive culture of 'freedom from'—in the language of phenomenology, with 'epoche' —there develops, or becomes evident, the 'intentions' or 'constructions' ('freedoms to') at successive retrogressive levels; (f) that all this is a matter of phenomenological awareness (*yogic* perception); and (g) that the process retrogressing that way will ultimately stop either with pure self 'intending' nothing (and, therefore, its individuality lapsing) or, alternatively, with an *ultimate* contentless *act* of Intention (as the Mahāyāna

Buddhists hold) or with the pure self with all possible 'intentions' (*vide* the Jaina notion of '*kevalin*' and others' notion of 'omniscience') or with the ultimate *act* of Intention that intends *everything*, though in embryo (*vide* the Mahāyāna notion of Bodhisattva). In a nutshell, this is all that is *transcendental* Indian philosophy, and it differs from phenomenology only at the last step 'g' which most phenomenologists would not agree to. Transcendental Indian philosophy would, precisely on that ground, demarcate itself as metaphysics from all that is sheer phenomenology. Kant of the *Critique of Practical Reason* would, in this respect, agree largely with the Mahāyāna Buddhists.

All these—'freedom from', 'freedom to' and, therefore, intention or construction, i.e. maturation of dispositions into experience with concrete shapes lent by impressions of past cognitions, and hence succeeding cycles of life as rewards and punishment for good and bad acts—are *primarily* matters of immediate spiritual awareness, very much like, though in an important aspect more than, the immediate awareness that gives us phenomenology or Kantian transcendental construction. If in Indian philosophy, all these have also been demonstrated through inference, it is all in the twin interest of safeguarding the spiritual intuitions and converting others. Ratiocination in this field can serve no other purpose; for if in the field of spiritual metaphysics it were our only weapon it would be a bad weapon for that, unless founded upon, or unpredictably yielding, some spiritual intuition; for one set of arguments is always refuted by another set and there is no need to this refutation and counter-refutation until the contestants agree to differ holding that the arguments on each side are based on a fundamental faith (immediate realization) differing from that on which the other's arguments are based.

This was how spiritual philosophy was understood in the *Upaniṣads* and *all* transcendental systems in their earlier days. Spiritual exercise in some form or another and steps of realization formed organic parts of such philosophies and minimum (just required) arguments were offered. This has been wrongly understood by some Western and present-day Indian thinkers as a stage of immaturity. It is only the non-transcendental systems like Nyāya, Vaiśeṣika, Mīmāṁsā and Jainism which drove, from the start, a wedge between the *life* of realization (with all appropriate exercises) and thematic argumentative philosophy. Non-transcendental philosophy was all based on *pramāṇa*, and how *śabda-pramāṇa* fared in their hands (even in the hands of the Mīmāṁsakas) we have already seen. However, in later days, say, since the thirteenth century, the entire Indian philosophy came somehow to accept these non-transcendentalists, 'particularly the Naiyāyikas' method of argumentation (*anumāna* and *tarka*) cum correct observation as the paradigm method, applied formally and *ab extra* even to transcendental concepts, necessarily with scant attention paid to the contents of these concepts.

III

Undoubtedly, in traditional Indian philosophy good (moral) action has been understood as what is done in accordance with what is socially, often just traditionally, prescribed or prescribed in authoritative works (often called scriptures, though of differing grades of authority); and bad (immoral) actions, correspondingly, are understood as those which are not in accordance with these or positively in accordance with what have been traditionally or socially prohibited or prohibited in similar texts. Yet, however, this is not the full Indian account of morality and immorality. *Dharmaśāstra*-s, including *smṛti*-s, and their Brāhmaṇic source, Mīmāṁsā, have indeed insisted on scrupulous performance of what is enjoined and avoidance of what is prohibited. (In doubtful cases there were always efficient interpreters.) But all this was meant only for the general mass of mankind (known as Hindus). Strangely enough, even Buddha who asked his followers to accept nothing in blind faith but judge, in every case, for themselves, laid down—and his disciples and later-day stalwarts elaborated—prescriptions and prohibitions not only for the Buddhist monks but equally for the ever-increasing laity. And it was so, similarly with the Jainas. The whole idea was that common people, even though otherwise educated, are not often competent to thrash out for themselves fundamental issues like what is good, what is bad, and why. If everyone is permitted to decide such issues by himself it would only result in all-round anarchy. Willy-nilly, rules have to be formulated by *competent* persons, and the more the rules tend to be fundamental the greater must be the competence of such persons. Who, now, are these persons ?

Proximately, they are, let us grant, those who are proficient in their scriptures. But this proficiency includes a sort of *original* thinking, viz. to interpret the scriptures according as newer and newer problems arise in newer and newer concrete situations. There are indeed formalized rules of such interpretation. But, certainly, the scriptures themselves did not formulate these rules. Obviously, they could be formulated only by those for whom the scriptures were an integral part of their being, whose living thinking was verily in the line of the scripture—in older language, those to whom the ultimate truths regarding man and the world came more or less to be revealed, or, if one admits an omniscient God, to whom God spoke more or less directly—in short, in our present-day language, those who are original thinkers on ultimate truths and values. For such thinkers (seers, one may say), moral and immoral actions are indeed what are prescribed or prohibited in the scriptures, but they are equally those which they think out (find) by themselves. In the *Gītā*, Arjuna has been repeatedly asked *to see for himself* the exact nature of action which is *niṣkāma* (categorically imperative), *nirabhimāna* (selfless), *lokasaṁgrahārtha* (altruistic) and, granting all this, *īśvarārpita* (about the results of which we need have no worry). Obviously, one who has this competence has transcended all worldly allurements, fear of others and selfish thoughts—one, in other words, who has learnt to resist effectively the compelling forces of nature (exactly what is known as 'freedom from') and, more than that, to tackle these forces from the point of view of conscious resistance, i.e., in effect, to control and utilize them for the benefit of others, ultimately of humanity as a whole (exactly what is known as 'freedom to').

Similar considerations hold with regard to moral and immoral actions understood as what are socially (or traditionally) prescribed and prohibited. Here, too, the prescriptions and prohibitions are mechanically binding on the general run of people. But it is admitted at the same time that at times of need these have to be changed—modified or even scrapped and replaced—by others, and who can decide about the matter except one who has cultured 'freedom from' and 'freedom to' the society and the tradition in question. Thus, freedom, understood in the proper sense of the term (not in its popular loose sense), lies at the root of the whole matter, though undoubtedly for the vast mass of mankind social and traditional prescriptions and prohibitions are binding. It may be noted that they have been binding equally on those who culture freedom, but till only new situations have not posed new problems or, better, till the corresponding solutions are found.[1]

IV

This explains the dominant tradition-or-social-centricity of the traditional Indian life. For the general mass the goodness or badness of an action is determined (almost) wholly by convention and reward and punishment meted out accordingly. Punishment has largely, indeed, been understood as preventive, i.e. in order that the society moves on as smoothly as possible. But what, after all, is wrong about that ? Is not this preventive theory still largely in operation even in 'advanced' countries of the present-day world—and that too even in peacetime ? If this is only a legacy of the past, nowadays consciously sought to be abolished, is that not largely a pious wish after all ? Moderation by other considerations does not necessarily make it less 'preventive,' though that way, undoubtedly, another point of view emerges, consciously or unconsciously, the whole idea being that punishment should not be *unduly* preventive. So far, indeed, as social stability is concerned—whatever be the form of the society in question—the *authorities* have always been, and are so even today everywhere, careful that it is not jeopardized, and punishment is largely meted out accordingly. The possibility or desirability of *educating* criminals has often been admitted, but authorities everywhere (including the old-day India) have, in social matters, been strict realists too. They have rather insisted on educating people *before* they turn criminals than wasting time over useless romantic projects. There is not much of difference between the traditional Indians and the more 'advanced' of the Western people in this matter, even regarding formulations of applied legal systems.

Whether punishment was a retributive measure in India or, for that matter, anywhere in the world depends on what precisely is meant by 'retribution'. If it means sort of *revenge*, as, we are told, many tribals are used to, this has never been a *formulated*

1. Is it any worse than the modern civilized life as *law-abiding* ?

motive in any civilized country anywhere, though such revengeful penalties have sometimes been imposed even by civilized people, specially at times of emergency, but oftener than not under the guise of some civilized measure. 'Retribution,' however, means quite another thing, viz. giving one his legitimate due; and in this sense punishment for bad deeds stands on the same footing with reward for good deeds. Punishment as retribution in this sense has always been a dominant theme in Indian mind and has followed, almost as a matter of necessity, from their theory of *karma*. Only, it has to be noted that it does not clash with any other theory of punishment, neither preventive nor educative. Indeed, retribution in this sense has always been understood as a sort of education. People in India have, through thousands of years, been taught by their *Dharmaśāstra*-s to accept punishment, humanly or divinely dispensed (exactly as in the cases of rewards) as their due and correct themselves accordingly. Thus there has never been anything 'tribal' in the Indian notion of punishment.[1]

Even this is not the whole account of the Indian notion of punishment—and, for the matter of that, of their notion of social control. Exactly as in the case of necessity *vis-à-vis* freedom, here too (almost) absolute social control was meant only for the ordinary mass of mankind. For, at critical periods of social turmoil—due, maybe, to war, large-scale invasion, natural calamities of various kinds, cultural conflict with neighbours or newcomers, etc.—social injunctions had to be relaxed or even changed, and this could be done only by those who had always had a taste of freedom, explicit or half explicit; and this means, which also was a fact, that some people (say, wise philosophers) were deliberately exempted from social control. But even in their case they got exempted either only after they had fulfilled (most of) their social obligations or, in exceptional cases, when they were found (by all concerned) to have been extraordinarily gifted for that (which was interpreted in India as that they had fulfilled those obligations in a previous cycle of life). The story of the traditional Indian life has to be understood from their social customs and injunctions, but their philosophy has to be

1. Exceptions in particular cases and in more or less prolonged periods of degeneration there must have been, as with every people in the world. But these are candid *exceptions.*

gathered from whatever these exceptional people have (or are reported to have) said.

Indeed, a central point of Indian ethics and socio-political philosophy is that the traditional Indians have distinguished three classes of action—good, bad and *niṣkāma* (the third, almost the same as Kant's 'categorical imperative'). For them, a good action is one that falls in line with authoritative social injunctions, a bad action is that which goes against such injunctions; and the *niṣkāma* is that which springs entirely out of freedom, freedom being understood in the transcendental sense discussed earlier. Good actions are invariably rewarded, either in this life by the society or in the next cycle of life through maturation of *adṛṣṭa*-s, and bad actions punished similarly—reward ultimately meaning some sort of worldly happiness and punishment some sort of worldly suffering. With regard to *niṣkāma* actions, on the other hand, there is no question either of worldly happiness or of worldly suffering, because, done without any sense of natural need and profit and so far without any sense of the 'natural' (empirical) ego as the agent, such actions do not produce any merit or demerit (*adṛṣṭa*). If, on the other hand, one who has developed this sense of freedom ('freedom from' and 'freedom to') does not yet act according to the categorical imperative (which is freedom itself formulated more or less concretely), that will be the grossest form of immorality, i.e. immorality proper, which is infinitely more serious than contravening any social injunction, because it would be flouting the basic humanity of man. Such flouting, depriving one of basic humanity, reduces him really to naught, i.e. just to an item of nature. This is what is meant when the traditional Indian says that the highest objective of life is to realize the *essence* of oneself. All the transcendental Indian thinkers have quite categorically announced this, and even the Mīmāṁsakas and the Naiyāyikas have permitted this. They have, of course, differed among themselves as to whether the so-called '*niṣkāma* action' is after all any form of *action*. Quite many of them have called it knowledge, of course, ultimate knowledge.

As with good, bad and purely moral (spiritual) actions, so exactly, one may hold, with true, false and absolute cognitions, and pleasure, pain and absolute bliss (and, if one likes, with the beautiful, the ugly and aesthesis—*rasa*—by itself). True knowledge is consciousness of something as existing (whether in the present or in the past or in the future) in this world, false knowledge, correspondingly, being the consciousness of what does not so exist—in either case there being some distance between knowledge (as subjective) and the thing (object) so known. Regarding 'absolute knowledge', on the other hand, transcendental philosophers hold that it is nothing but self-evident consciousness itself as either Being or pure Act of Consciousness (= pure Intention) having no object other than and standing over against itself.

So is the case with pleasure, pain and absolute bliss. Pleasure and pain have corresponding *objects* that we enjoy or suffer; they also have *causes* which, as in case of true and false knowledge, may not be their *objects*. But absolute bliss as transcendental has, like absolute knowledge and *niṣkāma* action, no other object over against itself, nor any cause except that which removes what had kept it covered (concealed) so long in the heart of ordinary pleasures, exactly as in the case of absolute knowledge or *niṣkāma* action which was kept covered in ordinary cases of true knowledge or in good actions. Thus, it is again, with the beautiful, the ugly and pure aesthesis (*rasa*).

All the three cases of the Absolute—absolute knowledge, absolute (*niṣkāma*) action and absolute bliss—are but freedom (either 'from' or 'to' or both) in three alternative forms. Considerations of this freedom is obviously much above that of tradition or convention (social or otherwise). If this freedom, in any of its forms, is transcendental, so is its consideration. While thus the goodness or badness of an action, the pleasantness or painfulness (one may say, the beauty or ugliness) of anything and the truth or falsity of a cognition are all determined by tradition, i.e. convention,[1] and are so far only relative, the absolute in none of its forms is ever so determined. Transcendental

1. Even truth and falsity are so determined, first, because observation is always selective and what has to be selected is determined as much by the conventional fund of knowledge we already have as by the constitution of our sense organs which, in its turn, is determined by their biological tradition, and, secondly, because every new theory (explanation) is to be judged by its all-round consistency with the fund of systematic knowledge already stored in convention.

knowledge, action and bliss (one may add aesthesis) are above all relativity.[1]

Anyway, the traditional Indian social-centric life does not negate its transcendental freedom. Social-centricity is meant for the vast laity. But the few savants at the top trace everything phenomenologically to freedom ('from' and 'to') as the ultimate guiding principle. The only difference between the traditional Indian attitude and that of the present-day people (particularly in the West) is (i) that with the latter freedom seems to be everybody's birthright and (ii) that the transcendental character of such freedom is naturally often missed there and very easily replaced by the empty naturalistic notion that one is free to choose (and do) anything he likes. Indians have traditionally been consistently against such (empty) freedom as a universal birthright : this, they insist, would only lead to all-round confusion. Are they wholly mistaken ?

V

We are often told that much regard for tradition, even though meant for the laity, has done immense harm to Indian philosophy because even the best talents have often spent their whole energy in writing commentaries and sub-commentaries. Good or bad, this, certainly, is in sharp contrast with the present-day Western philosophy since the days of Descartes and Bacon. One must not forget, however, that even in the West, in the days before Descartes and Bacon, *schools* of philosophy were greater realities

1. Anti-transcendentalists, like the Naiyāyikas and the Mīmāṁsakas, are not indeed afraid of this (according to them, only 'so called') relative acceptance of truth (and falsity) and the good (and the bad) (and—though this they have never discussed—the beautiful and the ugly). The Naiyāyikas hold that if we accept a cognition as true or false or an action as good or bad we do not accept it as *relatively* so. Although the possibility of its proving later to be otherwise is never denied, that is not also asserted consciously. Anything taken to be true (or false or beautiful or ugly) is taken to be really so with the further admission that if later it proves to be false or ugly our former judgment has to be relinquished; and yet this never means that we should take it only provisionally. The Mīmāṁsakas also hold the same view, though on a ground which the Naiyāyikas would never admit : they hold that every cognition *is* true till it is proved to be false. (But can one similarly hold that every action *is* good till it proves bad or everything is beautiful till, through careful additional study, it proves to be ugly ?)

than in subsequent days. There were only a few philosophers who started the schools and then talents after talents were engaged in writing commentaries and sub-commentaries or at the most independent treatises that were, after all, on the same old topics of their schools and with the same presuppositions. *Commitment* to schools of philosophy was thus no novel feature in India only. If this starting commitment has gone out of vogue in modern times it is because with Renaissance, Reformation and development of science and technology, there occurred not only a sharp break with the then tradition but also with tradition in general : tradition everywhere came to be suspected. True, with new independence permitted to every thinker people had greater scope for the (free) play of their intellect and perceptivity, but that was not always a gain. It was a gain only where there was sufficient methodological control and cooperative thinking, as in science and technology and in pursuits that were in line with science. Otherwise, however, this control and co-operation ceasing, the whole thing was thrown out of gear. This was abundantly evident in the field of philosophy and most of the humanities, and this anarchy paralleled another equally developing in social life in general where rapidly the idea of loose empty freedom, discussed above, came to be considered a fundamental birthright. *Listening*, with an open heart to what others say, came to be considered a weakness, smacking of the old-day allegiance to tradition, and everybody took it to be his birthright to *speak out* whatever occurred in his mind. Reason and observation were indeed requisitioned, but that mainly to support what the speaker wanted to *say*, not necessarily to strengthen what he *learnt* (*heard*). Science, being constitutionally a cooperative pursuit with a binding methodology, is an exercise as much in speaking as in hearing and is, therefore, a model of communication. But not so is philosophy that grew after Renaissance. Philosophical ideas may, quite many of them, be extremely fascinating, but not necessarily intellectually convincing therefor. *Such* philosophy grew side by side with modern science, but almost ever since its emergence it is being pushed to the background or permitted only, to whatever extent, the office of playing a second fiddle to, i.e. being a general 'commentator' (and often an incompetent one, for that) on scientific pursuit in general. This plight of philosophy was evident even in the days of Kant, and everyone (except probably the philosophers themselves) knows to what plight it has been brought today, unless, of course, one turns to the irrationalists of yesterday, to Kant's *Critiques*, to the phenomenologists and existentialists of today and probably also to all *genuine* 'humanists' who seek to build philosophy on some genuine ground, viz. 'transcendentalism.' And, surprisingly enough, these very philosophies tend to be each a *joint* venture, forming always a genuine school, developed jointly by various explorers in various aspects and *committed to* from the start. The idea of solitary explorers, each almost starting anew—so much esteemed in the present days in the name of equality in capacity and individual freedom—has done no substantial good to philosophy. This *commitment* of thinking people to this or that school—this insistence more on listening than on speaking—and this acceptance, in addition, of a more or less common methodology (logic) for communication, thus rendering the whole venture cooperative (i.e. social), made philosophy so valuable a pursuit throughout the entire premodern age whether in Europe or in India or anywhere else. For every thinking man this initial commitment is in fine adjustment with reason: reason not only seeks to confirm the commitment, it seeks equally to initiate others—and, what is more in the interest of human dignity, it can also convert a man of one faith into another if there is more rational support for the latter.

VI

This attitude of *commitment* and more insistence on listening than on speaking, i.e. insistence on cooperation more than on solitary venture, explain the apparently 'unusual' fondness of the traditional Indian mind for learning from authority (*śabda-pramāṇa*). This is so not merely in the transcendental field—where, of course, it is a must, but too often in our mundane life also. It is just a pointer that we learn at least as much in cooperation as through solitary ventures. Learning to speak is itself primarily a matter of listening. (It is not denied, however, that there is an original urge to *speak*, though that is, first of all, inchoate so far, taking concrete shape only through listening to others, and, secondly, speaking itself is meant for others to listen to, and, thirdly, where, as in many cases, speech (=thought) is meant apparently for clarifying and/or strengthening, i.e. systematizing, one's own ideas, even there, the self has bifurcated itself into one who speaks and another who listens ; and all strengthening, clarification and systematization is, thus, at least narcissistic communication). *Śabda-pramāṇa* is just that which generates knowledge in the mind of the listener. All Indian theories of language (and judgment)—except those of the Buddhists, and that understandingly enough, because the Buddhists who were constitutionally against authority as a source of genuine knowledge were more for speaking than for listening—were thus from the point of view of listening. The difference, in this respect, from most of the Western theories of language (and judgment) is evident to whosoever sees through the matter, the Westerners having relied almost entirely on the point of view of *speaking*.

Śabda-pramāṇa is critically relevant for all transcendental Indian philosophy (except Buddhism, as we shall immediately see) and also, as we have insisted earlier, for much of Indian ethics (life of action). This is why all forms of Vedānta, Sāṁkhya, Yoga, Jainism and Mīmāṁsā—the former four mainly for transcendental knowledge and the fifth for all injunctions and prohibitions in (Hindu) social life—spoke so much, and in such finest details, on *śabda-pramāṇa*, taking the scriptures (of various sorts) as (probably) the only anchorage ground for all that is transcendental and ethical. It is the Buddhists, as we have already seen, who, largely against testimony at least in their early days, exhorted people always to think for themselves—of course, as much in cooperation as possible—and not to rely solely on scriptures, not even on what Buddha himself said. This was probably a revolt similar to one that occurred in Europe with Renaissance, and this is why there is so much similarity, between Buddhism of various brands—as much in their metaphysics as in other departments of philosophy—and the post-Renaissance modern Western philosophy. However, on the Eastern soil—whether in India or in South-East Asia or in the Far East—Buddhism could not long maintain this attitude. Or, probably this attitude cannot for long maintain itself, when it comes to see the plight to which philosophy as individual ventures is reduced to, as, for example, is so much the reaction noticed in the present-day European mind with regard to philosophy.

Nyāya-Vaiśeṣika and almost all later-day Indian philosophy under the influence of Nyāya have offered arguments to show why testimony has to be accepted as a valid method of knowing. But exactly as in the case of Nyāya or Nyāya-like inferential validation of transcendental truths (discussed earlier), the attempt has practically ended in a fiasco, the philosophers concerned never appearing to be as serious with these problems as with others.

VII

It is a fact that neo-Nyāya and under its influence all later-day Indian philosophy have developed staggering hair-splitting almost at every step—a sort of subtle analyses and distinctions that would surprise *beyond bounds* (we say this very deliberately) even the subtlest of the present-day analysts in the field of philosophy. If, however, on this ground one feels like stricturing the later-day Indian philosophy as all *useless* hair-splitting, that would apply equally against the Western analysts of today. If, again, the latter are permitted to justify their venture on the ground that after all they are making an honest attempt to do away with (nonsensical) metaphysics as far as possible, the later-day Indian thinkers would justify their venture on an apparently better ground, viz. that, far from doing away with (transcendental = allegedly nonsensical) metaphysics, they are rather translating the transcendental truths in the language of the empirical as far as possible. If the Western analysts demand that people should first read what they have written before forming any favourable or unfavourable judgment, the same would be the claim of the later-day Indian analysts, too easily branded as hair-splitters. It is all useless hair-splitting only to those for whom the transcendental can be experienced in some spiritual attitude, but not to one who would admit these truths on empirical grounds.

VIII

As for the distinction between self and mind, so universally accepted in traditional Indian systems (even, in a way, in Buddhism, as we shall immediately see), there is nothing unusual about it. Whether the corresponding 'substances' are admitted or not, there is a clear distinction admitted by all, except diehard empiricists, between conscious states (or acts) that are psychological in the sense that they are experienced as objects, and somehow as 'over against' in introspection, this introspection as the (subjective) awareness of the psychological states cannot itself be a psychological state experienceable as an object by another introspection. That would evidently lead to *vicious* infinite regress, the basic phenomenon of 'awareness of the psychological state' being not explained at all : whatever can be pointed out as that *awareness* is again an object to another awareness (and, so far, again a psychological state), and so on *ad infinitum*. The only way out is to take the very first introspection as but self-revealing subjectivity that is never an *object* experienceable by another subjectivity. There is, thus, a fundamental distinction between psychological state as object and introspection as subjectivity proper, i.e. between psychological objective consciousness and self-revealing subjective consciousness. The first—the psychological—is mental and whatever connects several such mentals into one individual system, called the states of 'one person', is *mind*, and the self-revealing ever-subjective consciousness, which is necessarily single (at least for each individual person, if not for all persons together) is *self*. The Hindu transcendentalists have admitted the 'one' principle in either case as a substance, and hence, for them, both mind and self are substances. The Buddhists, on the other hand, who do not admit a substance anywhere, would talk only of a series (somehow 'one' series) of mental states on one side and a single (at least for each so-called 'person') self-evident act, function, power or dynamism,[1] on the other.

Such doctrines are not at least unknown in modern Western philosophy that has begun with Descartes and is not foreign even to the present-day philosophers. Phenomenologists of various brands and quite many of the existentialists often hold similar doctrines. One peculiar phenomenon may be noted in this connection. Somehow, during the whole period of pre-Cartesian Western philosophy, and even in the early Greek days, we seldom come across any notion like 'pure subjectivity', even

1. The burning 'power' of fire, as distinct from that fire—whether that fire as a substance is or is not admitted—is no pinpointable entity as that fire could be. It is therefore *indefinite*. It may be noted that Kant, too, in the *Critique of Pure Reason* understood 'transcendental apperception' (the pure subjective act) as nothing *existent* (theoretically cognizable reality) and yet at the same time not 'nothing' therefor.

in systems known as transcendental. There are often indeed talks of 'pure self'. But that is more or less a substance (maybe, transcendental) that holds together all modes of consciousness as objects, and, therefore, itself an object (even when it is transcendental).

This older Western notion of self agrees with how the Nyāya-Vaiśeṣika thinkers have understood it. They hold that all that is real, including modes of consciousness (which are largely described as attributes of self) and, therefore, their substratum—the Self—too, is object in the sense that it is always a possible *object* of some cognition. That second cognition too is equally an object to another cognition, called introspection, that too is a possible object to another introspection and so on.[1] These Nyāya-Vaiśeṣika thinkers have never recognized anything that is pure self-evident subjectivity, whether as self or even as (pure) consciousness. What is called 'subjectivity of knowledge' is, according to them, only the *relation* which that knowledge (as an object among objects) bears to the object *of which* it is the knowledge—just the counterpart of the relation known as 'objectivity of the object known' which that object bears to the knowledge in question. Older Western philosophy seldom went beyond this notion of self and consciousness.

Most of the Indian transcendentalists hold that this pure subjectivity remains, at two extreme ends, in two different forms—one the purest and the other wholly fused. In its purest form, somehow apprehended as pure subjectivity by itself, it stands as wholly other than the psychological states, though nevertheless, even in that form, it may view the psychological states all dispassionately, and in their true relation to one another. This dispassionate viewing is more or less like what the phenomenologists call 'intention' and a Kantian 'transcendental construction'. This is the state of subjectivity called, in Indian philosophy, *sākṣita* (witness-consciousness, i.e. pure consciousness as forward-looking, object-oriented). The other extreme form of subjectivity (pure consciousness) is its full fusion (absolute non-dissociation) with mental states and their substratum, the objective mind.

1. Some Naiyāyikas have, however, stopped with the first introspection, holding almost in the Advaita line, that it is self-evident. This they have done, obviously, to avoid vicious indefinite regress. But other Naiyāyikas—and they constitute the majority—differ.

In that form it is in no way a realization of its autonomy, its only function in that form being to make the objective psychological states (appear as) subjective (conscious) and their substratum, the mind, (appear as) the subjective (conscious) self. Equally, in this form, pure subjectivity (consciousness) misrepresents itself as but the psychological states and the mind.

The two extreme forms are at two opposite ends. In between, there are stages through which pure subjectivity realizes itself *progressively* as what it precisely is—in the language of phenomenology, it realizes objects as purer and purer 'intentions' (essences) or 'construction'. The study of subjectivity through these various forms of self-realization, i.e. through progressive 'phenomenalization' of nature,[1] constitutes a major part of all the transcendental philosophies.

Why the traditional Indian philosophy has been so eloquent about self and its distinction from mind we have just seen. As for its separate treatment of the concepts of *dik*, *deśa*, *ākāśa*, *parimāṇa*, *dūratva*, *antikatva*, etc. as though they are unconnected with one another, having nothing common among them, this the Indian thinkers have done for the simple reason that actually there is nothing common to all of them. In Western philosophy (written at least in English) space is so easily meant to stand now for *dik* (direction), now for *deśa* (extension), now for *ākāśa* (the entire empty space or ether = substratum of sound), now for *parimāṇa* (size), now for *dūratva* (distance) and now for *antikatva* (nearness) etc., that no one there has taken pains to point out what exactly is common to these different entities to entitle them to the same name 'space'. Something common may perhaps be worked out, but nowhere in the entire Western philosophical or scientific literature has this been even attempted. So if these Indian philosophers have kept them apart, even though some of them may have some obvious agreeing features, they have not at least bungled more than their Western partners. What, on the other hand, goes in favour of Indian philosophy is that there each of these concepts has been elaborated in all its niceties.[2]

1. The methodology of the entire Indian transcendental philosophy is, obviously, phenomenological realization, though in systematic philosophy, and in the later-day traditional Indian philosophy ratiocination made its appearance more and more abundantly.

2. I have to admit, however, that inspite of all my study of Indian philosophy

IX

The charge brought against traditional Indian science, developed within the traditional Indian philosophy, that it is primitive would, even if true, apply equally against its Greek counterpart and, more legitimately, against the cosmology, say of Hegel, in case the latter is taken as science. As a matter of fact, the whole point is about how cosmology stands related to science.

Whatever be the judgment passed on cosmology, the Indians had, even in much older days, an elaborate science, systematically developed and tested all through by its application, as evident in Indian chemistry, medicine, mathematics (including astronomy), etc.; and so far as physics is concerned one may just be referred to some Jaina texts. If a large part of our scientific literature has disappeared it is mainly because of long disuse or, perhaps, because science, a dangerous weapon in the hands of the unscrupulous, was never wholly written down and was handed down orally from teachers to reliable learners only.

Anyway, the relation between sciences and cosmology is as intriguing a problem today as it was ever in the past. Cosmology has never been just a piecing together of different scientific truths into a romantic account supposed to be unitary. That would seldom stand above 'science fiction.' Cosmology as a serious study has oftener been a synthetic approach to nature from the point of view of how mind accepts or rejects it or responds to it in other ways, and, at its height, an account of nature as a whole from the transcendental point of view. And, exactly as there are different levels of subjective approach from the gross physio-psychological response right up to the highest spiritual (phenomenological) attitude, so too has cosmology been of

and inspite of all my talks with the scholars in the traditional Indian philosophy I have failed to understand what they would mean by '*parimāṇa*' to have enabled them to understand self (and some other entities) to be of *vibhu parimāṇa* (infinite size), unless they have meant by '*parimāṇa*' the extent of graspability. But even then, the verb 'grasp' turns out to be as ambiguous as 'space'. The same consideration would apply against the verb 'cover'. The only way out would be to understand '*vibhu*' as '*infinite*' in the sense in which God is said to possess infinite intelligence, infinite power, infinite kindness, etc. Still, however, there would remain difficulties about the *parimāṇa* called 'infinitesimal'. And, should we at all admit all the three kinds of *parimāṇa*—infinite, finite and infinitesimal ?

different grades. In the older days, whether in India or in the West, it was largely transcendental and partly, of course, physio-psychological (including what is just 'conventional'). And in modern times, romantic cosmology apart, every branch of science, as much in its micro and as in its cosmic studies, is, because of its necessary relation to other sciences—in fact, because of its sliding into these—automatically turning into naturalistic *cosmology* of different grades; and at every such grade there is a denial of the eighteenth and nineteenth century idea that man, and even lower living beings, are constitutionally only passive entities affected by nature and responding to it as passive matter acted on reacts mechanically. With the rapid elimination of this idea, all sciences are coming closer to one another and developing into a grand unitary science which may not be very different from the genuine cosmology of the older days.

It would, therefore, be highly improper to brand *a priori* the traditional Indian concepts of *kṣiti* (soil, with smell and hardness as its essential properties), *ap* (water, similarly, with taste and liquidity as essential properties), *tejas* (fire with colour, i.e. incandescence, and heat), *marut* (air with tactile qualities and motion) and *vyoman* or *ākāśa* (ether with sound and empty space that permits accommodation of other entities) as primitive in any derogatory sense of the term without first studying them with all the seriousness they deserve—particularly as they have occurred in Vaiśeṣika, Sāṁkhya, Yoga, Vedānta, Śaiva-and-Śākta Tantras and the philosophy of the Jainas.

X

The charge, often levelled against the traditional Indian philosophy, that it has not developed any detailed psychology of wish, desire, will, impression and imagination is largely true, though, paradoxically enough, traditional Indian thinkers have never underestimated their importance for philosophic (particularly, epistemological) pursuit and spiritual realization and, as is evident from their literature, have known very well their distinctions from one another and from like psychological phenomena. It is difficult to understand why they—even the Nyāya-Vaiśeṣika thinkers—have not studied these phenomena in greater detail and more systematically. The other charge, however, that Indian thinkers have often unnecessarily spoken a lot on the concept of self-evidence of knowledge (consciousness) or self is wholly unmerited. This we have thoroughly discussed in connection with the charge 'viii'.

9

A NEW APPROACH TO INDIAN PHILOSOPHY

RAM SHANKAR BHATTACHARYA*

What is meant by Indian philosophy?

IT is necessary to state what we understand by the term 'Indian philosophy'. According to us Indian philosophy invariably accepts the existence of certain supersensuous (*atīndriya*) entities and certain unworldly means or processes for realizing them. The contention that philosophy is by nature incapable of experimental verification is not to be applied to the field of Indian philosophy. It would be wrong to define Indian philosophy as a *vidyā* which simply endeavours to reach a conception of the universe with all its elements and parts and their interrelations; or, as the rational knowledge from the concepts; or, as a science of principles. It is quite logical to designate Indian philosophy as a *mokṣa-darśana*, for it is essentially connected with *mokṣa* (release from pain). This is why we invariably find the idea of the absence of pain in all the varying conceptions of the highest goal as conceived by the different systems of Indian philosophy.

The following points are to be noted in this connection. In Indian philosophy inference (*anumāna*) plays the most important part. It is chiefly used to prove the existence of supersensuous entities stated in the promissory assertions (*pratijñā-vākyas*) of

*R. S. Bhattacharya is a traditional Indian scholar who lives in Varanasi, India. He is editing the *Samkhya-Yoga* volume (with Gerald Larson of the University of California, Santa Barbara) in the monumental *Encyclopaedia of Indian Philosophies* series.

the great authorities of the philosophical schools. Indian philosophy takes pain (and no wonder or doubt) as the source of philosophical inquiry. It does not disregard physical experiment and observation; yet it takes them as valid in a very limited field only. Duties or acts to be performed (*dharma*) fall under the external aspect of philosophy (*mokṣa-darśana*). Properly speaking, *dharma* is connected with the means for realizing various goals conceived by different philosophical systems. *Artha* and *kāma* do not fall under the field of philosophy. Though these two do not properly fall under *dharma*, yet they are not regarded as quite independent of *dharma*.

According to us, the *Cārvāka* system does not fall under the field of proper *darśana*, i.e. *mokṣa-darśana* (philosophy) as it is totally silent on supersensuous entities and unworldly means. Since it vaguely considers the nature of the subject (knower) it is regarded as a *darśana* in a secondary sense only. Its disregard for inference is also a ground for not taking it as a proper system of philosophy. In fact it is a pseudo-philosophy (*darśanābhāsa*).

We have nothing to say here about the origin and development of Indian philosophical systems. Our purpose for writing this paper is to show the ways or means which can remove the present lamentable state of Indian philosophy and can render it useful to the persons of modern times. All will agree that if the present state of Indian philosophy continues for three or four decades, there will be none who will take trouble to study Indian philosophy and, consequently, Indian philosophy will die a natural death. It is we (i.e. persons who teach Indian philosophy and who declare themselves to be the followers of different philosophical systems) who should be held responsible for this death. There is no doubt that our ignorance (i) of the character of *mokṣa-darśana* and (ii) of the experiences and experiments on which the philosophical doctrines and the arguments are based is the fundamental cause of the present lamentable state of Indian philosophy.

Objections against Indian philosophy :

The following are some of the objections often raised against Indian philosophy by persons of modern times :

(1) Indian philosophy does not solve any problem concerning economic or political life.

(2) Indian philosophy hardly discusses the grave problems of individual or social life (e.g. marriage) seriously.

(3) Indian philosophy does not clearly and intelligibly show the way through which a man can get rid of sorrow, though it assiduously holds that its main aim is to attain the state which is absolutely devoid of sorrow.

(4) The works on Indian philosophy are found to contain such views on gross physical objects which are disproved by scientific investigations.

(5) Fictitious or imaginary causes are sometimes conceived to explain a real phenomenon.

(6) All schools of Indian philosophy have considerable number of arguments and doctrines that hardly have any apt examples.

(7) Philosophers are often found to support their own views by referring to supernormal powers, though they never explain these powers intelligibly.

(8) Authoritative sentences are often found to be explained in contradictory ways by the teachers of different schools of Indian philosophy, and this fact tends to show that Indian philosophy has no strong foundation. I have often found highly educated persons to say that no argument in Indian philosophy is so powerful as to refute the views of the opponents conclusively and that almost all views of philosophical schools may be equally refuted or supported, for they are nothing but empty speculations only.

That some of the aforesaid objections are based on ignorance of the nature of Indian philosophy is beyond doubt. Some, however, are valid, though they are concerned with the later phases of Indian philosophy. In the following pages we are going to consider those ways or means that can successfully remove the present state of Indian philosophy.

What we premise?

Before going to consider the ways, we want to draw the attention of all concerned to the fact that the existence of philosophy solely depends upon the propounders or the followers of the philosophical systems. Unless these persons take the responsibility of at least a gross part of the philosophical views they try to propound, it is impossible to establish Indian philosophy in a glorious position. Failure to take responsibility for the philosophical views points to failure to understand their significance, value and validity. The lovers of Indian philosophy should always bear in mind that some of their fundamental doctrines are formulated by observing highly developed mental stages. The Advaitins are found to prove the falsity of the world on the basis of the act of crossing sorrow.[1] If the example of 'crossing sorrow' is not found, the falsity of the world becomes a false assertion. The character of Indian philosophy may be determined by this example.

It is to be noted in passing that I have no hesitation in declaring that a considerable number of erroneous views about the nature, function, quality, etc. of physical things arose in the medieval period on account of the absence of higher scientific investigations, some of which were accepted by the authors of philosophical works. All views properly disproved by scientific investigation must be accepted as invalid, for scientific investigation falls under *pratyakṣa-pramāṇa*. Similarly, many yoga-works of later teachers are found to contain wrong views on physical objects and bodily functions (e.g. air taken through the nostrils enters the abdomen), which must be shunned. Such views were maintained either by non-yogins or by those who belonged to the initial stage of yoga practice.

I may further add that I do not at all subscribe to the view of some thinkers that persons of modern times are not quite competent to understand philosophy (*mokṣa-darśana*) for it takes into consideration such entities as are supersensuous. All of us are eligible to follow the ways prescribed by ancient philosophers and to realize the goals conceived by them. It is our natural right to verify the results of practices enjoined by the sages.

The ways or means to be followed or applied to render Indian philosophy useful :

1. Immediate attempt should be made to show the validity of philosophical views on some of the gross mental fields with which we are intimately acquainted, e.g. the field of dream,

1. *Vivaraṇa-prameya-saṁgraha*, Chapter I; *Vedānta-paribhāṣā*, Chap. on *Arthāpatti*.

sleep, distractions (*vikṣepa*), attachment (*rāga*), aversion (*dveṣa*), violence (*hiṁsā*), memory, etc., instead of holding discussions on various forms of *samādhi* (concentration), the state of isolation or emancipation and the like about which scholars of modern times do not seem to possess experience of any kind. If these persons are convinced about the validity of *śāstric* views on the known fields of experience, they would not take the *śāstric* assertions on the unknown fields as totally invalid or absurd. I assure all lovers of philosophy that the ancient works on *darśana* contain such views on the aforesaid subjects as are still unknown to modern world and that they would solve many difficult problems that have arisen as a result of modern scientific investigations.

2. A similar attempt is necessary in the field of the object of senses, i.e. the objects known as *bhautikas* ('matter' of the scientists). It is to be noted in this connection that words like *pṛthivī*, *ap*, *tejas*, *vāyu*, etc. must be taken in the senses in which they are used in the philosophical systems if we want to show the validity of *śāstric* assertions and that these words do not convey the same sense in all the systems of philosophy. Objections are often raised on the *śāstric* views on gross objects taking words like *pṛthivī*, etc. in non-*śāstric* senses. It is highly improper to raise an objection on the Sāṁkhyan view on the *vāyu-bhūta*, taking it identical with air or gas.

3. An attempt should be made to verify the results (especially the gross perceptible results) of the acts prescribed by ancient philosophers. If the external results of *prāṇāyāma* (yogic control of breath) are found to be true, the higher experiences of a mind strengthened and purified by *prāṇāyāma* cannot be regarded as fanciful without showing cogent reasons. It is to be noted that all yogic means are inseparable from yoga metaphysics.

4. Much attention should be paid to those remarkable views of ancient philosophers which disclose unknown or little known capability, potentiality or powers of sentient beings or non-sentient things. The statement of the scholiast Vātsyāyana (on *Nyāyasūtra* 1.1.7) that all the four kinds of *pramāṇas* (instruments of valid knowledge) are applied by gods, human beings and *tiryaks* (animals of all kinds) is one of those assertions. It shows that an amoeba also applies not only *śabda-pramāṇa* but also *upamāna-pramāṇa*. If *sthāvaras* (the vegetable world) are

included in the *tiryaks* (as is found in Sāṁkhya; *vide Sāṁkhya-kārikā*, 53) then we are to accept that trees also possess the knowledge known as *anumiti* (inferential cognition), *upamiti* (cognition of similarity) and *śābdabodha* (verbal cognition). If this and other similar assertions are found to be correct, *mokṣa-darśana* will be discussed with reverence even by those who have no interest in *mokṣa*.

5. Classification of those factors which seem to be mythical is also necessary so that the philosophical ideas would be more intelligible to modern scholars. An example like 'the conjunction of a pillar and a ghoul' (*stambha-piśāca-saṁyoga*) often stated in the works on Nyāya is highly unsatisfactory as the character of a ghoul is absolutely unknown to modern persons. Such examples create doubt about the validity of *śāstric* assertions. If it is difficult to clarify such examples, they should be replaced by intelligible ones.

6. The followers of Indian philosophy should never apply any philosophical doctrine either to justify a wrong view or to conceal their inability in analyzing a fact correctly. The examples of this tendency are found abundantly in the writings of the philosophers of the medieval period. One makes philosophy ridiculous by asserting that the divergent views about the length, height, altitude, magnitude, etc. of rivers, mountains, etc. are to be reconciled in accordance with the Advaitic doctrine of *anirvacanīya-vāda* (*vide* Nīlakaṇṭha's commentary on the *Mahābhārata, Bhiṣma Parva*, pp. 673-75).

7. The true followers of Indian philosophy should never deny a fact with a view to supporting blindly the doctrines of any philosophical school. Advaitins are found to hold that since in sleep the internal organ gets dissolved, the perception of the act of respiration in a sleeping person must be taken as illusory (*Vedānta-paribhāṣā*, Ch. 7). The contention of these 'philosophers' is philosophically untenable, for so long as one takes his perception of a sleeping man as valid, he cannot take the perception of the act of respiration as illusory. All blind sectarian beliefs are to be shunned. Such beliefs are not based on the statements of the *Upaniṣads*, the source of our philosophy.

8. The confusion of ideas or notions is one of the causes for the degraded state of Indian philosophy. Scholars are often found to mix popular ideas with *śāstric* ideas. The confusion

of the worst kind arises at the time of comprehending the nature of Īśvara and the like. Usually scholars take the Īśvara of the *Yogasūtra* not in the yogic sense but in their own sense, thus making the yoga philosophy ridiculous. The *śāstric* conceptions look absurd if they are understood in a non-*śāstric* way.

9. The tendency of identifying the views of Indian philosophy with those of Western philosophy is an obstacle in understanding the merit of Indian philosophy. This reconciliation has destroyed the sharpness of the views of Indian philosophy. To take *nirvikalpa pratyakṣa* of Nyāya as the same as the 'indeterminate perception' is an example of wrong identification. The persons, taking this identification as correct, simply fail to comprehend the depth of the Nyāya view of perception and consequently consider some of the Nyāya views on perception inconsistent or invalid. The Nyāya philosophy loses its spirit when it comes to be taught by these persons. The coherence of the views of Indian philosophy cannot be known if the views are wrongly identified with the views of Western philosophy.

It is advised that the tendency of applying Western method of research indiscriminately to the field of Indian philosophy should be checked so that no confusion would arise in understanding the value and mutual relation of the views of different systems.

10. In conclusion, we want to draw the attention of all lovers of Indian philosophy to an external work that will be useful to the readers of philosophy. We are speaking about the composition of books for we think that the books are more easily accessible than teachers. We are of the opinion that fresh works on *mokṣa-darśana* require to be composed by following the modern method of treatment. Almost all existent works on Indian philosophy are more or less useless to modern persons, for the method of treatment in these works is not suitable to them. These works are useful to the persons of past ages when the system of education was largely different from that of our times. This is why modern persons feel bewildered when they read any text on Indian philosophy. The present idea of 'a graded course' was unknown to the ancient teachers. Some of the old examples given in these texts do not seem to be suitable or convincing to modern minds. New examples, especially examples from the scientific field and a vivid description of the experiments on which

the arguments are based must be given in these books. I have already stated that it is wrong to hold Indian philosophy as incapable of experimental verification.

10

INDIAN PHILOSOPHY BETWEEN TRADITION AND MODERNITY

J. N. MOHANTY*

ONE who is asking "What is Indian philosophy? What is 'Indian' about it?" has already situated himself outside of that tradition which we call 'Indian'. None of the philosophers who shaped that tradition, and with whose writings we are acquainted, ever asked such a question. They lived and thought within that tradition, which today we are, by the very questions we are asking, thematizing. In that very act of thematizing, a rupture has taken place. Or, rather, it is only such a rupture that could make thematization of the tradition possible. To ask "What is Indian philosophy?" is, in that very questioning, also to contrast Indian philosophy with non-Indian philosophy. Unless one transcends the tradition, one cannot, and need not, ask such a question. Yet, unless one understands the tradition *from within*, one cannot answer it. We are thus confronted by a paradox, a paradox which we need not *resolve*, but, by the very nature of what we, modern Indian philosophers, are, we have to *live* through. We cannot escape this tragedy.

I.1. And yet what sort of concept is the concept of "Indian *philosophy*"? The fact that this thinking is being carried out in

*J. N. Mohanty is George Lynn Cross Professor of Philosophy, University of Oklahoma. His important books include *Edmund Husserl's Theory of Meaning, Phenomenology and Ontology, The Concept of Intentionality, Gangesa's Theory of Truth.*

the English language, making use of the western concept of *philosophia* cannot be totally ignored. Is it not the case, as western thinkers have time and again insisted, that the concept of philosophy, not merely as the love of wisdom, but also as the first science, marks "the *telos* which was inborn in European humanity at the birth of Greek philosophy."[1] On the other hand, if philosophy is the highest and the purest form of rational enquiry, is it at all permissible to speak of "European rationality" ? Does not such an adjective ("European," in this case) impose a limitation which destroys the very sense of "rationality" ? If rationality is a universal, not limited by geographical regions, historical epochs or cultural relativities, then philosophy as the purest form of rational enquiry must be, in its very conception, capable of being a universal pursuit of mankind. Such a claim to universality is fully compatible with a great diversity of internal differentiation. European philosophy itself is not a homogenous domain, but rather, contains methodological, substantial and meta-philosophical differences of every imaginable degree and radicalness. It is, therefore, possible to speak of an over-arching sense of rationality and so of 'philosophy' which shall contain, within it, internal differentiations such as Indian *darśana* and Greek *philosophia*.

I.2. But Greek *philosophia* is love of wisdom, an *eros* which by its nature generates ceaseless enquiry and search aiming at wisdom. Indian *darśana* is systematic elaboration of truth, or an aspect of it, which has already been seen. It is not *search* for truth but elaboration of it, intellectual vindication, conceptual fixation and clarification of what has been received. In Greek *philosophia*, the individual thinker, captivated by the love, plays the decisive role. In a *darśana*, the individual thinker, great or small, plays a subordinate role, he does not found a system but carries its explication forward. The *darśana* is a perception of truth, or a possibility of its perception, which antedates any individual thinker or expositor. Criticism, clarificatory-explicative as well as destructive, is either intra-systemic and inter-systemic. Common to both, the *philosophia* tradition and the *darśana* tradition, is critical thinking, thinking which looks

1. E. Husserl, *The Crisis of European Sciences and Transcendental Phenomenology*, English Translation by David Carr (Evanston: Northwestern University Press, 1970), p. 15.

for evidence—empirical and rational—justifying cognitive claims, which elaborates principles of such justification, logic in the one case and *pramāṇa-śāstra* in the other, and which, using the tools thereby made available, reflects on the nature of what *is*, resulting in ontology in the one case and *prameya-śāstra* in the other.

I.3. The concept 'Indian philosophy' owes the other half of its problematic character to the difficulty of ascertaining what is in general meant by 'Indian' and what is meant by it in our specific context. If it is to a geographical region that we are referring, it is only well-known that political vicissitudes do not permit us to delimit that region in a historically invariant manner. Even when one speaks of 'Indian philosophy today,' do we mean philosophical works written by Indians or works on Indian philosophy written by anyone, Indian or non-Indian? (One may have to extend the scope of 'Indian' to 'Indian by descent' for obvious reasons.) But today Indians write on western philosophy as much as non-Indians write on Indian philosophy. Thus it is clear that authorship cannot be used to delimit Indian philosophy. A more promising attempt would be the following: we start by ostensively listing the *core* source-material in the various *darśanas*, and, then, extend the scope of 'Indian philosophy' to include any philosophical work which self-consciously takes up that core-tradition, and *perceives itself as continuing* the discussion of the *themes*, *issues* and *problems* formulated in, and arising out of, that tradition, no matter in what language and irrespective of the geographical and socio-political loyalty of the author. Note that this account makes use of the idea of 'self-consciously taking up and continuing a tradition.' A tradition does not function, maintain itself and grow by way of external causality. It is true that a tradition consists, in large measure, of sedimented meanings which need to be rescued from anonymity, reactivated and appropriated, but that is not incompatible with saying that a tradition is a tradition for one only insofar as it is self-consciously taken up by the latter. To say the latter, is *not* to say that for one who self-consciously takes up, lives and continues a tradition, all elements of that tradition are transparent, or that large areas are not either anonymous or obscure or ambiguous. The process of living in a tradition is also a continuing process of interpreting it and interpreting oneself in the light of it. Most of us, naïvely participating, accept, in the measure suited to our understanding, some handed down interpretation or other. The task of philosophy is to overcome the naïveté of this acceptance. But are not we talking now, not of Indian tradition in general, but of the tradition of the Indian *darśanas*? This already belongs to a higher level of self-conscious and reflective acceptance and participation, not in the sense that the participator distinguishes it from non-Indian traditions (he, in fact, in the past knew very little, if any of them), but in the sense that he knows, justifies and plays the rules of the game as laid down, developed and professionally practised through the centuries.

I.4. Against the explication of 'Indian philosophy' suggested above, two criticisms may be made. In the first place, it may be pointed out that it makes 'Indian philosophy' into an *open-ended contexture*, in the sense that anything would count as belonging to its scope if only it self-consciously pursues, extends and perceives itself as continuing the thoughts of the core-tradition. And, secondly, one may also want to argue that restricting the tradition to 'themes, issues and problems' tantamounts to denying that the system-centred nature of the *darśana*-tradition which was brought out by implication in I.2. To reply briefly: it would be un-illuminating to restrict the tradition to the *texts*,[1] for, first, we do not know how narrowly circumscribed that core corpus has to be. Assuming that we have a core corpus, we still have the problem of identifying what the texts say apart from the interpretations which have historically unfolded themselves. The orthodoxy of returning to the texts themselves is laudable, but the confidence that one can capture the sense of the texts themselves independently of interpreting them is a sign of either dogmatism or naïveté. Our only access to the texts is through interpretations, and the sense of the texts may well be said to have unfolded through such interpretations.[2] Orthodoxy may go along with this, and yet want to close the acceptable interpretations at some point of time. But again such a move

1. For the problems concerning the idea of the text, see M. Foucault, *Archaeology of Knowledge*.

2. Here Hans-Georg Gadamer's idea of "effective historical consciousness" is useful. cp. Gadamer, *Truth and Method* (New York: The Seabury Press, 1975).

is arbitrary. Why close the acceptable Vedic interpretation with Sāyaṇa, and why not admit Sri Aurobindo and Dayananda? Admitting then the *normative* role that the return to the core texts should play, it is nevertheless desirable to leave room for creative possibilities of interpretation, and this is what we wanted to do. As regards the systematic nature of the *darśanas*: it is again true that the *darśanas* are systems, but it would be a mistake to suppose that they were closed, absolutely self-justifying, systems. The basic conceptual framework for each *darśana* received some defence within it as well as by way of inter-system dialogues and disputations, but the defence of a conceptual framework (the list of *padārthas* and the list of *pramāṇas*) could not be radical[1] when carried out from within, for such a defence has to use the *pramāṇas* as formulated within that framework. The defence is rather *post facto*, a *defence* of what has been *received*. One may at this point genuinely ask, whether a radical justification of a system is at all possible. With the Mādhyamikas one may reply in the negative; with Husserl one may want to shun philosophical system and do a different sort of philosophy aiming at radical self-reflection and self-criticism. It is in view of such possibilities, one ancient and the other contemporary, and it is also in view of the inevitable weakening of belief in *śabdapramāṇa*, the source of the basic conceptual framework in each case, that today, in the global philosophical situation in which we, the Indian philosophers, find ourselves, it may be necessary to salvage, in the face of decay of the systems, the 'themes, issues and problems' and to go on from there.

II

It is considerations such as these that lead us to reflect on the concepts of tradition and modernity and on the situation in which the Indian philosophers find themselves today. There is a simple chronological sense which trivialises the deeper issues —the sense according to which in every age the latest to arrive on the scene is the modern while the old, the not-yet in the living present but stored in memory, is the tradition. Such a shifting distinction is taken care of by the flow of time, as the

1. For a more detailed treatment of this, see my "Understanding Some Ontological Differences in Indian Philosophy," forthcoming in *Journal of Indian Philosophy*.

living present recedes into the past, the latest to arrive becomes old and vanishes into the dimness of recollection. Our problem is not simply the formal problem of temporality. 'Modernity' has a specific sense here, and, in the Indian context, tradition has a special role. Both need to be looked into.

II.1. I think it is important to distinguish between tradition and orthodoxy. Orthodoxy consists in hypostatizing tradition into a lifeless, unchanging structure. Tradition, as distinguished from orthodoxy, is a living process of creation and preservation of significations. When a tradition is alive, it continues to grow, to create and to respond to new situations and challenges. When it is no more alive, it requires an orthodoxy to preserve its purity as against possible distortion and de-sanctification. A living tradition is ambiguous in the sense that it allows for growth and development in many different ways. It is false to oppose tradition to freedom of rational criticism, for rational criticism takes place, not within a vacuum but from within a tradition. What we are trying to capture, then, is not the opposition orthodoxy-modernity, but tradition-modernity.

II.2. If modernity means outright rejection of tradition, then, of course, there is no promise of a fruitful dialogue and mediation. Insofar as philosophy is concerned, modernity in this sense would amount to courting every modern fad or style, school and movement. But such an attitude, quite apart from whether it is genuinely *philosophical* or Indian or both, can only exhaust itself in chasing after the most recent, the ultra-modern for its own sake i.e. just because it is the most recent. It is to that extent self-defeating and self-destroying.

II.3. There are two other more promising lines of understanding 'modernity'. The first of these is that modernity consists in addressing oneself to what is *contemporaneous*. This is a fundamentally different attitude from that cursorily set aside in the just preceding paragraph. More responsible, it is not excited by the newest, but is *challenged* by the contemporary on-going dialogue. That makes it more philosophical. Philosophical thinking, in an important respect, is a dialogue, and even when it is monological, the monologue consists in appropriating and internalizing a possible dialogical situation. But with whom can I converse, who can ask me questions, challenge my convictions, question my arguments, excepting one who is a contemporary? While this appears to me unexceptionable, I must add, however, that it does not exclude tradition from being a dialogical partner. My tradition *can* be contemporaneous with me. What is more, this is particularly true of the situation of an Indian philosopher. A *living* tradition, to the extent it is living, challenges the thinker. The Indian tradition is contemporaneous with the Indian philosopher, for one thing, it offers the most important challenge to him, a challenge to understand, interpret and communicate with it. In the recent past, the philosophers in India assumed a false, unphilosophical role in relation to the tradition, the role, namely, of interpreting that tradition *to* the west, *to* the so-called modern world. This is unphilosophical, for it is not the task of philosophy to interpret something *to* some audience. The philosopher interprets the text, such interpretation being the way his thinking answers the questions and the challenge the text offers to him, or rather the meeting of his questioning and that of the text. What is more, in the special circumstance of Indian situation, the tradition permeates the life-world in which the philosopher finds himself, it in fact constitutes his life-world—not merely a subject matter for scholarly research. Promising as it is, the notion of contemporaneity, then, succeeds in mediating between 'tradition' and 'modernity,' and reveals that opposition to be not after all an unbridgeable gulf and our situation not to be demanding an 'either-or' choice.

II.4. The other promising clue lies in the idea of 'criticism'. The modern spirit is the critical spirit. Tradition demands respect and conformity. In view of the wide appeal of this way of formulating the contrast, it may be worthwhile to look deeper into its validity and limitations in the Indian context. To be fair to the Indian philosophical thinking, we need to reformulate the contrast thus: it is not true that Indian tradition knows of no *critical* thinking. What is at stake vis-à-vis modernity is, *whether there are universal norms of criticism*—logical, epistemological or axiological—which can be applied *indifferently* to any mode of thinking.

II.4.1. The traditionalist may argue that, in truth, any critical norm should be internal to a tradition, so that although it can and should be relentlessly applied within that tradition it cannot coherently be used to question the basic framework of that tradition itself. In the context of Indian philosophical tradition, for example, it is misconceived to apply the norms derived from formal logic, or epistemological norms derived from either empiricism or rationalism of the western tradition. According to the fundamental framework of that tradition, scriptural texts are epistemologically 'stronger' than either the purely logical considerations or sensuous evidence. Furthermore, the 'logical' itself is conceived as ancillary to and parasitical upon the perceptual and the scriptural, so that the tradition did not recognize the autonomy of the logical, be it in the sense of an autonomous, self-subsistent mode of being or in the sense of having an autonomous type of truth (i.e. 'formal validity', 'analyticity', etc.). With the subordination of the logical to the perceptual and of the perceptual to the scriptural texts, the framework rules out any purely formal-logical or sensualistic, empirical criticism *from within*, and, of course, criticism *from without* is in any case inadmissible.

II.4.2. Against this powerful self-defence and also self-interpretation of the tradition, one may point out that it operates with too rigid a conception of the tradition to begin with, one which transforms a given tradition into a self-sufficient whole, a windowless monad. But such a view flies in the face of the historical growth, not merely of ideas within a tradition, but also of its own supposedly basic framework. There is no *a priori* reason against—and some empirical evidence in favour of—interaction with alien traditions as a factor contributing to that historical growth. Consider, for example, the six *āstika darśanas* (excluding the *nāstika* ones, for the sake of simplicity alone) which define the range of variations within the tradition of Indian philosophy, and therefore also the invariant conceptual, logical and epistemological framework for those variations. Neither the six *darśanas* nor their basic frameworks were there in the scriptural literature. They were later-day growths, their expositors and advocates found for them footholds within the scriptures. To suppose that *only* these systems, and none others, could have developed within that tradition, that any other would have been basically incompatible with it, would be to insist on the possibility of an *a priori* deduction of the *six*—which is an unsubstantiated and unsubstantiable claim. In fact, each *darśana* has grown and developed far beyond what was anticipated by the early masters.

II.4.3. Faced with such a challenge, the traditionalist will no doubt fall back on what is indeed a valid point: through all the variations in systematic discourse, the basic *questions* continued to be the same while only the answers differed. There also persists a unique *style* of philosophizing. The *darśanas* derived their fundamental *concepts,* if not doctrines, from the pre-systematic scriptures—concepts such as '*prakṛti,*' '*karma,*' '*ātman,*' '*mokṣa,*' '*guṇa,*' and were elaborating the secret intentions of those texts (or at least thought themselves to be doing so). The validity of this last contention should be considered together with what is seemingly its counterpoint: many thinkers from within the tradition proved revolutionaries by challenging the basic framework (if there was one). Gautama, the Buddha, challenged the *Ātman*-tradition, Nāgārjuna challenged the metaphysical-epistemological framework, Raghunātha Śiromaṇi inherited the Vaiśeṣika categorical scheme from within, Vācaspati and Vijñānabhikṣu earned the title "Sarvatantrasvatantra" by cutting across party-lines and by seeking to reconcile systems, which certainly is ill consistent with the traditional either-or conception of the *darśanas.* When a culture is living, it does not take refuge under the name of a 'tradition' but indulges in adventures of thinking; when it is dead or dying, the idea of protecting a tradition from 'corruption' poses itself as a vital concern.

II.4.4. While recognizing the uniqueness of the *style* and, in some cases, of the *content* of philosophizing that went on in the Indian tradition, we still need to reject the attempt to hypostatize that tradition into such a self-sufficient, autonomous whole as to render it immune to *radical* (as distinguished from internal) criticism. For, whereas in the context of other sorts of systems (mathematical, and even cultural) genuine criticism is internal, it appears to be repugnant to the spirit of *philosophy* to limit criticism to the internal standards of a system. Nothing intrinsic to philosophizing can stop it from being radical questioning, i.e. questioning the basic presuppositions including the historical-cultural accomplishments. Thus, there is, in the very nature of philosophizing, a universality which one ignores, if one restricts it to the parameters of the *darśana*-tradition, as much as if one restricts it, as many western thinkers tend to do, to those of the *philosophia*-tradition.

One may want to argue, in response to the above contention, that such universality is very nearly achieved in abstract sciences such as formal logic, but even there a logical or mathematical system is conventionally founded and admits of alternatives to it. Where thought is not empty or formal, when one thinks about oneself and one's world, our aim shall be, not the abstract universality which is at home in all contents and so in the empty region of content in general, but the concrete universality which seeks the universal *in* the concrete and the particular: that precisely is assured by a well-founded tradition. It provides the content within which thought should search for the universal. Where indeed has philosophical thought been able to transcend the bounds of a tradition? Is not European philosophy, despite all claims to the contrary, despite all claims to new breakthroughs, innovations, 'destructions' and 'constructions,' still within the horizon which opened up with the Greeks and was, subsequently, determined by Christianity and the rise of modern science—all three of them historically accomplished traditions?

I agree that there is a difference between philosophical thinking concerned with oneself and one's world and the abstract thinking expressed in the formal sciences, so that the former, as concrete reflection, cannot start with, or even aim at, the empty universality of the latter. Nevertheless, two remarks may be in order: one with regard to formal-logical thinking and the other with regard to concrete philosophizing. As to the former, although it is true that there are alternate systems of logic, yet a logical system is not all arbitrary and the different alternate systems are not such that they have nothing to do with each other. In fact, one may very well ask, why are they *logics*? Insofar as they are logics, they share certain common features and satisfy certain common requirements. If this is true, what we learn is that the contention that even in formal systems there is no common norm and that all norms are internal to a system, is not quite tenable. As to concrete philosophizing, although here thought moves within the horizon set free by a tradition, no tradition can, with finality, set limits to the reaches of critical-philosophical thinking. It is precisely the greatness of a living and developing tradition that it can turn its reflective glance at itself. Both in self-reflection of a tradition and in an individual's reflection upon his own prejudices, a transcendence is achieved, without which philosophy would remain immanent criticism of culture. Neither the *darśana*-tradition nor the *philosophia*-tradition limit philosophy to this fate.

II.5. If the foregoing reflections have aimed at the thesis that tradition and modernity are not irreconcilably opposed to each other, that is because Indian philosophical tradition, with its emphasis on *pramāṇa*, contains enough of the critical spirit, and also because no responsible modernism could help taking seriously that alone on which it can build.

In the context of Indian philosophy, the relation to tradition *today* is all the more complex. This may be shown by bringing in the concept of the Indian *life-world*.[1] There is no doubt that that life-world is traditional; the beliefs, perceptions and practices which constitute it are rooted in structures of meaning sedimented long ago. The relation of the *darśanas* to this life-world has never been thematized, but it would seem that the law of determination holds good here as everywhere else : systematic philosophical thinking does not determine, but rather *idealizes*[2] the perceptions and beliefs constitutive of life-world, which, on the other hand, under-determines the systems. Given this law of determination, we need only to recognize that a radical transformation is taking place in that life-world—a transformation which, to be sure, is uncertain as to its relation to the underlying meaning-structures. This transformation consists in part in the introduction of western technology, and in part in the injection of political, economic and social ideologies from the west. While the rural-agricultural-traditional base remains unchanged, a technology grafted on it is not only bringing about vast changes but inevitably generating tensions in value and meaning systems. The political-democratic ideology, the consumption-oriented economy, and ideas of social egalitarianism are in conflict with the hierarchical, caste and class-ridden, and subsistence-oriented structures. The large question to which the Indian philosophers

1. For the concept of 'life-world,' see Husserl, *Crisis*. For problems in this concept, see J. N. Mohanty, " 'Life-world' and 'A Priori' in Husserl's Later Thought," *Analecta Husserliana*, III (1974), 46-65 and D. Carr, "Husserl's Problematic Concept of the Life-world," *American Philosophical Quarterly* 7 (1970), 331-39.

2. Husserl introduces this concept in the *Crisis* in connection with his account of Galilean physics.

today cannot but respond is, can such a transformation of their own life-world leave them untouched? Should it not demand a re-examination of the traditional modes of thinking, if not to reject them, surely to re-interpret them, if necessary, from the vantage point of the present situation. Such re-interpretation may be serious or cheap. It is serious, when it is accompanied by competence in traditional learning and guided by *genuinely philosophical motivations.*

III

Genuinely *philosophical* motivations can arise from out of the philosophical situation we inherit, not from the life-worldly situation in which we find ourselves. To understand the philosophical situation we inherit, we need to ask about the *essence* of Indian philosophy, an essence in which not merely its Indianness but also its being philosophy are preserved. As most textbooks of Indian philosophy will show, our predecessors, during the first half of this century, understood this essence to lie in the spiritual-practical intention of the *darśanas.* Our generation does not share this understanding of the philosophical tradition, and rightly so. For, in the first place, it is not as though western philosophy, in its beginning, did not have a spiritual-practical goal in view.[1] In the second place, the characterization in terms of spiritual-practical goal by itself does scant justice to the purely theoretical issues and discussions which dominate the *darśanas* so much that even the idea of a spiritual-practical goal itself receives a purely theoretical treatment. Moreover, locating such an intention in the essence of Indian philosophy helps us little by way of understanding the logical structure of the thinking which constitutes it. In the absence of such a global feature, and in view of the fact that the Indian philosophical *world* presents a bewildering variety of views, theories and concerns, the best we can do is put forward less ambitious hypotheses and try them out to see if they work. I, therefore, propose here for my limited purpose and within the limits of this essay, several such hypotheses.

III.1. One may distinguish between two conceptions of philosophy. Philosophy may be regarded as a science, as an

1. cp. J. Habermas, *Knowledge and Human Interest* (Boston : Beacon, 1971).

objective body of knowledge about the nature of things, statable in objectively true sentences. Or, philosophy may be regarded as man's historically developing self and world understanding. Only in the latter sense does philosophy have a history. In fact, in this sense, philosophy is a historical enterprise rooted in the alleged historicity of man's understanding of himself and his world, which itself is historical-cultural. Indian philosophy, we may begin by noting, understands itself to be philosophy in the first sense. It is a body of knowledge about the nature of things. But this is a self-understanding, it shares with ancient Greek thought as well. Historicism is a specifically modern concept, coming to its own somewhere around the birth of Hegels' 1807 phenomenology.

III.2. Since Aristotle defined 'metaphysics' as the science of being *qua* being, western thought has kept philosophy and science apart. If the sciences were gradually emancipated from philosophy, that was a destiny foreshadowed in the origins of philosophy as metaphysics. Indian philosophy does not, in that manner, separate itself from the sciences. It is true that the period of the *darśanas* was still before the rise of experimental science in the modern sense of the term. It is also true that European science was, in its Aristotelian phase, speculative natural philosophy. But a distinction between metaphysics and physics did not, in the Indian tradition, anticipate the clear-cut distinction of today. The Nyāya-Vaiśeṣika and the Sāṁkhya remained scientific, and dealt not alone with being *qua* being, but with beings in their various regional aspects as well. This closeness to natural, empirical science had its salutary as well as unwholesome effects. It kept philosophy closer to experience, but it also led to an almost unlimited role of the *causal* enquiry. The causal question was asked, even within epistemological and logical discourse.

III.3. The Judeo-Christian tradition brought to the western tradition two major components which superseded some earlier strands of thought in antiquity. These are : the idea of creation out of nothing and the conception of a linear temporal order. The former, on the surface only of theological relevance, has been of decisive influence in all aspects of thinking. (Consider, for example, one such consequence: the idea of pure possibilities as being prior to the actual world, a thought which itself has determined western logics and metaphysics.) The latter, seemingly secular, is really of theological origin. One needed a unique point of origin and an eschatological world-view in order to make sense of a unique, linear time, and both were supplied by Judeo-Christian thought. Now, Indian thought lacks both these components. How these lacks have influenced the total Indian mode of thinking is a question that needs to be pursued at many levels, something that need not be done here.

III.4. Next, I want to emphasize a nexus of moves which, at a deep level, characterize Indian philosophical thinking. Each of these requires an extent of elaboration and textual support which I cannot give within the limits of the present essay. But even at the risk of appearing to be dogmatic, I propose to state them in order to draw attention to their nearly pervasive presence.

(a) Consider, first, the concept of definition (*lakṣaṇa*). It is highly extensional. A definition does not seek to articulate the *essence* of the definiendum, but rather aims at uniquely identifying it. Any expression which succeeds in unique identification, which does not over-extend or under-extend, is a good definition, even if the properties in terms of which the definition is constructed be accidents and so neither genus nor differentia.

(b) This extensional concept of definition fits well with an overall denotative, referential theory of meaning, so that a (Fregean) concept of *sense as distinguished from* reference is almost lacking in Indian thought. Three remarkable theories hover on the horizon *suggesting* a theory that is not referential, the theory of *sphoṭa*, the theory of *apoha* and the grammarian's device of self-reference, but none gives a full-fledged intension.

(c) This extensionalism in theories of definition and meaning is combined with an intensional feature : analysis of sentences in terms of cognition, *jñāna*, that is expressed. This intensional feature goes well with the overall extensionalism because the cognition that is expressed is not a *sense*, but an occurrent (property, act or substantial modification, depending upon which system one happens to be talking about) belonging to someone's soul (*ātman*). Consequently, Indian logic is a logic of cognitions—inspite of its preoccupation with sentences and sentential contexts.

(d) A logic of cognitions, insofar as it is concerned with cognitions (which are occurrents), affiliates itself to psychology *of a sort,* but insofar as it is logic gives universal *rules* of the occurrence or non-occurrence of cognitive events of various types, given the occurrence or non-occurrence of cognitive events of other types. Thus although logic and psychology are not distinguished, we have neither psychologism not logicism, but an almost unique way out.

(e) In the absence of formalization, a conception of purely formal validity as contradistinguished from material truth never emerged. As is well-known, an inference is tested for its conformity to rules which include what *could be* called formal and non-formal requirements, but since the latter distinction was not made the best we can say is that an inference was regarded as true if the conditions for its occurrence as a cognitive event were given [see (d) above] and if the state of affairs is as one infers it to be.

(f) The concept of truth is so formulated that it does not leave room for a further differentiation into necessary truth and contingent truth, or into analytic and synthetic truth. There is a most fascinating but enormously complex set of features centring around and connected with the role of the modal concepts in Indian thought. The basic extensionalism and non-essentialism suggest that the modal concepts should as well be absent, and, in fact, this appears to be the case. The Indian philosopher is not concerned with bare possibilities, with counter-factual conditionals (the Nyāya looks upon *tarka* which makes use of counter-factuals as *a-pramā*), with possible worlds, but rather with what allegedly *is* the case. Everything can be doubted, provided the appropriate causal conditions of the cognitive occurrent called '*saṁśaya*' are present.[1] But this possibility of doubt does not constitute pure possibilities; rather, it constitutes what may at the most be called *motivated* possibilities.[2] But this theory of doubt does rule out of existence a class of truths that are indubitable and so necessary in the modal sense.[3]

1. See J. N. Mohanty, "Nyāya Theory of Doubt," *Visva Bharati Journal of Philosophy,* III (1966), 15-35. Reprinted in *Phenomenology and Ontology* (The Hague: Martinus Nijhoff, 1970).

2. I take this idea of motivated possibility from Husserl.

3. A full substantiation of this would need a discussion of the nature of *vyāpti*. In my view, *vyāpti* is understood extensionally, with the possible

At the same time, a universal scepticism is ruled out on grounds of contradicting the day to day practical life. While such a fallibilism clearly characterizes the Nyāya-Vaiśeṣika logic and epistemology, it is not otherwise in Vedānta insofar as empirical knowledge is concerned.[1]

(g) Although asserting causal relations in conceptual matters is hazardous, one may, without taking considerable risk, say that the features (a)-(f) are closely connected with the fact that none of the Indian epistemologies recognized mathematical knowledge as a type of knowledge that is *sui generis*. One often finds amongst possible candidates to the status of *pramāṇa* what is called *sambhava* (or, 'the possible'). Examples given of this mode of knowing are generally arithmetical truths. All epistemologists who mention it reduce it to the standard form of inference, and so deny it the status of an irreducible type of knowledge. In effect, mathematical knowledge played no role in the Indian epistemologies, not to speak of the paradigmatic position it occupied in the thinkings of the Greek rationalists. It may be noted that when the Nyāya logicians did find a place for numbers in their ontology, the resulting conception of number was a curious blend of intensional (insofar as number was regarded as a '*guṇa*' or quality) and extensional (insofar as this quality has a peculiar relation of *paryāpti* to all members of a group) elements.[2]

(h) If mathematical knowledge was not a *pramāṇa*, neither was history. Again, we find, in the literature, the claim of *aitihya* or tradition to be a *pramāṇa* set aside by reducing it to either *śabda* or inference or both.[3]

exception of the Buddhist understanding of a subclass of *vyāpti* in terms of (partial) identity (*tādātmya*).

1. For limitations to this fallibilism, see my "Indian Theories of Truth: Their Common Framework," forthcoming in *Philosophy, East and West*.

2. cp. D. C. Guha, *Navya-Nyāya System of Logic* (Varanasi : Bharatiya Vidya Prakasan, 1968) esp. ch. VII on "Paryāpti".

3. Again any hasty explanation of *why* this is so should be suspected. Possible explanations are : a general belief in the unreality of time (but all *darśanas* did not regard time as unreal), conception of time as cyclic (not all emphasised it, the Greeks nevertheless concerned themselves with history, there can be a philosophy of history compatible with the conception of cyclic time and cyclic time did not assert recurrent events, but only recurrent patterns), conception of spirit or consciousness as non-intentional and non-

(i) Possibly connected with the non-recognition of historical knowledge as a *pramāṇa* is the status of memory in the epistemologies. Memory was excluded from the scope of '*pramā*,' either because it is not an originary mode of knowledge but is rather parasitical upon a past knowledge, or because what it apprehends, viz. the past, is no more.[1]

III.5. In (a) through (i) under III.4., I have drawn attention to several features of Indian philosophical tradition, which have been—by way of comparison with the western tradition—described as 'lacks'. This locution is certainly misleading, particularly because the talk of 'lack' carries the sense of deficiency. My purpose, on the contrary, has been to bring into clear relief the nature of Indian philosophical thinking, as a matter of fact its originality. Here we find a thinking that cuts across many of the dichotomies that have presented themselves before western thought as though they are jointly exhaustive, and mutually exclusive, alternatives from amongst which one cannot but choose. These are: rationalism and empiricism, logicism and psychologism, extensionalism and intensionalism, causal and descripture enquiries, logical thinking and the ineffability thesis. Some of these dichotomies are being challenged in contemporary western thought, both analytic and phenomenological. It is exciting to find that the Indian philosophers totally bypassed these restrictive options. In the present philosophical situation, that by itself is instructive and promising. It holds out the promise, not merely of studying Indian thought from the point of view of the western philosophies, but also by reversing that strategy, of critically studying the western philosophies from the vantage points of the typically Indian modes of thinking.

IV

A task which the Indian philosopher of today has to face, which our immediate predecessors either overlooked or took for granted, is: what is living and what is dead in Indian philosophy? It is true that philosophical problems have many lives and some are known to have arisen from their graves. But there is also no

temporal, and the dominance of the a-historical, individualistic concept of *Karma*. Some of these are briefly discussed in J. N. Mohanty.

1. cp. J. N. Mohanty, *Gangesa's Theory of Truth* (Santiniketan, 1966), Introduction, pp. 39-40, esp. fn. 33.

doubt that *today* with the natural sciences separated from their ancestry, it is no longer feasible to think of the sciences as *belonging to* philosophy, howsoever otherwise one may want to understand the relations between the sciences and philosophy. Consequently, a large part of Indian philosophical literature, the part dealing with the atomic theories, theories of physical composition and chemical reaction, classification of living beings, to mention some from a host of themes, should be excised and relegated to the study of history of science.

IV.1. To give another example, possibly a more controversial one : the theory of *śabda* as a *pramāṇa,* indeed as the one mode of knowing which can override all others, needs to be looked at afresh. It is here that tradition and modernity come headlong into conflict. Even if it is true that the life-world does not fully determine the philosophical problems, it nevertheless appears that for a people whose faith in the infallibility of the scriptures is considerably weakened (or if it continues to survive unscathed, it is on the defensive as against the onslaughts of science, technology and modern social and political ideas), *śabdapramāṇa* cannot any longer provide the theoretical basis for a satisfactory philosophy. But that is *not* to reject *śabda* altogether as a *pramāṇa.* What is necessary is to re-examine the priorities and relative strengths and weaknesses. To be sure, no other age since antiquity has been, sheerly on theoretical grounds, more congenial to the idea of recognizing the centrality of linguistic texts in a culture's self-understanding and of language in cognitive, moral and religious lives. But one also needs to recall the distinction between understanding a sentence *p* and knowing that *p*,[1] the *different ways* in which language is central to cognitive enterprise and to moral and religious life,[2] and the problems connected with the notions of a text and its interpretations.[3] These methodological insights would, I believe, rehabilitate the tradition's self-understanding, without returning to that naïve use of *śabdapramāṇa* to which a return is just impossible.

1. cp. J. N. Mohanty, "Language and Reality" in : *Phenomenology and Ontology*.

2. cp. J. N. Mohanty, "Indian Theories of Truth : Their Common Framework" (forthcoming).

3. For this refer to the works of Gadamer, Ricoeur, Derrida and Foucault.

IV.2. Finally, it is also necessary to recognize those areas in which the Indian philosophical tradition made achievements on which we can continue to build. A tentative list of these would be: theories of consciousness, large parts of theory of knowledge and logic, spiritual psychology in the sense of descriptive psychology of mental functions, and grammar, syntax, semantics and phenomenology of language. These, and the specific themes coming under each, provide opportunities for both fruitful encounter between Indian and western thinking, and for possibilities of creative thinking for the Indian philosopher from within the tradition.

IV.3. It is also necessary to bring to our consciousness, the themes and concepts which, though richly available in the larger body of texts in the tradition, failed to come to the forefront in the classical *darśanas*. If there are such themes and such concepts, rescuing them from their 'philosophical anonymity' could provide a strategy for gaining a new look at the tradition itself. To give only two examples : the concepts of body and action. In the *darśanas*, (excepting possibly the Sāṁkhya-Yoga) the human body is but a thing, physico-chemical and living; but in the large mass of Vedic literature as well as in the literature of the Yoga, body is talked about as symbolizing cosmic and subjective principles, as occupying the ambiguous middle region between nature and freedom. Likewise with the concept of action : the domination of the concept of (the law of) *Karma* and an overriding interest in the role of action vis-à-vis knowledge as a means to salvation, did not permit the full development of a theory of action itself, although all its elements were present before the Hindu mind. To attempt such a theory, one needs to consider not merely the logical, and epistemological and psychological sources in the *darśanas*, but also the semantic discussions of imperative sentences as well as legal literature on the permissible and the not-permissible.

IV.4. Not surprisingly, there inevitably are many problems of great philosophical importance, which the Indian philosophical tradition did *not* concern itself with at all. Not all of these can be illuminated from sources within the tradition. In such cases, the Indian philosopher, without abandoning his Indianness, may, and in fact is bound to, go beyond the resources available from within. In an enterprise such as this, he will be a direct participant in a larger dialogue with a larger philosophical community. Indirectly, any philosopher—the Indian philosopher, even when he is engaged in interpreting and creatively developing his tradition—insofar as he is philosophizing, is participating in, and contributing to, a larger global tradition.

V

In conclusion, I should add that it is for the individual thinker to make his own decision as to how he shall resolve the tension between his sense of tradition and his sense of modernity. No authentic thinker can follow, or give, a general recipe. Decisions and commitments are made by individuals. They should be made, with an openness to creative dialogue and with a sensitivity to the 'contemporaneity' of both the tradition and the chronologically contemporary. What is essential is to generate the dialogue.

11

INDIAN PHILOSOPHY : IS THERE A PROBLEM TODAY ?

BIMAL KRISHNA MATILAL*

I have found the expression "Indian Philosophy" puzzling more often than not. For one who has spent most of his life writing books and papers and editing journals on Indian Philosophy, this is an odd admission. But one brief look at the titles of the papers presented in this anthology will vindicate the fact that the expression "Indian Philosophy" is utterly ambiguous and that genuine doubt is entertained by many as to its exact significance. If we contrast "Indian Philosophy" with "Greek Philosophy" or "Chinese Philosophy" then we tend to have a particular understanding of the phrase. We may understand it in such a context as the philosophical thoughts of classical or medieval India, or the philosophical schools or systems called *darśanas*. But the study of Indian philosophy in this sense will be looked upon as a mere philological exercise than a philosophical discipline. At best one can say that this belongs to the discipline of the history of philosophy, or perhaps more correctly to the history of ideas rather than to philosophy proper. I do not think this argument to be always valid.

*B. K. Matilal is Spalding Professor of Eastern Religions and Ethics, Oxford University, England. Studied in Calcutta and Harvard University. Author of *The Navya-Nyaya Doctrine of Negation*; *Language, Grammar and Meaning in Indian Philosophy*. He is also editor of *Journal of Indian Philosophy*.

The classical texts of Indian Philosophy can be studied in a way that may fall under the discipline of the history of ideas. But often history of ideas is primarily *history*, and hence such a study will involve essentially a historical enquiry. But the history of philosophy is, as one modern philosopher has put it,[1] philosophy before it is history. Therefore, if the study of the classical Indian philosophy, or as the moderners call it, 'traditional Indian philosophy',[2] is regarded as falling within the discipline of the history of philosophy, as opposed to the history of ideas, then it can hardly be separated from the general study of philosophy. I shall come back to this point later.

Sometimes "Indian philosophy" is contrasted with "Western philosophy", and immediately the phrase takes on a new shade of meaning. This meaning is, however, by no means clear; it has, I venture to add, an amorphous nature. For some people, Indian philosophy has a distinct character, namely, it is overwhelmingly spiritual (and some critics say "euphoric"), and, therefore, is in sharp contrast with the materialism of the West. Some say that it is other-worldly while the Western philosophy is this-worldly and hence scientific. The attitude toward this other-worldliness or the *mokṣa*-orientedness of Indian philosophy may vary from being one of over-enthusiasm to that of utter disapproval and condemnation. Over-enthusiasm for this other-worldliness need not detain us long. For this is generally found in un-informed dreamers who generally believe that Oriental mysticism is the answer to all the ills of modern Western civilization. In almost the same way, we may dismiss the other extreme view about Indian philosophy. For those who condemn Indian philosophy as not being philosophy at all but a bundle of dogmas and mystifying and unproductive statements about man and the world, are equally un-informed about the wealth of genuinely philosophical material contained in the classical texts of India.[3]

There are, however, some serious formulations of the above views about Indian philosophy, which cannot be easily dispensed with. For it is undeniable that the classical systems of Indian

1. Bernard Williams : *Descartes : The Project of Pure Enquiry* (Penguin, 1978), p. 9.

2. Kalidas Bhattacharyya's paper in this volume, Chapter 8.

3. Antony Flew : *An Introduction to Western Philosophy* (London : Thames & Hudson, 1971), p. 36.

darśanas are *mokṣa*-oriented whereas the concept of philosophy has a different origin in the West. Philosophy, as the etymology of the word indicates, was connected with 'the love of knowledge' or 'the love of wisdom'. But a little investigation shows that each *darśana* holds that the so-called *mokṣa* or the ultimate freedom of man is achieved, directly or indirectly, on the basis of our knowledge of the reality (*tattvajñāna*). In other words, each *darśana* was engaged in constructing a metaphysical system and adhered to the belief that our knowledge of the reality (as captured in its metaphysics) leads to the ultimate freedom of man. Thus, the *darśanas* of India were not very strikingly different from the old-fashioned philosophies of the West.

Besides, from A.D. 400 onwards, Indian philosophers showed genuine interest in the analysis of knowledge and argument, in the criteria of knowledge that reveals reality, in the theories of logic and dialectics, in the search for a sound philosophical argument, and so on. The literature on these issues is very rich and varied. But unfortunately most of this material lies buried under the treasure-chest of Sanskrit. This also proves that sound philological research is very useful even for genuine philosophical purpose. In my own view, to be sure, for research in traditional Indian philosophy, philological competence is almost indispensable. In any case, one thing is clear. The material that deals with the above issues cannot be but philosophical even in the modern sense of the term. Therefore, concern for *mokṣa* was not in any way detrimental to their philosophic interest. And some even argue that this concern actually adds to their special charm.

It may be argued that since the goal of *darśanas* was *mokṣa* or *nirvāṇa*, they were primarily therapeutics of *mokṣa*, and the philosophical, epistemological or logical issues discussed therein were only incidental. In other words, one may say, repeating an old argument that the *darśanas* were 'therapeutics' first before they were philosophies, just as the history of ideas is history before it is philosophy. If this is conceded then, the argument continues, to the extent our concern for *mokṣa* diminishes or wanes in modern human societies, these therapeutics lose their value or usefulness, and, consequently, the philosophic discussions that sustained such therapeutics become myths or museum-pieces. It will not do to point out, as against this position, that much of medieval Western philosophy was inextricably mixed with theology, soteriology and religious beliefs, for that point is already conceded. The balance is said to tilt in favour of Western philosophy partly because of the 'resilience' of the philosophic issues discussed by the medievals and partly because of the rational reconstructions of the ancient and medieval doctrines that modern study of them demands and delivers.

I will cite two arguments to refute the above position. First, it is not true to say that *darśanas* were primarily *mokṣa-śāstras,* and hence philosophy was only incidental to them. For the ancient and medieval writers on *darśanas* were consciously and deliberately participating in philosophic discussions and using what may be called philosophic methodology. What Vātsyāyana says of *Nyāya-darśana* holds generally true of other *darśanas* as well. Referring to the four-fold classification of disciplines which form the subject matter of study, the Vedic scriptures (*trayī*), agriculture and commerce (*vārttā*), politics and law (*daṇḍanīti*), and philosophy (*ānvīkṣikī*),[1] Vātsyāyana comments that each discipline has its own distinct *prasthāna* or method (Vācaspati glosses "*prasthāna*" as "*upāya*"), and this distinct method of the fourth one, *ānvīkṣikī,* or philosophy, is illustrated by its special examination of the sixteen categories which include means of knowledge, objects of knowledge, validity or invalidity of arguments, determination of truth and so on.[2] It may be said that I have taken here an unwarranted liberty in translating "*ānvīkṣikī*" as "philosophy." But this is not true. For Kauṭilya, who first talked about the four-fold classification of disciplines and from whom Vātsyāyana quoted, clearly used the term in the general sense of philosophy. For example, he cited three schools as examples of *ānvīkṣikī*; the metaphysical school of the Sāṁkhya, the twin school of Nyāya-Vaiśeṣika and the materialism of the *Cārvākas.*[3]

Vātsyāyana, in fact, argued that it is this distinct 'method' (*prasthāna*) that is essential to ānvīkṣikī (=philosophy), for otherwise this discipline would be indistinguishable from *adhyātma-vidyā* or *mokṣa-śāstra.*[4] I argue that this is true of the classical

1. I take the liberty of translating "*ānvīkṣikī*" as "philosophy".
2. Vātsyāyana on *Nyāyasūtra* 1.1.1.
3. Kautilya : *Arthaśāstra* (ed. Kangle), Bombay.
4. Vātsyāyana, *op. cit.*

darśanas in general, not simply of Nyāya. The Vedic scriptures along with the *Upaniṣads*, undoubtedly, constitute the *mokṣa-śāstra*. But the *darśanas* followed a distinct methodology, and formed an entirely separate discipline. Thus, my point is that the classical texts of *darśanas* were not therapeutics for *nirvāṇa* but dealt with philosophy properly and in all seriousness that their time, society and environment allowed.

Second, it must be pointed out that, even if, our concern for *nirvāṇa* wanes and consequently the therapeutics for such *nirvāṇa* lose significance, it does not necessarily follow that the philosophical bases of such therapeutics undergo total collapse or become automatically museum-pieces. In fact even a brief perusal of the contents of such texts as Dharmakīrti's *Pramāṇavārttika*, Jayanta's *Nyāyamañjari*, or Śrīharṣa's *Khaṇḍana-Khaṇḍakhādya*, shows clearly that the philosophic issues discussed by these classical thinkers are not altogether dead horses today. The concern of these classical Indian thinkers was genuinely philosophical even in its present-day sense, and their additional concern for *mokṣa* was hardly able to overshadow their genuine philosophical interest. Thus there is hardly any real reason, except, perhaps a parochial one, to argue in favour of the 'resilience' of the philosophical issues discussed by the medievals in the Western tradition, and the lack of such resilience in the case of the philosophic problems pondered over by the classical Indian thinkers. To put the matter strongly, if the study of Plato, Aristotle, Descartes, Hume and Kant, is useful for a modern student of philosophy, the study of Uddyotakara, Kumārila and Udayana is also relevant for him in the same way, provided, of course, he can overcome "the language barrier" that stands in the way. If a rational reconstruction of Descartes or writing a modern commentary on Aristotle's *Metaphysics*, is considered as part of creative philosophic activity today, I do not see why such a rational reconstruction of Diṅnāga or a modern commentary on Gaṅgeśa cannot be regarded as falling within the discipline of philosophy.

It must be noted that I have used the word 'philosophy' so far in a particular sense. This is the sense that is usually attached to 'philosophy' by the modern academic philosophers, specially by those who consider themselves as belonging to the modern analytic tradition in the West. But philosophy, it may be argued, is not just analyses and logic, epistemology and theory of meaning. It is also rational speculation and metaphysics, existentialism and phenomenology. It is arguable, however, that the study of certain classical Indian systems such as Advaita Vedānta or Mahāyāna Buddhism provides useful insights even when 'philosophy' is understood in this sense. But one does not need to labour this point any further.

This brings us to yet another sense that may be attached to the phrase "Indian philosophy". By this term we may be asked to record the recent philosophical activities in India. We may be required to consider what the Indian professional philosophers, academics, and thinkers today have been doing vis-à-vis their Western compatriots. What contributions, if any, have they made recently to the field of 'philosophy' by which one may understand simply Western philosophic tradition? The use of 'philosophy' in the exclusive sense of Western philosophy is quite widespread, and, therefore, such a question is quite reasonable for one to ask. Western philosophy, like Western education and Western science and technology, is, after all, being studied by the Indian professionals for over a hundred years. In reply to the above question, one may point out that creative and critical writings by the Indian professionals on Western philosophy may be rare, but not altogether non-existent today. We have metaphysicians like Kalidas Bhattacharyya, phenomenologists like J. N. Mohanty (whose interest in Frege and Quine is also well-known), logicians like Sibajivan and P. K. Sen, and Marxist-Socialists like S. N. Ganguly, economist philosophers like A. K. Sen. One may understandably raise the question of the 'Indianness' of the writings of these philosophers. In reply we can say that at least some like Mohanty and Sibajivan have consciously indulged in creative-comparative thinking for they have sound grounding in the classical Indian systems. In the case of others one can probably talk about an unconscious influence of the Indian background of their authors, and such an influence is not always intractable.

Let me emphasise again that one does not need an apology for justifying the study of classical Indian philosophy today, nor one needs to puzzle about the 'Indianness' of any philosophic writings. As my own training and research have been in the field of classical Indian philosophy, I wish to comment briefly about the research method in this particular field. In an earlier writing[1] I had referred to two particular barriers for the modern student to the study of Indian philosophy : the language barrier and the prevailing misconception (not necessarily altogether Western) about what Indian philosophy is. I still believe firmly that sound philological scholarship is a highly desirable requirement. Besides, it is necessary to have a good understanding of what counts as a philosophic problem discussed in the classical texts. Such an understanding should be supplemented by a reasonably thorough study of the relevant problems discussed in contemporary philosophic circles. Thus, a modern student of the classical Indian philosophy need not fall between the two stools.

'Comparative philosophy' has acquired a bad reputation mainly because of the failures and lack of depth of the early comparativists. The early comparativists not only misunderstood the nature and the extent of the problem they were trying to grapple with but they also lacked insight and adequate preparations. But the task of explaining and translating classical Indian philosophical texts in a Western language by a modern scholar involves automatically a sort of comparison and contrast between the moderners and the ancients. I have called this method 'comparative philosophy in a minimal sense' in the absence of a better term. In fact, 'comparative philosophy' in this minimal sense, may be seen as falling within the discipline of the history of philosophy in the global sense. Since it has already been argued that the history of philosophy is philosophy primarily, the above task should also fall within the general discipline of philosophy.

The purpose of the Indian philosopher today, who chooses to work on the classical systems, is to interpret and thereby offer a medium where philosophers, using the word to mean those who pursue rationally arguable answers to meaningful questions, both Indian and Western, may converse. For such philosophic research I strongly recommend the above method, for I have taken time to convince myself that there does not exist a world of difference between a considerable portion of the problems discussed by the ancients and those discussed by the modern philosophers today.

1. B. K. Matilal : *Epistemology, Logic and Grammar in Indian Philosophical Analysis* (The Hague : Mouton, 1971), pp. 9-10.

12

INDIAN PHILOSOPHY AT THE CROSSROADS

J. S. R. L. NARAYANA MOORTY*

INDIAN philosophy is at the crossroads. It has been there for the past five decades or so, since the British system of university education opened it to the influence of British and Continental philosophy. Now it is being influenced by both the Analytic and Phenomenological movements. Most contemporary Indian philosophers are still rooted in their tradition, yet they feel incumbent to meet the challenge of Western philosophy. In the process they are engaged in a variety of responses : (i) they are impressed by the Analytical and Phenomenological methods of the West and ask what in their tradition is salvageable and comparable to the Western system of ideas;[1] (ii) they try to impress their Western counterparts by presenting an apologetic of their favourite system or systems of Indian philosophy *vis-à-vis* Western criticisms of them;[2] (iii) they construct their own

*J. S. R. L. Narayana Moorty teaches philosophy at Monterey Peninsula College, Monterey, California. He has contributed articles to the Philosophy and Religion Volume of the *Telugu Encyclopaedia* and papers to *Indian Philosophical Quarterly*, *Visva Bharati Journal of Philosophy* and other magazines and newspapers in India.

1. I have in mind philosophers like Professors Bimal Krishna Matilal and J. N. Mohanty.

2. Professors Sarvepalli Radhakrishnan and T. M. P. Mahadevan are typical examples of this sort of philosophers.

systems of philosophy based on Indian intuitions, but present them in a Western garb.[1] Other Indian philosophers who specialize totally or partially in one branch or another of Western philosophy[2] think that there is nothing really genuinely philosophical in the Indian tradition, or they just are not interested in it.

Outside of these academic philosophers, we have seers and thinkers who may or may not be accorded the recognition of being philosophers, but who, nevertheless, have taught philosophies of various kinds and even built systems of their own within the framework of the Indian philosophical tradition.[3] They are the traditional '*guru*' type teachers. In addition to all these there are also one or two teachers who at least claim they disregard all tradition and present their intuitions of life and Reality but are not recognized as philosophers by the academic world because they do not write in a recognized systematic philosophic form.[4] Their teachings are, however, full of insights, and there are some similarities of content and method between their teachings and some of the teachings of the *Upaniṣads* or of the Buddha.

Here I shall examine two of these typical responses as to what Indian philosophy is or ought to be, argue that both of these views suffer from shortcomings, and offer my own alternative to them.

The following passages from a recent book by Professor B. K. Matilal illustrates one contemporary view of Indian philosophy :

> "Indian philosophy has unfortunately come to denote a group of occult religious cults, a system of dogmas, and an odd assortment of spirituality, mysticism, and imprecise thinking concerned almost exclusively with 'spiritual liberation.' "[5]

1. Professors K. C. Bhattacharya, Kalidas Bhattacharyya and K. S. Murty are examples of philosophers who have philosophized in the Kantian, Phenomenological or Existential mode, respectively.

2. Professors Sibajivan Bhattacharya and Rajendra Prasad belong to this category of philosophers.

3. Sri Aurobindo, Sri Ramana Maharshi, Sri Ramakrishna, Swami Vivekananda, Ma Ananda Mayi are teachers of this kind.

4. For instance, J. Krishnamurti.

5. B. K. Matilal, *Epistemology, Logic and Grammar in Indian Philosophical Analysis* (The Hague : Mouton, 1971), p. 10.

The historical reasons for this emphasis on spirituality are given by the author as follows:

> "...India, after a period of stagnation followed by several centuries of foreign domination, was facing the challenge of modern civilization and the superior technology of the West, and, as a result, desperately looking for an identity and a way of self-assertion. Some of the national leaders of India at this stage sought an escape in the mystical awe of so-called Indian 'spirituality'. All these are unfortunate historical facts—unfortunate because Indian philosophy, as a result of this movement, has remained identified with mysticism and mistakenly thought to be inseparable from religion."[1]

In contrast to this tendency, Professor Matilal construes a serious study of Indian philosophy to consist of

> "...a number of rigorous systems which are more concerned with logic and epistemology, with the analysis and classification of human knowledge, than they are with transcendent states of euphoria. Verification and rational procedures are as much an essential part of Indian philosophical thinking as they are in Western philosophical thinking."[2]

These passages betray a sense of impatience with anything in Indian philosophy which the Western analytical trend does not recognize as authentic human knowledge. Unfortunately, the same historical reasons which the author attributes to the emphasis on spirituality can just as well be attributed to the preoccupation with logic and epistemology and with "the analysis and classification of human knowledge". It is clear that what was central to a great portion of Indian philosophy for centuries, and around which numerous philosophies have been built—the Brahman experience in Vedānta, or the experience of *Nirvāṇa* in Buddhism, to mention only a couple of examples—gets thrown overboard because it does not fit the fashionable definition of knowledge acceptable to Professor Matilal. Moreover, even some eminent Western philosophers like Heidegger, Marcel or Jaspers would not limit the definition of knowledge to what is publicly verifiable, and might consider such transcendent experiences as authentic.

To what exactly is Professor Matilal referring when he says that Indian philosophy has "unfortunately come to denote..an odd assortment of spirituality, mysticism"? Does this mean, for example, that the *Upaniṣads* and the Buddha's teachings and the philosophy of Nāgārjuna or Śaṁkara are no longer to

1. B. K. Matilal, *Epistemology Logic and Grammar in Indian Philosophical Analysis* (The Hague : Mouton, 1971), p. 11.
2. *Ibid.*

be considered as serious philosophy? Is only Nyāya to be considered as serious philosophy? What justification is there to ignore everything else? Because there are no rational arguments. Is the presence of such argument essential to every form of philosophical opinion? If so, then Vedānta, Buddhism, Sāṁkhya and Yoga, etc., all have arguments to bolster their positions. So they too ought to be considered as philosophy. What about the *Bhagavad Gitā* which stands in between the teachings of the *Upaniṣads* and the systems? And what of the sources of inspiration of these systems? For instance, what makes one think that the series of investigations into the nature of Reality in the *Upaniṣads* made by the seers and the investigations of the Buddha into the nature, cause and removal of suffering, are not philosophy? The only reason why one would not consider these as philosophy seems to be that some of these opinions do not seem to be subject to empirical verification. But by the same token, the Nyāya theory of knowledge which seems acceptable to Professor Matilal and which considers knowledge as a quality of the soul must also not be considered part of philosophy because the existence of the soul is unverifiable.

A consequence of such an attitude is that teachers like the Buddha who are alive today are not even recognized as philosophers. Only what their grand-followers might say two centuries later in interpreting and defending them through rational argument would alone be considered philosophy. The function of philosophy in this understanding would amount to a critical examination of propositions concerning knowledge, meaning, or consciousness, and testing them for their internal consistency and cogency. At least one of the main functions (if not *the* function) of philosophy, namely, as a means of liberation or attaining Brahman or *Ātman* experience or *Nirvāṇa*, is discarded in this understanding. These passages also ignore the fact that in the Indian tradition, although logical and epistemological studies are important, they are only ancillary to other studies, say the study of Vedānta.

There are some further consequences of this view. Traditionally, moral and value theories were developed as part and parcel of a metaphysical theory. Values and morals are all made generally subservient to a theory of liberation. If we debunk spirituality and liberation then we are not left with any theory of morals or of values. A philosopher of the persuasion of Professor Matilal would not be able to provide, if he had situated himself in the Indian philosophical tradition as he would like to do, any moral or value theory of any guidance to contemporary problems. At best, he would, through his analytical and verificationist persuasions, provide a meta-ethical theory of ethics, but not a normative theory which might be of value to contemporary man.

In contrast to Professor Matilal's view of Indian philosophy, let us consider a more conservative response which would like to preserve Indian tradition in its entirety, as in the following contemporary interpretation of the Vedānta:

> "(1) The Self is different from the mental modes because it is the witness of those modes, whatever is not different from the modes is not the witness thereof, as, e.g. a mental mode, etc. (2) The Self is real, because it is the substratum of what illusorily appears, as nacre is of the illusory silver. (3) The Self is of the nature of consciousness, because it illumines what is inert, as e.g. a pot. (4) The Self is the supreme bliss, because it is the seat of absolute love; what is not the supreme bliss does not become the seat of absolute love, as, e.g. a pot. (5) The Self is plenum, because it is related to or is the basis of all, like ether.
>
> The Self that is the reality is the supreme value in the sense that there is nothing else that can serve as the ultimate human goal (*parama-puruṣārtha*) or release (*mokṣa*)."[1]

The passage above seems to be telling us what the Self is, and how we can prove it exists. But somehow the words in it seem to have lost their meaning to us. We might verbally understand it, yet we do not get the faintest idea of what the Self really is. The passage may just as well be compatible with the idea that there is no such thing as the Self. For instance, we have no idea of what 'absolute love', 'witness' and 'supreme bliss', etc. mean, because these notions are not given any concrete content. When we look under the heading "*Release*" in the same article, we read that "release is attained and bondage 'destroyed' when nescience is removed."

> "Release is eternal, and it is the ever attained. On account of nescience it seems to be unattained as it were. Similarly, bondage is not real, being nescience-caused. At the rise of knowledge, it is removed as it were, being already removed."[2]

1. T. M. P. Mahadevan, "The Insights of Advaita," in Margaret Chatterjee (ed.) *Coutemporary Indian Philosophy*, Series II (London : George Allen & Unwin, 1974), p. 129.

2. *Ibid.*, p. 130.

Again we have no idea of what is being talked about in any concrete way. Generalities and vaguenesses plague such passages. This may be the source of philosophical disillusionment with and alienation from tradition that exists in contemporary India. The passages do not supply the connecting links between man's current life experience and the experience of the self. No wonder, words like *māyā*, *avidyā*, *karma*, *ātman* and Brahman have become such banalities in modern India. Passages like the above form part of a traditionalist understanding of Indian philosophy, viz. that the scriptures contain the truth concerning Reality and the Self, and the business of philosophy is to expound, interpret and defend the scriptures.

The above two views concerning the nature and function of Indian philosophy are neither mutually exclusive nor exhaustive of the field of Indian philosophizing. The present essay presents a third alternative as to the function of contemporary Indian philosophy, an alternative which combines some elements of both the views and goes beyond them. This alternative preserves what is unique to Indian philosophy, yet makes it methodologically more acceptable to the contemporary mind. It also addresses itself to the contemporary needs of man, thus supplying a direction to the Indian philosopher at the crossroads.

Philosophy must remain true to its origins and its original mission. Philosophy arose, both in the West and in the East, in man's attempts to find answers to some fundamental questions concerning the nature of the universe and human existence. But gradually philosophers also had to pay attention to the question of how to communicate these answers to other men, particularly other philosophers, once they had found them. In the course of history, Western philosophy and to a degree Indian philosophy, also, have increasingly given way to a discussion of the means of communication and questions of epistemology. Such problems of communication and knowledge arose when there was no consensus as to whether a certain answer was the right answer, or when others doubted whether that answer was an answer at all. There has been an excessive preoccupation with refining tools of communication, analysis, and argument to the neglect of the answers that philosophers could have sought. The reasons for this preoccupation is that philosophers have come to think that purely rational and speculative systems of philosophy do not and cannot yield indisputable results, and what can be known must be publicly verifiable, or found in one's immediate contents of consciousness (*á la* Phenomenology). At least in the Analytic tradition, philosophy does not bake any more cakes than science.

In the West, for reasons of public life in a democracy, no demands are placed on the personal life of the philosopher *qua* philosopher except those of a purely professional ethics. We have imported this into India and said it does not matter how a philosopher lives, as long as he teaches and writes philosophy according to the officially accepted norms. While professionally no demands can be placed on his personal life, morally, I think, a philosopher, at least in the Indian philosophic tradition, is abdicating his responsibility as a philosopher if he separates his life from his philosophy, if he does not at least try to live the way he preaches, making every effort to get back to the experiencing of Reality and to communicate to his fellow men in an idiom they can understand.

At least one fundamental characteristic of Indian philosophy (and Indian tradition in general) is a recognition of an Ultimate Reality, of some sort of experience of it, and of such an experience providing liberation from the humdrum of everyday life, while at the same time providing a fundamental solution to the problems of living and of the intellect.

It is quite possible that some philosophers, owing to whatever influences from the West, might not recognize any of these, indeed any experience out of the ordinary, and find a solution to problems of living and of the mind through empirical and rational methods. But does this mean that this should be the only serious study of Indian philosophy ?

Of course, philosophers have no specially privileged access to Reality. Poets, artists, scientists and even common folks have their own access to Reality. Only the means of access chosen by the philosopher are different. A philosopher experiences Reality and communicates his experience to his fellow men in a philosophical idiom and thus makes Reality (or Being, if you will) accessible to them. But just because he does not always choose to express his experience in a systematic or argumentative form, it is sheer prejudice not to consider him a philosopher.

And then, of course, we will have interpreters of such expressions, in terms of system-building, and defenders, etc., and the logicians who are only interested in the instruments of communication. They too are philosophers, but only in a borrowed sense. For if we remove the source of inspiration of philosophizing, which is the experience of Reality, all the rest become puerile exercises of reason. Their products may be applicable in various walks of life, but somehow they lack substance. At that point the Indian philosopher, like his Western counterpart, would be caught in the world of common experience, leaving the important problems of the meaning of our existence and the fundamental solution of them to the priest, the psychoanalyst, the politician and the charlatan.

Although philosophers in the full sense of the term can and do have access to Reality themselves, they or other philosophers can spend their time formulating the conditions of access to Reality. They set forth somewhat systematically the positive and negative conditions for access to Reality, such as, for example, that one has to become at least temporarily free from dualistic thought and the field of the known to have access to Reality. Such formulations have to be constantly revised in view of the latest logical refinements, and re-expressed in the current idiom. While the philosopher formulates conditions of access, an artist provides access through the work of art, and the scientist through his scientific discoveries. None of these means of access to Reality is necessarily superior to any other.

So, inasmuch as they themselves have access to Reality, the artist, the philosopher, the scientist and the common man might be considered philosophers in the original sense of the term, while the philosophers who only interpret such an experience, analyze it, and communicate the conditions of access to others are philosophers only in a secondary sense. Their means of providing access to Reality is different from those of others. Technically speaking, this is what makes them philosophers. They have the unique logical capabilities of making explicit what is implicit in the positive and negative conditions for such an experience of Reality, while the artist or the scientist provides the means without bothering to tell us how or why the means do or should provide access to Reality.

It has been shown time and again in the history of human thought, particularly in the Indian tradition, that the experience of Reality does provide answers to the most fundamental metaphysical and psychological problems of man. The search for unity in man's understanding of the universe and the search for a unifying experience are both satisfied in such an experience of Reality. Instead of trying to provide an answer in a rational system, the experience dispels the questions. Only when the experience is translated into a rationalist, dualistic garb of thought does it cease to be unifying, but this does not mean that the experience itself is dualistic. Of course, any formulation of it has to be necessarily dualistic, due to the nature of thought and concepts, as has been repeatedly demonstrated by philosophers like Nāgārjuna.

An objection can be raised at this point, in the spirit of the Analytic tradition, viz., what empirical evidence is there for saying either that such Being or Reality exists or that anyone has an experience of or access to it ? Notice that this objection does not (or at least should not, except in terms of the logical cogency of any formulation of such experience) arise from the phenomenological tradition, for if that tradition accepts the immediate evidence given in one's consciousness as final, and if there is no contradiction in the concept of such an experience, then there could not arise any objection against its possibility. Only in the Analytical tradition we have the requirement that in order for someone to meaningfully talk about any experience it must be publicly verifiable. But such verification applies only to experience of finite things, and when the experience is of the unlimited, which by definition Reality is, it fails to apply. It may very well be that this experience occurs in a non-interpretative or non-categorizing mode. But such a characterization of the experience lands us in a difficulty, namely, that of the dualism between the subject and the object, which the experience of Reality by definition transcends. If we interpret the experience as an experience which is free from the categories of thought, and therefore one of pure sensation, then again we land in a difficulty, viz., of limiting Reality to what is given in sensation only, while Reality by definition is not so limited. For example, what about the mental givens, like feelings, emotions and so forth ? Or, again, if we describe the experience of Reality as a non-intentional, self-luminous intuitive consciousness, etc., as the Vedāntists might do, this is itself a distortion of such an experience which cannot be comprehended in *any* of the known categories. As we said above, from this it does not follow that no conditions can be set forth for the access to Reality. That precisely is part of the work of philosophy. For example, one way of experiencing Reality is by transcending thought which can only comprehend the limited. This can itself be achieved by any of various means.

If such conditions are followed and Reality is still not experienced, one has the right to ask why the means did not work, how they could be further improved, or whether alternative means could be proposed, and so on. But just because one personally has not had access to such Reality, one has no right to debunk the experience itself as merely speculative, unverified and superstitious. Also, to deny a philosophical formulation of a certain experience as being incoherent or logically untenable is not necessarily to have a right to deny the experience itself which is thus formulated. In fact, in philosophies like Buddhism, we have persuasive demonstration that such a Reality cannot be comprehended by rational means, and its experience cannot be described by any philosophical system or set of ideas.

Another objection might be raised here, namely, how can such an experience of Reality be distinguished from any extraordinary experience? How do we know, for instance, whether it is Reality we experience and not just a state of mind, perhaps induced by drugs or someother means? How do we know that there is an object corresponding to the experience of Reality?

The urge to verify one's experience is part of our ordinary experience of finite objects. Experience of Reality in that sense cannot be verified. We can never *know* that we experience Reality; for one thing the process of verification by its very nature alienates one from the experience itself and renders it by definition dualistic. One who has such an experience must realize that it does, however, satisfy his metaphysical and psychological urges and at the same time, to some degree or other, transform his life. If a person shows signs of such a transformation (or even if he does not, but has some other way of indicating that he has achieved an integration of his thought or of his psyche), that is a kind of pragmatic verification that such an experience has indeed occurred, or at least is possible in some people.

A third objection takes off on the second and says that if there is no necessary connection between experience and transformation of oneself, i.e., if one can occur without the other, then we cannot use the transformation as a test for the occurrence of such an experience.

It may be true that experience of Reality in someone may not necessarily result in the transformation of his life in the sense that he lives creatively, lovingly and harmoniously with other people. However, it is highly unlikely that a person whose life is completely transformed, has not experienced Reality.

Another critical objection that can be raised in this context is what sense does it make to say that some experience which cannot be translated into any dualistic thought is an answer to all our fundamental metaphysical and psychological questions ? The answer to this question lies in an admission that dualistic, separative thought is precisely the reason for and the source of the fundamental questions and that these questions cannot be answered fundamentally by the dualistic thought itself, but only in a state of being where such thought is absent. One can further admit that such a state of being is in reality not as much an answer as a state in which the questions are dissolved, (where such questions do not arise any more). Moreover, such a state provides an insight into the nature of dualistic thought itself which prompts us to ask such questions.

A question here can also be raised as to whether this sort of philosophical enterprise does not limit philosophy to just spiritual matters, while the problems of the mundane world such as moral ones are left untouched.

The answer is that just the contrary is true. It is the analytical and verificational approach to philosophy that would neglect moral matters and matters of value, because it has no fundamental way of deciding between conflicting ethical claims, except for some purely formal requirements, as a consequence of which we have in the West purely meta-ethical discussions. Some Indian philosophers, as illustrated above, are not even interested in discussing ethical matters because they have no way of dealing with them.

What moral guidance can the experience of Reality provide then ? The answer can take any of a variety of forms, depending on how one construes such an experience. One can say that through identification with various things, ideas and persons, all human problems arise out of the dualistic mind which sets one in opposition to other men and creates conflict, and, therefore, the primary aim of all morality must be to encourage men to become free from their self-centredness created by the dualistic mind by means of some kind of de-conditioning self-knowledge. Or one can take the approach that access to Reality, being the most ultimately satisfying experience, would, once obtained, turn one's attention away from mundane pleasures, and at the same time provide the necessary harmony among human beings, because the ordinary motives of seeking pleasure and avoiding pain and other selfish motives, which alone create the strife and disharmony between oneself and others, are no longer operative.

In this context, I would like to mention J. Krishnamurti, who is not even considered generally as a philosopher in the academic world, as an example of a philosopher who not only reports on his personal experiences of Reality,[1] but also draws the consequences of such an experience for human problems and living.[2] Another important figure is Professor Paul F. Schmidt who questions his own Analytical and Logical Positivist background, draws some consequences for living from his own experiences of Reality, and sets them in the context of Existentialism and Buddhism, etc.[3]

It seems to me that the contemporary Indian philosopher at the crossroads has a choice. He can embrace the Analytical and verificationist approach of the West and abandon the uniquely 'spiritual' character of Indian philosophy and its ethical consequences. If he is still interested in Indian philosophy, it would be to make a historical study of it by translating texts, analyzing them and comparing some of the ideas in them with ideas in the philosophies of the West. He may even incorporate them in his philosophizing in a Western form. Such studies would have a value similar to that of doing any history of philosophy. The philosopher certainly has a right to choose what

1. J. Krishnamurti, *Notebook* (New York : Harper, 1973).

2. J. Krishnamurti, *Flight of the Eagle* (New York : Harper, 1971).

3. Paul F. Schmidt, *Rebelling, Loving and Liberation* (Albuquerque: Hummingbird Press, 1971).

interests him in the history of philosophy and ignore the rest. This does not imply, however, that he has a right to debunk the spiritual element of Indian philosophy as non-philosophy.

Or, the Indian philosopher can choose to rejuvenate the tradition of Indian philosophy by attempting to experience Reality first hand, if possible, and, if not, to attempt to make sense of what other philosophers, artists, scientists and common men claim about their experience of Reality. When one does not believe that such an experience is possible, one goes to the other alternatives. But if one sees it as possible, then I think, one has a responsibility of preserving what is valuable and unique in Indian philosophy.

Even if a philosopher temporarily chooses to ignore the spiritual aspects of the Indian philosophical tradition, metaphysical and psychological questions will keep haunting him, and sooner or later he will turn and return to these questions which demand answers. And the answers can, ultimately, be found only in the experience of Reality in which he transcends conditioned existence and in which his psyche can find inexhaustible nourishment. A philosopher who has not paid heed to his original quest has perhaps not been true to his calling.

13

INDIAN PHILOSOPHY AT THE CROSSROADS OF SELF-UNDERSTANDING

DEBABRATA SINHA*

I

THE expression 'philosophical culture', that I have borrowed from Edmund Husserl,[1] may be used to indicate the broad frame of reference, within which a philosophic tradition originates, flourishes and continues. For a particular philosophic tradition can hardly be viewed apart from the total cultural orientation. There is an essential interaction of the two—a two-way movement—philosophic tradition reflecting the foundations of the culture at large, and at the same time finding its expressions in and through the various culture forms and institutions, in terms of which the whole life of a people is crystallized. The intent of such a tradition would depend, to an essential measure, on how the tradition *understands* itself, at certain critical phases of its development. And, of course, the older and, to that extent,

*D. Sinha is Professor of Philosophy, Brock University, Canada. He is the author of *The Idealist Standpoint : A Study in the Vedantic Metaphysic of Experience*; *Studies in Phenomenology*; *Phenomenology and Existentialism : An Introduction*.

1. Husserl speaks of "philosophische Kultur" in one of his manuscripts (hitherto unpublished), with reference to which I introduced a 'comparative' discourse on the theme of theory-practice relation. The present context of my use of the expression, however, is not exactly the same as Husserlian one. See my article, "Theory and practice in Indian thought : Husserl's observations" *Philosophy East and West*, XXI (July 1971), 255-64.

more complex a philosophic tradition grows, the more 'critical' is the task of its self-understanding.

In this regard, the Indian philosopher today would find himself between tradition and contemporaneity combining an awareness of heritage with a sense of distantiation from the same. It could yet be challenging and interesting, as any paradoxical situation could be. Only it goes beyond a theoretical paradox, it touches the very mode of our living—it is an existential challenge too. Completely exposed to Western philosophical discipline(s), the Indian philosopher today, when he looks to his own thought tradition, is apt to find himself in a strangely ambiguous position. For he partakes of the great tradition of the *Darśanas* in a direct or indirect manner, and yet sees himself more or less alienated from that tradition. Whether he recognizes or not, the question of identity and continuity seems to be inevitably present in his mind, as he sways between the polarities of tradition-involvement and of participatory response to the *Zeitgeist.*

How, then, does and should, the present-day philosopher of India take his position in respect of his own philosophic tradition? Before coming to the question, I might consider certain phases in the interaction of the Indian mind to the impact of Western thought. (a) At one end, the scholastic-Sanskritic tradition of the Pundits, with all its rigour and authenticity, yet posed a complete indifference to the intellectual-scholarly climate of the modern world, without any effort to relate with the latter. (Few exceptions in this regard could only prove the general rule.) (b) The second form of this encounter may be characterized as a partially 'defensive' approach, which seeks to discover Western parallels to the concepts and strands in ancient and classical Indian thought. The thrust in such endeavour has been mainly to translate Indian notions, problems and doctrines in terms of Western philosophical idioms and conceptual framework, as far as the latter are readily available. The eagerness to find ready parallels often meant an effort to read certain typical Western theories and standpoints into Indian thought. Thus, for example, a characterization of Advaita Vedānta as 'absolutistic' (Hegelian) or as 'absolute idealism' of the Bradleyan type, or to line up Buddhist Vijñānavāda with the subjective idealism of the Berkeleyan type, could be cited as attempts in this direction.

Such semi-defensive expository treatments of the historical systems were still a worthwhile step towards an understanding of the philosophical heritage of India in the modern philosophical language, particularly, considering the historical-political context of the Indian subcontinent in that period. Yet the zeal for bringing the older thought in line with modern Western thought quite often amounted to a juxtaposition of doctrines and concepts pertaining to the two traditions of thought and culture. But in that enterprise, the genuine perspective of Indian thought, with its typical 'ethos', was not necessarily brought into focus, nor was the social and historical background (as far as available) taken into consideration.

A third approach, not often to be met with, concerns itself with a thematic-problematic reflection in terms of the system in view, looking for genuine *philosophical* problems and questions therein. The exposition here does not involve a mere 'comparative' interpretation, in an effort to find out parallels, but rather an attempt to understand the particular standpoint from within and to relate it to certain strands of Western thought only in respect of thematic relevance. Krishna Chandra Bhattacharyya is the outstanding example, and a rare one, of this type of endeavour in recent Indian philosophy. In this connexion the observations of Kalidas Bhattacharyya in his editorial introduction to *Recent Indian Philosophy* may be worth mentioning. Bhattacharyya sums up the broad trends in the contributions of the Indian philosophers during the second and third decades of the century as follows :

> "The history of modern Indian philosophy thus presents the picture of even the best brains applying themselves seriously to the fundamentals of the Western and the old Indian philosophy to see if they could completely reconcile the two philosophies but finding, many of them, that for the most part they remain only parallel maintaining a good distance from each other."[1]

This oscillation between the two areas seems to characterize generally the movement of philosophical thinking in modern India. A more exclusive preoccupation with either of these

1. cf. Kalidas Bhattacharyya (ed), *Recent Indian Philosophy : Papers selected from the Proceedings of the Indian Philosophical Congress,* 1925-1934, Volume One (Calcutta : Progressive Publishers, 1963), p. viii.

areas, along with a relative neglect of the one or the other, has been a more recent phenomenon.[1]

In the modern Indian philosopher's treatment of his own tradition of thought certain shortcomings might be observed. Firstly, as already pointed out, an element of alienation from the tradition, even when the philosopher is otherwise sympathetic to the latter, is often to be found present. Towards an understanding of the thought tradition *in its own terms*, what largely came in the way is the total involvement in the conceptual apparatus and idioms, theories and doctrines, of Western philosophy. Consequently, what is apt to be missed are the accents and nuances of the original reflexions themselves. This seems to have been the inevitable price for the otherwise necessary and useful strides of the Indian philosopher towards modernity.[2]

Secondly, in the various attempts to expound or interpret the philosophical content and intent of the *darśanas*, what is generally ignored is the question of method or methodological presuppositions. The latter is often not spelt out, either in respect of the philosophical translation of the contents of an older thought, or of the method (explicit or implicit) of philosophic reflexion in terms of the system which is sought to be understood.

Thirdly, the socio-cultural presuppositions and constants of Indian thought, in their historical perspectives, in general contrast to the Western cultural history, are not properly taken into consideration. The modern Indian intellectual, half distantiated from the moorings of his traditional culture, looks to the heritage of thought almost as detached from the concrete setting of life-praxis. Consequently, the total relevance of the philosophical culture could not find a fitting recognition in the midst of indifference at one end and romantic idealization on the other. In the Indian philosopher's preoccupation with Western thought too, the same lopsided approach in respect of the total historical-cultural context usually tends to prevail.

1. Almost an exception to this common attitude, K. C. Bhattacharya offered in his *Studies in Vedantism*, as he put it, "problematic constructions on Vedantic lines intended to bring out the relation of the system to modern philosophical systems". Krishna Chandra Bhattacharya, "Introduction to Studies in Vedantism" in Gopinath Bhattacharya (ed), *Studies in Philosophy by Krishna Chandra Bhattacharya*, Vol. I (Calcutta : Progressive Publishers, 1965), p. 1.

2. For example, B. K. Matilal's *The Navya-Nyāya Doctrine of Negation*, and J. N. Mohanty's *Gangesa's Theory of Truth*, etc.

II

Where does the Indian philosopher stand today—between his own tradition and the contemporary climate of thought? In his effort to move forward in the current of creative thinking in response to contemporary philosophic situation, is he expected to forgo the burden of traditional thinking? Or should he rather reinforce the strength and foundations of his thinking by creative appropriation of the on-coming movement of philosophic tradition? Such questions would beset the Indian philosopher today, placed as he is at the crossroads of understanding his philosophical culture and coming to terms with it. Almost unawares, he is moving to a point wherefrom he would be constrained to take his position between the alternatives of either disregarding the native tradition of thought altogether or taking a total cognizance of the latter in its authentic background. The question of the viability of a completely culture-neutral mode of philosophizing apart, the Indian philosopher has got to come to terms with his heritage of thought, even if he takes up a negative position. At least, he cannot pose non-committal indifference on this point. On the contrary, he has to be ready for a profound re-thinking and re-understanding of the tradition in terms of its own original beginnings.

This confrontation with tradition could operate in two phases, which are apparently contrary—namely, participation and critical reflexion. A participatory understanding of one's own tradition, that is, of oneself situated (along with his fellow-beings) within the genuine continuity of tradition, has to be joined with a critical awareness of the very issue of authenticity of what is being handed down to us, incorporated into our present-day situation. The integration of these two moments in the selfsame activity of understanding the tradition in its own terms, but from our present-day situatedness, could find its resonance in the so-called 'global situation' of our time. The political, economic and communications developments in the world today, along with travels across the continents, have all worked towards minimizing the barriers dividing the Western world from the Eastern, and within the continents themselves. Cross-cultural perspectives in thinking of fundamental problems and issues are not only recognized to be desirable, but sometimes recommended as a necessary step in the re-understanding of one's own philosophic tradition.

Such recognition of 'global' perspective need not, however, imply the easy model of a 'comparative philosophy' outright, or a superficially worked out 'synthetic' philosophy. It is most important that the distinctions in fundamental accents of the two traditions, with their respective overtones and undertones, be properly grasped, before looking for points of similarity, even when the latter could apparently be observed. That need not, of course, mean that we go on repeating such platitudes as that Indian philosophy is 'spiritual' and the Western 'materialistic', or one 'theoretical' and the other 'practical' and so on. The mutuality of these polarities of distinction has to be taken into consideration along with the genuine differences themselves. The latter, even when heuristically formulated, could help towards discovering thematic relevance and points of contact and effect an in-depth dialogue between the two traditions concerned. Thus when we, for instance, conceptually line up *padārtha* with 'category' (Aristotelian or Kantian or otherwise), *dravya* with 'substance', *ātman* with 'self' (or 'soul'), *ahaṃkāra* with 'ego', *manas* with 'mind', *jñāna* with 'knowledge', *ajñāna* with 'ignorance', and so on, we have to spell out the distinctive conceptual-doctrinal context and orientation in the Western thought where the concepts occur.

Mere exercise in comparison could spell almost a movement in circularity, from which it would be hard for contemporary Indian thinking to escape, unless a great deal of self-critical caution and methodological awareness prevail. Nevertheless, I might venture to say, in the field of Indian philosophy at the moment a certain climate of freedom could perhaps be felt—freedom, on the one hand, from a sheer demand for self-justification of the tradition looked at as history, and on the other hand, from the conceptual and doctrinal stereotypes transmitted and adapted from the West. In this context it might be interesting to note J. L. Mehta's observation, while working on the line of Heideggerian mode of thinking towards a re-understanding of Indian thought, that the Indian philosopher, concerned with systematic and speculative thought, has to use certain basic Western Concepts (like 'Absolute', 'Transcendence') with the recognition that he is "creating a new domain of meanings".[1] Whatever may be the Western model concerned—whether classical, modern or contemporary (some of the latter though perhaps relatively more pertinent)—it cannot be pushed too far in the enterprise, except as operative models for explicating the foundational insights, in terms of which the superstructure of thought becomes meaningful. But in any case the thought concerned has to speak for itself.

Paradoxical as it might sound, the philosopher in India today owes the phenomenon of self-criticism, if not skepsis which promises to be constructive, largely to the impact of the Western disciplines not merely in philosophical thinking but also in rigorous indological works. A work like Karl Potter's *Presuppositions of India's Philosophies*, for example, contributes towards making the philosopher-scholar more awake to the task of taking a closer look at the characteristically *Indian* perspective (s) of philosophic thinking, "to push the limits of the presuppositions of Indian thought".[2] Such presuppositions, formally enunciated as they are, would have value as heuristic recommendations. In the final analysis, however, they have to be traced back as implicated within the originary moments of intuitional insights which thought incorporates (a point I will subsequently introduce, though briefly).

III

Towards exploring the characteristics that mark out the typical outlook and thrust of Indian thought (vis-à-vis Western), we have to address ourselves to certain basic questions.

III.1. How far is it appropriate to characterize Indian philosophy strictly as 'metaphysical' in the typical Western sense ? One could perhaps at once reply : even if not in the original European (Greek) sense, it is certainly applicable in its general import. But then, there arises the question : are we critically aware of the genuine difference in perspectives in the two cases ? Basically the Greek (Aristotelian) model of metaphysics as 'first philosophy' of being as being has dominated in the philosophical

1. cf. J. L. Mehta, "Heidegger and the comparison of Indian and Western philosophy" : *Philosophy East and West*, Vol. 20 (July, 1970), 303-17.

2. cf. Karl Potter, *Presuppositions of India's Philosophies* (New Jersey : Prentice Hall, 1963).

thinking of the West till the present time, even where there is radical opposition to metaphysics. That is admittedly a rational-theoretic model of logically constructed superstructure, in terms of which the varieties of experience could possibly be interpreted and organized. (The radical programme of Heidegger is an exception; the proposal of 'descriptive metaphysics' of Strawson, for example, is a variation.)

How then, would the Indian tradition of philosophical thinking differ in this regard ? Does it not also offer world-views which are equally entitled to be called 'metaphysical' (what they are, in fact, usually called) ? Could the Indian enterprise to comprehend the being and meaning of the world, life and existence be looked upon as 'scientific' (in the original Greek sense), that is, rational-cognitive theory of reality ? *Darśanas*, in their original phase, embody intuitive insights (*anubhava*) into the nature of things—they are put forward as the truth of things, life and being. Thus having necessarily the acclaimed evidential basis in some set of 'heard' insights, that is *Śruti*, such philosophies were not primarily offered as possible models of 'rational' thinking. Not to speak of the *Upaniṣads*, the seminal source of all philosophic developments in the subsequent age of the systems—a truism too often ignored in the academic interest in classical thought—even the *Darśanas* were not primarily meant to be speculative investigations into first principles, established as axiomatic truths, with deductive-derivative bearing upon various aspects of experience.

Yet *Darśanas* could be called 'metaphysics', only if we employ the concept in an intuitional rather than a purely constructional sense. Accordingly the central drive of metaphysics would be towards an intuitional grasp of the essences behind the given experience-continuum, rather than any hypothetical (or semi-hypothetical) construction of models. With the former approach could be tied up the notion of metaphysics (that is, metaphysics of experience) as the 'transcendental' enquiry into presuppositions—those of ordinary experience, knowledge and language, and so on—taking 'transcendental' in a broadly 'phenomenological' sense.[1] As a paradigm of the typically Indian approach to

1. An attempt to interpret the central thesis of Advaita Vedānta (doctrine of *Cit*) on broadly transcendental-phenomenological lines can be found in the

metaphysics, we have Śaṁkara's characterization of Truth as *vastutantra*, i.e., pertaining to the nature of things, to reality, and not *puruṣavyāpāratantra*, i.e., dependent on the (mental-intellectual) effort on the part of the inquiring individual.[1] Be it in Vedānta or Vaiśeṣika or Sāṁkhya, or even the Buddhist systems,[2] the accent is on the modes of intuitionally given (to the reflecting mind) rather than on a rational frame of reference, in terms of which the nature of reality is to be interpreted or hypostatised. What these systems of thought originally intend to deal with are not bare concepts, with conceptual relations formally worked out—although the latter obviously operate within the process of demonstrative thinking—but rather the real nature of things as they are (*tattvas*) presented, in their inherent modalities, at deeper levels of reflexion.

III.2. The attitude towards metaphysics brings up at once the question of the *method* of reflexion—the method that might be centrally operative in the original motivation of Indian thought. Here again the polarities of easy 'mysticism', on the one hand, and over-intellectualism, on the other, have to be steered clear of, focussing on the characteristic mode of reflexion itself. As already observed, we can characterize the Indian approach to reality basically as intuitional rather than as constructional. It goes back, in fact, to the Upaniṣadic tradition of the threefold steps of *Śravaṇa*, *Manana* and *Nididhyāsana*. The significance of this model within the parameter of philosophical discourse tends to be ignored—taken either as an antiquated stereotype, which has lost its relevance for modern understanding, or as something shrouded in 'esoteric' practice beyond the scope of philosophical discourse. But what we are apt to overlook is the climate of a deeper sense of reality, and the reflectional discipline directed towards opening up the mind to that presence —be it the foundational essence of being, or be it the *tattvas*, in terms of which the acclaimed essence of essences could be possibly

author's *The Idealist Standpoint : A Study in the Vedantic Metaphysic of Experience* (Santiniketan : Visva-Bharati, 1965).

1. cf. *Śaṁkara-bhāṣya* on *Brahma-sūtra*, I.i.1.

2. In the Mādhyamika school, though, of all the Buddhist schools, the *negative* critique of metaphysics, of any metaphysical position (*dṛṣṭi*), has been radically worked out. Whether it still leaves any room for a positive metaphysic of experience (as in Advaita Vedānta, for example) is an open question.

envisaged. Even when thought moves *via negativa*—as most conspicuously in Mādhyamika, and partly too in Advaita Vedānta (in its 'negative phenomenology' in respect of *Avidyā* or *Ajñāna*)—what is intended is not an abstract negation (in the shape of *Śūnyatā* or *Ajñāna*, as the case may be) as a *mere* formal possibility, but rather a 'transcendental' presence.[1]

In other words, the whole procedure may be characterized as 'transcendental reflexion', where the movement of thought is not from certain concepts, or definitional statements of concepts, to the derivatives and deductions in the world of experience, but rather from the experienced continuum of phenomena to the over-empirical essence or essences in which they are grounded. The accent is thus on originary experience—'essence-intuition', translated is terms of Husserlian phenomenology (though not in the same context or sense). That implies an inwardized deepening of the cognitive attitude in the direction of the 'transcendental' dimension, where things and beings could be viewed in their unitary perspective.[2] The role of *anubhava* (or *anubhūti*) has been recognized in all the Indian systems to be the foundational stratum for a metaphysics of experience. Śaṁkara's accent on this issue is quite unambiguous : knowledge, he urges is to culminate in complete comprehension—*avagatiparyantaṁ jñānam*.[3] (The root *ava-gam* etymologically signifies 'to reach', 'to obtain' —which is of particular significance in this context.)

The motivation of alignment with the rationalist-metaphysical or recent analytical currents of Western thought has led, in a

1. I cannot undertake a demonstration of this point, which may be somewhat contentious, within the short purview of this paper. What I do here is just to indicate the proposed line of treatment.

2. It is interesting to note that K. C. Bhattacharya introduces and develops, in *The Subject as Freedom*, the model of "transcendental psychology", as he prefers to call it, in his exposition of the philosophy of pure subjectivity on the basis of the Advaitic notion of *Cit*—a model to be carefully distinguished from metaphysics, mysticism, epistemology or even introspective psychology. See K. C. Bhattacharya, *Search for the Absolute in Neo-Vedanta* ed. by George B. Burch (Honolulu : The University Press of Hawaii, 1976).

Also compare Bhattacharya's remarks : "There is properly no metaphysics of the subject, if by metaphysics is understood an enquiry into the reality conceived as meanable.", *The Subject as Freedom*, Ch. 1, sec. 11.

3. *Śaṁkara-bhāṣya* on *Brahma-sūtra*, I.i.1.

way, to the ignoring of the original drive and concern of the Indian philosophical tradition. On the other hand, the focus of serious scholarly interests has very largely shifted more and more to the later phases—logical-dialectical, conceptual-analytical as they gradually turned to be. The ontological modes of understanding tied up phenomenologically with originary intuitions, somehow tended to recede from the foreground of philosophical expositions. And that resulted practically in sort of dichotomy in later-day understanding between esoteric obscurantism at the one end and abstract formalism at the other. For what was in a way lost sight of is the mode of reflexion which could make sense of the originary insights in terms of our experience of things and beings.

In emphasizing the transcendental-intuitional dimension, however, the role of formal analysis and reasoning cannot be overlooked. The question of *pramāṇa* and of *prāmāṇya*, and the universal employment of *anumāna*, though not so rigorously formalized as in later age, have been present quite early in *darśanas*. But analysis of thought and language, and the process of inferential reasoning, need not as such run contrary to the said process of intuitive apprehension, unless the right perspective of ratiocination is missed. All modes of analysis and reasoning (including comparison, postulation, etc.) are denied the status of self-sufficient guides to truth; but in no case are they denied the valuable instrumental role in the explication and elaboration of philosophical truths. As Śaṁkara characteristically urges : all empirical demonstration and logical reasoning have got to culminate in intuitive apprehension, because through that alone are we presented with reality—*anubhava-avasānatvāt bhūtavastuviṣayatvāt ca.*[1] Epistemologically speaking (although we cannot, strictly speaking, mark out epistemology as an independent discipline in the Indian context), Indian philosophy commonly recognizes the priority of perceptual immediacy to any of the indirect (*parokṣa*) *pramāṇa*—even subordinating the strength of *anumāna*, which is otherwise acknowledged to bear a high degree of validating capacity.

At least two significant implications of this methodological position should be considered. Firstly, the notion of *a priori*,

1. *Śaṁkara-bhāṣya* on *Brahma-sūtra*, I.i.2.

in the sense in which it has so centrally been employed in the history of Western thought, is conspicuous by its absence in Indian thought. The latter has not generally proceeded in terms of universal necessities of pure thought or reason, nor is 'rational intuition' or 'intellectual intuition' counted as central to philosophical reflexion. The concept of universals (*sāmānya*)—even when 'realistic' in its orientation (as in Nyāya-Vaiśeṣika, for example)—is not tied up with the notion of pure rational necessity. It could, however, be worthwhile to explore how far the philosophy of the Grammarians (*Vaiyākaraṇa*) uphold the ontological *apriorities* of language (*Vāk*).

Secondly, the attitude to language in the Indian tradition has to be reviewed in its authentic perspective. On this issue too, we have to direct our attention right from the early beginnings of the *Darśanas*, rather than being guided by the later developments—particularly in Navya-Nyāya and other schools largely adopting its semantic approach and the formalized technique of linguistic analysis and inferential arguments. Following in the trail of the Upaniṣadic attitude to language (both natural and 'metaphysical') in the context of the quest for enlightenment, language comes to assume, on the ontological dimension, a non-semiotic role, just as thought, as authentic reflexion, turns to be essentially non-representational. To put the situation in a different way, thought as well as language prove to be in a way 'symbolic', in the sense that words or notions do not mean any objectively definable states of affair, but rather aid the reflecting consciousness in deepening its intuitive comprehension. As I have discussed elsewhere,[1] language, understood in this perspective, would show a 'forward-looking' stance, as it were, in pushing the mind further into an encounter with the presence of reality. The paradigmatic statement (which could otherwise simply be called 'mystical') of *Tat tvam asi*, for instance, admits of no semantic-syntactic breakdown on the model of an ordinary proposition of identity. The words themselves consummate, so to say, into the concrete (existential) actualization in consciousness. In fact, that is the whole thrust of *śabda*-generated immediacy (*śabdāparokṣa* in *vākya-janya-jñāna*).

1. cf. D. Sinha, "Reflections on some key terms in Advaita Vedānta" in *Language in Indian Philosophy and Religion* (Canadian Corporation for Studies in Religion, 1978).

The structure of language as such has provided a very important key to philosophic reflexion and theory, whether in the East or in the West. But, unlike in the dominant Western tradition, language or the grammatical structure, has not been generally considered in the Indian tradition as a necessary step towards constructing a metaphysical theory. In the latter, linguistic explorations are mostly used as heuristic guide to thinking in its search for constitutive essences underlying linguistic usage. As previously pointed out, we hardly come across metaphysical language proper in the *Darśanas*. Unlike in European rationalistic metaphysics, mathematics or mathematical language ('mathesis universalis') never became the model of philosophic certainty in Indian thought—the former being at least implicitly adopted even in modern non-metaphysical philosophy of the West. But in the West, the rationalistic language of metaphysics and its absolute cognitive claim were also radically questioned by Nietzsche—Hume and Kant having preceded in certain ways. On the Indian scene, starting with the Upaniṣadic reservation regarding the efficacy of language in respect of *parāvidyā*, the skepsis towards metaphysical language took a radical shape in the Mādhyamika school of Buddhism.

III.3. We now come to the very question of *knowledge* as treated in early and classical Indian thought. The Upaniṣadic teaching of *jñāna* as *parāvidyā* indicates the paradigm of supreme insight where the dichotomy of subject and object should no longer prevail. To have a closer look at the guiding notion of *jñāna*, the admittedly highest point of the said philosophical culture, it is basically looked upon not as 'theoria', that is the Greek idea of the view of things and beings as contemplated by the reflecting mind. It is rather the total illumination of the seeking mind, culminating in identity that is self-evidencing. The translation of *jñāna* as 'knowledge', within the obvious framework of cognitivity model, could be too simplistic, if not misleading. (Of course, the very expression *jñāna* has also been extantly employed in the philosophical discourses of the *Darśanas* in the limited epistemological context where it is equivalent to *pramā/pramāṇa*, or *buddhi*, or *vṛtti-jñāna*, and so on.)

For all theoretical and practical purposes, however, the epistemological level of *pramāṇa* is accepted in all its ramifications. Not only in Nyāya-Vaiśeṣika and in later developments of the schools, but in the Vedānta of Śaṁkara and his immediate successors, like Padmapāda and Prakāśātman, inferential and other mediate forms of reasoning were amply used. However, the ulterior efficacy of such cognitive processes, ratiocinative and demonstrative, lay in their efficacy to lead the reflecting movement onto the focal point of immediate presentative apprehension (*aparokṣānubhūti*). Such meta-cognitive presence (not *pramāṇa*-operated, as they are ideally supposed to be) is uniformly recognized to be of a non-objective (not subjective, for that matter) nature—or one that does not strictly conform to cognitive determination.

We have to reckon with a very unique orientation of the noetic model explicitly or implicitly present in all the major schools. It is the basic recognition of an immediate openness to the presence of the foundational essence of the reflecting subject himself. Such ideal terminating phase of transcendental reflexion is sought to be carefully differentiated from the framework of objective categories (or categories of objectivity), in terms of which our systems of knowledge (science and metaphysics) normally operate —reflexion itself having a negative thrust. Even the system of Nyāya-Vaiśeṣika, marked by realistic-objectivistic direction of ontological analysis and construction of *padārthas*, still focus, on final analysis, on *ātman* and its immediate apprehension (*upalabdhi*).[1] This central motive and direction of enlightenment (*Mokṣa*) through the unfoldment of the essence of self could be found not only in the *āstika* systems, but in Jainism and in Buddhism as well, though in an indirect (perhaps retroactive) manner.

IV

A recognition of the marks and characteristics discussed above might still leave traces of an 'apologetic' attitude on the part of an Indian student of the philosophic tradition of India. Let us have a closer look into the matter. (a) The original drive of Indian thought is admittedly not a theoretic one; if not so, how could it, then, at all justify its claim to be a philosophy at all? This question presumably arises in view of the central Western stress on 'theory'—right from the Greeks down to the

1. See note 2 on p. 282.

present-day. Does the Indian life-motivation in spiritual freedom (*mokṣa*)—an acknowledged value-orientation tied up with the highest model of self-unfoldment—imply a deficiency in the philosophic enterprise itself? Without going into the question of theory-practice relation, which I have discussed elsewhere,[1] we may recognize that there is a movement of theoretic freedom in going about philosophizing, theoretically posing puzzlements in our understanding of things and analyzing and answering them theoretically. On the other hand, when thought appears to move within a fixed frame of reference as defined by *mokṣa* or *ātmānubhava*, or *bodhi* or *prajñā*, a repetitious movement and a constraint on the autonomous activity seems to be the consequence. To this negative critique it may be pointed out, as our discussions above would show, that *Śruti*, so far as it is accepted as the firm centre of reference, the acclaimed alfa and omega of reflective endeavour, presents the profound challenge to the modern Indian philosopher to be engaged in the on-going process of understanding, interpreting and relating what was originally meant to be 'heard'.

(b) Taking, on the other hand, a closer look at modern Western thought itself, we could well observe certain deeper currents of skepsis regarding the very rationalist tradition itself. Nietzsche urged his radical critique of the Western paradigm of knowledge, that is, knowledge as 'theoria', as Science, as Truth. He sought to explode the very claim of knowledge as 'disinterested', and attacked the norm of 'pure' objective knowledge by pointing to 'the illusion of objectivity'. To come to recent times, Heidegger attacked the whole tradition of conceptual metaphysical thinking, and offered his new conception of philosophy as an autonomous inquiry guided by non-conceptual non-representational 'meditative thinking' (*Denken*).[2] Husserl, again, by introducing the methodological discipline of phenomenological philosophy, combined with his critique of scientific objectivism, opened a new avenue for explaining the region of consciousness, with its modes of intuitive-eidetic givenness. I am not proposing or recommending here that any of these philosophical currents be adopted as *the* model for interpreting ancient Indian thought.

1. See note 3 on p. 282.

2. cf. Martin Heidegger, *What is called Thinking*? (Translation of *Was Heisst Denken*?), trans. by J. Glenn Gray (Harper : Colophon Books, 1968).

What I would rather suggest is that existential and phenomenological philosophies in broad—oriented, as they are, to experience in depth—offer to break through the usual Western dichotomies of reason and experience, intellect and intuition, logic and mysticism, rationalism and irrationalism. And to that extent, they could possibly offer a more appropriate and relevant idiom and language to translate the content of Indian thought, in its authentic accents and nuances.[1]

Besides these conspicuous movements in contemporary thinking, certain cultural (or 'counter-cultural') trends have recently been showing up in the Western world, if not elsewhere too in some degree, sharing some discontent with the all-engulfing dominance of the rationalistic-scientistic tradition and its technocratic orientation in the overall life-pattern of the Western man today. At various levels—ranging from dilettantish lip-service to a serious involvement—interest in the perspective (s) of Eastern thought, even as a viable alternative, is a phenomenon to be reckoned with. Whatever enduring value such interest might carry in themselves, they indicate at least some openness, on the part of Western consciousness, to the credibility and promise of the Eastern insights towards meeting the challenges of the contemporary human situation, along with some skepsis regarding the total relevance of the Western tradition in this respect.

Whether, and how much of, such phenomena in the West are passé, is a different consideration. What concerns us here is how the Indian philosopher today would respond to these. Is

1. (i) Comparable, in this context, is George Burch's observation : "Neo-Vedānta is existentially oriented but phenomenologically grounded in experience." (Burch, though, has not spelt out either of these modes of thinking in reference to Neo-Vedānta, or for the matter of that, original Vedānta.) See his Introduction, *loc. cit.*, p. 54.

In *The Idealist Standpoint* though the author has attempted a "phenomenological reconstruction" of the Advaitic metaphysic of experience, the inadequacy, on the final analysis, of the strictly Husserlian model in a fuller understanding of the total import of Advaitism has also been indicated. Mention may also be made of Kalidas Bhattacharyya, *A Modern Understanding of Advaita Vedanta* (Ahmedabad : L. D. Institute of Indology, 1975).

(ii) Looked at in this perspective, the attempt to formalize the whole area of logical-epistemological literature (particularly later) in terms of modern semantics and logical analysis, as have recently been done by competent scholars, Western and Indian, can be viewed as a parallel enterprise which has its undoubted value, but in a limited and partial context.

he prompted to the task of exploring the possibility of a newer dimension of thinking—maybe, a revision of the very idea of reason (ratio) and the scope of philosophic rationality itself—in terms of which a more authentic and holistic understanding of the philosophic tradition could be possible? At the same time such re-discovery (if the expression could be used) might possibly offer a more fruitful and effective mode of reflexion, where the demands of formal reasoning are integrated to the supposed intuitive moments of reflexion, and, consequently, provide some sort of a meta-formal (or 'transcendental') paradigm for meeting the challenging questions of our time, theoretic as well as existential. How far the present-day Indian philosopher, as the genuine representative of his tradition, could meet this 'global' demand for newer dimension in thinking, is an open question. But the demand at this hour is for self-understanding as much as self-criticism on his part. To understand (or rather, re-understand) his tradition of thought in its own terms, shedding off the 'idols' inherited from within and without, is an immense task and responsibility.

One essential step towards this encounter of self-understanding would certainly be a turning back to the sources themselves in the ancient texts concerned. Rigorous philosophical translations of the respective Sanskrit (also Pāli, and eventually Tibetan too) texts have to be undertaken by philosopher-Sanskritists (or Pāli or Tibetan scholars, as the case may be). The translations have to be as much authenticated and systematic (internally, in terms of the system concerned) as critically and thematically oriented. For the objective would not be primarily a philological-linguistic one, but a philosophical recovery of the original import and the contextual meaning of the concepts, idioms and expressions in use, and to relate them, in terms of their inherent relevancy, to current philosophic problems and themes. Some of the basic texts pertaining to the different *darśanas* in their relatively earlier stages of *bhāṣya* and *kārikā*, along with the significant *Prakaraṇa* texts and *Ṭikās*, have to be taken up afresh for intensive first-hand philosophical translations. They alone could provide the groundwork for a programmatic re-understanding of Indian thought.

In fact, the programme of translation should be vital to the total task of self-understanding. But translation, in this context, would be interpretation as well. For it would not imply here objective disinterested textual rendering of the words or sentences; it should rather be a participatory, 'interested' translation. The latter could best be signified as 'hermeneutic'.[1] Questions are to be put, as it were, to the texts in consideration, and responses extricated therefrom; in a truly dialogical situation, the texts themselves would answer the questions put to them. Such an approach could possibly relate the modern scholar-thinker more intrinsically to the ancient minds, ought to be understood in and through the texts. Through a phenomenologically-explorative understanding of the texts, the implicit metaphysic or critique of experience may be envisaged and worked out in the steps of (transcendental) reflexion-cum-analysis.

All that I have ventured to suggest here, in a programmatic way, is a broad framework for a fresh and more integral approach to the study of India's philosophical traditions. This might work towards the possibility of on-going dialogue, on the scene of contemporary philosophy, between the two sets of philosophical language pertaining to the two traditions, broadly defined, of the West and the East. It is not meant to be just 'comparative philosophy', as so often rather glibly spoken of, but something more essential and organic to the living practice of philosophic reflexion. It might even emerge into a possible 'global' self-understanding of human thought itself—a goal and a dream, which we could perhaps look forward to from our present situation.

1. cf. Hans-George Gadamer, *Philosophical Hermeneutics*, translated and edited by David E. Linge (University of California Press, 1976).

14

TRADITION, FREEDOM AND PHILOSOPHICAL CREATIVITY

RAJENDRA PRASAD*

IT is almost definitional that every nation has its own traditions, philosophical as well as non-philosophical. Traditions are, by and large, crystallizations of some of the important, surviving, modes of thought or action, prevalent among a people, or a group of people, for a considerable period of time in its history. It is also true that every nation takes pride in and respects at least some of its traditions. Perhaps this is necessary for the preservation of its identity in the commonwealth of nations. To say all this is not to deny or be oblivious to the fact that no tradition is eternal. Some traditions *change*, or give place to others, in a natural, silent, process, while others *are changed* or replaced as a result of deliberate efforts made by some members of the group they belong to. Since in this paper I am concerned only with the philosophical traditions of India, I shall talk only about them, and unless otherwise stated, my use of even the unqualified 'tradition' should be taken to mean 'philosophical tradition'.

Every country which today has any philosophy also has some philosophical traditions, and one can discover some relationship

*Rajendra Prasad is Research Professor of Philosophy in the Indian Institute of Technology, Kanpur, India. He has published a large number of research papers and co-edited Proceedings of the *International Institute of Philosophy*; *Bhagwandas Commemoration Volume* and *Marathi Encyclopaedia of Philosophy*. He was also the editor of *Indian Review of Philosophy*.

between the two. It is not at all a startling truth to say that every modern philosophy can be said to be seated on the shoulders of some philosophical traditions, and the traditions which support or have inspired it could be wholly or partly indigenous. It very often happens that philosophical activity takes its inspiration from both indigenous and non-indigenous traditions. The latter could be such traditions which cohere, or even such which provide a contrast, with the former. Such an interaction between or intermingling of traditions has become very much natural particularly after the Second World War, because of the fact that since then information about what has happened or is happening in one country has become easily available to others.

That India has a very vast philosophical heritage is admitted by all, though there may be some disagreement about the assessment of that heritage or about the comparative evaluation or significance of its various parts or constituents. But the philosophical traditions of some other countries, particularly those traditions which are accessible or approachable through the medium of English have also been quite readily available for a fairly long period of time, and are still so, at least to those Indians who completed their formal education by the year 1955, or before the time English ceased to be the major medium of instruction in schools and colleges. The importance of English as the chief window through which the foreign sky enters the horizon of Indian philosophers cannot be overemphasized, because even the philosophies done in foreign languages other than English are read generally in English translations. For nearly a decade, some Indian philosophers have started writing on, or in the manner of, continental existential and phenomenological philosophies, but almost all of these scholars depend more or less exclusively on works available in English, and not on their French or German originals. It is because of unavailability in English of works in Chinese and Japanese philosophy that their traditions have not had any mentionable impact on them; otherwise generously receptive as they are, they would not have remained so unaffected by what has happened or is happening in those parts of the globe. In fact, besides their own classical and contemporary traditions, it is the Anglo-American philosophical traditions which have been a major source of (philosophical) feeding to them.

Since any philosophical activity is done almost always in the setting of some tradition (s), the modern Indian philosopher may also be naturally expected to be doing his philosophizing in the setting of the traditions available to him. But the relationship between the *Indian philosophical traditions* and *modern Indian philosophizing* seems to many philosophers, Indian as well as non-Indian, to possess a unique type of philosophical importance To them it seems to be incontrovertibly true that the philosophizing of a modern Indian will not be really Indian unless it is of a piece with some classical Indian tradition or traditions, and there is very often implicit in this view a specific opinion about the genius or spirit of the Indian traditions. Those who hold, implicitly or explicitly, this view consider it to be a philosophical characterization when they deny or doubt the Indianness of some of the writings by some modern Indians (including the present writer). That is, the phrase 'Indian philosophy' (or even the word 'Indian') is treated by these scholars as denoting a philosophical concept, and a concept of paramount importance. Concealed in all this, there is also the unexpressed, or dimly expressed, presupposition that somehow or other an Indian philosopher is obligated to be an 'Indian' philosopher, to philosophize in that specific style which is taken to be the 'Indian' style, because, some liberals would say, he is an Indian, or because, some extremists would say, that is the real, genuine, way of philosophizing. In this way the relationship between the Indian traditions and contemporary (or future) Indian philosophy has assumed the status of a philosophical, or at least quasi-philosophical, controversy. It has been fed upon some confusions or misunderstandings of a general nature pertaining to the nature and goal of philosophy as well as upon some others pertaining specifically to the genius of the Indian traditions and their role in contemporary philosophizing. How adversely all this has affected philosophical creativity and freedom of thought will hopefully be made clear in the sequel ?

In an obvious sense 'Indian philosophy' should be taken, or allowed, to denote any kind of philosophy done by an Indian in the past, present or future. But it has become almost conventional to mean by it classical Indian philosophy or of any segment of it. Thus, none of the thinkers, e.g., Radhakrishnan, Dasgupta, Hiriyanna, Chatterjee and Datta, Vidyabhusan, Jwala

Prasad, etc. has cared to suitably qualify the title of his work with the word 'classical' or any other word connoting the ancientness of the views discussed by him. Both or either one of the following two beliefs seem to be responsible for this glaring historical inaccuracy. Perhaps, these authors believe (a) that classical philosophies are all which India has done, or would be (re-) doing, or (b) that there is something eternal, timeless, sacrosanct, in the classical philosophies which, therefore, have to be described without being given a temporal designation. It is needless to say that both of these beliefs are sheer prejudices.

The classical Indian schools of philosophy have been considered by several modern writers as being not only historically or geographically Indian, but as constituting philosophy of a special type, and the phrase 'Indian philosophy' has therefore been taken to denote a particular concept of philosophy. Furthermore, this concept of philosophy has been taken to distinguish Indian from Western philosophy and by some as also the right, or most proper, concept of philosophy *per se*.

According to such writers—and they constitute a large class including some prominent and professionally or extra-professionally influential names—the genius of Indian philosophy consists in its *spiritualism.* This line of thinking has been given wide publicity at home and abroad, in a very persuasive and forceful manner, by Radhakrishnan:

> "philosophy in India is essentially spiritual."[1]
>
> "The dominant character of the Indian mind which has coloured all its culture and moulded all its thoughts is the spiritual tendency. Spiritual experience is the foundation of India's rich cultural history. It is mysticism, not in the sense of involving the exercise of any mysterious powers but only as insisting on a discipline of human nature, leading to a realisation of the spiritual."[2]

Generally the Sanskrit word '*darśana-śāstra*', or simply '*darśana*' is used as the Indian equivalent of 'philosophy.' *Darśana*, meaning spiritual experience, is said to be the basis of *darśana-śāstra*, meaning philosophical speculation or study. "A '*darśana*' is a spiritual perception, a whole view revealed to the soul. This soul sight, which is possible only when and where philosophy

1. S. Radhakrishnan, *Indian Philosophy*, Vol. I (London : George Allen and Unwin, 1923), p. 24.

2. *Ibid.*, p. 41

is lived is the distinguishing mark of a true philosopher. So the highest triumphs of philosophy are possible only to those who have achieved in themselves a purity of soul."[1]

Several later writers uncritically followed Radhakrishnan in emphasizing the spiritualist interpretation. The writers of almost all the text-books or introductory books on classical Indian philosophy, perhaps with the unique exception of Chattopadhyaya,[2] have accepted it as something like the standard or official interpretation of the Indian conception of philosophy, with the result that a collegiate student of Indian philosophy is imperceptibly conditioned into believing that it is wholly incontrovertible or unquestionable. Some writers even present it as the only right or the most satisfactory conception of philosophy. For example, Malkani holds that philosophy "is a science of the spirit, if we may so call it. It is *ādhyātmic vidyā*. This *vidyā* has nothing hypothetical or speculative about it. It is *more properly a way of direct seeing or darśana.* Imagination misleads. The pure light of reason does not mislead. Philosophy is the operation of this pure light of reason.

> *This is the concept of philosophy that was current coin in ancient India. We need to revert to it, if philosophy is to justify its place of honour among all other human activities, both theoretical and practical.*"[3]

By 'pure light of reason' Malkani means intuition, spiritual vision, and not rational cogitation. Since science is taken by Malkani (and others holding the spiritualist position) to be a concern of sense and logical reason, his condemnation of science is natural.

> "Science also pursues truth. But its approach to the problem is unreflective. It does not consciously seek truth. . . Scientific truth is factual truth only. And all factual truth can be questioned. . . It is not science that is the glory of man. Science, in fact, has always the tendency to turn man into the worst of animals. It is the symbol of physical power, not of any spiritual power. We add no great quality to animality by reasoning more efficiently than the mere animal does."[4]

1. S. Radhakrishnan, *Indian Philosophy*, Vol. I (London : George Allen and Unwin, 1923), p. 44.

2. Debiprasad Chattopadhyaya, *Indian Philosophy : A Popular Introduction* (New Delhi : People's Publishing House, 1964).

3. G. R. Malkani, "Philosophical Truth," *Philosophical Quarterly*, Vol. 22, No. 4 (1950), 208 (Italics mine). "*Ādhyātmic Vidyā*" means "spiritual inquiry."

4. *Ibid.*, pp. 206-07

It is clear that Malkani carries further the Radhakrishnan tradition of the spiritualist interpretation of the classical Indian conception of philosophy by claiming it to be also the best conception of philosophy, since, according to him, philosophy can "justify its place of honour among all other human activities" only when it functions as a *darśana*, a spiritual pursuit.

Chubb makes the spiritualist conception even thicker by linking philosophy almost definitionally with *sādhanā*.

> "Philosophy may be understood," he says, "either as actual knowledge of the Real in a transfigured consciousness, or as an aspiration towards such knowledge. *The thought system of the unregenerated consciousness which claims to be knowledge of Reality, without acknowledging that sādhanā is an essential part of the process that leads to such knowledge, is not philosophy in the proper sense of the word. It is what passes for philosophy in the* Western universities, and unfortunately, as a result of a wholesale import of Western ideas in our educational systems, in Indian universities as well."[1]

By '*sādhanā*' Chubb means

> "any action or series of actions done by an individual with the conscious aim of achieving union with God or realizing the highest and unconditioned truth. 'Action' here includes the state of 'passive alertness,' in which one steps back and witnesses the total contents of the mind, until the Mind, its support withdrawn, lapses into Silence."[2]

Chubb thus brings to the surface, in bold light, the religious or mystical element in the spiritualist position. To give the weight of unquestionable authority to his position, Chubb begins his account with a quotation from K. C. Bhattacharya, reading : "Philosophy is for meditation and is not knowledge."[3] That Bhattacharya also follows the Radhakrishnan tradition is testified by his son, Gopinath Bhattacharya, when he interprets his father to hold that "philosophy is the elaboration of different kinds of spiritual experiences."[4] It is Bhattacharya's spiritualism which has attracted Malkani towards his way of thinking, as Malkani also interprets Bhattacharya to hold that philosophy is a

1. J. N. Chubb, "Philosophy and Sādhanā" in *Proceedings of the Indian Philosophical Congress*, 24th Session, 1949, Part I, pp. 5-6 (Italics mine).
2. *Ibid.*, p. 1.
3. *Ibid.*
4. Krishna Chandra Bhattacharya, *Studies in Philosophy by Krishna Chandra Bhattacharya*, ed. by Gopinath Bhattacharya, Vol. II (Calcutta : Progressive Publishers, 1958), Introduction, p. xii.

> "spiritual business of finding the meaning of concepts not in the objective use made of them, but in the corresponding personal or spiritual experience."[1]

I have quoted Gopinath Bhattacharya and Malkani because they are accepted even by the admirers of Bhattacharya as completely authentic and very sympathetic, or rather, devoted, interpreters of the latter's philosophy. All of the above thinkers, Radhakrishnan, Malkani, Chubb, and Bhattacharya, are considered as eminent, even creative, modern Indian philosophers. But all of them are traditionalists in the sense that what they consider to be the correct interpretation of the Indian tradition of philosophizing is for them the right kind of philosophizing; that is, what is to them the traditional Indian concept of philosophy is also the right concept of philosophy. I shall refer to this interpretation as the ST conception which is a short form of 'the spiritualist interpretation of the traditional or classical Indian conception of philosophy.' Very often when one refers to Indian philosophy, not in a regional but philosophical or conceptual sense, he means by it the ST conception. It is in this sense that some thinkers, Indian as well as non-Indian, expect modern Indian philosophers to do, or charge them to be obligated to do, *Indian* philosophy.

The ideas which go, though quite loosely, with the ST conception are the following : Ultimate reality is spiritual in nature, it is some sort of a self or spirit; the empirical, natural, world has only phenomenal reality; the way to know ultimate reality is not sense or reason but some kind of direct seeing, some sort of religious, mystical, experience, a kind of becoming one with the known; this becoming is also man's final destiny or salvation (*mokṣa*) and the goal of philosophy or *darśana*; philosophy derives its importance from being *mokṣa-śāstra*, a pursuit leading to *mokṣa*; the link between the philosophic pursuit and *sādhanā*, spiritually or religiously disciplining the philosopher's mind and body, is very close because *sādhanā* is necessary for the achievement of the philosophic goal. All this is very much akin to the religious aspects of the Vedāntic or Advaita Vedāntic point of view. It is no wonder, therefore, that all of the champions of the ST conception are advocates of or sympathetic to some form of the Vedānta.

1. G. R. Malkani, Some Points in K. C. Bhattacharya's 'Concept of Philosophy,' *Philosophical Quarterly*, Vol. 23 (July 1950), 50.

Some scholars make a distinction between *darśana* and *darśana-śāstra*, and maintain that philosophy is *darśana-śāstra*, and not *darśana*. '*Darśana*,' being derived from the root '*dṛś*,' etymologically means visual perception, but has acquired the conventional meaning of spiritual vision or experience and, therefore, '*darśana-śāstra*' would then mean a study of or inquiry into spiritual vision or experience. But this distinction, though semantically tenable, has been knowingly or unknowingly ignored by the followers of the spiritualist interpretation. It has become (almost) invisible or non-existent as a result of their linking philosophy with meditation, *sādhanā*, salvation, etc. Moreover, even if they make philosophy a study or elaboration of spiritual experiences, their interpretation remains a spiritualist, theological, interpretation, as philosophy even then remains inexorably and almost exclusively bound up with spiritual experiences, thus retaining all the implications of the ST conception I am going to discuss in this paper.

There is a historical reason which is, at least partly, responsible for the emphasis and importance given to the ST conception. The movements for religious revival in the nineteenth century India needed some theoretical or philosophical support. Obtaining such support from Western ideas or theories which were then available was likely to have hurt the nationalistic pride of the leaders of the movements as well as the sensitivity of the Indian people. Therefore, the leaders turned to India's past, to its classical philosophies, particularly to the Upaniṣadic, Vedāntic, philosophies.

The religious revival, by and large, took the form of the claim that real, genuine, Hinduism was not what in practice it was then found to be. It was maintained by the leaders that the prevailing evils of casteism, untouchability, disrespect for women, dry and rigid ritualism, etc., were not in any way essential to Hinduism. To present Hinduism in what was considered to be its pristine purity, they went back to the Vedic or Upaniṣadic sources, and claimed that in its original form, as discoverable from the classical works and practices, it was completely free from the prevalent evils mentioned above. The spiritual interpretation of classical Indian philosophy seemed to lend a theoretical support to all this, and that is why it was emphasized in a manner which exhibited nationalistic zeal more than objective scholarship. This cause was most eloquently championed by

Radhakrishnan who went to the extent of claiming that spiritualism is not only the bedrock of the entire ancient Indian culture but the main saviour of the Indian nation. According to him,

"philosophy in India is essentially spiritual. It is the intense spirituality of India, and not any great political structure or social organisation that it has developed, that has enabled it to resist the ravages of time and the accidents of history. External invasions and internal dissensions came very near crushing its civilization many times in its history. . .yet it has its head held high. India has not been finally subdued, and its old flame of spirit is still burning."[1]

Historians may not agree with Radhakrishnan in his claim that it is India's spirituality which has enabled it to hold its head high, or that the flame of spirit is still burning. But if anyone who is led to believe what Radhakrishnan says of India's spirituality, it is very likely that his patriotic sentiment, if not duly disciplined by his philosophical objectivity, will assert itself to make him follow the band-wagon of the spiritualist interpreters.

In course of time the historical occasion, the religious, nationalistic, motivation, was forgotten, and later writers on Indian philosophy started believing, more as a result of conditioning than as that of any independent, objective, interpretation, that Indian philosophy, or rather philosophy *per se*, was essentially spiritual. Even some, like Chubb, to whom Western philosophy did not seem to be spiritual in their sense or the Indian sense, did not hesitate to call it non-genuine philosophy. The conclusion from all this is evident : if Indian philosophy is essentially spiritualistic, then the philosophy of an Indian which is not spiritualistic is not by definition Indian philosophy, and if genuine philosophy is spiritualistic, Western philosophy which is not is not genuine philosophy. This unhealthy trend was, as I have said earlier, led by Radhakrishnan, and his influence on those who wrote after him was very great, more on account of his eloquent and nationalistic, patriotic, style than on account of his logic. His status as a teacher, administrator, and statesman, as well as the fact that his books were published abroad—a fact still considered to be highly respectable—contributed a great deal to his philosophical influence.

Since Radhakrishnan's books were published abroad, they enjoyed for a pretty long time the privilege of being the chief

1. S. Radhakrishnan, *Indian Philosophy*, Vol. I, pp. 24-25.

source of information to Western scholars about classical Indian philosophy. Consequently, his viewpoint also influenced Western interpreters of Indian philosophy a great deal. For example, in *A Source Book in Indian Philosophy* (ed. by S. Radhakrishnan and C. A. Moore, Princeton University Press, 1957), selections from the writings of only two modern Indian thinkers, Radhakrishnan and Sri Aurobindo, have been included and Sri Aurobindo is no less an advocate of the ST conception than Radhakrishnan. In fact, in modern India, among non-professional thinkers, he has contributed a great deal towards identifying philosophy with theology, or at least towards blurring the distinction between the two.

Coupled with all this, there is another factor which also contributed to the predominance of the ST conception. Among the early Western writers on Indian philosophy, the majority consisted of Christian missionaries or Orientalists who were interested more in the religious or moral (in the practical, not theoretical or conceptual, sense) aspects of Indian thought than in its technical logic, epistemology, or even ontology. The ST conception which very nearly converts philosophy into theology, appealed to them very much.

To many Indians what makes the spiritualist interpretation look so plausible, or motivates them to interpret Indian philosophy in the spiritualist fashion, is the (so-called) close association between religion and philosophy in ancient Indian thought. But since religion and philosophy are not in fact isomorphic pursuits, in interpreting classical Indian philosophy a modern interpreter must keep in his mind the distinction between the two even if they have not been kept sufficiently distinct in ancient writings. But the spiritualist interpreters either fail to recognize this distinction or to give to it the importance it deserves, and they are led (or misled) to believe that the end or objective of Indian philosophy is the same as that of (Indian) religion. As the religious end is in some sense spiritual perfection, it is natural for them to conclude that the aim of Indian philosophy is also spiritual perfection. The religious goal is very often called *mokṣa* (*kaivalya*, *nirvāṇa*, etc., meaning salvation) and hence *mokṣa* is said to be the goal of philosophy as well, without caring to explore the possibility that the philosophical salvation may not be non-distinguishable from the religious salvation. The result of this is not only to make the spiritualist interpretation of Indian philosophy look plausible but also to encourage philosophers to be indifferent to ascertaining the exact status of the concept of *mokṣa* as a philosophical concept. The latter is an important philosophical, axiological, besides being a religious, concept, and it was introduced in Indian value theory to play the theoretical role of the final justifier for the entire system of morality which, for some good logical reasons, it cannot play.[1] But on account of the interpreters' incorrectly and inadequately distinguishing between the role it was expected or required to play in philosophical theory and religious life, its philosophical role was not properly understood.

It is true that most of the classical schools refer to *mokṣa*, or something like *mokṣa*, as the highest value (*puruṣārtha*). But it is not necessary to give it a religious or spiritual connotation. It can very well be interpreted to mean attainment of happiness, peace of mind, equanimity of the soul, discriminative knowledge, freedom from ignorance, etc., and in any one of these senses it can be a non-spiritual, non-religious, earthly, noetic goal. Moreover, even if one may say that according to *Indian value theory* the final aim of man is *mokṣa* in its spiritual sense, it seems to be quite far-fetched to hold that it is also the objective of studying such technical philosophical disciplines as logic, philosophy of language, epistemology, etc., in each one of which classical Indian philosophy is extremely rich.

It is Radhakrishnan again who has very greatly contributed to the theologisation of the Indian conception of philosophy. In the final chapter of his two-volume work on classical Indian philosophy, he concludes by saying that according to the classical masters "the discipline of philosophy is at the same time the fulfilment of a religious vocation."[2] This is in effect the final conclusion of the spiritualist interpretation. Some overly patriotic enthusiasts, who think that the Indian conception of philosophy is the only proper conception of philosophy, when told by men like Radhakrishnan that Indian philosophy is "essentially

1. For a detailed substantiation of this point, see my "The Concept of Mokṣa," in *Philosophy and Phenomenological Research*, Vol. XXXI, No. 3 (1971), 381-93.

2. S. Radhakrishnan, *Indian Philosophy*, Vol. II, p. 771

spiritual," or that it is the "fulfilment of a religious vocation,"[1] very smoothly slide on to the generalized conclusion that any philosophy is real philosophy only if it is theology. For a modern Indian who, because of merely being an Indian, belongs to such a glorious tradition, to do any different kind of philosophy would definitely be, to say the least, inglorious !

All these factors, combined with the unavailability of good, conceptual, English translation of an adequate number of technical philosophical works, have helped the prevalence of the ST conception both in India and abroad. This has worked as a dissuader to many, particularly Western, logicians, epistemologists, conceptual analysts, rather theoretically oriented non-religious philosophers in general, with the result that the number of such persons exhibiting any serious interest in Indian philosophy is quite negligible. By emphasizing the mystical, theological side of Indian philosophy the ST conception has led many to believe that spiritualism is its strongest point, and in consequence its purely technical, secular, parts like logic, epistemology, ethical and meta-ethical theory, philosophy of language, even ontology, etc., have been deplorably ignored. A patriotic Indian may feel uplifted to hear from one who values religiosity more than intellectual illumination that Indian philosophy is superior to Western philosophy. But this feeling of superiority and exaltation does not stay long since he very soon discovers that one who treats philosophy as an autonomous inquiry, not bound to theology, condescends to call Indian philosophy 'philosophy' only as a matter of etiquette.

The ST conception has some very important, though pernicious, philosophical implications.

1. It leads to, as suggested above, the downgrading of such technical branches of philosophy as philosophy of science, philosophy of language, formal or philosophical logic, theoretical ethics, meta-ethics, etc., as they are not concerned with spirituality or self-realization. Malkani's condemnation of science is a good pointer in this direction.

2. It also encourages dogmatism or unproductive traditionalism, and tempts one to attach undue importance to purely interpretative, exegetical, studies of classical Indian philosophy.

1. S. Radhakrishnan, *Indian Philosophy*, Vol. II, p. 771.

If philosophy is spiritual wisdom which is stored in classical Indian philosophy and which can show men the path to self-realization, then what else can be a more laudable objective than recounting, reporting, propagating, or meditating over, the spiritual truth or truths of classical Indian philosophy? By doing *śravaṇa* (reception of the truths), *manana* (reflection over them), and *nididhyāsana* (meditation) one can attain one's destiny. There would be no need for creative or critical thinking, and philosophic freedom and progress would become vacuous concepts.

Some scholars have openly admitted that Indian philosophy does not need to make any further progress, and several eminent scholars have devoted themselves to restating, explaining, or justifying some classical philosophies with the explicit or implicit conviction that they represent the ultimate truth. Malkani is very candid in denying the need to progress beyond the ancient masters.[1] He himself being an Advaitin, whenever he has an occasion, he tries to expound and defend an Advaitic view. For example, when engaged in presenting a comparative study of consciousness, he does not hesitate to make an attempt "to explain and justify the Advaitic view as the only right and consistent view of consciousness."[2]

But even better examples of glorifying merely interpretative studies of Advaita Vedānta are found in the various writings of Mahadevan. His traditionalism, or dogmatism, born out of his adherence to the ST conception, is clearly visible in his declaration, or reiteration, made very recently in the style of a committed Advaitin, that "such insights as the ones we have tried to explain" (i.e. Advaitic insights) "will be found to illuminate man's path to perfection. They will never be outmoded or become obsolete."[3]

1. *Philosophical Quarterly*, Vol. XXII, p. 198.

A well-known professor of philosophy once reported to me that his elder brother, who was an equally well-known professor of philosophy, was against doing any philosophical writing because he held that all that was worthwhile in philosophy had already been written or said by classical Indian philosophers (Author).

2. G. R. Malkani, "Comparative Study of Consciousness," in W. R. Inge, et. al. (ed), *Radhakrishnan : Comparative Studies in Philosophy* (London : George Allen and Unwin, 1951), p. 231.

3. T. M. P. Mahadevan, "Contemporary Relevance of the Insights of Advaita," in M. Chatterjee, (ed), *Contemporary Indian Philosophy*, Series II (London : George Allen and Unwin, 1974), p. 132.

A traditionalist need not be an Advaitin. If one believes that in the classical philosophical traditions are stored the *darśanas*, the spiritual visions, of people whose veracity is unquestionable, one can consider it his duty to reinterpret and revive the tradition of whichever philosophy it is that has appealed to him. An emphatic assertion of this standpoint has very lately been made by Chari. "Is there a distinctive Indian philosophical tradition bound up with the hoary Indian culture ? And must the Indian philosopher of today be concerned with reviving and reinterpreting tradition ?" "My answers," he says, "to these questions are in the affirmative." Chari also interprets the Indian tradition *à la* the spiritualists.

> "The Indian philosophical enterprise is at once metaphysical, ethical, religious and mystical. The differentiation of religion and philosophy, and the delimitation of their respective spheres, is a Western phenomenon, not an Indian trend."[1]

Chari does not care to mention that the Indian philosophical enterprise, along with being at once metaphysical, ethical, etc., is also logical, epistemological, critical, analytical, empiricist, etc.

If one's attachment to a philosophical tradition becomes sentimental, it does tell upon his intellectual (and/even behavioural) freedom, and it is very likely to become not only sentimental but even obsessive if the tradition concerned has been given a religious or nationalist colour. The ST conception did both. It dressed up classical Indian philosophy in a theological garb and, helped by some historical factors, seemed to boost nationalistic pride. It gave the impression that any counter-interpretation would be unpatriotic or anti-national. If the West was superior to India in science and material advancement, claim the champions of the ST conception, India was much superior to the West in having spiritual philosophy, a philosophy much superior to Western philosophy, since the former was a sure way to self-realization, a value higher than which there was no other value (*niḥśreyasa*) and which all that the West had—science, philosophy, material prosperity—would never be able to give.

It would be unusual for anyone who accepts this style of thinking to retain his philosophic freedom, the freedom to look at and

1. C. T. K. Chari, "Culture, Language and the Philosophical Enterprise in N. K. Devaraja (ed) *Indian Philosophy Today* (Delhi : Macmillan, 1975), p. 93.

make use of classical traditions in an independent, objective, creative, manner; in a manner that does not forbid him to make new departures which may not be in keeping with the traditions as understood in the ST conception. If he would come into contact with some non-Indian or non-spiritual traditions, it is very likely that he would feel inclined to proceed to defend the superiority of the Indian traditions over the latter, or to show that whatever is worthwhile in them is already present, or anticipated or implied by something already present in the Indian traditions. Radhakrishnan, in most of his writings and, many others, have taken this path. Mahadevan's essay "Contemporary Relevance of the Insights of Advaita," already referred to, exemplifies that this practice is considered honourable even in the seventies.

Excessive, uncritical, respect for the classical philosophies have made interpretative, exegetical, works acquire a kind of dignity which definitely is not theirs; and this dignity, by some, perhaps as a result of conditioning, or generalization, to *any* interpretative work, no matter the philosophy interpreted is Indian or Western, classical or contemporary. Editors of works which should have contained only creative, or at least genuinely critical, pieces, do not feel any incongruity or compunction in including in them, nor do authors in contributing to them, purely exegetical essays.[1]

Contemporary Indian Philosophy, first series, edited by Radhakrishnan and Muirhead[2] is perhaps the first coordinated work

1. To mention only a few examples, one can refer to Banerjee's "The Foundations of Advaita Vedānta," Parikh's "The Humanism of Roy" and Varadachari's "The Search for Integrated Life," in K. S. Murty and K. R. Rao (ed), *Current Trends in Indian Philosophy* (Waltair : Andhra University Press, 1970).

Also see Mahadevan's "Contemporary Relevance of the Insights of Advaita," Devasenapati's "God, Man and Bondage," and Ray's "G. E. Moore and the Autonomy of Ethics," in M. Chatterjee (ed) *Contemporary Indian Philosophy*, Series II.

What goes on in the name of comparative philosophy is also in point of philosophical substance exegetical. For example, Sinari's "The Experience of Nothingness in Buddhism and Existentialism" in M. Chatterjee (ed) *Contemporary Indian Philosophy*, Series II.

2. S. Radhakrishnan and J. H. Muirhead (ed), *Contemporary Indian Philosophy*, First Series, 2d ed. (London : George Allen and Unwin, 1952).

exhibiting the dominance of the ST conception on the philosophers and philosophically oriented thinkers of India in the thirties. The overwhelming majority of its contributors are adherents of the ST conception and under the influence of the Advaita Vedānta. What dismays an open-minded, secular, observer of contemporary Indian philosophizing is the fact that even in the seventies the ST conception and its child, the exegetical tradition, are exercising their grip on the minds of some Indian writers without any sign of loosening. This trend of thinking has tended to obliterate, at least for most of its adherents, the distinction between exegetical scholarship and philosophical creativity, between doing history of philosophy and philosophy. Its general dampening effect on intellectual freedom, on the urge for creativity and innovation, is natural. Almost all of the followers of the ST conception are led by its own logic to accept *śruti* (scriptures) as the ultimate, unquestionable, source of the knowledge of spiritual truths which are the real truths for them. To quote Malkani :

> "But truth must be absolute truth or it is no truth. This is the truth that philosophy seeks; and when it finds it, there is no subjectivity about it. Truth speaks and we listen. Verily is *śruti* or hearing the way to truth."[1]

In a latter article also he sticks to this position. Indian philosophy, he says,

> "*replaces imagination by some kind of spiritual experience as the starting point*... Philosophy is supposed to be concerned with a knowledge of the supersensible ground of empirical reality. It is supposed to be concerned with metaphysical truth...How is the knowledge of this truth possible ? Not through reason alone which is not an original or an intuitive source of knowledge. The senses are intuitive, but they cannot grasp the supersensible. There is only one way in which the reality of the supersensible can be indicated to us. This indication comes to us from the scripture as a revelation from above."[2]

Thus, neither empiricism nor rationalism, nor even intuitionism as ordinarily understood, can be regarded as a correct theory of knowledge. Not even intuitionism as normally understood because it does not have to regard scriptural authority as the basis or starting point of the philosophic pursuit. Malkani is one of those for whom, as I have already shown, the actual

1. *Philosophical Quarterly*, Vol. XXII (1950), 209.

2. *Ibid.*, Vol. XXIV, p. 139

objective of Indian philosophy is the proper objective of philosophy *per se*.

It may be urged, in support of the spiritualist, interpretative, activity, that the great masters like Śaṁkara and Rāmānuja also assumed the veracity of the scriptures and presented their philosophies by way of interpreting or commenting upon them. But it is important to remember that they did not merely attempt to restate, interpret, defend, or justify a philosophical position already presented by someone else in a full-blown form. Rather, they tried, and with great success, to evolve or develop one out of ideas not fully systematized or intelligible in one and only one way. Their work can be compared with a sculptor's carving out of a block of marble a particular human figure which is not already there to be discovered or seen by any eye, or the only one which can be carved out of that block. In a sense the figure is contained in the block and in a sense it is not, since it is a well-known fact that carving it out of the block is an imaginative, creative act and not just an imitative, mechanical one. The classical masters like Śaṁkara are in a sense commentators, but their commentaries are creative and innovative, and not merely exegetical or justificatory. It is true, however, that had a genius like Śaṁkara not bound himself to the task of writing commentaries on the scriptures, his philosophic freedom would have been much greater and his creativity would have soared to still greater heights.

The modern spiritualists and scripturalists (followers of scriptures) do not attempt to do to the writings of, say, Śaṁkara, what he did to the scriptures, not to speak of going back to the scriptures themselves. Their exegetical writings are, therefore, not, truly speaking, in keeping with the classical traditions of Indian philosophy. The classical commentators were *creative* in their commentaries, whereas their modern followers feel themselves glorified by trying simply to be *faithful* to them.

Too much respect for any classical tradition is a sign of decadence, or at least of stagnation. It makes one backward-looking, and prevents one from becoming forward-looking; it makes one rest in the past and dissuades him from making any serious effort to create a new future. It obstructs and distorts, even his perception of the present. It has been greatly responsible for modern Indians not paying adequate attention to, or not being critically aware of, the demands, needs, and problems of modern Indian life, with the result that they are not getting such fresh philosophical questions which the facts of life pose before a perceptive philosopher. If by sheer chance one happens to read such a question correctly, he turns to some classical Indian, or modern Western, philosophy for an answer. The result is, as expected, further thickening of the already too thick traditionalism and imitativeness.

The reverential attitude towards classical traditions stifles one's creativity also in another way. By constantly keeping before his mind the works of the great masters and with unqualified admiration, the modern Indian philosopher feels himself to be like a pigmy, too frail and small a creature to rise to the august heights reached by the masters. He then starts consoling himself by devoting his energies to the mere exposition and interpretation of their views.

I am not saying that classical traditions, or any traditions for that matter, should be indiscriminately condemned or shunned. That will be a suicidal move. Rather, one should have towards them an attitude of objective, critical, understanding and assessment. One should have the willingness to retain, modify, or even drop certain parts of them, and the freedom to make honest efforts for the creative extension of what is worthwhile in them in new directions. Only such a person would be *truly* following the tradition of classical masters, and not he who prepares an apologetic for them. In such enterprises, traditional ideas may get very greatly changed, even misinterpreted, mutilated or replaced by new ones, but the net philosophical gain resulting out of the creative process will do more than merely compensate for any loss caused by the distortion of the traditional heritage. This type of work can be congenial to open-minded, free-thinking, Indian scholars and provide them a good avenue for contributing to philosophical progress. Another, related type of activity, equally creative, would be to undertake purely theoretical, logical, studies of some of the basic ideas, theories, or presuppositions of classical Indian philosophy, not for the sake of discovering their historical origin, or tracing their development, or assessing their local importance in the body of the school they belong to, but for bringing out their conceptual capabilities, relationships, and importance, determined by independent, objective, philosophical, considerations.

The above two are good avenues for the expression of creativity for those philosophically free, non-committed Indians who have the aptitude to make use of classical Indian ideas as their resource materials. And, for this kind of work, it is the relevant attitude that is more important than expertise and scholarship in classical Indian philosophy, since the goal here would be philosophical reflection and not authentic exposition. The first step the modern Indian philosopher needs to take in order to undertake in a meaningful way either one of the above activities is to *free* himself from blind attachment to any philosophical tradition, classical or contemporary, indigenous or foreign; he would have to make special efforts to obtain freedom from the ST conception because of, as already mentioned, its religious and (seemingly) nationalistic appearance.

The predominance of the ST conception should not, however, make one forget that it is *not the only* possible interpretation of the classical Indian conception of philosophy; empiricist, non-spiritual, analytical, trends can very well be discovered or read into the writings of several classical masters. Almost every school offers good specimens of purely analytical, secular, non-mystical, studies, as, for example, Dharmakīrti's *Nyāya Bindu.* Even in the writings of Śaṁkara there are several tracts exhibiting good examples of penetrating logical analyses, e.g. his commentary on the first four aphorisms of the *Brahma Sūtra.* In fact almost any variety of philosophy can be located in one or the other of classical writings which constitute an infinitely rich stock. It is a misfortune that due to some historical reasons the plausibility of the ST conception alone attracted the attention of modern Indian thinkers with the result that it was given undue publicity.

Even if the spiritualist interpretation is historically correct, it deserves to be rejected, or if retained, retained with caution, because, as shown above, it contains built-in mechanisms to curtail philosophic freedom and thereby discourage philosophical creativity and novelty. When its champions require a modern Indian philosopher to be *Indian* in his philosophizing by making the latter cohere with the ST conception, they forget to ask themselves which one, trying to be Indian, or trying to be philosophically free and creative, is (philosophically) more important.

The ST conception is not a right conception of philosophy because it amounts to denying the academic autonomy of philosophy by making it either subservient to, or coterminus or isomorphic with, religion. It does not matter whether this place of honour is given to Hinduism or to some other religion. Since every religion claims to possess a set of absolute truths about some supersensible reality, all that a philosopher of this orientation needs to do is to interpret the philosophies he is interested in, in the light of the set given to him by his religion. This is what some modern Christian missionaries interested in Indian philosophy are doing. Father De Smet's essay "Towards an Indian View of the Person" in M. Chatterjee (ed) *Contemporary Indian Philosophy* (Second Series) is a good example.[1] Being impressed by the importance given to the concept of person in Christianity he tries to show that "materials for an Indian recognition of the person are present both in the theologies and in the various anthropologies of the Indian tradition."[2] By referring to the Vedas, Brāhmaṇas, Upaniṣads, Jainism, Sāṁkhya, Buddhism, the Bhagavad Gītā, Śaṁkara, etc., he claims to have shown that the concept of person is not foreign to classical Indian philosophy even though "it has no adequate rendering in any of the Sanskritic languages."[3] It is not at all obvious to me in what way this contributes to philosophical progress. Apart from giving satisfaction that Christianity is not at loggerheads with the theologies and anthropologies, i.e., the philosophies of God and man, of India, what else can such an essay achieve?

But the Indian philosophical scene is not all bleak. Contemporary Indian philosophy does exhibit some signs of slow but gradual emancipation from commitment to the ST conception and the traditional bonds in general. It is also becoming more and more mature. Although creative work on a large scale may not be available, there are visible at least some definitely optimistic indications. The tradition of committed scholarship in respect of traditional spiritual Indian philosophy, as we find, for example, in Malkani's or Mahadevan's committed Advaitism, is gradually becoming less and less fashionable, and along with it is also getting weaker the tradition of historical scholarship. Good,

1. M. Chatterjee (ed), *Contemporary Indian Philosophy*, Series II, p. 54.
2. *Ibid.*, pp. 51-52.
3. *Ibid.*

expository, historical, works may not be written for some time to come. This is likely partly because purely historical scholarship is slowly ceasing to enjoy the respect it once enjoyed among philosophers and partly because most of contemporary Indian philosophers do not possess the necessary expertise in Sanskrit.

Some contemporary thinkers are moving in the direction of using some traditional Indian ideas in their own ways and in consequence some good specimens of creative writings are becoming available. To make use of one's native philosophical traditions in one's creative thinking is to make the most profitable use of them. This is also their most honourable use because the traditions then pass on to new generations in a living manner, and do not remain stored in the history of the country as antiques are in its national museum.

But it is worth recollecting that it is in no way obligatory for an Indian philosopher to make use, in his philosophizing, of Indian or only Indian philosophical traditions. As I wrote more than a decade ago,

> "the correct relationship between philosophical traditions and philosophical reflection is very much like the relationship between food and health. We eat because we want to be healthy. The right food for a man is only that which keeps him healthy, and it is meaningless, from the dietetic point of view, to ask where it comes from. It is also not necessary that the same food suit everybody. Further, even the best food will do a person good only if it is properly digested and assimilated by him, and not if it is only carried as a precious headload."[1]

In a section of the philosophical community in the country, there is current the seemingly patriotic prejudice that even the creative philosophical contributions of a modern Indian can be genuinely Indian only if they are *rooted* in some classical philosophical tradition or traditions of the country.[2] Moreover, the

1. "Tradition, Progress and Contemporary Indian Philosophy, *Philosophy East and West*, Vol. XV, Nos. 3 & 4 (July-October, 1965), 257.

2. According to this criterion, one may declare that what has been contributed by Daya Krishna to Murty and Rao (ed) *Current Trends in Indian Philosophy*; or by Deshpande and Sen to M. Chatterjee (ed), *Contemporary Indian Philosophy*, Series II; or by the current author to Murty and Rao (ed) *Current Trends in Indian Philosophy*, M. Chatterjee (ed) *Contemporary Indian Philosophy*, and N. K. Devaraja (ed) *Indian Philosophy Today* is not genuinely Indian. On the other hand, the contributions of S. S. Barlingay, Sibajivan Bhattacharya in *Indian Philosophy Today*, or N. K. Devaraja's contribution in *Contemporary Indian Philosophy* or Kalidas Bhattacharya's article in *Current Trends in Indian Philosophy* are genuinely Indian. It is difficult to defend this criterion on sheer academic or logical grounds.

traditional philosophies are not, in their original, easily available to modern Indians because of linguistic difficulties, and that is why most of those who claim to make use of them have to depend on secondary sources. Therefore, the attempt to house contemporary philosophizing so inextricably in the bosom of the classical is not in general going to yield happy results.

An Indian may make some classical philosophy or philosophies of India the background of his philosophizing, or derive his conceptual tools therefrom. But there is nothing obligatory in his doing this, nor is there anything wrong if he turns to some non-Indian philosophy or philosophies instead. One should make use of a philosophical tradition only if it is philosophically rewarding, and not simply because it is indigenous. Even some Western scholars, particularly those who subscribe to the ST conception, seem to maintain that contemporary or future Indian philosophy in order to remain Indian should be rooted in classical Indian philosophy. But they offer no good reason, as there cannot be any. If a departure from the tradition in Western philosophy made by a Western thinker can be welcomed as a revolution, why should one from the Indian tradition made by an Indian be ignored as an imitation of the West or condemned as blasphemous ? To hold such a view is like admiring modern India for its improved Khadi but ignoring or treating with contempt its synthetic fabrics on the alleged ground that they are like Western fabrics.

The future of Indian philosophy will be determined, to a large extent, by its independence from the classical Indian traditions. But it must not in this process hook itself to any non-Indian tradition. Bondage to a tradition, whether indigenous or foreign, is always destructive of philosophic freedom. Philosophical creativity does not take place in a vacuum. What G. E. Moore once said of himself is true of the majority of philosophers: it is the serious study of another philosopher's work which very often stimulates one to intelligent criticism or creative thinking. Not all philosophers receive their stimulus from the problems of life. The average modern Indian philosopher also has to get his stimulus from the study of some other philosophers, Indian or non-Indian; it does not matter what their nationalities are. It is very likely that a contemporary Anglo-American philosopher is found to be a more convenient source of stimulus than a classical Indian, not only because of the language but also because of nearness in time. The classical mode of thinking and the classical problems may not be as attractive as the modern ones because of the brute fact that we are not living in classical times. But it is also possible that one discovers modern problems, or better ways of solving modern problems, in classical writings, Indian or non-Indian. Contemporary or future Indian philosophy can be really and satisfactorily creative only if it shakes off its almost pathological attachment to traditionalism, Indian as well as Western. To support this severance one needs to have the feeling of national self-confidence as well as of national self-respect. Philosophy can have natural growth only in an atmosphere of openness and freedom, shackled neither by adherence to the spiritualist tradition generating the superstition of the superiority of Indian over Western philosophy, nor by a similar adherence transferred to phenomenology, existentialism, or linguistic analysis, etc., with its own equally undesirable consequences.

The various types of philosophical activities current in contemporary India are : (1) reportive-descriptive studies, (2) comparative studies, (3) synthesis of ideas from different philosophies, (4) problem analyses, and (5) theory-construction. The reportive-descriptive studies still outnumber others, and even comparative studies in effect turn out to be descriptive. Synthetic studies have been encouraged by those who believe in some practical good, coming out of putting together reconcilable ideas from the East and the West, in respect of cultural understanding between nations. Therefore, if it is possible, it would be more relevant to international understanding than to philosophical progress. Only the last two are directly in the direction of the latter.

PART III

THE FUTURE OF INDIAN PHILOSOPHY

15

WHITHER INDIAN PHILOSOPHY : A SEARCH FOR DIRECTION AND SUGGESTIONS FOR RECONSTRUCTION

DINESH C. MATHUR*

INDIAN philosophy, like any other philosophy, is best understood in its concrete historical context. It is the cultural enterprise of the Indian people beginning with the poetic outpouring of the Vedic Aryans in the ancient past. It includes the speculative ventures of the Upaniṣadic thinkers, the systematic philosophical treatises of the *sūtra* period including those of the Buddhists and the Jainas, the full-blooded philosophies of the epics, the ethical codes, the later commentaries on the *sūtras* as well as the logico-polemical literature initiated by Navya-Nyāya which lasted until the end of the sixteenth century. In view of the extreme complexity, subtlety and long historical span of Indian philosophizing it will be naïve and hazardous to "understand" it in terms of any neat formula. By the end of the sixteenth century all possible viewpoints, such as idealism, realism, naturalism, materialism, scepticism, transcendentalism, absolutism, theism, atheism, etc. had been represented in India's

*D. C. Mathur is Professor of Philosophy, State University of New York at Brockport. Published several research papers in *The Journal of Philosophy*, *Philosophy and Phenomenological Research*, *Philosophy East-West*. He also authored two books : *Modern Logic : Its Relevance to Philosophy* and *Naturalistic Philosophies of Experience* (Studies in James, Dewey and Fraber against the background of Husserl's phenomenology).

philosophies. Since I have abstained from any dogmatic definition of philosophy in order to avoid a veiled stipulation about its "correct" nature, I would include within the compass of Indian philosophy the writings of those Indian scholars who endeavoured to recover and reinterpret India's philosophical heritage after its eclipse during the period of British occupation. Here belong the writings of Raja Rammohun Roy, Dayananda, Vivekananda, Tilak, Gandhi, Tagore and Aurobindo. This was the period of Indian renaissance roughly spanning from the middle of the nineteenth to the middle of the twentieth century. Among those who occupied university chairs in philosophy in India S. Radhakrishnan stands foremost for his comprehensive and eclectic scholarship, adoption of a modified version of Advaita Vedānta, and for his impact on other younger philosophers of India's post-independence period. Contemporary Indian philosophy is reflected in the writings of those who have combined varying degrees of acquaintance with classical tradition with a knowledge of Western philosophy in all its aspects. A perusal of some anthologies recently published shows no overall unified perspective as some of them continue to deal with classical problems of the nature of *Brahman* and its relation to *Jiva* and the world, or of human suffering and final liberation (*mokṣa*), while others pick up philosophical problems and puzzles here and there and adopt the analytical method of ordinary language philosophy following Wittgenstein and Ryle, and still others manifest the influence of phenomenology and existentialism in their writings.[1]

Lest I should give the impression that Indian philosophy has been the exclusive concern of Indian scholars past and present, let me hasten to add that quite a few Western Orientalists, belonging to Germany, England and France, played a crucial role in rehabilitating India's philosophical heritage from its dormant state for two centuries preceding India's independence.

1. (a) K. Satchidananda Murti and K. Ramakrishna Rao (eds), *Current Trends in Indian Philosophy* (Waltair : Andhra University Press, 1972).

(b) Margaret Chatterjee (ed), *Contemporary Indian Philosophy*, Series II (London : George Allen and Unwin, 1974).

(c) N. K. Devaraja (ed), *Indian Philosophy Today* (Delhi : Macmillan, 1975).

(d) Donald H. Bishop (ed), *Indian Thought : An Introduction* (New York: John Wiley, 1975).

Their *perception* of India's religio-philosophical tradition and its influence on Indian scholars during that period is of great interest for a sound understanding and reconstruction of Indian philosophy. And lastly, any philosophy which is confined within the four walls of the classrooms, or is buried in the stacks of university libraries is bound to be effete—fit to be relegated to the museum of antiquities. Therefore, an overall appraisal of Indian philosophy should include a study of its impact on the socio-historical problems of the common man in India who, though not having the benefit of academic training, has nevertheless been reared in the cultural climate of its tradition. Keeping in view all these aspects of Indian philosophy, it is the intention of this paper to evaluate its contribution in the past and suggest directions for its reconstruction so as to make it live and relevant to the concrete issues of modern India.

As pointed out above Indian philosophy as a historical and cultural phenomenon has been extremely complex presenting a rare combination of bold speculative sweep in its earlier phase and subtle logical and dialectical reasoning in its later systematic phase. So seductive has been its charm that not only Western orientalists like Schopenhauer, Deussen and Max Müller but, following their lead, Indian scholars of repute as well were taken in when they identified the whole of Indian Philosophy with Upaniṣadic Idealism and Advaita Vedāntism. When Neo-Hegelianism of T. H. Green, F. H. Bradley and John and Edward Caird was the reigning philosophy in England it was fashionable among Indian philosophers to look with pride on their brand of philosophical idealism and regard it as the last word in philosophy. Śaṁkara was compared to Kant or to Bradley and this performed the historical function of bolstering our national ego and infuse confidence in our own cultural past. This is precisely the reason for the widespread belief shared by a large number of scholars that the quintessence of Indian philosophy is its "idealism" and "spiritualism." Radhakrishnan is the most influential and typical representative of this sweeping interpretation of Indian philosophy when he says : "Philosophy in India is essentially spiritual."[1] That American scholarship

1. S. Radhakrishnan, *Indian Philosophy*, Vol. I (London : George Allen and Unwin, 1927), p. 24.

did not remain far behind in sharing such an adulatory version of Indian philosophy is shown by the fact that in the first half of the nineteenth century Emerson, among other transcendentalists, turned in an amateurish fashion to the Upaniṣads and the *Gītā* for inspiration. And by the end of the century Royce, the last of the Neo-Hegelian idealists in America was a great admirer of the "spiritual" and "idealistic' tradition of India. In our own times, specially during the late sixties of this century, there has been a phenomenal resurgence of interest in India's philosophies among the youths of America. Disillusioned and alienated by the blind drift of modern technology, the hectic "rat-race", the brutal Vietnam War and the unintelligent destruction of the environment, a large number of American youth sought an escape into a romanticized version of Indian "spiritualism". This was the heyday of the drug sub-culture, romantic experimentation with everything exotic and the radically novel, and an exaggerated emphasis on "do your own thing." No wonder, they turned to Transcendental Meditation, chanting "Hare Krishna," Zen Buddhism, and other "spiritual" panaceas advertised by various *gurus*. This was their perception of oriental philosophy in general and Indian philosophy in particular. However, besides all this popular brand of Indian philosophy there has been and there is a more serious, academic and critical interest in Indian philosophy among well-informed American scholars at various universities. Such an interest was stimulated by the impact of Swami Vivekananda's lectures and the founding of the Ramakrishna-Vivekananda Centers in America at the turn of the twentieth century as well as by the various East-West Philosopher's Conferences commencing with the first one in 1939 in Honolulu under the able leadership of the late C. A. Moore. As a consequence there is a more realistic and "pluralistic" interpretation of Indian philosophy among American scholars today. It will be worthwhile to consider a few serious interpretations of India's philosophical tradition by a few contemporary Western orientalists, refute prevailing cliche's and misconceptions and bring out their limitations before attempting a possible reconstruction of some basic categories and concepts of India's philosophies.

Recently attempts have been made by some Western orientalists to interpret Indian philosophy in terms of some single neat formula. Some of these are variations of the eulogistic characterization of Indian philosophy as being essentially "spiritual" even though they do not necessarily imply such an adulatory endorsement. For example, Ninian Smart has put forward the thesis that Indian metaphysical systems have been dominated by religious motives.[1] Another such interpretation is by Karl H. Potter who has argued in his recent book that philosophies in India have been mainly concerned with *mokṣa* or transcendental freedom, and that speculative arguments were used as means for eradicating doubts arising from skeptical and fatalistic positions.[2] He has reiterated this thesis in another paper in which he has seriously suggested that idealistic and transcendental philosophies of Nāgārjuna and Śaṁkara "provide attractive candidates for the role of true philosophy" as an escape "between the horns of contemporary dilemma between theology and technology, faith and reason."[3] Such panegyric interpretations of India's philosophies have been critically examined recently by Daya Krishna who found them largely mythical.[4] These "spiritualistic" and "religious" interpretations suffer not only from the fallacy of sweeping oversimplification but also from the egregious blunder of taking India's philosophies piecemeal in an unhistorical manner. They completely ignore the socio-historical context of philosophical ideas and thus end in mystifying and confounding people rather than enlightening them.

As a counterweight to such an "idealistic" interpretation of Indian philosophy there is the other extreme of "understanding" the entire corpus of philosophical literature of India in terms of a radically different but still a simplistic formula, namely that of Marxist "historical materialism." Here we have the writings of N. P. Anikeev, Dale Riepe, Debiprasad Chattopadhyaya and

1. Ninian Smart, *Doctrine and Argument in Indian Philosophy* (London : George Allen and Unwin, 1964), p. 16.

2. Karl H. Potter, *Presuppositions of India's Philosophies* (New Jersey : Prentice-Hall, 1963).

3. Karl H. Potter, "Indian Philosophy's Alleged Religious Orientation," *Philosophic Exchange* (Brockport, New York), Vol. I, No. 3 (Summer, 1972), 159-74.

4. Daya Krishna, "Three Conceptions of Indian Philosophy," *Philosophy East and West* (1965), 37-51, and "Three Myths about Indian Philosophy," *Quest* 53 (1967), 9-16.

D. D. Kosambi.[1] No doubt, a socio-historical interpretation of ideas is more enlightening than a piecemeal one. It puts ideas in their historical context and performs the painstaking task of detailed analysis rather than making sweeping generalizations. On the contrary, a piecemeal approach to philosophical systems is unenlightening precisely because ideas do not appear suddenly from the blue air or pop up ready-made from people's heads. Therefore, to describe the whole of Indian philosophy as "spiritual" or "idealistic" is to betray historical ignorance or manifest blatant selective bias. However, this does not mean that a Marxist interpretation in terms of historical materialism can do full justice to the complexity of philosophical ideas and disputes, if it assumes a one-sided dependence of ideas on productive forces of a particular period. I do not think that Marx intended such an interpretation to be put on his philosophical position. It is well-known that Marx and Engels devoted a good deal of thought on the mutual relationship between what is called the "infra-structure" and the "super-structure" in any social analysis. A monolithic analysis of ideas whether in terms of "idealism" and "spiritualism" or in terms of "reductive" materialism is too simplistic and as such, is no more than a dogmatic interpretation of social history. An actual study of the cultural and social history of various peoples shows that the concepts of society and history are complex and are best understood in the plural than in the singular. There is not one single

1. (a) N. P. Anikeev, *Modern Ideological Struggle for the Ancient Philosophical Heritage of India* (Soviet Indology Series No. 1) (Calcutta, 1969).

(b) Dale Riepe, *The Naturalistic Tradition in Indian Thought* (Seattle : University of Washington, 1961).

—*The Philosophy of India and Its Impact on American Thought* (Springfield, Illinois : Charles C. Thomas, 1970).

—"On the Proper Interpretation of Indian Religion and Philosophy," *Philosophic Exchange* (Brockport, New York), Vol. I, No. 3 (Summer, 1972), 177-91.

(c) D. D. Kosambi, *Ancient India : A History of Its Culture and Civilization* (New York : Pantheon Books, 1965).

(d) Debiprasad Chattopadhyaya, *Indian Philosophy* (New Delhi: People's Publishing House, 1964).

—*Lokayata : A Study in Ancient Indian Materialism* (New Delhi : People's Publishing House, 1959).

—*What is Living and What is Dead in Indian Philosophy* (New Delhi : People's Publishing House, 1976).

society. There are various social groups. Nor is there one History with a capital "H". There are multiple histories. It would be naïve to regard history as a mystical force governed by a single iron law of dialectical materialism. Socio-economic factors do play an important part in giving rise to ideologies but man's awareness of these factors adds a new and significant dimension to the historical process. Ideas once arisen exercise a *critical* function in reorganizing and reinterpreting historical experience as is exemplified by the impact of the historical Buddha's teaching in the sixth century B.C. At the same time ideas are capable of dialectical development too. In other words there is a history of ideas also. There is, therefore, not only an on-going dialectical interaction between socio-historical experience and philosophical ideas but a relatively independent dialectical development of ideas as well, giving rise to various conceptual problems. The long history of philosophical disputes between rival systems of India's philosophies during the *Sūtra* period, and the philosophical debate between Buddhist logicians and idealists following Dignāga, and Nyāya-Vaiśeṣika philosophers following Uddyotkara, for almost six hundred years from the 5th century to 11th century A.D. amply illustrate how ideas are capable of generating their own problems. Though a study of these philosophical disputes in the context of socio-historical factors can be enlightening, yet they cannot be "explained" without residuum merely on such an analysis.

In the light of what I have said above it follows that basically philosophical problems have a cultural and historical genesis. Viewed concretely in terms of actual historical development philosophy does not set out from scratch and philosophical problems do not grow in a vacuum. It always starts with an existing set of beliefs, values and attitudes which have been challenged by fresh experience or novel ideas. This encounter between novel ideas and traditional beliefs gives rise to fresh philosophical thinking leading to a reorganization and reinterpretation of ideas and experience. The historical Buddha, Śaṁkara, Vivekananda and Gandhi are obvious examples of creative thinkers who performed such a critical function, forced people to reconsider their fundamental assumptions, and provided a new focus and a new vision from which to interpret their experience. Methodologically speaking, therefore, philosophy has always been the intellectual expression of the process of social and cultural change. Only when Indian civilization became stagnant by the end of the seventeenth century, it ceased to be creative and produced no fresh philosophical thought for a long time. Historical scholars have wondered why Indian philosophy till today has remained mostly sterile—either submerged in scholastic interpretation of classical texts or preoccupied with problems which have become irrelevant to our own times. There must have been some inherent weaknesses in Indian civilization and culture which made it an easy prey to Muslim invasions in the tenth century A.D. and later to Moghul conquest and British occupation. Such a long period of political subjugation did certainly play a significant role in the cultural and intellectual stagnation of India. However, either because of this political conquest or independently of it there was another factor which kept Indian thinking unhistorical and backward looking. This was the lack of the development of experimental temper which, by contrast, had produced a powerful impact on the Western world since the seventeenth century. It may have been a historical accident that a galaxy of scientists and mathematicians as Francis Bacon, Galileo, Kepler and Newton arose in the Western world to create that powerful combination of experimental science and mathematics which not only revolutionized our knowledge of nature but also produced a great impact on the philosophies of the seventeenth and eighteenth century Europe. Another such revolutionary idea which had still a greater effect on philosophy was Darwin's theory of evolution published in the middle of the nineteenth century. Philosophy in the Western world has not remained the same since, but has incorporated these scientific ideas in their pursuit of the central questions concerning the nature of the world and the meaning of life, the methods of acquiring knowledge, the place of values in a world of facts, and the nature and the possibility of the good life for man. Such a historical connection between the analytic as well as speculative functions of philosophy on the one hand and man's growing knowledge and changing social experience on the other has been lacking in India since its cultural decadence by the end of the seventeenth century. It is hardly surprising that no new and comprehensive philosophical outlook responsive to those new scientific and evolutionary concepts emerged in India. Indian philosophical thinking in the recent past either ignored this growing scientific knowledge or debunked it as "materialistic" in contrast to its alleged "timeless" spiritual truths declared once and for all by our ancient sages based on their "intuitive" experiences. However, such inflexible posturing and fixation on the past is not only unnecessary but is positively detrimental to the emerging social and moral needs of modern India. A new comprehensive philosophical outlook is called for which would reinterpret our traditional philosophical heritage, retain what is of lasting value in it, and yet adapt itself to the cumulatively growing knowledge made possible by the rise of science and technology. In other words it would have to take time and history seriously.

What would qualify for such an outlook? My suggestion is that a comprehensive, critical and imaginative naturalism based upon the firm foundations of all aspects of human experience—scientific, moral, aesthetic and religious, and supported by reason in the sense of critical intelligence as opposed to blind faith in scriptural authority, sheer prejudice or emotion, would alone do justice to the complexity, the possibilities and the limitations of the human condition. This would require a proper understanding of the meaning and interrelation of experience and reason and give them a firm footing in nature without positing a hypothetical "transcendental" realm of super-nature. It would avoid the untenable dichotomies of nature and super-nature, the secular and the spiritual, the material and the ideal, and yet find a proper place and function for *all* areas of human concern. It would steer clear of "reductive" materialism which attempts to explain man's ideal pursuits in terms of mechanical and physical categories, and at the same time would provide a more defensible interpretation of man's spiritual dimension without reifying it to an ontological realm apart from the natural. Such a critical naturalism would regard experience as neither purely subjective nor purely objective but rather an active and interactive relation between the whole person and his changing environment. Reason on such a view would not be an onlooker or outsider but an integral part of on-going experience as articulated and clarified by an active, selective and inquiring mind. The term "nature" in this sense would not designate an entity such as a ship or sealing-wax, nor would it be conceived anthropomorphically as a giant organism. Rather, it would have to be understood as a collective term for all the actualities and possibilities revealed by the total thrust of on-going human experience.

The above-mentioned view of nature is defensible on the basis of a reflective analysis of our *total* experience supported by the organized sciences and supplemented by our moral and aesthetic sensibilities. Nature so understood is neither a succession of discrete and chaotic particulars nor an eternal timeless being like a "painted ship on a painted ocean." All natural existences —physical, biological, psychological and social—are events with a historical or temporal dimension. They are episodic, having a beginning and an ending. They are changing structures involving both continuity and novelty. Contingency and continuity are real pervasive features of all existence. Human existence marks no radical break from the rest of natural existence though it has its own *emergent* characteristics. If Indian philosophy has to become alive and responsive to this progressively correctible knowledge it would have to reinterpret some of the basic concerns and categories of its tradition. I would like to suggest here some of the ways in which our traditional concepts need alternative interpretations.

Adoption of a socio-historical approach to the study of India's philosophies would necessitate the dropping of a number of dogmas which have been taken for granted by classical scholarship. One such dogma has been the pervasive belief that the Vedas, Upaniṣads and the *Gītā* are embodiments of eternal infallible truths and wisdom. Notwithstanding the bold speculative teachings of the Upaniṣads and moral insights of the *Gītā* such a claim to infallibility is not only indefensible but is a positive hindrance to the proper understanding of their doctrines. It is not only possible but proper to understand these scriptural doctrines in the light of natural and historical experience of the early Aryan settlers in India. The Aryan hordes after settling down in the tropical climate of the Indo-Gangetic plains were faced with the task of conquering the native tribes and of learning the arts of agriculture. Ṛg-Vedic outlook, to begin with, was naturalistic, expansive and optimistic. Most of their prayers to the gods were for material goods and happiness in this world. But soon their whole outlook underwent a change as the old tribal unity and solidarity was lost and a new socio-economic structure based on class distinctions emerged producing a gulf between those who were engaged in productive manual labour (the *Vaiśyas* and the *Śūdras*) and others who constituted the leisure class of the rulers (the *Kṣatriyas*) and the *Brahmin* priests who led a parasitical existence on the patronage of the rulers. Surely, the latter two classes freed from productive work enjoyed the leisure to speculate on the nature of ultimate reality which was posited as pure consciousness. Such was the socio-historical background of Upaniṣadic idealism which asserted the primacy of consciousness over natural reality. And yet it would be simplistic to "explain" this search by the Upaniṣadic thinkers for unity behind the bewildering variety and multiplicity of changing phenomena *merely* in terms of socio-economic factors. Indubitably, socio-economic change provided a stimulus and functioned as an occasion for fresh thinking. But we cannot rule out the factor of curiosity for understanding the inexhaustible mystery of existence and the immensity of the universe. Impressed by the constant flux and transience of things and events those early thinkers should have wondered whether there was a unified principle, an ultimate ground and creative source of *all* existence which would render this diversity intelligible. It was also a search for ultimate freedom from the rigmarole of coming into being and passing out of being—the so-called worldly cycle of birth and death (*saṁsāra*). Ṛg-Vedic optimism, naturalistic happiness and hope for living for hundred years, and a life of joy and material expectations gave way to existential anxiety and pessimism. In this quest for certainty, they hit upon the concept of *Brahman* as the ground and the creative source of the universe and identified it with *Ātman* as the innermost transcendental self of man. Concepts of *karma* and *māyā* became prominent, and gradually the emphasis shifted from plurality to unity, from objectivity to subjectivity and from natural reality to spirituality and ideality. Thus, it appears that once those thinkers raised the question of the ultimate creative source of the ceaselessly changing panorama of nature they could not be satisfied with half-way principles of explanation. Their bold speculative inquiry was guided by its own internal logic. They were in search of a unifying principle of intelligibility behind the multiplicity of objects and the flow of events. And they hit upon *Brahman* or *Ātman* as the transtemporal ground of the phenomenal order. This fulfilled their quest for certainty and satisfied their need for ultimate freedom (*mokṣa*). Such a unifying principle could not be a numerical entity. It would be logically incoherent to regard it as an object, a thing, an event or a person. The identity of *Brahman* and *Ātman* (the eternal "I") was meant to emphasize that such a principle was real (*sat*) and not merely a figment of the imagination, and also that it was the ground of *all* existence including man, gods, animals and physical nature. This conception could plausibly be interpreted in naturalistic terms—taking nature in an imaginative, comprehensive, and deepened sense as suggested above. But, unfortunately, this naturalistic insight was missed by classical commentators who turned the doctrine into absolute idealism by interpreting *Brahman* and *Ātman* in terms of pure consciousness, and relegating the natural world and the empirical selves to the position of *māyā*—an illusory order of reality. Such an interpretation created the well-nigh insoluble problem of relating such a transcendent conscious principle to the empirical world of change, and implied a wholesale devaluation of the natural world and empirical human pursuits. As a consequence of such an idealistic interpretation, the commentators and scholars over the centuries wasted precious time, energy and ingenuity in grappling with this pseudo-problem. Śaṁkara, Rāmānuja, Mādhava, Radhakrishnan and Aurobindo, among others, marshalled their erudition and acumen in working out a satisfactory solution of this problem. But it should be recognized that the task of relating *Brahman* to the world of change and to individual selves is a hopeless one because it makes the untenable assumption that *Brahman* is a conscious ontological *entity*. In this respect the *Bṛhadāraṇyaka Upaniṣad* rightly declared the *neti-neti* (not this, not this) character of *Brahman*. If *Brahman* is understood as representing man's imaginative quest for unification, certainty and intelligibility without reifying it into an *antecedent* ontological spiritual Reality (with capital R), then the true task is to use it as a heuristic principle for forging the unity of man and the world through painstaking, concrete and practical social measures and individual efforts rather than get lost in a theoretical puzzle which is conceptually insoluble because of the way it is posed.[1] In any case it makes no sense to apply the anthropomorphic category of consciousness to such a principle of unification.

Other philosophical concepts and beliefs which are peculiarly Indian and are in need of clarification and re-interpretation are those concerning the "law of karma," the doctrine of rebirth, and the nature of bondage and ultimate freedom (*mokṣa* or *nirvāṇa*). Because of considerations of space no detailed examination of these concepts can be undertaken here. And yet it will not be out of place to suggest some needed revisions and re-assessment of these basic Indian concepts. In this context, it is worth pointing out that despite the existence of powerful realistic and logical systems of classical times the one impression which has persisted and has been perpetuated by a number of scholars is that the absolute idealism of *Advaita Vedānta* represents the quintessence of Indian philosophy. In a recent book,[2] contemporary Indian philosophers have tumbled over one another in eulogizing the Advaitic concept of *Brahman* as the pinnacle of Indian philosophical idealism. Writer after writer has repeated the assertion that such a transcendental reality can be "known" only through supersensuous and supra-rational intuition without examining the concept of such an alleged intuition critically. They have repeated the Upaniṣadic belief that one knows *Brahman* by "becoming identical" with it.[3] None has raised the critical issue here of the logical distinction between "having" the experience of being one with *Brahman* and *knowing* it. They have taken the identity statement literally without unpacking its implications. Not only Indian scholars but quite a few Western orientalists have been so dazzled by the dialectics of the Mahāyāna Buddhist philosopher Nāgārjuna and the Advaitic philosopher Śaṁkara as to concur in their relegation of the whole rational enterprise to the realm of appearance against the

1. For elaboration of this view, see D. C. Mathur, "The Concept of Self in the Upanishads," *Philosophy and Phenomenological Research* (March 1972), 390-96.

2. Donald H. Bishop (ed), *Indian Thought : An Introduction* (New York : John Wiley, 1975).

3. S. S. Barlingay, "Indian Epistemology and Logic," in Donald H. Bishop (ed), *Indian Thought : An Introduction*, p. 160;
G. N. Joshi, "Metaphysics," Ibid., p. 180;
T. M. P. Mahadevan, "Śaṁkara," Ibid., pp. 288-90;
Donald H. Bishop, "Epilogue," Ibid., pp. 368-69.

background of a transcendental reality which remains impervious to rational modes of inquiry. They have been taken in by the subtle logic of these dialecticians without being aware of their assumptive use of the concepts of "reality" and "phenomena". The *Śūnyavāda* of Nāgārjuna and the *Advaita* of Śaṁkara both assume a particular view of "reality" as something eternal, unchanging and permanent. Here is a quest for certainty and a desire to escape from change and transitoriness of all worldly things and pursuits. Even the ingenious "no-view" doctrine of Nāgārjuna implies unconsciously a particular view of "reality", and idealistic philosophers like T. R. V. Murti have been quick to interpret Nāgārjuna's concept of *Śūnyatā* as the transcendental Absolute.[1] All such absolutistic philosophies have given rise to the untenable dichotomy between the trans-social realm of Reality on the one hand and the natural socio-historical world as mere appearance (*māyā* of Śaṁkara and *Saṁvṛti-satya* of Nāgārjuna) on the other. Panegyrical endorsement of Śaṁkara's doctrine "*Brahman* is real, the world is illusory" cannot simply wish away the rugged world of nature and socio-historical experience as is evidenced by the adoption of an ambivalent attitude by such writers towards the alleged "illusoriness" of the world. Since the natural world cannot be "thought away" they clarify their position through dubious arguments by asserting that it is "empirically" real but "transcendentally" unreal. One can imagine what effect such a disjunction has on the unwary masses of India on the one hand, and on unscrupulous and hypocritical opportunists on the other. Perhaps all such wholesale denigration of the natural world and the rational enterprise of knowing it could be obviated if our idealist philosophers had correctly grasped the function of reason vis-à-vis experience. Certainly the function of reason is not to "digest" and "devour" experience but to articulate, clarify and organize it. No doubt, the whole cognitive enterprise in terms of conceptual categories is not a substitute for "having" a full-blooded, concrete and vivid experience. But this does not mean, as has been asserted by Śaṁkara, Nāgārjuna and their followers, that since conceptual problems and paradoxes arise in the course of such articu-

1. T. R. V. Murti, *The Central Philosophy of Buddhism*, 2d ed. (London : 1960).

lation the whole rational enterprise, therefore, belongs to a "lower" order of reality—"mere" phenomena—as against the absolute reality given in a mystical intuition. Such conceptual philosophical problems may arise because of unexamined assumptions, inadequate attention to the nature and function of language or failure to refer back these concepts to the bar of immediate experience. In any case, the crucial distinction between illusions within the world and the world as an illusion has to be understood, and it is to be clearly realized that the truth of the former assertion does not imply the truth of the latter. Once such philosophies of "transcendence" and "withdrawal" are abandoned and understood in their socio-historical context, Indian philosophers would have on their hands the crucially important task of developing a critical theory of ethical and social philosophy.

In the light of the above-mentioned task Indian theory of *puruṣārtha* the fourfold scheme of values (*dharma*, *artha*, *kāma* and *mokṣa*), *Varṇāṣrama dharma*—the fourfold classification of society into *Brāhmaṇas*, *Kṣatriyas*, *Vaiśyas* and *Śūdras*, as well as the four stages of life would have to be critically appraised in the light of modern India's problems. The hoary belief in the "law of karma" and the whole concept of action would have to be examined afresh in order to determine their impact and relevance to social change in India. All these beliefs have shaped the Indian psyche and have become an integral part of Indian culture. The epics *Rāmāyaṇa* and the *Mahābhārata* and the *Gītā* have played a major role in shaping the beliefs and attitudes of the Indian people. These are great works, and thinkers, past and present have rightly derived their inspiration from them. Mahatma Gandhi, inspired by the activist teaching of the *Gītā* organized and awakened the supine masses of India from their stupor and led them through non-violent mass action to the goal of independence from the British yoke. Surely Gandhi contributed more to dispel the belief in the illusoriness of the world (*māyāvāda*) by his social action than a host of academic philosophers could ever do. Nay, he boldly challenged the hierarchical class structure and vehemently condemned its virulent and disastrous modern garb of casteism. Though theoretically he believed in the so-called "law of karma" and the theory of rebirth, and ultimate freedom (*mokṣa*), yet through his practice, he broke down the *fatalistic* interpretation of the whole doctrine. Our philosophers could perform this task of re-interpreting the *karma* doctrine on theoretical grounds what Gandhi had done by actual practice. Certainly, it could be done if one linked man's deeds to their consequences—individual and social—in this world, rather than tracing the causes of events in this life to deeds performed in a hypothetical previous birth. The latter hypothesis would involve the tough philosophical problem of personal identity between successive births and the need for postulating a "subtle body" (*sūkṣma-śarīra*) besides the physical to account for causal continuity. Moreover, without solving the crucial problem of empirical evidence such a belief in rebirth would remain in the mystical haze of the occult. And lastly, despite an attempt to interpret the "law of karma" in such a manner as to make man himself responsible for what happens to him because of his free decisions in a previous existence, and granting him freedom to change the future course of his life, the doctrine has in actual practice been taken fatalistically by the poor and illiterate masses of India. As a matter of fact, the belief in the theory of karma and the existence of mass poverty have been historically involved in circular causation. It, therefore, appears that the pernicious effects of this doctrine far outweigh any explanatory value it might have had in the past. Once socio-historical causes of events are understood the need for such a theory would be obviated.

The doctrine of ultimate freedom (*mokṣa*) and its relation to the three other values of moral duty (*dharma*), pursuit of wealth and economic prosperity (*artha*) and pleasure (*kāma*) would have to be critically examined. The most important problem in this connection is how to understand *mokṣa* which is put toward as a trans-social and trans-empirical goal in contradistinction to the three social goals of duty, pursuit of wealth and pleasure. There is a tension between the social goal of the performance of one's duty according to the principles of *Svadharma* and *Svabhāva* as preached by the *Gītā*, and the pursuit of the transcendental goal of *mokṣa*. Krishna's teaching to Arjuna in that revered book did not satisfactorily solve this problem. Arjuna's situation as depicted there was revolutionary, fraught with the gravest of consequences but the advice given by Krishna was in terms of a static code of duties determined by *Svadharma*.

Such a static code of duties is hardly an appropriate response to meet the dynamic situation faced by Arjuna, otherwise he would not have asked for any moral advice at all. One has the feeling that *Krishna*'s advice to Arjuna and his exhortation to him to fight the war were in terms of an esoteric doctrine of an external *Ātman* who is never born and who never dies. But then from the point of view of such transcendental heights *all* actions might be justified. Krishna did not convince Arjuna through a rational reflection on the social and moral consequences of acting one way or the other but initiated him in the mysteries of a metaphysical doctrine. And it is because of this metaphysical intrusion into the solution of dynamic moral situation that the *Gītā* preaches a serene unconcern for and non-attachment (*niṣkāma-karma*) to all consequences personal and social. This tension between the need for being goal-oriented on the social plane where rationally justifiable moral and social action is called for, and the need for an ultimate concern for the serene *Ātman*, has characterized Indian culture ever since. Such an unresolved tension has meant for the vast mass of people either a lip-service to the *Ātman* and a consequent withdrawal from the field of responsible social and moral action, or an opportunistic pursuit of selfish, individualistic goals. In either case it has been detrimental to effective social change and improvement, and to some extent it is responsible for the relatively static character of Indian society.[1] Is it not time, therefore, to drop the transcendental dimension of *freedom* and relate it to man's socio-historical situation as well as his capacity for conscious reflection. To call attention to man's situational rootedness in the physical, biological and socio-historical infra-structures is not, however, to reduce him to a thing or a mere product. This would be fatalistic determinism. Freedom and individuality (in the sense of being capable of choice and initiative) are matters of growth, education and reflection. They are not "given" in advance but are matters of achievement through conscious effort. Man's freedom, though rooted in socio-historical situation, is a *real possibility* in the sense that he can become reflectively aware

1. For elaboration of this point of view, see D. C. Mathur, "Doctrine of Nishkama-Karma : An Alternative Interpretation," *Quest*, No. 42 (1964), 23-25.

of his situation, given the right circumstances, and overcome his limitations through personal effort and endeavour. Such a realistic concept of freedom is certainly more honest and relevant to the awakening of the apathetic masses of India for the realization of their hitherto untapped potential than any make-believe notions of "transcendental" freedom.

To sum up, what India needs today is an integrated philosophical outlook best described as *naturalistic humanism* which steers clear of the dogma of "reductive" materialism on the one hand and the "withdrawal" philosophies of transcendental idealism and *māyāvāda* on the other, and which does not commit the all-too-common error of confusing ethical and moral idealism with the speculative theory of metaphysical idealism that derives the whole of natural reality from Absolute Spirit. Such a modern outlook involves a new set of values and a new way of life which has got rid of religious dogmas and superstitions of all kinds, has eschewed all notions of casteism and fanatical communalism, and is based on progressively correctible personal and social experience, reason and verifiable knowledge. It takes an integrated view of man as having physical, mental, moral and spiritual capacities which have a footing in nature and yet which mark him off from the rest of nature as a conscious being capable of transforming nature through science and technology, and creating new values of truth, honesty, love, beauty, brotherhood, and freedom. It believes that moral and spiritual qualities are not automatic by-products of socio-economic factors and cannot be fostered on a large scale without adequate changes in the social, economic and political structure. It takes a realistic view of man's freedom as a matter of achievement through education and conscious acts of choice and valuation. It regards all "transcendental" notions of freedom which have no footing in nature and society as romantic moonshine. It believes that within the limitations of the total environment man is capable of becoming aware of his conditions, can review his past, learn from history, and finally use this knowledge to act cooperatively with his fellow beings to change his destiny. India today is utterly in need of such an intelligent activistic, socially-oriented, unselfish and humane outlook if it is to dispel the current mood of apathy, frustration, hopelessness, fatalism and cynicism in Indian society. It is hardly an exaggeration to say that India is passing through a period of horrendous moral and spiritual crisis. While the so-called leaders are engaged in the worst kind of self-aggrandizement, naked pursuit of power and money and the worst kind of Machiavillian chicanery, the masses are sinking deeper and deeper into misery, suffering, poverty and fatalistic resignation. Such a revolutionary and explosive situation can be met neither by a withdrawal into the "ivory tower" of transcendentalism and mystic contemplation of the "inner" self, nor by enclosing oneself in the "glass chambers" of *mere* linguistic analysis. Philosophers have to step out of such havens of safety into the market-place of the real world, study the causes of the prevailing atmosphere of despair and offer a constructive social and moral philosophy which when implemented through intelligent social planning within the democratic framework, can produce the needed change for the better. It would require that combination of integrity and effectiveness in our leaders which is as rare as it is indispensable in the context of the contemporary situation in India. It should not be forgotten that precisely when there is complete breakdown of order in society, when there is widespread corruption and self-aggrandizement, gross inequalities and untold misery for the large masses of the people that the democratic structure collapses giving rise to despotic dictatorship. And India recently had a brush with such a catastrophe. Indian philosophers could render an invaluable service by disseminating a new philosophical outlook as a guide to intelligent social action so as to turn things around and usher in an era of peace, prosperity and happiness for all regardless of caste, creed, religion, and sex. Will they rise to the occasion or let it pass ?

16

THE RESPONSIBILITIES OF MODERN INDIAN PHILOSOPHERS

N. K. DEVARAJA*

I

THE situation in philosophy in contemporary, i.e. post-independence, India is one of mixed appearance to cultural observers. Looking at the surface, there seems to be no visible change in the activities of scholars working in the departments of philosophy in numerous universities and colleges. For one thing, there is marked continuity of interest in the exploration and interpretation of India's rich heritage in philosophy. In particular, great classics of Mahāyāna Buddhism—some of them recovered and reconstructed from Tibetan and Chinese sources—have engaged the attention of some of our leading scholars. Scholars of Jainism, mostly the Jainas themselves, have edited and published practically all their classical works in Sanskrit as well as in Prākrit. Among the Hindu systems, Realistic Schools, Tantra works, classical writings in Kashmir Śaivism, Philosophy of Grammar and Navya Nyāya have claimed special

*N. K. Devaraja is presently U.G.C. Research Scholar, Lucknow University, India. He was a Senior Professor in the Department of Philosophy, Banaras Hindu University, India; Sayaji Rao Gaekwad Professor of Indian Civilization and Culture; Director of the Center for Advanced Study in Philosophy, Banaras Hindu University. Written several articles and books including : *An Introduction to Sankara's Theory of Knowledge*; *The Philosophy of Culture*; *The Mind and Spirit of India*; *Hinduism and Modern Age*; and edited *Indian Philosophy Today*.

attention. Among the twentieth century thinkers, Gandhi and probably Sri Aurobindo have attracted the largest number of exponents and commentators. On the other hand, there has grown up a generation of scholars in philosophy by and large out of tune with traditional Indian thought due partly to their ignorance of the classical languages, specially Sanskrit, and partly to the influence of the anti-metaphysical trends in recent Anglo-American and even Continental philosophy.

This latter influence, particularly the influence of Anglo-American Analytical Philosophy, it may be noted, has produced a rift, a sort of crisis of communication, between scholars wedded to the tradition and those interested primarily in contemporary Western thought. Before we proceed to discuss some important consequences or manifestations of this rift, we should like our readers to notice and appreciate the fact that no such rift divided the scholars of philosophy in pre-independence India. For during the four pre-war decades of the present century, while the Marxist gospel had begun to influence a section of our intelligentsia, that influence was confined mostly among political workers. This is not to say that teachers of philosophy were in any sense indifferent to the political aspirations of the Indian people; on the contrary, the majority of them were intensely patriotic and greatly attached to the Indian cultural traditions, particularly in philosophy and religion. However, these scholars contributed to the national struggle for independence mainly by strengthening the forces of cultural renaissance inaugurated during the nineteenth century by such illustrious leaders of thought as Raja Rammohan Roy (1772-1833), Dayananda (1824-83), Ramakrishna (1836-1886) and Vivekananda (1863-1902). One important factor that sustained religious and philosophic leaders of the Indian renaissance in their work was the respectful attitude towards our religio-philosophic heritage shown by Western orientalists. Another factor, equally important in that it largely conditioned the attitude of aforesaid orientalists, was the predominance of idealistic philosophies in Europe during the last quarter of the nineteenth century and their general resemblance to the better-known traditions in Indian spiritual thought.

The resemblance in question ceased to be a significant factor linking the Indian philosophic tradition with the Western shortly after the downfall of idealism in the West. India, no doubt, had its tradition of realistic thought that experienced a sort of revival after the advent of Moore and Russell in England and the New and Critical Realists in America. But this revival was too short-lived to materially affect the attitudes of Indian scholars. On the contrary, the rise of anti-metaphysical, analytical schools of thought—whose influence penetrated into the Indian mind only gradually and was articulately felt more or less after the Second World War—directly led to the rift or schism, referred to above, among the ranks of Indian philosophers. This schism, as we shall see, has adversely affected both the parties concerned.

II

The exponents and interpreters of our classical spiritual thought, who ushered in and lent support to the forces of Indian renaissance, were inspired on the one hand by honest faith in the relevance and regenerative power of that thought particularly for contemporary India; and, on the other, by the patriotic motive of instilling cultural self-confidence in the Indian people fighting for their independence. However, in the face of the new, emergent factors on the cultural horizon of the civilized world dominated by scientific technology on the one hand, and the positivistic thought-currents, both sustained by and giving sustenance to the predominantly pragmatic-scientific outlook of the age, on the other, scholars exploring Indian heritage no more command the faith and confidence of their forbears belonging to the last decades of the nineteenth and the earlier decades of the twentieth century. Undoubtedly, an important factor responsible for their loss of self-confidence is the attitude of the fellow scholars claiming to represent the modern scientific-analytic currents of thought. On the other hand, it is being noticed that this latter brand of scholars has not so far succeeded in making any notable constructive contributions to Indian philosophic thought. This is not to say that the so-called modern or modern-minded scholars of philosophy have been sitting idle and not doing writing and research work each in his own way. However, the work done over years by most of them seldom amounts to more than a record of stray reactions to issues raised and discussions conducted chiefly by Anglo-American philosophers. As a consequence, an observer of the philosophical (or broadly cultural) scene in contemporary India would scarcely come across a work attempting a bold, innovatory synthesis of problems or data agitating the minds of contemporary thinkers and their interested readers all over the world. This situation obtains not only in the field of philosophy but in most of other fields of inquiry in today's India. Partly, no doubt, the situation may be due to the relatively unsettled and unsatisfactory conditions, political and economic, prevailing in the country. But probably there are other factors that influence the course of philosophy in the country today.

Lack of proper communication between the exponents and admirers of the tradition and those having preference for modern Western thought tends, we believe, to obstruct the growth of significant constructive thought in our midst. Such thought should satisfy the two conditions of being Indian as well as modern. In order to qualify to be called "Indian", our thought should in the first place have roots in our age-long tradition; in the second place, it should in some sense express and fulfil the needs of modern India. Indeed, the thought that arises from and belongs to the soil of a country cannot but be an instrument of its self-awareness; as such its main task consists in the articulation of the aspirations and values cherished by the people. That the thought should be modern implies that it should proceed under the guidance of a proper sense of evidence characteristic of our scientific age. These statements invite some elaborative comments.

Our philosophic tradition spreads over more than two millennia. It is marked by intense spiritual seriousness and depth of conviction on the one hand and acute dialectical temper bordering on scepticism on the other. It also exhibits an immense variety of viewpoints particularly in the analysis of moral-spiritual matters and logico-epistemological issues. The long history of Indian philosophy in its three major manifestations, Buddhistic, Jaina and Hindu, has, with varying degrees of articulation, raised and discussed most of the problems and issues that agitate or trouble the modern minds. This will be evident to any unbiased connoisseur of contemporary thought who cares to acquaint himself with the philosophical reflections of the several Buddhist schools, i.e. the Sarvāstivādins, the Mādhyamikas and the authors of logical texts; the Mīmāṁsakas and the

Grammarians; as also the more important critics and controversialists in the Nyāya and Vedānta camps who fought dialectical battles with the great Buddhist thinkers.

A careful perusal of even a few among the major dialectical treatises in Sanskrit is enough to puzzle the minds of those trying to understand the nature and assess the role of philosophical thought and reasoning in the direction of man's cognitive culture. In our opinion scholars, who confine their attention mainly to contemporary thought, are likely to miss the baffling puzzlement, and the deep intellectual and spiritual disturbance, that arise in consequence of a thinker's intimate encounter with such a rich and varied tradition in philosophy as the Indian. This is not to suggest that a similar familiarity with the Western tradition is not equally rewarding. That familiarity, however, is more or less presupposed by intelligent participation in contemporary discussions carried on in the West. But it seems that too much absorption in these discussions tends to blur the historical perspective; indeed, but a few contemporary thinkers, especially in the Anglo-American world, seem to command that perspective. Now the Indian philosophical tradition happens, in some respects, to be distinct and different from the Western particularly in the order of issues raised by it and the amount of time and emphasis given to them severally. While sharing some of the interests of medieval European thought, Indian philosophy differs from it, first, in its approach and methods, and second, in the major, operative conceptions developed and the more important conclusions as to the wisdom of living reached by it. For these reasons that tradition, so peculiarly indifferent to the modern man's secular and scientific concerns and so thoroughly committed to a transcendent goal while yet employing ruthless dialectic in its service, is more likely to force on us the perspective of historical and cultural relativism.

By virtue of being Indians born to a mature yet varied tradition, we are bound to find ourselves in sympathy with some of the attitudes embedded in it. We owe it, first, to ourselves to articulate our awareness of these attitudes and the varied perceptions, partly moral—religious or spiritual—and partly conceptual and aesthetic, accompanying and engendering or determining those attitudes; we also owe it to other cultural traditions of the world to invite them to share with us the wealth or the burden of the perceptions and attitudes peculiar to our inheritance. But, in no case should we allow ourselves to think either that it is possible for us to steer clear of the tradition in thought and practice, or that it would benefit us in any way to disown it. In view of the latent influence that the tradition exerts on the course of our socio-cultural and moral-spiritual life, it will not do for us to denounce it with a view either to proclaiming our distinction from or superiority over our compatriots or to gain entry into another tradition rated superior to our own. There are several important reasons why a person alienated from his own culture should, rather than repudiate it, seek to reform and modify it from within. For one thing no civilized human being can completely rid himself of the attitudes and values inherent to his tradition; the reason is that the attitudes and values in question enter into the very blood and texture of the being of the individual as the latter grows into cultured manhood—a condition necessary even for the experience of alienation. For another thing, the attitudes and values unconsciously imbibed from one's tradition are likely to interfere with effective acquisition and absorption of the perceptions and values informing a significantly different tradition. In the third place, as a convert to the new tradition the person concerned is not likely to achieve as inside view—comparable to the view he has in relation to his own culture—of the *contradictions* or *shortcomings* of the alien culture or tradition towards which he is attracted. As a consequence of this, it will not be easy for him to make a genuine contribution to that tradition in terms of its own accepted norms and attitudes. It may be contended that there are some purely technical areas in philosophy, comparable to mathematics and also to the physical sciences, that have no intelligible connection with one or other tradition in culture; and that such areas may be cultivated equally well by gifted individuals irrespective of their different cultural backgrounds. It is also contended by some that philosophy as a whole may be treated as a technical subject like mathematics and various scientific disciplines, the implications being that its pursuit by a person need not be influenced by his cultural affiliations. This view of philosophy is, by and large, unacceptable to us. For, unlike mathematics and the sciences, philosophy is concerned chiefly with the analysis and critical assessment and appraisal of value attitudes cherished by the elite in a society. It follows that there cannot, e.g., be a philosophy of morals, or art, or religion—even a philosophy of history or physics—which is wholly unrelated to the perceptions and assumptions relating to values entertained by a society. While it may be granted that the pursuit of some technical subjects, such as symbolic logic, is eminently free from cultural influence, it is doubtful if the *energy* and the *enthusiasm* needed for the pursuit would be made available to workers in equal amounts by different cultures. For a worker in any field can hope to receive support from the people and culture to which he belongs only when there exists a minimum of harmony of interests between him and the latter.

These, probably, are the reasons why the scholars working wholly without reference to the indigenous tradition have not been able to produce noteworthy schemes of ideas acceptable to the Indian people. The last important scheme of this type was produced by Sri Aurobindo during the pre-independence decades. No comparable scheme, acceptable to the new generation of Indians—with stricter standards of evidence and proof characteristic of our time, and with requisite degree of intellectual maturity and moral seriousness—has so far been offered to the intelligentsia.

The metaphysical system of Sri Aurobindo, while lacking the logical subtlety and rigour of Hegelian philosophy, bears a general resemblance to it. Like the German idealist, Sri Aurobindo uncritically presupposes the reality of spiritually directed evolution, as also that of an Absolute regarded both as the Originating Agent (First Cause) and the Goal of evolutionary process. Needless to say, both these assumptions became progressively more repugnant after the re-emergence of the positivistic current of thought in the early twenties. The assumptions in question render tenuous and ineffective Sri Aurobindo's lengthy reflections on society and politics, history and progress.

This, of course, does not imply that the *subjects* and the *issues* touched upon by such idealistic thinkers as Hegel and T. H. Green, Bradley, Bosanquet and Sri Aurobindo are not important. The point is that in the changed intellectual climate of today, when peoples and governments have greater faith in planning than in a providential design and when many a prediction about history, claiming to be eminently scientific or in accordance with the governing principles of the (human?) cosmos, have already come to grief, the reflections about the problems and the issues in question need a thorough re-modelling and re-orientation. Nor is it a good reason for ignoring those questions and issues since they are not being debated by contemporary Anglo-American or, for that matter, the Continental thinkers. Here, indeed, is a matter regarding which the Indian thinkers may profitably follow a different line. Having devoted centuries of thought to normative ethics and cultural history, European thinkers may legitimately ask for a holiday or a period of repose from that type of work; but the same cannot properly be claimed by the thinkers in our country where empirical matters, socio-political, moral and cultural, have long remained neglected by the acclaimed leaders of religio-philosophic thought.

Regarding the aforesaid questions and concerns, the philosophers in modern India are faced with a new challenge, which they may convert into a new opportunity. In the new technological environment created by the progress of science, mankind finds itself hammed in by numerous and diverse problems of adjustment, psychological and moral-spiritual, no less than economic and political. The challenging question is : In the light of our experience as an ancient race that has withstood the storms and stresses of a variegated history, are we in a position to suggest some new yet tried remedies for the ills of the modern world? I, for one, believe that as inheritors of a diversified tradition in age old wisdom, we can help ourselves and our fellow-humans if we learn to translate that wisdom into modern terms. This means that we resist the temptation to revive today the metaphysical idiom that the ancients used in support of the wisdom in question. The enterprise may require us to look for and invent new conceptual bases for supporting the insights and/or values recommended by a galaxy of our wise men.

The foregoing considerations together with the circumstance that no person or culture today can afford to ignore the methodological triumphs of science as also its technological achievements that have brought about the meeting of peoples and cultures belonging to different parts of the globe, should enable us to see our responsibilities at this juncture in history. The problems facing the modern man are so complex and of such magnitude that he needs all the resources of knowledge and understanding, will and character to tackle them. Our first responsibility as custodians of traditional wisdom and as privileged participants in modern adventures of ideas is to our own people. Instead of trying to forcibly uproot their minds from unhelpful tradition, we should try to introduce them to modern attitudes towards the universe and the human society in terms intelligible to them with reference to their own tradition suitably represented through reconstruction or reinterpretation. These activities need not involve either falsification or misrepresentation of the past; they should rather mean redistribution of emphasis in representing the more sensitive areas of value-perception. Both the reconstruction and the reinterpretation in question have to be accomplished with an eye mainly on the requirements of the modern age and modern mind. It is not implied that modern scholars and thinkers driven, like politicians soliciting votes, by needs and requirements of the moment should proceed to deliberately falsify history. The suggestion is that, assuming that the tradition actually contains some insights both valid and valuable for our age, competent scholars and thinkers should endeavour to identify and uncover them, and then proceed to incorporate them in a world-view relevant for our times. By these processes the insights in question can both be preserved and be made helpful to the onward march of man's higher culture.

It seems that even the more important and valid insights embedded in a rich tradition of long-standing can be transmitted and preserved for posterity mainly through the agency of people born to the tradition. It is also true that people belonging to such a tradition cannot easily be persuaded either to discard, for good or bad, the insights and emphases enshrined in that tradition, or to give acceptance to attitudes and values contradictory to or radically different from those propagated or endorsed by that tradition. One of the assumptions of this paper is that such attitudes and values, with a kernel of meaningful relevance for all mankind, cannot fail to affect the minds of even radical thinkers inheriting the tradition.

It is far from our intention to make out a case for traditional outlooks and values and to plead for orthodoxy either in religion or in morals and politics. All that we are mainly concerned with is to spell out the conditions that make for effective communication between the truly original thinkers and their compatriots having varying degrees of understanding of, and admiration for, traditional doctrines and values. In the context of present-day conditions in Indian life and culture, one of our tasks is to prepare the people's minds for the acceptance of new ideas and valuational attitudes by familiarizing them with scientific findings and achievements with a bearing on their day to day life. This objective is partly achieved by the processes of industrialization of the country and the exposure of the villagers to city life. Intellectuals, particularly the philosophers, can contribute to the acceleration of the processes of modernization of the Indian mind in two ways. First, they should accustom the national mind to questioning and critically examining the tradition by highlighting the differences and mutual criticisms of thinkers present within the tradition itself. Thus a modern scholar and teacher of Indian philosophy may sympathetically expound and present the criticisms levelled by the Buddhists against the "Ātman" or substance tradition of the Hindu philosophers; criticisms of Śaṁkara's Advaita by rival Vedāntic commentators; criticisms of theistic god by the Jaina and Buddhist philosophers, and so on. It maybe presumed that even anti-metaphysical thinkers will be more sympathetic to some positions in traditional Indian philosophy than to others. At least as a teacher he should be able to use his modern bias for the liberation of the pupils' minds. But, in our view, he has no right to pose to be indifferent to the rich and varied heritage of his country's philosophy.

Every original thinker has to reckon, by way of criticism and/or accommodation, with one or other tradition before proceeding to expound his own views. There is no reason why an Indian thinker should seek to avoid this work in relation to his own tradition. For one thing the thinker concerned is likely to injure the prospects of his own thought system by his refusal to bring it in relationship with the indigenous tradition. Nor is it easy for an Asian thinker, however original his conceptual scheme or conceptions, to secure a footing as an effective contributor to or continuator of an alien tradition. It seems to us that such footing may be gained only by a scholar or thinker working in the fields of such formal disciplines as symbolic logic and mathematics as also the physical sciences.

Do the above considerations imply that contemporary Indian philosophers have no responsibility whatever towards philosophy as a subject or towards mankind in general? I see no contradiction whatever between serving the cause of effective philosophizing in India and that of world philosophy or of philosophy as a subject; nor do I see any conflict between being useful to the Indian people and to mankind at large. It will be granted that the ancient Greek thinkers, who thought and wrote for their own people, left a legacy in philosophic and political thought that has been useful to future generations all over the world. Similar claims may be made on behalf of significant ideas developed either in ancient India or in ancient China, Egypt or Persia.

The point of these assertions is that, there being no conflict or opposition between serving one's own tradition and people and humanity at large with its varied traditions, needs and ideals, the best way to assist in the growth of world thought is through strengthening the growth of important ideas and values within the tradition to which one belongs. In this connection it may be noted that Mahatma Gandhi, who never yielded to the suggestion to visit and preach his gospel in Western countries, has probably exerted greater influence on the world's ethico-religious and socio-political thought than any other modern Indian thinker. While working within a tradition a competent scholar or thinker helps to build up and promote a significant variant of man's creative possibilities in a particular field; this variant is attended to with respect and advantage by people belonging to other traditions. Even so, the literary productions of people as different as the Chinese and the Greeks, the Indians and the Arabs, the Italians and the Germans, etc., are read and enjoyed by one another. Any deeply felt and powerfully portrayed emotional situation in a novel or play, whatever the language or the tradition wherein it belongs, proves to be interesting to connoisseurs all over the world. The same seems to be true of significant intellectual problems and perplexities and the attempts made to solve or resolve them. This is the reason why the dialectical arguments against, e.g. motion (or plurality), advanced by such brilliant thinkers of antiquity as Zeno and Nāgārjuna, continue to intrigue and puzzle us today, even as the works of Homer and Vālmīki are enjoyed by modern lovers of literature.

Indian thinkers can serve modern philosophy better if, having properly acquainted themselves with their powerful tradition, they draw sustenance from it in producing conceptual wholes having a distinctive flavour which, whether recognizable as Indian or not, will play a supplementary role in relation particularly to Western currents in contemporary thought. To take an instance, while Zeno finds fault with the categories of motion and plurality, to Nāgārjuna those of rest and unity are equally repugnant. What Nāgārjuna seeks to discredit in his *Mādhyamika Śāstra*, is not this or that single category, but the pairs of contradictory categories in all possible combinations. His dialectical onslaught, indeed, is directed to all concepts or conceptual ways of thought made possible by the use of language. For the *Tattva* or the Real, according to him, lies altogether outside the range of our linguistic categories which, as *Vikalpas*, serve merely to distort it. While F. H. Bradley believed, like Hegel, that our thought systems progressively aimed at building up and reflecting the harmony of the Absolute, no such concession to human thought is granted by Nāgārjuna or even by his successors, e.g. Diṅnāga and Dharmakīrti. To take one more instance the Judeo-Christian tradition, which holds sway even today over the Western religious mind, has never visualized the possibility of a religion without God conceived as First Cause or Creator. On the contrary, India has produced great religious teachers from Mahāvīra and Buddha onwards who bequeathed to posterity some of the noblest traditions in religious thought and practice without reference to such a God.

In ancient and medieval India it was the passion for religion or passionate involvement in religious quest that furnished both energy and motivation for vigorous philosophic thinking; in ancient Greece the problems of morality and socio-political organization formed the main concerns for responsible philosophers. As regards cosmology and theory of knowledge, these constituted the necessary basis for speculations in other fields. In modern Western thought while questions concerning the moral-religious life or the spiritual destiny of the individual dominate Continental philosophy, those relating to the exact meaning and significance of the cognitive concepts in science and everyday life occupy the minds of Anglo-American philosophers. It seems to us that, for some decades to come, Indian philosophers may not be able to make important contributions in philosophy of science. But they can certainly develop passionate interest in issues with a bearing on socio-political life and with those concerning the destiny of man and the course of human civilization and culture. The special problem facing contemporary Indian thinkers is to forge powerful links between traditional moral-religious or spiritual reflections on the one hand and the socio-cultural issues arising in our present-day democratic society with diversities of language, belief, custom, etc., on the other. I am persuaded that the desired links can be established by bringing to the fore and strengthening the humanistic elements in our mixed heritage. I have no doubt that our considerable heritage particularly in philosophic and religious thought, approached and exploited in the right spirit, will prove to be the source of renewed self-confidence and of new points of departure in our discussions of quite a few important problems relevant for our times.

17

FUTURISM AND INDIAN PHILOSOPHY

V. NARAYAN KARAN REDDY*

IN India the science of Futurology or Futurism persisted from times immemorial in one form or another. Originally it started as 'reverie' of the perfected individual and the perfected society. The man who had an overall view of the future situation was called a "*kāla-jñānī*," and a person who can foresee the future in all its details was a '*dṛṣṭi-dhārī*'. An insistent interest in future man has been the most novel, the most fruitfully distinguishing characteristic of the common writers and thinkers in India.[1] Futurism is thus an intent aspiration for growth and progress and futurology is the creative science of evolution and fulfilment.

In Indian philosophy, if carefully viewed, we see a number of expressions and interpretations which directly or indirectly refer to the science of futurism. It was never a history of philosophy in its dealing as in most of the other cases. On the other hand, it has been a copious record of rich and luxuriant visions and perspectives.[2] The age-old history of Sanskrit literature

*V. Narayan Karan Reddy is Professor and Head of the Department of Philosophy, Osmania University, India. He is the author of *Sarvodaya Ideology and Acharya Vinoba Bhave*; *Thoreau, Gandhi and Vinoba*; *Universalism and Essentialism.*

1. Sri Aurobindo, "The Future Poetry," in *The Movement of Modern Literature—2* (Birth Centenary Library, Vol. IX) (Pondicherry : Sri Aurobindo Ashram, 1972), p. 108.

2. Futurism and Indian Philosophy run parallel to each other in their deeper quest after perfection. All the seers and the sages of the Upaniṣads were gifted visionaries who were always concerned with the basic problems of Realization, Perfection and Human Destiny.

is the true testimony and repository of faith in futuristic ideas and beliefs. Let us examine the following words and phrases at random and analyze their basic intentions to interpret the 'aims and purposes' of human life in terms of human destiny.

In Sri Aurobindo, we come across the word '*aṣṭa-siddhi*' which means eight siddhis. *Siddhi* is perfection, realization and experience. The two *siddhis* of knowledge are *vyāpti* and *prākāmya*; the three *siddhis* of power are *aiśvarya*, *īśitā* and *vaśitā*; the three *siddhis* of the body are *mahimā*, *laghimā* and *aṇimā*. *Vyāpti* means reception or communication. *Prākāmya* is the full *prakāśa* of the senses which tends to suppress the ordinary limits of the body. It enters into the sphere of *tanmātras* transcending the normal limits of *jñāna-indriyas*. *Aiśvarya* is the effectiveness of the will acting on the object or event through thought. *Īśitā* is the effectiveness of will acting on the subject or event through *citta* or temperament. *Vaśitā* is the control of the object in its nature for effective and desired action.

Mahimā is the power of increasing the physical mass and density at will. *Laghimā* or lightness is the power of making the body light, reducing the gravity at will. *Aṇimā* or subtlety is the power of making the body subtle, reducing the physical mass and density at will. The last three definitions are taken from the glossary of *Yogic Sādhanā* by Uttar Yogi first published in 1911.

In ancient India, the practice and the attainment of *aṣṭa-siddhi* was considered as the acquisition of the highest knowledge, i.e. *buddhi*.[1] *Buddhi* is true understanding which is not subservient to the senses. It concerns itself with the pursuit of pure truth and right knowledge based on the inner instrument, the *antaḥkaraṇa*. Once man attains the level of *buddhi*, he becomes a *dṛṣṭi-dhārī*, the wielder of the vision. The vision of the future was veiled by the seers and sages of the *Upaniṣads*. Even to have this vision, some path is prescribed in Indian thought, i.e. *aṣṭa-siddhi*.

1. *Jñāna* or realization of experience is *bhāva* or perception of things in Indian philosophy. Carrying out of the *Jñāna* in *bhāva* is *satyadharma*. The special faculty of *jñāna* which is explained in terms of the past, present and future of the world as it exists, has existed and will exist in time is commonly signified as *trikāladṛṣṭi*. *Aṣṭa-siddhi* was considered as the necessary condition for the acquisition of highest knowledge, i.e. *buddhi*. *Aṣṭa-siddhi* is of three orders : two *siddhis* of knowledge, three *siddhis* of power and three *siddhis* of the body.

In classical Indian thought, *cit* is the pure consciousness and *citta* is the mixed stuff of mental, vital and physical consciousness out of which are born the impulses or movements of thought, emotion and sensation. *Cit-śakti* or *cit-tapas* is Consciousness-Force. It is present in man as mental will and knowledge as the Supreme Force. It is free in its rest or action. It is not bound by any of the impulses of *prāṇa*. It is the supreme and the sovereign force next to *buddhi*.[1] This force helps in our knowledge of the unknown future. In addition to this, Indian philosophy refers to a secret circumconscient or environmental consciousness in which are determined our unseen connections with the world outside us. It is through this environmental consciousness that the thoughts, feelings, etc. of others pass to enter into one. According to Integral Psychology, the sublimal projects itself beyond all *kośas* or sheaths and forms a circumconscient consciousness through which it receives the contacts of the world and can become aware of them and deal with them before they enter. This is indeed a future vision of events and objects in Indian thought.[2]

The Gnosis is the effective principle of the Spirit and the highest dynamis of the spiritual existence. A totally self-aware, all-aware intelligence is also signified as gnosis in the integral philosophy of Sri Aurobindo. It is a power of self-possessing divine knowledge. Thus gnosis is all-consciousness that is based upon Truth of Being and not upon ignorance or nescience. On the other hand, grace is something spontaneous which flows from the Being of the Divine Consciousness. Divine Grace is not always based upon the natural aspiration of the individual. Divine grace can supersede the Cosmic Law. It is an all-pervading act of the Divine presence. According to Sri Aurobindo, gnosis is a process of self-transmutation at the level of the Overmind. It helps in the descent of the Supermind over the Overmind. At the level of the gnosis, there is nothing like the past, present or the future. Everything becomes self-revealing and self-transforming. Grace is the all-enveloping consciousness of

1. Sri Aurobindo, Supplement in *Trikaladrishti* (Birth Centenary Library, Vol. XXVII) (Pondicherry : Sri Aurobindo Ashram, 1972), p. 371.

2. Sri Aurobindo : *The Life Divine*, vide *The Knowledge by Identity and Separative Knowledge* (Birth Centenary Library, Vol. XVIII) (Pondicherry : Sri Aurobindo Ashram, 1970), p. 541.

the Divine. When this is dawned, all secrets of both the self and the world are revealed in one span of consciousness. Gnosis and Grace are thus two aspects of the same Reality called Total Transformation.[1]

Vijñāna is the essential knowledge by identity. It is all-embracing consciousness. It also amounts to total comprehension in Indian thought. It is the original comprehensive consciousness which holds an image of things in its essence. It is also the true and complete view of things. It is the inner vision which can see objects and events through the forces of vibration. Visions and realizations are its emanations. There must be in the nature of things a faculty or principle which sees the Truth unveiled. Thus eternal faculty of knowledge which corresponds to the eternal fact of the truth is Truth-Consciousness. According to the *Vedas*, there is the principle called Truth-Consciousness which sees the Truth directly and is in possession of it spontaneously. Past, present and the future are meaningless divisions in the context of the all-pervading scope of Truth-Consciousness. The 'essential' knowledge is never isolated from the direct knowledge in any sense in Indian philosophy.[2]

Intuition is a power of consciousness nearer to the original knowledge by identity. When consciousness touches the truth of things and beings, a spark, a flash and blaze of intimate truth-perception is lit in its depths. Intuition is an outleap of a superior revelation. Intuition is self-consciousness, feeling, perceiving, grasping in its substance and aspects. Intuition in Sri Aurobindo's philosophy is an edge of light thrust out by the secret Supermind. Revelation is a part of the intuitive consciousness. Revelation is direct sight, the direct hearing or inspired memory of Truth, i.e. *dṛṣṭi*, *śruti* and *smṛti*. Revealed knowledge is always superior to the intuitive perception of knowledge. In Indian philosophy, almost all the Upaniṣadic sages and saints were the sources of revealed knowledge. Many thinkers and

1. In Indian Philosophy, Total Transformation is the transformation at all levels—physical, vital, mental, psychical and spiritual. In addition to all this, the element of Grace is all-important. Aspiration and Grace are considered as twin mediums of all transformation. It is on this basis the *Vedānta* says that 'not a blade of grass moves without the grace of God.'

2. Sri Aurobindo : *The Upanishads*, vide *Kena Upanishad* (Birth Centenary Library, Vol. XII) (Pondicherry : Sri Aurobindo Ashram, 1972), p. 182

writers of ancient India used to predict intuitively many things and events of the future. The whole Indian mythology is full of fruitful intuitions and revelations.[1]

In a democracy, we come across with many mediums and mechanisms. The dominant channels or mechanisms which tend to condition or govern the public opinion today are 'emotional initiation' and 'rational persuasion.' The method of 'emotional initiation' is adopted by popular political leaders, whereas the method of 'rational persuasion' is used by statesmen, writers, artists and social realists. On the whole, where there is ignorance and illiteracy, the method of 'emotional initiation' works well and where there is increased education and urbanization, 'rational persuasion' operates adequately. In future democracy, the areas of 'emotional initiation' decreases and correspondingly the scope of rational persuasion is bound to increase.

Democracy in India as it is practised is not the last or penultimate stage. Even a perfect democracy is not likely to be the last stage of social evolution.[2] But democracy in one form or the other is necessary for the flowering of self-consciousness of the social being. In a democracy, each individual will be allowed to govern his life according to the dictates of his own reason and will. Democracy is non-interference and mutual toleration. It is a way of life, i.e. *vyavasthā.* So, in a democracy, the reason and will of every individual will be on par with the reason and will of every other individual and even one and all tend to share the ideals and benefits equally. According to Sri Aurobindo, the democratic tendency in humanity has long been there. This tendency has been pressing forward victoriously to self-fulfilment throughout the ages. In this specific context, democracy is a sure preservative of liberty. However, we see today the democratic system of government march steadily towards such an organized annihilation of individual liberty as could not have been dreamed of even in the old aristocratic and monarchical

1. Sri Aurobindo : *The Hour of God,* vide *Thoughts and Approaches* (Birth Centenary Library, Vol. XVII) (Pondicherry : Sri Aurobindo Ashram, 1972), p. 89.

2. Sri Aurobindo : *Social and Political Philosophy,* vide *The Drive Towards Legislation and Social Centralisation* (Birth Centenary Library, Vol. XV) (Pondicherry : Sri Aurobindo Ashram, 1971), p. 434.

systems. According to Sri Aurobindo, most governments either have now or have passed through a democratic form, but nowhere yet has there been a real democracy; it has been everywhere the propertied and the professional classes and the bourgeois who governed in the name of the people.[1]

Nevertheless there was always a strong democratic element in Indian polity. All institutions in one form or other exercised democracy in India. But

> "in recent times, liberty and democracy have been, and still are, a cant assertion which veils under a skilfully moderated plutocratic system, the rule of an organised successful bourgeois over a proletariat."[2]

In India, the future of democracy may not be mere 'equality', 'liberty' and 'fraternity' but a feeling of togetherness, cooperation, participation and above all a sense of growth and progress. Democracy may not be for the sake of democracy. It is bound to aim at nobler causes and hopes to have some higher individuals and social ideals apart from its common community purposes. It is probably for this reason alone that we tend to conclude 'the good individual is essential requisite of a good democracy.'

In the future education of India, man is not bound to any fixed traditional norms. There will be complete openness of mind towards ever-new revelations of knowledge based upon one's own experiences in age. Moral and emotional development is as much important in education as the psychical and the spiritual. In the future, education has to be rooted in the psychical and the spiritual, if it has to complete its cycle of perfection. Reformation of man will be a smaller ideal. On the other hand, his transformation into a New Humanity will be the sole object of integral education and perfection. It is in this context, Sri Aurobindo said :

> "An Integral Education which could with some variations, be adapted to all the nations of the world, must bring back the legitimate authority of the spirit over matter fully developed and utilised."[3]

True education must begin even before birth. Education will no more be an outer training of the individual. On the other hand, it will be more and more a perfection of inner life. If

1. Sri Aurobindo : *Social and Political Philosophy*, vide *Some Lines of Fulfilment* (Birth Centenary Library, Vol. XV) (Pondicherry : Sri Aurobindo Ashram, 1971), p. 377
2. *Ibid.*, vide *Self-Determination*, p. 600
3. Sri Aurobindo and the Mother : *On Education*, Part I, vide *A National Education for India* (Pondicherry : Sri Aurobindo Ashram, 1972), p. 4.

education is to serve man by perfecting his inner life, it has to fulfil five principal aspects.

> "Education to be complete must have five principal aspects relating to the five principal activities of the human being, the physical, the vital, the mental, the psychical and the spiritual."[1]

The ancient and the modern, the classical and the recent will not have any definite place in the future scheme of education. Sri Aurobindo rightly declares,

> "In the future education, we need not bind ourselves either by the ancient or the modern system, but select only the most perfect and rapid means of mastering knowledge."[2]

In the present system of education the progress is from below upward through ascending levels. But in the supramental education of the future, it will be from above downward. 'Consciousness based knowledge' will invariably be always superior to 'mind-based acquisition'.

Science and technology, from the Indian standpoint, cannot perfect our life. They can at best organize and stabilize our environment. Sri Aurobindo, in *The Life Divine* clearly mentions that

> "our science itself is a construction, a mass, of formulas and devices; masterful in knowledge of processes and in the creation of apt machinery, but ignorant of the foundations of the being and of world-being, it cannot perfect our nature and therefore cannot perfect our life."[3]

It has its own infinite limitations. Like most other mental and external knowledge, it gives us only the truth of process and not the real truth. In the words of Sri Aurobindo,

> "one might ask whether science itself has arrived at any ultimate truth; on the contrary, ultimate truth even on the physical plane seems to recede as science advances."[4]

It is likely that in the future science, there is bound to be goals and purposes. There will be a happy blend of science and spirituality. If science is to turn its face towards the realization

1. Sri Aurobindo and the Mother : *On Education*, Part I, vide *Integral Education* (Pondicherry : Sri Aurobindo Ashram, 1972), p. 8
2. Sri Aurobindo, *The Hour of God*, vide *Simultaneous and Successive Teaching* (Birth Centenary Library, Vol. XVII) (Pondicherry : Sri Aurobindo Ashram, 1972), p. 213
3. Sri Aurobindo, *The Life Divine*, vide *The Divine Life* (New York : India Library Society, 1965), p. 917.
4. Sri Aurobindo and the Mother : *On Science*, vide *Drawbacks and Limitations* (Pondicherry : Sri Aurobindo Ashram, 1972), p. 12.

of higher life, then it will be a new science. It ought to deal with the forces of the Life-world and not the bare-Matter. In fact, we need new science for the new world of tomorrow. Taming technology is not controlling or harnessing its forces. But it invariably means setting up of new goals for life. Nevertheless, this will be the sole mission of the future science in India. It will prepare us for an age of wider and deeper culture. The present industrial or commercial 'barbarisms' will have to be dislodged by the new scientific humanism of the future. In every philosophy of the world, the individual is the one supreme consideration. By revitalizing the aims of the individual, we can restructure the aims of society. Man is the maker of his destiny. He can even bring heaven on earth, provided he channelizes his talents and energies in a proper way. When Mahatma Gandhi says "rise yourself" and the "sum total of mankind is not to bring us down but to lift us up," it amounts to a social futurism of the higher order. But this social futurism has to be well harnessed, organized and directed towards the goals of perfection.[1]

In Indian tradition, conscious survival and existence are altogether different concepts. In future, motion of matter in space and change in time may not be the sole condition of existence. We are bound to ascend from Matter through a developing life towards Divine being. It is on this basis Sri Aurobindo said, conscious survival is altogether a different grade of existence. It is meant for some higher purpose than Matter and material life. Seeking after values, pursuit of norms and aspiring for a spiritual ideal, etc. come under the broader category of conscious survival. The planes of survival or the planes of 'higher life' are much discussed concepts in Indian thought. Though the baselines of survival differ differently from individual to individual, the fundamental goals of life are common to everyone. So, it is the aspiration of man which tends to influence or condition the different levels or planes of his survival. No amount of 'situational groupings' and 'personal stability zone' will come

1. Gandhi's philosophy of *sarvodaya* rooted in *śoṣaṇa-vihīna-samāj* aims at the liberation of the individual, i.e. *jīvan-mukta*. 'Work for the world' and 'liberate yourself' is the main burden of his teaching. 'Rise yourself' above the daily routine and at the same time work for the masses implies a social futurism of the highest order. . .

to our final rescue, particularly when there is 'psychic disparity,' or psychological crisis or decadence within the natural framework of human personality. The word 'complete survival' has altogether a different connotation and significance in Indian thought. 'Complete survival' is synonymous to 'whole living.' In Indian philosophy, conscious struggle is aspiration and all problems of life and existence are problems of awareness, growth, perfection and fulfilment. According to the span-of-consciousness theory, every moment man is making progressive leaps towards higher and ever higher levels of human existence. It is for this reason not all problems of existence are problems of discord and disharmony. On the other hand, they are essentially problems of harmony. "For all problems of existence are essentially problems of harmony,"[1] says Sri Aurobindo in his *Aims of Evolution.* Today we speak of the evolution of Life in Matter and the evolution of Mind in Life. In future, there is bound to be evolution of Spirit in Mind. This spirit is variously explained in Sri Aurobindo. Spirit is Supermind; Spirit is Consciousness; and Spirit is also Transformation. The future man will evolve new strategies of survival which behove his true status, dignity and destiny. These strategies are no other than the conscious mediums or instruments of life and reality. On this basis, the man of the future is bound to witness many eventful happenings in his very life and that he is bound to be classed or categorized under the 'new species' or 'new creation'—the Supermanhood.

According to Indian thought, "the individuals who will most help the future of humanity in the new age will be those who will recognize a spiritual evolution as the destiny and therefore the great need of the human being."[2] The general aim of man in future will be to attain the advent of a progressing universal harmony. The aim of a

> "spiritualized society would be to live like its spiritual individuals, not in the ego, but in the spirit, not as the collective ego, but as the collective soul."[3]

1. Sri Aurobindo and the Mother : *On Evolution* (Pondicherry : Sri Aurobindo Ashram, 1972), p. 10.
2. Sri Aurobindo : *Social and Political Thought*, vide *The Advent and Progress of the Spiritual Age* (Birth Centenary Library, Vol. XV) (Pondicherry : Sri Aurobindo Ashram, 1971), p. 250.
3. *Ibid.*, vide *Conditions for the Coming of a Spiritual Age*, p. 239

A spiritual human society of the future would realize three things : God, Freedom and Unity. Future society is based upon these three essential truths of human existence.

> "A spiritual human society would start from and try to realise three essential truths of existence which all Nature seems to be an attempt to hide by their opposites and which therefore are as yet for the mass of mankind only words and dreams, God, Freedom, Unity."[1]

The perfection of environment is not based upon any other medium or machinery except the individual himself. It is for this reason that social futurism according to the Indian mind, may much depend upon the individual reformation and perfection.

> "This erring race of human beings dream always of perfecting their environment by the machinery of the government and society, but it is only by the perfection of the soul within that the outer environment can be perfected."[2]

India has always dreamt of its future society, with all hope and optimism. It has envisaged that in the future, people may like to transcend all barriers of races and cross all boundaries of nations to live in such a place where they will be treated as free citizens of a 'new world.' According to the teachings of Sri Aurobindo and the Mother, "there should be somewhere upon earth a place that no nation could claim as its sole property, a place where all human beings of goodwill, sincere in their aspiration, could live freely as citizens of the world. . .a place where the needs of the Spirit and the care for progress would get precedence over the satisfaction of desires and passions, the seeking for material pleasures and enjoyment."[3] When we tend to repeat 'the goal ever recedes from us' and the 'full efforts is full victory' it amounts to a new social futurism. It is clear that never before, has the present looked so persistently and creatively forward toward the future. The past has its own role in the making of the present and the present has its own role in shaping the future. But relying too much on the past for purposes of social futurism is not only wrong but false and preposterous. When past is a drag, the future is a force. It is on this basis the

1. Sri Aurobindo : *Social and Political Thought,* vide *Conditions for the Coming of a Spiritual Age* (Birth Centenary Library, Vol. XV) (Pondicherry : Sri Aurobindo Ashram, 1971), p. 239.

2. Sri Aurobindo, *The Hour of God*, vide *Thoughts and Aphorisms—Karma* (Birth Centenary Library, Vol. XVII) (Pondicherry : Sri Aurobindo Ashram, 1972), p. 120.

3. The Mother : On the Future Society, Bulletin International Centre of Education (Pondicherry) (August, 1954), 113-15.

whole edifice of futurism is built up in India. It is not wholly true to say that man moves into future; but it is the future which drags man into its fold every time it is the correct expression, according to Indian interpretation of futurology.[1]

Sri Aurobindo, the author of *The Life Divine* and the prophet of the New Race on earth, was a great visionary who visualized many radical changes in the very life of the individual and structure of society through basic Aspiration and Transformation. He hoped for a better world in future for man and humanity from all aspects and levels of perfection and fulfilment. According to him, on no occasion were we so conscious of the future as today. The swing from the past to the present is sudden and abrupt. This can be viewed as an unprecedented adventure of man into ever-new possibilities of his race. In his own words,

> "the Futurist outlook has never been more pronounced than at the present day; on all sides, in thought, in life, in the motives and forms of literary and artistic creation, we are swinging violently away from the past into an unprecedented adventure of new teeming possibilities."[2]

Future is a two edged weapon. It is an admixture of hope and despair. It is like a sphinx, with two minds. Sometimes, it elates and enlivens and at other times it discourages and even disappoints us with great rage and fury. "The future is a sphinx"[3] he says "with two minds, an energy which offers itself and denies, gives itself and resists, seeks to enthrone us and seeks to slay."[4] This conception of future is sometimes deeply repulsive and sometimes irresistibly attractive with new hope. The repulsion is due to our own natural recoil from the unknown.

1. According to Indian thought, it is the future which draws the aspirant or seeker towards his goal. The normal expression is that man through effort, moves into future. In fact, the 'nisus' of future runs into diverse ways only to lift the race of humanity to desired goals of perfection. It is only on this basis we say 'future is a force.' There is no such thing as 'lag phase' or retrogression in the social futurism in India.

2. Sri Aurobindo : *The Future Poetry*, vide *The Movement of Modern Literature*—2 (Birth Centenary Library, Vol. IX) (Pondicherry : Sri Aurobindo Ashram, 1972), p. 108.

3. In Sri Aurobindo's explanation, Sphinx is a monster in Greek mythology with the head of a woman and the body of a lioness that proposes riddles to travellers and strangled those who could not solve them.

4. Sri Aurobindo : *The Supramental Manifestation*, vide *Conservation and Progress* (Birth Centenary Library, Vol. XVI) (Pondicherry : Sri Aurobindo Ashram, 1971), p. 318.

According to Sri Aurobindo, perfection cannot be brought about by imperfection. Perfection can be aspired by perfect men alone. Such individuals, however few in numbers, can lead the entire humanity to right destiny.

> "A perfected human world cannot be created by men or composed of men who are themselves imperfect."[1]

The individuals who help the future of humanity are those who believe in the truth of spiritual evolution as the destiny. In fact, true charity begins at home. If the instrumentation is inadequate, perfection is bound to be ineffective and inadequate and so it invariably implies imperfection. The truth of spiritual evolution lies in its movement towards perfection. This, at its best, is also designated as Supramental Manifestation.

> "A spiritualised society would live like its spiritual individuals, not in the ego, but in the spirit, not as a collective ego, but as the collective soul."[2]

Sri Aurobindo emphasizes on the inner rather than the outer environment as a tool of perfection. Outer environment is bound to be imperfected again and again if it is not assisted by its inner environment. By effecting a change in the inner life, we are bound to effect a change in the outer life but not vice versa.

> "The erring race of human beings dreams always of perfecting their environment by the machinery of government and society : but it is only by the perfection of the soul within that the outer environment can be perfected."[3]

Our attachment with the known always contradicts with our fascination towards the 'unknown'. Every step into the 'unknown' is indeed a wager between life and death. The decisions we make amount to either destruction of our present name and form to which we are closely attached or the great fulfilment of what we are going to be in future in the realm of the unknown. Sometimes the elements of the future evolution are foreshadowed and striven after in the course of our 'human aspiration towards personal perfection and the perfection of the life of the race.'

1. Sri Aurobindo : *The Life Divine*, vide *The Divine Life* (Birth Centenary Library, Vol. XIX) (Pondicherry : Sri Aurobindo Ashram, 1970), p. 1022.

2. Sri Aurobindo : *Social and Political Thought*, vide *Conditions for the Coming of a Spiritual Age* (Birth Centenary Library, Vol. XV) (Pondicherry : Sri Aurobindo Ashram, 1971), p. 239.

3. Sri Aurobindo : *The Hour of God*, vide *Thoughts and Aphorisms* (Birth Centenary Library, Vol. XVII) (Pondicherry : Sri Aurobindo Ashram, 1970), p. 120.

Evolution is not a new manifestation other than the individual or race perfection. Nevertheless, perfection supersedes evolution in all respects and means. It even moulds and transforms evolution from diverse angles. In fact, evolution and perfection are one and the same aspects of one reality.

Sri Aurobindo teaches that one should not look backwards on any occasion in the course of life. This habit of back introspection hinders our progress towards the future.

> "One should always have one's look turned forwards to the future—retrospection is seldom healthy as it turns one towards a past consciousness."[1]

'One cannot go back to the past; one has always to go in the future' has been the main theme of the difficulties of Yoga in *Letters on Yoga*. Even otherwise, passive thoughts of the past are not so helpful in the conscious evolution of man. So also, if the ideas and thoughts about the future come as mere memories and imaginations, they are not useful to us from the point of view of Yoga or Futurism. Sri Aurobindo further asserts that the past has not to be stored. Man must learn to go into the future realization and all that is necessary in the past for the future must be taken up and processed into the given or desired form of the future.[2] This is a clear-cut optimistic view of human destiny in Sri Aurobindo. According to him, in the cosmic evolutionary process, man is a stage and not a goal. He cannot, however, be considered the consummation of the above process. The stage of mind to Supermind cannot be treated as light out of darkness but 'light out of light.' For this reason, Sri Aurobindo declares that "a clear and more inspiring vision of the destiny of the spirit in man will be a larger part of the poetry of the future." Writing on the Future Poetry, Sri Aurobindo says that in future, there will be the true growth of the power of the spirit in the humanity of the future.

1. Sri Aurobindo : *Letters on Yoga,* vide *Difficulties of the Path* (Birth Centenary Library, Vol. XXIV) (Pondicherry : Sri Aurobindo Ashram, 1970), p. 1726.

2. In Indian philosophy, past is never a drag. On the other hand, it is a dynamic reality in its essence. It is never isolated from the rest of its categories. The spirit of the age in its conscious movement towards its endless destiny blends all the 'essence' of life and reality into one process of becoming and growth. It is on this basis, Sri Aurobindo says that 'all that is necessary in the past for the future' must be taken up for a better and a higher future.

"And whatever poetry may make its substance or its subject, this growth of the power of the spirit must necessarily bring into it a more intense and revealing speech, a more inward and subtle and penetrating rhythm, a greater stress of sight, a more vibrant and responsive sense, the eye that looks at all smallest and greatest things for the significances that have not yet been discovered and the secrets that are not on the surface. That will be the type of the new utterance and the boundless field of poetic discovery left for the inspiration of the humanity of the future."[1]

In addition to these specific remarks, Sri Aurobindo tends to make certain general remarks regarding the future of man. Future man will be endowed with a larger cosmic vision. He will realize the divine power and his divine possibilities will lift him up to the level of Superman. The nations of the future may actualize these dreams and most of them may make real these things in their life and culture. These nations of the 'coming dawn' will have a peculiar status in the world of events and will have the privilege of witnessing the dawn of the new consciousness called the 'integral' or 'supramental' consciousness in all its fullness and wholeness.

"It is in effect a larger cosmic vision, a realising of the godhead in the world and in man. . . The nations that most include and make real these things in their life and culture are the nations of the coming dawn and the poets of whatever tongue and race who most completely see with this vision and speak with the inspiration of its utterance are those who shall be the creators of the poetry of the future."[2]

According to Sri Aurobindo, the cycles of evolution move forward and upward. But these cycles are most cyclical in their action. This process of evolution gives us an impression of a series of ascents and descents. The gains of evolution, if they seem to be suspended for some time, 're-emerge in new forms suitable to the new ages.' Thus, the concept of progress in Sri Aurobindo is teleological. The goal is the ideal of perfection. In *Human Cycle*, Sri Aurobindo envisages three major stages of social evolution. The infra-rational stage in which the society is rooted in its physical and vital consciousness is the first phase. In its second phase of evolution, i.e. the rational stage, the society is governed by mental consciousness and in its third phase of

1. Sri Aurobindo : *The Future Poetry*, vide *The Power of the Spirit* (Birth Centenary Library, Vol IX) (Pondicherry : Sri Aurobindo Ashram, 1972), p. 256.

2. *Ibid.*, vide *Conclusions on The Future Poetry*, p. 288

social evolution, i.e. in the supra-rational or spiritual stage, the life and institutions are moulded in the truths of the spiritual consciousness. Thus, human society in its growth has to pass through the three stages of evolution before it arrives at the "completeness of its possibilities".[1] Sri Aurobindo explains in his *Human Cycle* that there are two important conditions for the awakening of the new spirit in society. First, there must be few qualitative or pioneering individuals who can realize the higher life and thereby try to recreate or transform the society after perfection; and, second, it is the deadliness or preparedness of the common mind of the people which is quite important in this process. The failure of most of the past social or spiritual movements to make an enduring impact in the lives of the individuals and societies has been mainly due to the fact that these two necessary preconditions of progress have never been rightly realized together.

Sri Aurobindo envisages the coming or dawning of New Humanity which might be called the beginning of a 'divinised life,' or the Supramental manifestation upon earth. He sees altogether a new category of higher life and consciousness in the future race of mankind,

> "a new humanity uplifted into Light, capable of spiritualised being and action, open to governance by some light of the Truth-Consciousness capable even on the mental level and its own order of something that might be called the beginning of a divinised life."[2]

In future, in the New Age, there will be no more religions. A new religion would be useless in the age of Supramental creation, says Sri Aurobindo.

> "In the Supramental creation, there will no more be religions. All life will be the expression, the flowering in forms of the Divine Unity manifesting in the world."[3]

1. Indian philosophy envisages perfection and completeness of possibilities for the entire race of mankind through integral consciousness—the vital, the mental and the spiritual at different stages and levels of civilization, i.e. infra-rational, rational and supra-rational. Nonetheless, the failure of most of the past social movements are due to the unnatural avoidance of these preconditioned stages by the social prophets of the age.

2. It is only in his last writings, Sri Aurobindo has explained in detail the significance of such a future civilization by using terms like "Mind of Light" and "New Humanity."

3. The Mother, *Bulletin of Physical Education* (Pondicherry) (November, 1957).

Speaking on the future of the family, Sri Aurobindo says that if the present needs and desires have any place in the future evolution of man, then the family will survive in some form or the other. If in case these desires and needs will have no place in his future life, then the present family will have no chance of survival. In this case, man will outgrow his ordinary levels of family life. Family is bound to break and disintegrate because its functions will be meaningless and even redundant in future. Family is needed as a primary 'impulse of life' for the fulfilment of vital consciousness. Second, the family may also serve collectively for the satisfaction of the life of a larger 'vital ego' in society: this is explained in terms of *kula dharma* in ancient India. In the latter case, family 'englobes the individual in a more effective, competitive and cooperative life unit.' Nevertheless, in future, man will have to transcend or outgrow his vital and egoistic nature. The family, along with all other social institutions of man, will break down and disappear in the process. Presently, the relation between man and woman is quite peculiar.

> "In their mutual relations, man and woman are, at one and towards each other, quite despotic masters and somewhat pitiable slaves. No law can liberate woman from man unless they are freed from all their inner slavery."[1]

In the view of Sri Aurobindo and the Mother, in the future supramental civilization, the complete breakdown of the family and all family relations is an indispensable condition specially in the case of exceptional individuals; but the general mass of humanity may continue to run after its vital and social benefits till they feel the incessant and urgent call for the higher or the spiritual life—the Hour of God. Sri Aurobindo declares that "man's greatness is not in what he is, but in what he makes possible."[2] Man is bound to fulfil himself either by producing

1. The Mother, "The Problem of Women," *Bulletin of Physical Education* (Pondicherry), Vol. VII, No. 2 (April, 1955).

2. The whole basis and foundation of Futurism in India rests on the 'possible' futures more than the 'probable' and the 'preferable' futures. The greatness of man does not merely lie in his intrinsicality or potentiality; but it is present in his natural capacity to make things and acts possible. This involves a positive direction. In this context, futurology or Futurism in India is oriented towards its applicability than predictability. It is in this sense Sri Aurobindo explains further, "If earth calls and the supreme answers, the Hour can be even now for that immense and glorious transformation." (Sri Aurobindo : *The Hour of God*, Sri Aurobindo Ashram Publication, 1959, p. 61).

out of himself a 'new and a greater being' or he himself will become a Divine Humanity by giving place to the Superman. The Mother foresees the supramental world in the following way :

> "The supramental world will eliminate what mental intervention in Matter has created as perversion, ugliness, all this deformation that has aggravated, suffering, misery, moral poverty, the entire zone of that sordid and repulsive misery which renders a whole section of human life something so horrible."[1]

Prospective Analysis

In Indian philosophy, we come across a number of expressions and interpretations which refer to the science of futurism in diverse ways. A visionary, i.e. *dṛṣṭi-dhārī* was a *kāla-jñānī* who wielded the full knowledge of the future. *Aṣṭa-siddhi* is the eightfold path of perfection prescribed to a person who aspires to become a *kāla-jñānī* by perfecting his *antaḥkaraṇa.* Nevertheless, the highest goal of this path of perfection was *vijñāna*, i.e. the knowledge of identity which transcended *kālajñāna.* Intuitions and revelations were always viewed as higher sources or mediums of futurism in Indian philosophy. In ancient India, all that was necessary as the past for the future was chosen and given a new form for the better and truer realization of life. Thus from the standpoint of Indian thought, the future was never an endless stream of events but an enormous flow of new consciousness.

In India democracy is a way of life, i.e. *vyavasthā.* It is more than a polity or a form of government. In this context, the future of democracy in India may not be confined merely to the common watchwords of 'equality', 'liberty' and 'fraternity'. On the other hand, democracy is bound to be a genuine feeling of collective and conscious participation with all sense of overall growth, progress and perfection. However, the democratic tendency in humanity is and has long been there and growing stronger and stronger with greater impetuosity towards the fulfilment of its final goal, i.e. the ideal of human unity retaining the indigenous assimilative character, i.e. *svadharma* and *ātmasatkarma.*

1. The Mother : *Bulletin of Physical Education* (Pondicherry) (August, 1955).

In the future, education has to be fixed in the psychical and the spiritual dimensions of human personality if it has to complete its cycle of perfection. It is the perfection of inner life which leads to the perfection of outer environment. Perfection of inner and outer spheres of human existence are invariably rooted in the 'consciousness-based knowledge' of the future which is altogether different from the present 'mind-based' acquisition of facts. According to Indian philosophy, that education which fosters *sādhanā*, (i.e. spiritual self-training) and forbids the practice of *anuṣṭhāna* (i.e. particular religious exercise) may serve the cause of *citta-śuddhi* (i.e. purification of the mind). It may not help in the creation of super-social man (i.e. *parivrājaka* or *siddha*, the fulfilled or perfected man). On the other hand, that education which is essential and spiritual can alone create a visionary or a genius. In the scheme of future education, classical and recent, the ancient and the modern will not have any specific or definite place. The people will try to choose only the most perfect and adopt the rapid means of mastering knowledge. The seekers of the future may develop new instrumentations of knowledge altogether. Thus, future education will invariably be free from all antinomies of thought and contradictions of language. It is bound to be the education of 'psyche' or soul more than the training of the senses or mind.

From the standpoint of Indian philosophy, science and technology cannot perfect our life; they can at best organize and stabilize our outer environment. If science is to concentrate on the realization of the higher life, then it is bound to be a new science. This new science may successfully deal with the forces of the 'life-world' and instal altogether a new social futurism with new goals of perfection for the entire race of mankind. Science and technology are common to all men in their ultimate analysis and conclusions; they are open to all nations in their methods, available to all races in their results and they tend to establish community of both thought and living at all levels of existence. In future civilization, 'laws of identity' will be preferred over the 'laws of contradiction' even in the field of physical sciences and the image of science will not be so hazardous and barbarous as today. Science is bound to assist in the overall evolution of society and the general progress of humanity by its synchronizing process of positive transcendence and synthesis.

It is likely that in the future science, the goals and purposes dominate over blind actions and accomplishments. We may not tame technology as we tame a wild beast, yet the aims of technology will run parallel to the aims of spirituality throughout the globe. This synthetic ideal will be explained to its last significance through the scientific humanism of the future. At present, man is subordinated to his scientific and technological innovations. In the future, he is bound to be the central figure in the whole universe and harness all energies to raise his status and evolve all strategies for his conscious survival and growth.

In Indian philosophy, conscious struggle is aspiration and all problems of life are problems of growth and perfection. In future, man will evolve new strategies of survival which behove his true status. For this reason, probably, he is bound to witness many eventful happenings in his very life and that he is bound to be classed under the category of 'new creation'. 'Situational groupings' and 'personal stability zones' will have little significance when compared to the collective aspiration, race-virtue and complete survival. Terrestrial transformation can be brought about effectively by the two twin processes of individual transformation and social transformation. In planning the oew strategies of survival, the planner ought to experience *abhaya*, that is, complete freedom from fear. Then alone is he capable of explaining the *avyakta* (unmanifest) as *akāla* (timeless). Nonetheless, science, while investigating life, discovered that the root nature of all living is a struggle for survival. This struggle for survival implies a happy blend of physical science and human happiness and perfection that is in the offing in future. True happiness lies in the true growth of our being in its allness and wholeness. Even our body is our means of fulfilling the *dharma* ('*Śarīram khalu dharma-sādhanam*').

Social futurism is not a combination of the few social trends but a meaningful co-existence of 'multiple choices' and alternatives, of aims and goals in life. The aim of future society will be to realize its real being, nature and destiny and travel towards divine perfection. The highest destiny is to express in the general life of mankind, the power, the light and the harmony and better the right conditions of progress and perfection. The aim of the spiritualized human society of the future, from the standpoint of Indian tradition, is to realize the three essential truths of existence, i.e. God, Freedom and Unity. The future society will regard man not as a mind, a life and a body, but as a soul incarnated upon earth for a specific purpose of divine fulfilment. In Indian thought, human fulfilment and the divine fulfilment are not isolated realities. *Svadharma* (the *dharma* of the individual self) is not divorced from the *dharma* of the age (*yuga-dharma*) and the same is not different from the *mokṣa-dharma* (dharma of highest liberation). In the light of these truths, the common life of the people of the future is bound to be more meaningful and purposeful. The future society will be free from common strife, greed and hatred. On the other hand, people will follow the altruistic ideals and pursue the spiritual goals and ideals. *Loka-saṃgraha* (working for the world) will not be different from the *daiva-saṃkalpa* (thinking about God). There is bound to be an integral perfection (*samagra-siddhi*) in the overall life of the society of tomorrow. Reformation of society and perfection of the environment will not, however, be rooted in any other medium except the individual himself. It is not always true to say that man moves into future; but it is the future with its structure moves into man's claims and draws him into its fold every time. In the years to follow, past will never be a drag as all past will be a moving future; both the past and the future will be ever-living forces of evolution and progress. It is for this reason, perhaps, man's real greatness lies in what he makes possible of his future and not in what he is at present. It is on this sound premise that the whole edifice of social futurism is built up in India.

According to Sri Aurobindo, on no occasion were we so conscious of the Future as today. The Future is like a sphinx with two minds. Nevertheless, it is an admixture of hope and despair. A perfect human world cannot be created by men or composed by men who are themselves imperfect. Sri Aurobindo visualized the transformation of even earth-nature here and now. According to him, the spiritualized society of the future would live like its spiritual individuals, not in the 'collective ego' but in the 'collective spirit' or soul. It is the inner life and the inner environment of the individual which tends to transform the outer living or existence. Evolution is never a new manifestation other than the individual or race manifestation. In fact, evolution and perfection are two sides of the same reality. One has always to move into the future and not go back to his past consciousness, if he really wants to grow in his life. If the ideals and thoughts about the future come as mere memories and imaginations, they are not useful to us from the point of view of both Yoga and Futurism. In the cosmic evolutionary process, man is only a stage and not a goal. Man is never a final consummation in the long process of evolution of his species. The transition from the stage of mind to supermind can be viewed as the 'Light out of Light.' Nevertheless, there will be the true growth of the power of the spirit in the humanity of the future. There will be more intense and revealing speech, more inward and subtle attributes of sense and sight in the future man. He will be endowed with a larger cosmic vision and new Consciousness—the integral consciousness. If the gains of cyclical evolution seem to have been suspended for some or other reason, they tend to re-emerge into new forms suitable to the new ages. The concept of progress in Sri Aurobindo is teleological. According to him, every society has to witness three major stages of social evolution, the infra-rational, the rational and the supra-rational before it arrives at the 'completeness of its possibilities.' Sri Aurobindo envisages two important conditions for the awakening of the new spirit in society. The 'pioneering individuals' and the 'preparedness of the common minds' are equally needed for a radical or an innovative change in society. Sri Aurobindo sees altogether a new category of higher life and consciousness in the future race of mankind. This is the beginning of a divinized life on earth called the 'New Race' or 'New Humanity.' In future, there will be no religion except spirituality. All life will be expression and the flowering in terms of the Divine Unity manifesting in the world. The family along with all other social institutions of man will break down and the disappearance is in process. In their natural relations, man and woman are, at one and towards each other, quite despotic masters and somewhat pitiable slaves. No law can liberate women from men unless they aspire to free themselves; men too cannot cease to be slaves unless they are freed from all their 'inner slavery'. In the case of 'exceptional individuals' there will be a breakdown of the family and all family relations. Man's greatness lies not in what he is, but in what he makes possible. He either produces out of himself a new and a greater being, or he himself will become a divine being—the Superman. In either case, there is bound to be a manifestation of higher life in the very race of humanity.

Indian philosophy, in its long journey from the ancient ages to the modern period has concerned itself equally with whatever is thinkable and knowable to us at the highest level of our experience, as well as with the lowest and the minutest ranges of our everyday life and observation. In the process, it has enlarged its boundaries of thought and aspiration; and its philosophical intellect has decidedly begun the work of 'new creation'. It has now almost assumed the status of an inalienable science of both being and becoming.

It is needless to mention that philosophy in India has always abhorred mere 'guessing' and 'speculation' in its intellectual canalization of spiritual knowledge. At the same time, it has never lost its secret sense of immortality and impulse towards perfection.

On no occasion, Indian philosophy and the science of futurism were isolated truths. The vision of the future was always linked up with the overall aspiration and growth of humanity. It is in this specific and broader context, that the present paper has been planned and attempted to include and encompass the varied aspects of modern futurology as anticipatory democracy, future education, taming technology, strategies of survival and social futurism as well-considered profiles of the future.

18

THE FUTURE OF INDIAN PHILOSOPHY

N. S. S. Raman *

TO ask questions about the future is after all a natural tendency, born perhaps out of curiosity to know about the shape of things to come. Indians, in particular, fall prey to the tendency to consult an astrologer before undertaking any important task. But to ask questions about the future of a type of philosophy (e.g. Marxism or Idealism) is by no means restricted to Indian culture. Colloquia, symposia, seminars, etc., have been organized to assess the existing status of a system of thought and to anticipate its future possibilities. One hears such titles as "Revolution in Philosophy" or the "Future of Philosophy" which indicate some anxiety on the part of the professional philosopher to look into the future in the light of the present. The student of Indian culture is aware of the three great Buddhist conferences in this country convened several centuries ago, with a view to review the then prevalent philosophical and religious situation and to suggest steps for the future. One also hears about the various "Party Congresses" in the Soviet Union with the same purpose, though many lead to unfortunate consequences like denunciations and purges. Unlike the party theoreticians, however, the intentions and the objectives of the academic philosopher are harmless, when he poses questions about the

*N. S. S. Raman is Professor and Head of the Department of Philosophy, Banaras Hindu University. He was educated at Mysore, Rajasthan, Glasgow and Mainz universities. He was a Visiting Professor at the University of Mainz. He wrote a number of articles and a book on *Karl Jaspers* in German.

future of his philosophy or of philosophy in general. It may be noted that the philosopher's vision of the future of his philosophy, in most cases, is optimistic.

In this paper, I am posing questions about the future not of philosophy in general, but of Indian philosophy *in India*. This question is vital because I feel that we are living in the midst of a culture in transition. We are also living in a country which is proud of its tradition, though it has only recently become politically free from foreign domination. The cultural and educational benefits this country has received from foreign political domination is a very controversial matter and I shall not waste much time here by argument. When asked about it, every educated Indian will immediately enumerate the following benefits—English language, discovery of our own past, science and technological revolution, introduction of democratic concepts and institutions converging towards a national unity never possible before, the introduction of an educational system not based on caste, etc. All of these must, no doubt, be regarded as worthwhile contributions of a foreign culture to India during the two hundred years of its rule. In the field of philosophical knowledge and education, one sees Indians taking to Western philosophical ideas as fish takes to water. They not only read great masters of the Western philosophical tradition like Plato, Aristotle, Hume, Kant and Hegel, but also evince keen interest in typically Western tendencies like analysis, existentialism, Marxism, etc. Approximately sixty to seventy per cent of the philosophy curriculum, that undergraduate and graduate students learn, is oriented by Western philosophical ideas and systems. About half of all dissertations written in philosophy are devoted to problems of European philosophy. When new trends like phenomenology, philosophy of language, etc., develop in the West, there is an immediate response in India to such trends.

I have no doubt that such a keen interest is not only unavoidable but also desirable. In a fast shrinking world, we have to make attempts to develop a global philosophy not chained to any particular creed or culture. True international brotherhood, of necessity, involves mutual appreciation of ideas and traditions by a continuous philosophical dialogue. In spite of the great ideological rift that marks the twentieth century cultural scene, we must also, at the same time, note the attempts towards bridging the gulf between the East and the West, regarded till recently as unbridgeable. And Indian philosophers have contributed, in no small measure, towards achieving this end.

Nevertheless, my own attitude to comparative philosophy has been somewhat negative, for reasons which I have elaborated elsewhere.[1] In particular, I have expressed a strong dislike for those who take to English philosophy as though all conceptual activity in this country is still moulded by what goes on in Oxford and Cambridge universities. I appreciate, of course, the remarkable contributions of the English intellect, but I cannot, at the same time, ignore the differences between the European and our own tradition. A sympathetic understanding of their systems of thought does not entail sacrificing our heritage. There is a tendency in this country to look down upon Indian thought, which may be due to the influence of the British ways of thinking, though we cannot ignore the historical fact that the British were in full control of all educational and cultural institutions in this country for more than 150 years of their imperial rule. They have bequeathed to us a language in which most Indians think and write, even if the domain of discourse is Indian philosophy. There were times when the British ways of thinking were attracted by the Teutonic trends, and Indian philosophers immediately followed suit. For a brief period, at the end of last century and the beginning of this century, British philosophy was attracted to Kantian and Hegelian idealism; indeed, it seemed to break away from its empiricist moorings, though not for long. British philosophy later on was attracted by analysis, to which it held on to this day. Indian philosophers, in recent years, have been following these British trends since the end of last century, though some Indians trained in their own ancient ways of thinking have indeed revived interest in the study of the traditional systems of thought. The 'Oxbridge' type of philosophy which some Indian philosophers today teach their students enthusiastically cannot be a part of Indian tradition, though Professor Ganeswar Misra of Utkal University has been trying to show that this type of analysis was already known to our

1. See my article, "Is Comparative Philosophy Possible?" in N. K. Devaraja (ed), *Indian Philosophy Today* (Delhi : Macmillan, 1975), pp. 201-17.

forefathers ! In spite of its denials,[1] English philosophy has been typically English, and it has not gone beyond the English-speaking countries, including those in the Commonwealth. English philosophical classics have no doubt been translated into some European languages, but I cannot here evaluate their influence on the European mind. It has been observed[2] that some of these translations have been successful, as the points made out by some of the English writers like Gilbert Ryle and A. J. Ayer are of a general kind and could be made intelligible to the non-English-speaking people also, although some of the illustrations in the original works are drawn from the English forms of idiomatic and non-idiomatic usage. But I cannot agree with those who maintain that J. L. Austin could command the same influence among the Continental European writers as the earlier philosophers like Hume and J. S. Mill. But many Indians have taken fondly to analysis of language in British style at the cost of their own heritage.

It is my firm belief that, with this kind of marriage to British philosophy, Indian philosophy has no future. I would maintain, in spite of the numerous suggestions to the contrary, that there are "objections in principle to this kind of linguistic philosophy ever moving outside the English-speaking world by the medium of translation" and that "this sort of concern with the everyday workings of a natural language must inevitably defy satisfactory translation : if English-speaking philosophy is linguistic, then it must inevitably remain the philosophy of the English speakers."[3] This certainly explains why it has not made any headway in Europe. It is my view that in India too it has not made much progress. Any apparent influence it seems to have had is only skin-deep.

Till the fifties of this century, Indian philosophy in the universities was attracted by neo-Hegelian idealism, and they saw in

1. I refer in particular to the very persuasive article about the application of analytical philosophy to Indian philosophy by G. Misra "Metaphysical Models and Conflicting Cultural Patterns" in N. K. Devaraja (ed), *Indian Philosophy Today*, pp. 155-68. Also see C. T. K. Chari's article "Culture, Language and the Philosophical Enterprise" in the same volume, pp. 82-99.

2. Bernard Williams and Alan Montefiore, "Introduction" to *British Analytical Philosophy* (London : Routledge and Kegan Paul, 1966), p. 9.

3. *Ibid.*, p. 7.

it a kind of wisdom similar to that to be found in the Vedānta. Here the Indians became, though indirectly, conscious of their own heritage. If one were to peruse the number of doctoral dissertations that appeared between 1930 and 1960, one would come across many works devoted to such comparative studies. The Indian interest in analytical philosophy, in contrast, does not make the student conscious of his ancient heritage not only because the language of analysis is foreign to his tradition, but also because the rejection of tradition by analytical philosophy is also a major cause for this indifference. An eminent philosopher of the West once remarked to me that Indian philosophers today were being quite articulate about their anti-British politics, but at the same time, showed a secret admiration for English philosophy, social and political theory and for English political and educational institutions. It is a great pity that British thinkers did not evince an equally keen interest in Indian thought and institutions. To them it was at best a second-rate culture. I have no doubt that this sort of admiration in the older generation of Indians is gradually waning.

II

Our own heritage in the linguistic sphere is by no means mean. Sanskrit language is admired by many Indians for its richness and depth. Philosophical expression in non-Sanskrit languages which is now being encouraged in some parts of India is not new. Many of the dialogues of the Buddha compiled more than two thousand years ago were written in the language of the common man. Many works were written in ancient Indian languages like Tamil, in which highly abstract ideas were expressed. Any language in which poetry could be written could also be used to convey philosophical ideas having great depth and intensity. Take the Upaniṣads, for example. Its thoughts are couched in poetic language, which any other Indian language would have been unable to express. Ancient Indian philosophers did not care much for the logical form as we do today. For that matter, no philosophy in any part of the ancient world cared much for logic. As all students of philosophy know, it was only after Aristotle that logic as such became a formalized science, a necessary adjunct of philosophy. As Collingwood has remarked in a similar context,[1] the philosopher must go to school with the poets in order to learn the use of language, in their way as a means of exploring one's own mind and bringing into light what is doubtful and obscure in it. This implies skill in the use of the various figures of speech in order to convey with greater power the various insights that may come to the thinker in a flash. He must show a capacity for moulding language by inventing new phrases and new metaphors, which must be capable of being understood with the same vigour in which they are expressed. They must be capable of being accompanied by an incentive to create and recreate meanings. In other words, language should not be treated in a rigid manner, as fixed in import, but 'infinitely flexible and full of life.' Ancient Indian thought having inseparable religious moorings is inconceivable apart from myths, metaphors, allegories and parables. Texts like the *Bhagavad Gītā* were continuously enriched by commentaries. Today, use of myths and metaphors in philosophical speech would be laughed at. In our search for logical clarity, we have allowed the literary qualities of philosophical ideas to fade away. We do not realize how rich our various languages are and are lost in the maze of the jargon of analytical philosophy. Just as we try to universalize religious experience and religious language by applying Western methods and norms of interpretation wholesale to Indian religions, we also apply the same methods of inquiry and interpretation to forms of philosophical thinking in India. This is the reason why attempts to express the Vedānta in English philosophical jargon has, in my opinion, totally failed. It is in this context that I deeply regret the declining interest in India in Sanskrit language and culture. Modern Indian languages, many of whom are successors to Sanskrit are groping in the dark. Literary output in them is extremely meagre compared to that in modern European languages. It makes me sadder to note that the philosophical works appearing in them are scanty and substandard, if anything. I cannot help feeling that we are fast heading towards a cultural vacuum in India.

1. R. G. Collingwood, *An Essay on Philosophical Method* (Oxford : Oxford University Press, 1953), p. 214.

The great German philosopher Karl Jaspers called art and poetry the 'germinating centres of language.'[1] In the religious experience of all cultures, we find poetry, myth and metaphor quite expressive. Thus the language of the Vedas and the Upaniṣads and of the early Buddhist texts is quite poetic, quite expressive; it is not even metaphysical and certainly not scientific or logical. Here the thinker is guided more by the symbolic, arising out of spontaneous inspiration rather than by the logical or the metaphysical impulse. The ancient man in general thought much less in logical or scientific terms, and more in terms of the symbolic and the mythical. Western philosophy for the last five or six hundred years has not known anything like it. Perhaps the logical and metaphysical tradition is much older and is traceable to Aristotle. The significance of the symbolic is nowhere so conspicuous as in Indian philosophy, and it is only in recent years that Indian philosophy has fallen into the habit of regarding philosophy as ontology, metaphysics, ethics, epistemology, logic, criticism of science, and so on. Therefore, if we have to revive an interest in ancient Indian ways of thinking, then we have first to preserve the symbolic and the poetic heritage. The task of future Indian philosophy is also to bring more into limelight the depth of this symbolism, and to create new avenues of expression of man's authentic inner experience (which Indian philosophy has always been). Naciketā's dialogue with death, Āruṇi's dialogue with Śvetaketu, the story of Śunaḥśepa, the Kṛṣṇa-Arjuna-saṃvāda in the *Gītā* are all examples of the many ways in which this authentic inner experience is expressed. It would be a pity if such a power of words is lost in the quagmire of conceptual analysis. If Indian philosophy has to have any future at all, other than that of being lost in the global current of conceptual analysis and of scientism, then it has to rekindle this power of our language. It is my firm belief that with our linguistic heritage, it would not be difficult to create conditions for the authentic expression of philosophical experience.

III

In my opinion, there are three ways in which language can express meanings : (a) to express matters of everyday life and

1. Karl Jaspers, *Von der Wahrheit*, Munchen, 1947, p. 917. The phrase he uses is '*Keimstätte der Sprache*'.

knowledge—this mode of expression is the least symbolic and embraces many types of expression, from journalistic to the language of empirical and social sciences; (b) to convey meanings of science and technology, where the set of meanings would be exact and go beyond the reach of the common man, and therefore would not be so intelligible as everyday language; and (c) to express meanings of man's deeper and inner life, in the language of poetry, religion and philosophy. It is the third mode of expression that brings forth completely the hermeneutical significance of philosophical activity. Such an activity would transcend the sphere of logic. Perhaps the modes of expression of meanings in language are more diverse than what I have just enumerated. I only want to emphasize here that it would be wrong to understand or interpret various types of symbolism through the same logic. Even Wittgenstein has shown in his later philosophy that subordination of language to rigid rules of logic would be unfair to language, philosophy itself being a 'fight against the fascination which forms of expression exert upon us' (*Blue and Brown Books* p. 27), though, from our standpoint this kind of 'bewitchment' of our mind by language should be looked upon not as a 'disease' which should be cured by philosophical analysis, but as the very glory of philosophy. On the other hand, one need not also be rigid like the Advaita Vedāntin, who regards all philosophies as leading to Advaita. This point of view would ignore the wide divergences in experience and expression. Some philosophical systems have taken refuge in mysticism, where language 'breaks down,' where 'thought cannot reach.' This kind of mystical ecstasy is sometimes 'expressed' through incommunicable silence. Such a philosophy of 'silence' can obviously have no interest for us, being incommunicative and static. All such philosophies are private and do a great deal of injustice to the dynamism of the Indian tradition. In spite of the great number of treatises and expository commentaries written on it, the Vedānta remains but a static philosophy, which has no relevance to communicative experience of men in the contemporary context. The fact of some Western intellectuals being attracted to the Vedānta does not at all prove its relevance to and capacity for facing intellectual challenges today.

Hence if philosophy is to survive and to have any future, it has only to be conceived within the framework of language. At the same time, if it is to have any significance at all, should produce a creative response, though within a limited circle. Unlike scientific truths, philosophical meanings can never be universalized because of two important factors : (a) understanding is linked to tradition, and (b) philosophical understanding is restricted to a closed circle of the initiated. The future of Indian philosophy is, therefore, bound to the questions of preservation of tradition, and of preventing it from being lost in the universalized language of science. Philosophical understanding must reveal what the German philosopher, H. G. Gadamer, has described as a "mysterious intimacy (*rätselhafte Innigkeit*) which is bound up with the way in which speech is contained, in a hidden way, in thinking."[1] It would be a full revelation of the power of words which must be renewed and expressed in every new act of thinking. There may be nothing wrong in adding new dimensions from without (in fact it may even be quite authentic to do so), so long as these new influences enrich the tradition. Hence, though I have questioned[2] the blind academic pursuit of comparative philosophy, merely for its own sake, I have not opposed the enrichment of our tradition from new dimensions of thought outside our own tradition.

But the danger of identifying philosophical culture with the scientific is obvious. It would kill any philosophical creativity, by identifying the two levels of language. Those who try to replace traditional thought by a scientific one might aim at developing a global philosophy divorced from individual historical traditions. But that would result in an identification of philosophy and science, and destroy the basis for any future Indian philosophy. But science and technology have given rise to a host of authentic problems regarding reality, man and his relation to cosmos, the meaning of life and of human powers and activity and the nature of the universe itself. A scientific and cultural revolution may have shifted the focus of attention of Indian philosophy. There has, therefore, arisen a great scope for a new philosophical dialogue based on the new needs

1. H. G. Gadamer, *Truth and Method* 2d ed. (Translation of *Wahrheit und die Methode* by William Glen-Doepel) (London : Sheed and Ward, 1979), p. 351.

2. See my article in *Indian Philosophy Today*, pp. 201-17.

of man and society, which the new scientific culture and temper are unable to deal with. Therefore, Indian philosophy of the future cannot but encounter these new challenges within the framework of its tradition.

When we speak of tradition, can India's religious heritage be forgotten ? Obviously, the entire range of language and thought in India must be seen as inseparably bound to our religious tradition. The content of our thought might undergo transformation, but not the tradition. To illustrate this point, one need only realize how Buddhism and Jainism have always been conceived within the framework of our tradition. Unfortunately, even in the study of our own religious tradition, we are guided and influenced by a Protestant or Catholic methodology of comparative religion, which clouds our mind to some of the distinctive features of our great religions. Added to this prejudice is another so-called ideological study of our tradition. The Marxist orientation in the study of history, politics, art, literature and, above all, of philosophy, belongs to the same class as religious prejudice. In either case, the pre-conceived set of notions and methods guide the study of our ancient thought and institutions. The outlook of the missionary has long tended to destroy objectivity and depth of approach, since the main aim is conversion to the fold and not impartial scholarship.

We have to remedy these injustices perpetrated by British-oriented philosophical outlook and the missionary and political ideological reading of Indian philosophy. Radhakrishnan took a serious note of the missionary outlook of some of the so-called interpreters of the Indian tradition (e.g. Albert Schweitzer). It is time we took note of others who stand in the way of developing our own tradition independent of Western systems. For philosophy is not like science; in my view, it is linked inseparably to language and culture. This does not mean that one should be indifferent to great philosophical ideas which have had a substantial role to play in the intellectual histories of other cultures. I reiterate that the student of philosophy has to re-orient himself in these tendencies, without being tempted to borrow them and apply them to the Indian tradition. Nor does this mean that we have to turn a deaf ear to the achievements of science and technology. Knowledge as a totality at a given stage in history of any culture—and this totality includes also scientific knowledge—will shape the emergence of new ideas and new philosophical experience. I do not also mean to suggest that we should revive our past traditions in order to achieve a philosophical renaissance; knowledge of the past is necessary, but it should not influence us to the point of damaging the authenticity and originality of new ideas.

This renaissance in philosophy, above all, requires a new national policy in our education. The new educational policy, in general, should not attempt to borrow Western ideals wholesale and it should not also aim at reviving outdated and culturally irrelevant ideas from our ancient heritage. The burden of our past heritage should not make us collapse under its weight. It should bear in mind the rich linguistic heritage of the country. India is placed in a convenient geographical and cultural position to play an original and authentic role in the shaping of a new philosophical consciousness, a new symbolism, and a new ethos, which might all contribute to the development of a new unity of philosophical experience.

19

ON TEACHING INDIAN PHILOSOPHY

S. S. Rama Rao Pappu*

IN recent years, philosophy teachers in the West are showing an increasing interest in problems of "teaching philosophy".[1] Typical problems which are discussed in this context are both "practical" and "philosophical". The practical problems which are discussed concern such issues as sharing classroom experiences, discussing curriculum development, the interest and importance of audio-visual equipment, computers, etc. as instructional aids, and so on. The philosophical issues which are discussed relate to the philosophy of teaching philosophy. Of course, philosophers ever since Plato were interested in what is called "philosophy of education". But the philosophical issues discussed in "teaching philosophy" are more specific. Some typical questions which are discussed in this connection are : "Can philosophy teaching be neutral ?" "Can philosophy teaching be objective ?" "Is teaching philosophy a moral activity ?" "What values ought we to promote in teaching philosophy ?" "Should men teach feminist philosophy courses ?" etc.

*S. S. Rama Rao Pappu is Associate Professor of Philosophy, Miami University, Oxford, Ohio, U.S.A. He studied in the University of Delhi, India, and Southern Illinois University, U.S.A. He has published articles in Indian and American journals and has co-authored a book *Gandhi and America's Educational Future*.

1. See, for example, specialized journals like *Teaching Philosophy*, *AITIA*, *Journal of Pre-College Philosophy*, "Newsletter on Teaching Philosophy" published by the American Philosophical Association.

Of course, it comes as no surprise to philosophers that there is a philosophy of teaching philosophy. And, like other philosophical disagreements, philosophers disagree on *what* the philosophy of teaching philosophy is. There is, however, a possibility of agreement on the following point, viz., that one's philosophy of teaching philosophy is dependent to a large extent upon one's conception of philosophy. If a philosophy teacher thinks that the aim of philosophy is to "show the fly out of the fly bottle," then his philosophy of teaching philosophy is guided by the ideal of showing the student how best to release the fly out of the fly bottle and how to prevent the flies from entering the bottle again. Or, if philosophy is considered to be a reverential hymn to the Creator, a philosophy teacher aims at teaching how to praise our Creator, the Lord.

In this paper, I shall explore some philosophical problems concerning the teaching of Indian philosophy. If, what is said above concerning the relation between teaching philosophy and philosophy is accepted, then the question of *teaching* Indian philosophy is essentially bound up with our views concerning the *nature* of Indian philosophy. In Part I of this paper, therefore, I shall briefly expound the generally accepted *traditional* view that Indian philosophy is spiritual and its aim or goal is the attainment of *mokṣa* or "spiritual liberation". If it is accepted that *mokṣa* or spiritual liberation is the aim of Indian philosophy, then our philosophy of teaching Indian philosophy ought to be directed towards this goal. In Part II, I shall attempt to draw some philosophical implications of this position. In Part III, I shall develop what I consider to be a "broad" interpretation of *mokṣa*. I shall argue here how *mokṣa* as I reinterpret it, could form a nucleus for a progressive philosophic pedagogy.

I

The term "Indian Philosophy" refers to a variety of schools and systems developed in the Indian subcontinent over a period of 3000 years. In its long, complex and rich tradition covering this period, despite sectarian, terminological, logical and epistemological disputes between different "schools" of thought, there is a fundamental agreement that the aim of philosophy is the liberation of the individual from his "earthly", phenomenal existence. For traditional Indian philosophers, philosophy is a *mokṣa-śāstra*, a treatise on *mokṣa.* Every major philosophical work begins with the premiss that the discussion contained in the book will lead the inquiring student to *mokṣa* or release. "Indian philosophy is freedom-intoxicated as it were. Every fibre of it is a protest against bondage."[1]

The agreement that the individual needs to be liberated also presupposes a broad agreement on some other aspects of the human condition. First, it was generally agreed that our earthly life is one of suffering. It is, of course, true that not all Indian philosophers have depicted the human condition in such tragic terms as some Buddhists did. For many Hindu philosophers, the state of human existence is one of boredom, if not outright anguish. At the least, our mundane existence is not as good as the transcendental existence. Second, the notion of *mokṣa* or spiritual liberation also presupposes that we are "bound". Since the Indian philosophers interpreted the notion of bondage (*bandha*) as essentially empirical, they were led to maintain some distinction between the empirical and transcendental modes of our existence. It is, no doubt, true that for some Indian schools of thought the distinction between the empirical and the transcendental exists only at the epistemological level; for others, however, it exists at the ontological level as well. Despite these differences, it is important to note that there is a distinction between the empirical and the transcendental for all Indian philosophers. Third, the concept of *mokṣa* also raises the question : What is it to be liberated ? For the Hindu philosophers, it is the Self which needs to be liberated and for the Buddhist philosophers who denied the existence of a Self, it is what we may call the "individual" (not his Self) who needs to be liberated.

Though there is no disagreement among Indian philosophers that the freedom of the Self (or the freedom of the *individual*, in the case of the Buddhists) is the *summum bonum* of all philosophy, they disagree about the nature of the Self, about the state of the Self when it attains *mokṣa* and about the means of attaining *mokṣa.* To mention a few of these differences : The Jaina philosophers maintain that there are a plurality of Selves, and these Selves differ in their phenomenal existence not only

1. Debiprasad Chattopadhyaya, *What is Living and What is Dead in Indian Philosophy* (New Delhi : People's Publishing House, 1976), p. 565.

in the degree of consciousness but also in size. For the Nyāya-Vaiśeṣikas, the Self is a spiritual substance which possesses the qualities of cognition, affection and consciousness. Consciousness, for example, is an accidental attribute of the Self. On the other hand, for the Upaniṣadic thinkers, Sāṁkhya-Yoga school and the Vedāntins, consciousness is the *essence* of the Self. In contrast to all these conceptions of the Self, the Buddhists deny the very existence of Self as a substance. Likewise, there are radical differences among Indian philosophers about the state of the Self when it attains *mokṣa*. Buddhism which denies the existence of Self states that no description of the state of *nirvāṇa* is possible. According to the Theravāda tradition, all that we can say about *nirvāṇa* is that it

> "is the elimination of craving (*tanhakkhaya*), hence a state of detachment (*virāga*). Because of this state of detachment, the *arahant* is free from suffering. Hence *nirvāṇa* comes to be characterized as the end of suffering (*dukkhass'anta*) and a state of perfect happiness (*parama sukha*)."[1]

In the Mādhyamika tradition it is maintained that *nirvāṇa* is neither a *ens* nor a non-*ens* nor both nor neither. In contrast, the Upaniṣads and the Vedāntins maintain that the state of the released Self is one of infinite knowledge, infinite consciousness and infinite bliss. The Nyāya-Vaiśeṣikas, however, differ from these views and state that since consciousness is an accidental quality of the Self, in its released state, the Self does not possess any consciousness. Lastly, there are also wide differences among Indian philosophical schools about the *means* for liberation—some advocating that knowledge (*jñāna*) is the sole means for liberation, others stating that it is action (*karma*) and still others maintaining that *both jñāna* and *karma* are necessary for liberation.

Mokṣa, therefore, with all the implications that this concept involves is *constitutive* of the philosophic activity of Indian philosophers. Just as political philosophy cannot be studied without necessary reference to the concept of "state"; biology cannot be studied without a necessary reference to the concept of "life" and; physical sciences without reference to "material object", Indian philosophy cannot be studied without reference to the concept of *mokṣa*. In this sense, *mokṣa* is the *constitutive* concept

1. David J. Kalupahana, *Buddhist Philosophy : A Historical Analysis* (Honolulu : The University Press of Hawaii, 1976), pp. 81-82.

of Indian philosophy. *Mokṣa* is also a *regulative* concept of Indian philosophy in the sense that philosophic problems and theories of language, logic, epistemology, ethics, etc. were regulated by the notion of *mokṣa.* Thus, take for example, Indian epistemology. It is the overarching principle of *mokṣa* which led Indian thinkers to subordinate reason to intuition, recognize verbal testimony (*śabdapramāṇa*) as a separate criterion of truth, direct realization (*sākṣāt-kāra*) of truth as the culmination of all intellectual endeavours, and so on. Likewise, since *mokṣa* is the realization of the Self, Hindu philosophers naturally tended to emphasize the spiritual over the material, the "inward" over the "outward", the so-called "mystical" over the "rational". Because of its central concern with *mokṣa,* Indian philosophy is often characterized as "spiritual". To say that Indian philosophy is spiritual does not mean that it is theistic, since many Indian philosophical systems are atheistic. Nor does it mean that it is religious—if by "religious" we mean a set of dogmatic divine truths which have to be accepted and acted on faith alone. The spirituality of Indian philosophy simply means that Indian philosophies originated with an analysis and understanding of the human condition and its phenomenal existence and show the way to man's transcendence. That Indian philosophy aims at *mokṣa* which is non-phenomenal makes it a "spiritual" philosophy, just as the medieval philosophers' concern with God, Scripture, Revelation, etc. makes it a "religious" philosophy. To be sure, the medieval philosophers' great contributions in epistemology, metaphysics or ethics could be considered independent of their religious concerns but a true understanding of medieval philosophy is possible only if we understand their philosophical contributions within the Christian framework.

In addition to the "spiritualistic" framework of Indian philosophy which is often asserted, it is also said that the aim of Indian philosophy is not merely to let people *know about mokṣa* but to enable them to *realize mokṣa.*

> Every Indian system seeks the truth, not as academic 'knowledge for its own sake' but to learn the truth which shall make men free . . . Every doctrine has been turned into a passionate conviction, stirring the heart of man and quickening his breath, and completely transforming his personal nature. In India philosophy is for life; it is to be lived. It is not

> enough to *know* the truth; the truth must be *lived.* The goal of the Indian is not to know the ultimate truth but to realize it, become one with it.[1]

Though it is often contended that Indian philosophy does not merely aim at *knowing* about *mokṣa,* but also aims at *realizing mokṣa,* it has not been made clear why it ought to aim at *mokṣa*-realization but not merely at *mokṣa*-knowledge. We may perhaps think of the answers in the following manner.

First, because Indian philosophy had its origins in finding a solution to the predicament of human existence, the solution of *mokṣa,* when arrived at, should not be contemplated theoretically but must be *applied* to the problem of human existence. It is similar to a medical researcher who is interested in finding a cure for cancer in order to save the people affected by cancer. When he finds a solution to the disease, his solution is not intended to be contemplated theoretically but must be *applied* to his patients at once. The role of philosophic theory is thus instrumental in finding solutions to the riddle of human existence—and perhaps philosophy is the most efficient instrument here.

Second, the goal that philosophy merely aims at a theoretical understanding and is not necessarily committed to practice is a Western conception of philosophy to which the Indian philosopher does not subscribe. For the Indian, philosophy is both theoretical and practical, the latter being more important than the former. An Indian philosopher is both a thinker and a doer, and mere thought without action does not qualify one as a philosopher.

Third, Indian philosophy may also maintain that the distinction between theoretical knowledge and practical realization is not applicable to the case of *mokṣa.* In Advaita Vedānta, for example, it is in fact maintained that he who *knows* Brahman *becomes* Brahman. To *know* the truth concerning *mokṣa* is, at the same time, to *attain mokṣa* or Self-Realization. The point emphasized here is *not* that one who knows the truth concerning *mokṣa does* something later to attain *mokṣa.* Rather, *mokṣa*-knowledge *is mokṣa*-attainment. They are not two distinct processes. A variant of this theme is the view (e.g. in Nāgārjuna's Mādhyamika philosophy) that philosophy as dialectical

1. S. Radhakrishnan and Charles A. Moore (ed) : *A Sourcebook in Indian Philosophy* (Princeton, N. J. : Princeton University Press, 1957), pp. xxiii-xxiv.

criticism shows the incompetence of Reason to attain Reality. Dialectic aims at the death of thought, which is, at the same time, the birth of Wisdom.

The points which have emerged from the above discussion may be summarized as follows. For the traditional Indian philosopher, *mokṣa* or spiritual liberation is constitutive of Indian philosophy. It is its *summum bonum.* Indian philosophy conceives of the role of philosophy as "practical". For the Indians, a philosopher is not merely a critical, reflective individual who *knows a lot* about man, world, man's place in the world and the means of man's spiritual liberation; or one who can talk, argue and discuss philosophic problems and arguments. The true philosopher is one who has attained spiritual liberation (or at least one who is committed to attain spiritual liberation from his phenomenal existence).

II

It is axiomatic in all teaching that *how* we teach is, to a large extent, dependent upon *what* we teach and what goals we want to achieve. If the subject matter is carpentry and our aim in teaching is the development of skills in the student, then we teach him *how* to acquire the skills of carpentry. On the other hand, if we teach history, and our goal is merely telling the student certain facts, we teach *that* certain facts are true.

Now the aim and goal of philosophic activity according to traditional Indian thought implies some philosophic models of teaching philosophy which we may bring out here. We have seen that Indian philosophy presents us with a distinct goal, the *summum bonum*, *mokṣa*, to which all philosophic education must be directed. An Indian philosophy student is not presented with a "presuppositionless philosophy" on which he has to creatively build his own philosophic system. Nor is he merely given the "arguments for and against" a philosophic position and left to himself to draw his own conclusions. Rather, the student is presented with a pre-established goal by appealing to which he should judge his progress. Of course, Indian philosophy is rich in its emphasis on argument and counter-argument, deliberation and weighing of evidence, and so on. Philosophic reasons and modes of arguments were studied for their own sake in Indian philosophical systems. What is called "*tarka*" in Indian philosophy is studied to prepare oneself to play the "logic game". Despite this, it was generally maintained by traditional Indian philosophic educators that *tarka* does not add to our fund of "knowledge". It serves the negative function of abandoning any incoherent argument. Though *tarka* plays an important role in philosophic education, the aim of teaching philosophy is not identified with imparting *tarkic* abilities in the student. A student who is well-versed in *tarka* may be a good debater and may have good forensic skills, but pursuing *tarka* for its own sake means that the student has lost track of his goal and is involved in a narrow-minded intermediate goal. An Indian philosophy teacher, therefore, cannot aim merely in the development of *tarkic* or critical-reflective faculties in his student. He should go beyond this and tell the student the importance of *nididhyāsana* (practical realization of the truth).

Second, the Indian philosophy teacher cannot also take a "democratic attitude" towards his students—i.e. taking the attitude that the student's opinion is as good as the teacher's. Since the goal of Indian philosophy is said to be "not *mokṣa*-talk but *mokṣa*-attainment," an *ideal* philosophy teacher is one who has himself attained *mokṣa*, who has an authentic first-hand experience of it. The teacher who has so attained *mokṣa* also speaks with authority, and the student reverentially accepts the authority of the teacher's words. It is well-known that in Indian philosophy verbal testimony (*śabdapramāṇa*), argument from the authority of trustworthy persons, is accepted as a criterion of truth. Of course, there can be argument, criticism and counter-criticism between the student and the teacher if the teacher is merely involved in teaching *about mokṣa*, but where the students are taught *in mokṣa*, the teacher becomes the final authority in the matter.

Third, an Indian philosophy teacher cannot remain "neutral" and plough a "no man's land" because Indian philosophy presents us with a distinct philosophic goal, viz. *mokṣa*, and *regulates* the content of all philosophic inquiry in this context. An Indian philosophy teacher, therefore, cannot be neutral about the goal of his teaching. However, because the goal of philosophic teaching is the attainment of *mokṣa*, an Indian philosophy teacher is neutral between the *methods* of teaching philosophy. For him, that method which produces a vision of *mokṣa* in the student is the best one. Which philosophic method produces the required vision is dependent upon the ability and capacity of the student whom he is instructing. Generally, however, like Western philosophers, an Indian philosopher also adopts the rational-critical method intending it to remove conceptual hurdles, intellectual difficulties and methodological doubts that a student confronts in his goal of attaining *mokṣa*. Some Indian philosophical systems (e.g. the Mādhyamikas) point out that we use the rational-critical method (dialectic reason) only to show the incompetence of rational-critical method to reach Reality. If the student does not make progress by following, say, the rational-critical method, the teacher does not mind adopting some non-rational (not irrational) method. The success of the student is not measured by the extent to which the student has mastered the method, but whether he has made progress in the attainment of the goal. Heinrich Zimmer, for example, says :

> The attitude toward each other of the Hindu teacher and the pupil bowing at his feet are *determined by the exigencies of this supreme task of transformation. Their problem is to effect a kind of alchemical transmutation of the soul.* Through the means, not of a merely intellectual understanding, but of a change of heart (a transformation that shall touch the core of his existence), the pupil is to pass out of bondage, beyond the limits of human imperfection and ignorance, and transcend the earthly plane of being.[1]

If the rational-critical method fails, the teacher may tell some parables to get the point across. Even if that fails, he may keep "silent" and convey the truth through silence. The philosophic model of teaching which an Indian philosophy teacher adopts may, therefore, be called the "vision model". Some attain vision after critical reflection (*manana*) on the Truths, others by hearing parables, and so on. In other words, the critical-reflective method is no more important philosophically than the method of parables, since the goal of philosophic teaching is to "pass the Light" from the teacher to the student enabling the student to attain the vision for himself.

In the vision model of philosophic teaching, the teacher of course does not teach the vision. The student can only be led to it. Every Indian philosophical system presents the student with a vision and (approximately) describes what it is like.

1. Heinrich Zimmer, *Philosophies of India* (Princeton : Princeton University Press, 1971), pp. 4-5. (italics mine).

The philosophic reasons and arguments presented in support of the vision are like steps in a ladder. The teacher can only help the student to climb the first few steps but he cannot follow the student all the way to the top. The *via negativa* (*neti-vāda*) method of the *Upaniṣads*, the *adhyāropa* and *apavāda* method of the Advaita Vedāntins, the dialectical method of the Mādhyamikas are some of the pedagogical methods ancient Indian philosophers have used to lead the student to attain the philosophic vision.

III

We have so far considered some philosophical implications of teaching Indian philosophy which is traditionally considered to be a *mokṣa-śāstra*. To some contemporary Indian philosophers, however, the very concept of *mokṣa* and the "vision model" through which it could be taught appears too mystical and bizarre. I have some sympathy with their complaint. I do not, however, agree with them when they advocate that the notion of *mokṣa* as the goal of Indian philosophy needs to be abandoned altogether. Nor do I agree with them that the concept "philosophy" should be restricted to the critical-rational discussion of ideas and arguments. In this section, I would like to maintain that *mokṣa* as the aim of Indian philosophy is a profound insight of the traditional Indian philosophers and if it is interpreted more broadly, it will have relevance and significance to the contemporary (and non-spiritual) student of Indian philosophy also.

We have seen that according to traditional Indian philosophy, the aim of all philosophic inquiry is *mokṣa* and philosophic education is *mokṣa*-oriented education. We have also seen that the state of *mokṣa* which is said to be non-phenomenal makes Indian philosophy a "spiritual" philosophy. Now I would like to state that the concept of *mokṣa* is so rich that there is no reason to restrict ourselves in interpreting it in the exclusively spiritualistic, non-phenomenal dimension alone. It seems reasonable to me to interpret *mokṣa* from a non-spiritualistic point of view also without doing undue injustice to the traditional Indian philosophical literature. Once we reinterpret *mokṣa* in a non-spiritualistic way, even those who are wary of accepting spiritual liberation as the goal of Indian philosophy may come around and accept it as a sound insight of the traditional Indian philosophers. We may distinguish here three important non-spiritualistic conception of *mokṣa*. These may be called : (a) *Mokṣa* as the "Liberation of the Person;" (b) *Mokṣa* as the "Liberation of the Mind;" and (c) *Mokṣa* as "Social Liberation."

(a) *Mokṣa as the Liberation of the Person* :

Mokṣa as the liberation of the person should be distinguished from the traditional conception of *mokṣa* as the liberation of the Spirit. Because the traditional Hindu philosophers thought that the essence of a person is his Spirit, they were led to conclude that *mokṣa* is the liberation of the Spirit. Even if we disagree with this identification of a "person" with his "Spirit," it is hard to maintain that the concept of a "liberated person" is unintelligible. When someone says that "My Spirit was liberated when I was forty" his statement is not directly verifiable, but when he says that "I was liberated (transformed, enlightened) when I was forty," he is making an intelligible, verifiable statement. We can verify this by observing whether or not his life-styles have changed, his perspective on the world is now different, whether his relationships with others are transformed, and so on. Following the *Bhagavad Gītā* (but without the *Gītā*'s metaphysical presuppositions) we may characterize the liberated person as one who has acquired self-mastery; who has conquered the "deadly sins" of anger, pride, fear and lust; who is not carried away by passions as the wind carries away the ship on the waters (*vāyur nāvam iva ambhasi*); who has conquered egoism (*ahaṁkāra*); who maintains an inner poise and is neither elated by successes nor distressed by failures; who is truly a *triguṇātīta*; and so on. In short, a liberated person is one who is not swayed either by "external" forces nor by "internal" passions and maintains a self-mastery. This is merely one example of the concept of a "liberated person" and Indian philosophy, particularly the *Gītā* and Buddhism are rich in providing us with several alternative descriptions of this conception.

(b) *Mokṣa as the Liberation of the Mind* :

Indian thought contains two kinds of liberation of the mind—one the yogic and the other philosophical. In yogic thought, concentration (*dhāraṇa*) and control of mind were considered essential steps leading to "stasis" (*samādhi*). Because the mind jumps and wanders incessantly, like a monkey jumps from branch to branch, it was considered an impediment to the goal of liberation. *Cittavṛtti* or "whirlwinds of consciousness" need to be destroyed before one transcends the human bondage and attains liberation. From a philosophical perspective, however, the liberation of the mind consists in our indefatigable pursuit of the truth; not accepting things merely on authority; thinking critically, rationally and coherently (following reason wherever it leads us to) and even questioning the limits of reason as the determinant of Truth. Śaṁkara, for example, despite his allegiance to Scripture, states that one should not accept the "truth" of the proposition that "fire is cold" even if a thousand scriptures unanimously proclaim it. Nāgārjuna, likewise, states that dialectic should be applied not only to test the truth of philosophical perspectives but also to examine the limits of Reason itself.

(c) *Mokṣa as Social Liberation* :

It is evident that it is society which civilizes, socializes, accultures and makes the *homo sapiens* into "persons". But it is also society which controls, tyrannizes and makes demands for conformity. A socially liberated individual is one who does not obey social rules and conventions because of their authority. When he obeys the social rules, it is only because he finds them reasonable and imposes these rules on himself, and not because society dictated him to do so. He subjects the social and customary codes to a critical examination and develops a critical social theory and a critical code of conduct for himself. The idea of a *sannyāsin* who is above ordinary social *dharma* is the Indian example of an individual who has transcended the authority of the society; who lives in society but cannot be controlled by it. This is what is meant by the characterization that a *sannyāsin* is *in* the society but is not *of* the society.

Having distinguished these three non-spiritualistic senses of *mokṣa*, I now want to state that the aim of philosophy is liberation and the goal of philosophic education must be directed to the liberation of the student in one or more of the senses of *mokṣa* (spiritualistic and non-spiritualistic) described above. Every beginning student of philosophy asks the question : "What is philosophy *for* ?" or "Why study philosophy ?" It seems to me that lying behind the notion of philosophy there is the idea of liberation which is valued for its own sake. Even if we agree with the analytic philosophers that philosophical activity consists of understanding "how silly people use silly words" or "showing the fly out of the fly bottle," there is implied the idea of liberation of the Mind mentioned above. Philosophic education which does not have liberation as its goal is empty, pedantic and inconsequential.

The idea that philosophy has a goal, namely liberation, may give the reader the impression that I have reduced philosophy to a practical science having practical ends. Philosophy, it may be contended, is a theoretical discipline, its problems are theoretical and its methods are theoretical. I do not, however, think that the distinction between theoretical understanding and practical pursuits is as clear as one would wish it to be. Take, for example, the Buddha's philosophic inquiries which originated when he "wondered" about the phenomena of suffering, birth, old age and death and found the "solutions" to these problems. Are the Buddha's inquiries then to be characterized as "practical" and therefore not philosophical ? Simply because a philosophic inquiry originates in a "practical" need and finds a solution to it does not make the inquiry itself less philosophical.

Now suppose a philosopher is interested in finding out why man suffers. Once his inquiries begin and he gets the knowledge (say, following Advaita Vedānta) that man's suffering is due to the ignorance of his real nature as Brahman, his suffering has already vanished ! Of course, in this case, the philosopher must be rationally convinced of the metaphysical system of Advaita Vedānta. A metaphysical perspective (as presupposed, for example, in *mokṣa* as "Liberation of the Spirit") cannot but have practical implications for the way we live. If it is true, as the Advaita Vedāntins argue, that Brahman is the only reality and the world we live in is neither real nor unreal, it makes a great difference to our lives. Metaphysical knowledge has a strong bearing on the way we live. He who knows that Brahman is the sole reality and the world is an illusion is logically committed to lead an appropriate way of life. As J. O. Wisdom says:

> "(There is) a close connection between a way of life and a *Weltanschauung*; for to advocate a certain way of life is also to reveal how one sees the world, and conversely if one spells out how one sees the world, one implies a way of life."[1]

1. J. O. Wisdom, *Philosophy and its place in our Culture* (N.Y. : Gordon and Breach, 1975), p. 206.

Of course philosophical inquiries need not begin with a "practical" problem like the solution to the problem of suffering. Following Aristotle, even if we say that it is through wonder that men began to philosophize, once the philosopher has rationally constructed a cosmological ontology, the truth of that ontology will have a practical bearing on the philosopher's way of life. From a pedagogical perspective, therefore, it is not necessary for the philosophy teacher to initiate the student into philosophy through a "practical" problem. Provided we impart the student a metaphysical system which could be justified, or the student himself is enabled to provide a system of his own, he is thereby liberated not only from his unreflective common sense metaphysics but is also logically committed to transform his way of life according to this metaphysical system.

Similar considerations apply to the other three senses of "liberation" distinguished above. For example, an individual who has a vision of the liberated life, who knows what it is to live the life of a paradigmatic individual is thereby logically committed to transform himself to lead that life. Likewise, the liberation of the mind works in three ways. In the ordinary case, as it often happens in teaching logic, when a student knows the distinction between fallacious argument and a valid argument, he is logically committed to avoiding fallacies in his thinking and reasoning. Ordinary logic thus liberates the student from reasoning incorrectly. At a higher level, the liberation of the mind consists of not accepting a proposition merely on authority, not accepting it because it is believed to be true by everyone, not accepting it because of one's instinctual beliefs, and so on. A liberated mind accepts a proposition only if it is based on evidence, based on his experience, and so on. At a still higher level, a liberated mind questions (like Kant and the Mādhyamikas) the competence of reason to grasp reality and arrive at truth. If it turns out, as it did for the Mādhyamikas, that reason is impotent to reach reality, the liberated mind must transcend reason itself.

In short, the highest vision of the ancient Indian philosophers is to conceive that the goal of philosophy is liberation, that philosophical knowledge logically commits one to liberation—and in some cases philosophical knowledge *is* liberation. The notion of liberation has two aspects—negative and positive. Take, for example, the liberation of the mind. When a student knows the distinction between valid and fallacious arguments, he is (negatively) "liberated from" fallacious thinking. On the other hand, when he knows, for example, the incompetence of reason itself to arrive at truth, he has attained (positively) the liberation of mind itself.

Because the aim of philosophy is liberation, it is so difficult to teach philosophy. (a) At the worst, philosophy teachers teach philosophy as if it were history, using a "teaching that" model. This seems to be particularly true about teaching Indian philosophy and hence the oft-repeated accusation that Indian philosophy is of "antiquarian interest". For many teachers of Indian philosophy, Indian philosophy is nothing but the *history* of Indian philosophy. As a historian of Indian philosophy, then, the philosopher becomes interested in topics like the date and authorship of a philosophic work, the structure, significance and influence on this and of this work, the kinds of arguments advanced and positions held in that work, and so on. The best teacher, on this model, is one who teaches these facts as faithfully as possible and the best student is one who memorizes and reproduces what the teacher told him. It is, therefore, no wonder that contemporary philosophical scholarship on the Indian scene is largely exegetical and not original and the "examinations" to the philosophy students are mostly "memorization tests". What the Indian philosophy teacher misses in this approach is to show the student that the Indian philosophical tradition consists of a series of bold insights and mind-boggling visions of the ancient Indian thinkers.

(b) Somewhat better are those Indian philosophers who accept the view that the essence of philosophy is logic and try to teach certain philosophic skills or *tarkic* abilities in clear and correct thinking. They conceive philosophy as merely an exercise in logical thinking. For them, however, it is just an accident that they are teaching, say, ethics, instead of metaphysics. The modes of reasoning they employ are the same; there is only a difference in terminology. Ethics, for example, is simply logic which uses the terminology of ethics. Metaphysics, likewise, is logic which uses the metaphysical notions. I claim that the development of *tarkic* abilities in the student is better than memorization of dates, works and facts of the Indian philosophical tradition because the former at least has the potential for liberating the mind (one of the senses of *mokṣa* explained previously).[1]

(c) Still better are those teachers who aim at *liberating* the student *from* accepted structures of thought and habitual modes of belief and unreflective ways of life. The best philosophy teacher is one who liberates the student, not just negatively, but positively so that the student develops for himself a perspective, a vision, a *Weltanschauung*, a *darśana*. The reason why philosophy teachers do not teach a vision is not because it is pedagogically impossible, but because they themselves do not have one. More often, the perspective they present to the student is someone else's perspective. Occasionally, if a philosophy teacher really happens to have a vision, he is afraid to teach it because of the fear of being accused of indoctrinating the student. What distinguishes the "creative period" of Indian philosophy from the "scholastic period" is the daring visions put forth during the creative period by the seers and founders of "schools" and other independent thinkers of Indian philosophy. Even the much abused *Cārvāka* had a vision which deserves greater respect than the hair-splitting arguments of the scholastics who had no vision. Indian philosophy has a future only if we are visionaries and not scholastics and if we encourage perspective and not expertise in our students.

1. This seems to be particularly the mode of teaching during the "scholastic period" of the development of Indian thought. In the teaching of Indian philosophy, says D. Ingalls, "the basic texts offer as it were a map of the universe. All the categories and the major types of relations are there precisely defined. The student is then tested with various sets of circumstances which he is asked, as one might say, to fit into the map. One student will take one point of view, another another, and at each step justification is given by reference to the rules of the game. A senior student acts as umpire with occasional reference to the master." Quoted in Ben-Ami Scharfstein (ed) *Philosophy East/Philosophy West* (N.Y. : Oxford University Press, 1978), p. 74.

20

THE RELEVANCE OF INDIAN THOUGHT TO THE EVOLUTION OF WORLD PHILOSOPHY

ASHOK K. GANGADEAN*

I

Introduction : In Search of a Hermeneutic of World Philosophy

IN this paper I shall sketch out my vision of the future of Indian Thought (IT) in the context of World Philosophy (WP). I wish to suggest that the future of IT is essentially tied to the evolution of WP, and conversely, that the emergence of WP is inseparable from the development of IT. In the preliminary clarification of this thesis it is desirable to explicate the notion of "World Philosophy".

The concept of "WP" becomes accessible in the context of the Philosophy of Worlds or Comparative Ontology. Ontology investigates the form, formation and transformation of worlds. A world is a reality which is constituted by a particular categorial structure, a configuration of categories which defines a system of possible experience. A world system is, therefore, at the same time a system of meaning which determines what is intelligible and prescribes a realm of meaningful experience. Thus, for

*Ashok K. Gangadean is Associate Professor of Philosophy, Haverford College, Pennsylvania, U.S.A. He has published several articles on Comparative Philosophy in *Philosophy : East and West* and other journals.

example, the Hindu world is a reality which manifests itself in a particular categorial form, defines a language of meaningful experience, prescribes a realm of possible facts and delimits the bounds of human understanding. By contrast, the Christian world arises in a different categorial form with a different reality, a unique language of experience, a different system of meaning, etc. What makes sense to the Hindu fails to make sense in the Christian world, and what is a possible fact for the Christian is not within the realm of possibility in the Hindu world. The diverse possible and actual worlds, ontologies or languages of experience involve such radically distinct structures of consciousness and being that different worlds appear to be incommensurable realities.

The history of thought, being precisely the articulation of diverse ontological languages, provides abundant examples of different worlds. Within the so-called "Western" tradition, for example, we encounter the emergence of different realities in the teachings of Plato, Aquinas, Descartes, Spinoza, Leibniz, Hume, Hegel, Wittgenstein, and so on. These creative ontologists led the way in forging new languages of experience. And in the Indian tradition alone we encounter a rich diversity of ontologies, the Hindu and the Buddhist worlds being two obvious examples.

While ontology is concerned with the structure of a given world, comparative ontology focuses on the transformation or reformation of a given world, as well as on intelligible transformations between different worlds. The Philosophy of Worlds is typically concerned with the following sorts of questions: How is intelligible discourse between different worlds possible ? What is the logic of ontological revolutions ? How can intelligibility itself be reformed ? How is religious conversion possible ? How is communication or ontological translation between different worlds possible ? Can there be common sense and cross-reference between different ontological languages ? Are there any absolute terms for all possible worlds ? And so on.

These typical transcendental concerns of the Philosophy of Worlds help us to appreciate the fundamental problematic of WP. For, on the one hand, Comparative Ontology recognizes a *diversity* of radically different worlds which inevitably leads to realities or languages which are incommensurable. This means that the terms of reference and the reference of terms are relative to a given ontology, so no terms are "neutral," common or absolute for all possible worlds. The incommensurability of worlds is synonymous with the relativity of sense and reference. This disclosure of Comparative Ontology leads to scepticism concerning the possibility of intelligible transformations between different worlds. But, on the other hand, the Philosophy of Worlds also arises in the primitive intuition that there is One world, one unified reality. This intuition, of course, collides with and challenges the converse intuition of radical diversity. The intuition of radical ontological *unity* offers a solution to the problem of intelligible transformations between worlds : for if, indeed, there is ultimately one world, one unified, universal ontological language, then incommensurability evaporates, and the alleged transformations between different worlds turn out to be internal changes within one common world. Both voices of Comparative Ontology —the voice of radical diversity and the voice of radical unity —appear to be primitively true and irreducible. It is here that we find the antinomy of Comparative Ontology : each thesis appears to be axiomatic, and one contradicts the other. It is in this dialectic of Ontology that the challenge of WP emerges.

The concern of WP has been alive throughout the history of thought. Stated simply, perhaps simplistically, it is the concern of negotiating the dual intuitions of radical diversity and radical unity. How is it possible at once to acknowledge that there is a diversity of realities *and* that there is one reality ? I wish to suggest that this is the generic perennial concern of philosophy—it is the concern of the nature of rationality itself.

WP is not *another* particular ontology among others; it is not a separate and distinct philosophical language which "ties" the diverse philosophical languages together. Rather, it is a rational mentality or hermeneutic which accommodates a diversity of worlds in "one" consciousness. The hermeneutic of WP must be rich enough to recognize the irreducible differences between realities or ontological languages, yet powerful enough to enter into discourse between possible and actual worlds. The perennial challenge for philosophy is first to recognize this and to explain how it is possible. The "Western" philosophical tradition, for example, has been exemplary in the articulation of diverse ontological languages and philosophical forms. But it has been deficient in the articulation of the possibility of common discourse between these diverse languages. Clearly it has *assumed* that rational discourse between ontological languages is possible, yet characteristically it has been negligent in exploring the logic of discourse between language forms. By being typically preoccupied with the excavation and articulation of particular ontological languages it has tended to overlook the form of rational consciousness which comes to the fore when attention is focused on a universe of diverse actual worlds.[1]

The recognition of a plurality of *actual* worlds seems to strain our ordinary rational sense. The rational heritage which emerged since ancient Greek thought has generally given the benefit of the doubt to the hermeneutic of duality—to the mentality of the *contemplative* attitude—which assumes a differentiation between consciousness and its object, as well as an irreducible differentiation between determinate objects. This hermeneutic of either/or requires the thinker to maintain that there can be only one true actual world, all other purported possible worlds being hypothetical or fictional. Thus, either the Cartesian world is correct and actual or else the Humean world is real, but not both. Either the Christian world is true or the Hindu world, both cannot be equally acceptable and actualized on rational grounds. In this hermeneutical mentality there can be one and only one true world, one reality, and all else is at best merely possible and at worst impossible. For this reason the *either/or* hermeneutic of the contemplative mind is not suitable for the rationality of WP.

On the other hand, the classical Indian tradition has tended to stress the *meditative* hermeneutical attitude, an attitude which insists that there can be no duality between consciousness and its object. The meditative mentality characteristically takes the duality of contemplative reason to be the essence of attachment, ignorance, bondage and suffering, and strives to overcome this in a transformation of consciousness which liberates reason and

1. In the context of Comparative Ontology a possible world is a coherent and intelligible world system and language form, and if a world is possible then it is actual. If, for example, we speak of the Hindu or Christian worlds as possible then this is the same as saying that they are actual, for to be intelligible is to be actual. And it is not here assumed that there can be only one intelligible or actual world.

enlightens understanding in the wisdom of detachment and non-duality. This hermeneutic is quite vocal in its celebration of silence, a silence which is the highest achievement of rational consciousness which emerges only when particularity in all of its forms is finally defeated.

The meditative transformation of rational consciousness beyond the bondage of particularity seems at first to offer an intriguing alternative for the hermeneutic of WP. The wisdom of non-dual consciousness appears to readily accommodate a plurality of actual worlds in the unity of one cosmic consciousness. The meditative posture takes reason to its highest regions where it witnesses the particularity of differentiated forms in "silence". But if meditative reason supports one primitive intuition of WP—that there is one world, one reality, one consciousness—it seems to do so at the expense of eclipsing the other primitive intuition of our dialectic. For the typical challenge for the "silence" of non-dual discourse is precisely the recognition of the irreducibility of differentiation and the particularization of forms. Meditative reason celebrates unity by reducing diversity to some form of appearance. The particularity of a given world is a function of ignorance, and alternative actual worlds simply compound and multiply the intrinsic illusion of dualized reason. If the meditative hermeneutic reveals one world, one reality, it is some transcendent non-worldly world which escapes the particularity of determinate names and forms. If meditative reason achieves a "universal" unified consciousness it is a peculiar form of cosmic universality beyond a plurality of determinate worlds. For this reason the "neither/nor" hermeneutic of the non-dual meditative mentality is not suitable for the rationality of WP.

It appears that both the contemplative hermeneutic *and* the meditative hermeneutic are necessary ingredients in the hermeneutic of WP. For we have seen that WP requires both voices in the antinomy of Comparative Ontology. Contemplative reason is essentially dualized and stresses diversity and differentiation while meditative reason is non-dual and accentuates *radical* unity and non-differentiation. The challenge for the hermeneutic of WP is to find a way to keep both voices alive, to negotiate dual and non-dual reason. The future evolution of WP essentially depends upon the success in mediating these two forms of reason.

Needless to say, various attempts to uncover a universal hermeneutic for WP have been made in the past. But any successful attempt must find a way to honour the *particularity* and uniqueness of a given world, and at the same time to celebrate the *universality* of cosmic unified consciousness or being. The depth of this challenge should now be clear—it is nothing less than negotiating the infinite ontological space between *finite* dualized reality and *infinite* non-dual being. How is it possible to acknowledge *both* at once?

We now begin to discern a pattern—on one side we find particularity, differentiation, duality and finite; and on the other we find universality, non-differentiation, non-duality and infinitude. But in the context of WP it is clear that the polarity of particular/universal (finite/infinite) must not be confused with the distinction as it is typically drawn within the hermeneutic of dual reason. For example, in the context of a particular ontological language or world the polarity of particular/universal remains *relative* to the particularity of that world. Thus, if with respect to a particular categorial world (and all worlds are categorial) the referent of "I" is some particular entity, then the universal relative to that particular is "personhood" or "humanity" or some such universal. A *categorial universal*[1] is, therefore, always relative and determinate in content (i.e. differentiated and dualized). Such a universal is relative to the meaning system of a particular world. For instance, the general term "person" would have one sense in a given world and a different sense in another. By contrast, universality in the context of WP must be absolute and valid for *all* possible/actual worlds—a transworld or *transcategorial universal*. Such a universal is non-dual and transparent or indeterminate in form—the form of all possible forms. So the polarity of particular/universal in the hermeneutic of WP is the radical one between *categorial particular* and *transcategorial universal*; a successful hermeneutic must hold both together in a healthy dialectic.

Let us pause for a moment to glance briefly at some previous attempts to negotiate this infinite space. In the "Western"

1. From a logical point of view any general term—"justice", "piety", "triangularity" etc. specify categorial universals. A categorial universal has determinate content and specifies a class of possible instances.

tradition we readily see several diverse approximations to the hermeneutic of WP. Heraclitus opened the way by seriously challenging the logical form of dual reason by questioning the fixity of essentialism and the rigidity of the principle of identity. Plato stretched contemplative reason beyond its bounds to the fulfilment of reason in the (transcategorial) "form" of absolute Goodness. This universal form or all possible forms, this transparent light of Reason, was clearly seen to be beyond the duality of Being and Non-Being. Here we find an exemplary transformation of consciousness to the "silence" of non-dual Universal Logos. In another context Nietzsche developed a radical critique of dualized rationality in his poetic and aphoristic injunctions beyond the polarity of "good and evil". Again, Kant pressed pure (contemplative) reason to its formal limits in the excavation of the intrinsic antinomies of worldly thought. He opened the way to (transcategorial) rational faith and reduced particularity to the realm of phenomena. In still another way, Hegel, in a brilliant stroke, lured reason into a dynamic essentialism which he took to be the cure for the antithetical fixity of ossified either/or reason. He attempted to save essentialism while questioning the logical form of dualized reason. In the dialectical self-transformation of *Geist* we find another approximation to a transcategorial universal. More recently, we find encounters with the hermeneutic of WP in such diverse writers as Heidegger, Whitehead and Wittgenstein. Heidegger traced the limits of dualized rationality in the phenomenology of Dasein; in his later writings he groped for an alternative hermeneutic which was closely akin to metaphysical poetry. Whitehead strove to go beyond the naïve hermeneutic of inorganic either/or logos in his ontology of organism; he sought an organic hermeneutic which was bi-polar, and in which an actual entity was at once fully determinate and particular and at the same time ontologically universal. And Wittgenstein, in two brilliant attempts, opened the way to the hermeneutic of WP. In the *Tractatus* he explored the limits of propositional logic and moved to the horizon of "silence". But in the *Investigations* he challenged the bondage of essentialism and absolutism and vindicated natural language as he attempted to liberate natural reason from its obsessive fixity. He showed that reason can have a plurality of forms, each involving a legitimate and unique form of life. In this way he moved closer to the kind of hermeneutic required for WP.

These are a few hints of transformations to transcategorial reason. Many other examples from the "Western" tradition may be given. The point to be stressed here is that the above attempts *begin* with the logos of dualized contemplative reason and move to its limits through an internal critique. These attempts *end* at the frontier of WP; for the hermeneutic of WP *begins* with the recognition of the limitation of dualized reason. The challenge for WP, we have seen, is to find our way "back into the cave" while remaining in Universal Light. Plato, for example, with his disdain for particularity and obsession with universality, traced the journey of reason to its transcategorial universal, but the way forward and onward into the "cave" remains cloudy and eclipsed. For the cave becomes profoundly transformed when exposed to Universal Light. It is no longer satisfactory to take the world of particulars to be the world of mere appearance. And Wittgenstein leaves us with a fragmentary array of diverse language forms with no hope of disclosing the logos which makes discourse between them possible.

Before turning to similar encounters in the Indian tradition it is timely to touch on one striking omission in the "Western" tradition. In the above inventory I did not mention the obvious attempt to negotiate the space between the finite and the Infinite in the being of Jesus the Christ. Christ-being, if approached in the dualized hermeneutic of categorial reason takes one form, but if approached in the hermeneutic of transcategorial reason emerges in a universal form. The Christ, viewed ontologically, is an exemplar of a being which is at once fully finite and particular *and* fully infinite and ontologically universal. Categorial reason is unable to cope with such a being; it requires that such a being be ontologically composite, i.e. two natures entails two distinct entities. On the other hand, transcategorial reason *requires* that such a being be a radical unity in the duality—Christ-being is a perfect example of transcategorial being : it finds the Divine crossing between the categorial particular and the transcategorial universal. It makes a world of difference whether we take the Christ to be a categorial universal for a particular Christian ontology, or a transcategorial universal for all possible/

actual worlds.[1] It is the hermeneutic of WP which alone acknowledges the transworld universality of the Christ. What must be a "mystery" for categorial reason is literal truth for transcategorial understanding. Thus, it makes all the difference whether one is a categorial Christian or a transcategorial Christian : the former requires that one affirms the categorial particularity of the Christian world and denies the validity of other worlds, but the latter discovers the way to celebrate the universal significance of the Christ (the Infinite Living Word) without denying the particularity of the "Christian" or any other world.

As we turn in this preliminary sketch to the Indian tradition, we find a characteristic orientation to the meditative hermeneutic. Of course, the Indian Tradition (IT) encompasses a vast array of ontological languages and language forms, and I do not wish to distort or naïvely oversimplify. For the purposes of this study, however, and at the risk of appearing arbitrary, I shall focus attention on what I take to be the most significant contribution of the IT to the evolution of WP. In this regard I find the preoccupation with the *meditative* transformation of consciousness to be typical and characteristic. More specifically, I find the teachings of the great Buddhist dialectician, Nāgārjuna, as well as the teachings of the great Hindu seer, Śaṁkara, to be the high-points of the evolution to WP.

While the contemplative tradition begins with duality and journeys through contemplative reason in the ascent to transcategorial Universal Reason, the meditative tradition typically *begins* with transcategorial Cosmic Consciousness and strives to instruct the categorial mind and make room for legitimate particularity. A measure of success for the hermeneutic of WP is the extent to which it can honour particularity in Universal Light. And it fails to the extent that it demotes or deprecates differentiated being.

1. Naturally, the universalization of the Christ within the Christian ontology (categorial universal) is taken by believing Christians to be absolutely universal for all reality. But Comparative Ontology reveals that any world inherently universalizes itself in this way and takes itself to be absolute. In the context of a plurality of actual worlds, however, it becomes clear that a categorial universal can be absolute only if other worlds are *reduced* to the terms of reference (meaning system) of the ontology in question.

It is precisely this challenge that we find in the classical Hindu teachings. In the *Bhagavad Gītā*, for example, Lord Krishna's instructions to Arjuna reveal that true action arises in yogic detachment. The yogi is the one who, through proper meditation, "enters" into Krishna consciousness which is beyond the duality of *saṁsāric* differentiated existence, and performs actions in ontological detachment. Krishna consciousness is, of course, the cosmic transcategorial awareness and being we have already spoken of. What baffles Arjuna, and in fact baffles us all, is the requirement that the yogi live and act "in the world". Lord Krishna insists that detachment in yoga does not mean inaction, and certainly does not entail the abandonment of one's *dharma*. In fact the highest state of the realized one is to live and act in the world. The challenge for this instruction is precisely the challenge for the hermeneutic of WP which we have discussed: how is it possible to be in (true, absolute) cosmic consciousness and at the same time live in the "cave" and respect the "particularity" of *saṁsāric* existence ?

One obvious response is to show that the mundane world, when seen in Universal Light, emerges in Divine particularity;[1] the "cave" no longer remains the realm of illusion, ignorance and appearance, but is revealed as sacred ground in transcategorial or Universal reason. The warrior on the battlefield in yogic awareness is the cosmic warrior, the sweeper in the street becomes the cosmic sweeper, the ferryman who crosses the river makes his cosmic journey, etc.

This has been the classical response, but from the point of view of WP it only multiplies hermeneutical problems. If cosmie or Krishna consciousness is non-dual and non-differentiated then why should there be any particularity at all for the yogi ? And why should there be a determinate world with any duties and injunctions for proper action ? If the yogi speaks, what is the nature of his non-dual speech ? If particularity and individuation is bound in ignorance how can the yogi have any identity whatsoever ? And so on. These are legitimate concerns, all of which cry out for some explication of the nature of non-dual discourse, transcategorial reason and yogic life in the world. It is in

1. It is desirable in this context to distinguish between the particularity of categorial thought and particularity or differentiated existence (the created world) as it is revealed in Universal Light.

this area that the meditative tradition has been deficient and needs further development and articulation.

Again, in the *Māṇḍūkya Upaniṣad* we find a brilliant example of meditative reason which begins with the Infinite transcategorial word : "All this is AUM." It is revealed that AUM is the non-dual Absolute "Word" or sacred symbol (name of all names, formless form of all forms) which at the same time is *everything* in the finite determinate world and *nothing*. This work teaches that in the order of meditative reason dream consciousness is of a higher nature—while in the order of contemplative reason it is lower. It presents a model of all possible states of consciousness (all of which are just AUM) and reveals that true meditative consciousness is beyond the three levels of dual awareness. The fourth (non-state) is AUM, which may be appropriately interpreted as transcategorial Universal Logos. And the three states are at the same time nothing but AUM (particularized, differentiated and spoken AUM). So here again, we find the dialectic (the antinomy) of WP; and the same sort of questions naturally arise : how can AUM be non-dual (i.e. non-differentiated, Absolute, non-cognitive, silent, beyond articulation and cognition, etc.) and at the same time constitutive of all differentiated existence, i.e. all possible states of consciousness and all possible existent differentiated beings ? How can AUM be both transcategorial *and* categorial at the same "time?" How can AUM be transcategorially infinite and finite at the same "time" ?

These and similar questions are addressed by Śaṁkara in his great *Brahma-Sūtra Commentary*. Here we find a major breakthrough to the hermeneutic of transcategorial reason. For Śaṁkara repeatedly struggles to explain how the Infinite Universal AUM can at the same time be manifested in the determinate existential form of the *saṁsāric* world. In his systematic articulation of Advaita Vedānta he introduces powerful hermeneutical devices to meet the dialectical challenge. For example, he begins his commentary with the device of *adhyāsa* (superimposition) to explain how all dualized categorial reason arises from an original "eclipse" of the Absolute transparent Infinite Word. Furthermore, he introduces a distinction between *nirguṇa* and *saguṇa* Brahman and uses this distinction together with the creative power of *Māyā* to "explain" how the Infinite transcategoric

AUM can at the "same time" be manifested in finite *saṁsāra*. And he labours to instruct the spiritual student that Self-realization (meditation on Brahman) cannot be conceived in categorial reason. But here, again, further difficulties are raised from the point of view of WP. The critical challenge becomes the articulation of the non-dual rationality of Scriptural or Divine discourse. The wonderful breakthrough offered by Śaṁkara in his *Commentary* is the instruction that Divine Logos or Scripture is non-dual discourse—that Scripture is the speaking forth of AUM. He opens the way to the articulation of transcategorial discourse. Nevertheless, we are left (as with Plato) with a realm of particularity which is a function of ignorance and delusion—for all duality and particularity arises from the eclipse or fall of Pure Consciousness.

In another way Nāgārjuna takes us *into* the unexplored territory of WP. As he demonstrates his powerful dialectic in the *Kārikās*, we discover that Absolute (transcategorial) consciousness is *non-different* from *saṁsāra* (particularized worldly existence). That is, he directly meets the challenge of the transcategorial hermeneutic by demonstrating that natural language (reason) works only in transcategorial or *śūnya* consciousness, and breaks down in incoherence in dualized categorial reason. The crucial breakthrough is the instruction that worldly discourse (*saṁsāric* existence) cannot be coherently approached in the hermeneutic of either/or rationality. But to present this radical teaching he introduces a critical ingredient in the hermeneutic of WP: he introduces the principle of dependent co-arising (*pratītya-samutpāda*) in the context of *ontological relativity*. Nāgārjuna had detected in the deep structure of reason the emergence of a formal bi-polarity. He noticed that in the development of the Indian philosophical tradition two complementary ontological languages had been articulated—one was the Hindu *Ātma* ontological language of Absolute Being (Self), the other was the Early Buddhist *Anātma* ontological language of non-Being (No-Self). The former was the language of Being, the latter was the language of non-Being. The brilliant contribution of Nāgārjuna was to have seen that these two complementary languages disclosed the bi-polar structure of rational consciousness. It is in this context that he demonstrated the "emptiness" of all possible "views" (assertions, theories, ontologies), and showed that natural reason was *already śūnya* or transcategorial. Thus, the world of particularity and duality (*saṁsāra*) becomes inherently equivocal in the context of Nāgārjuna's dialectic : it means the pre-meditative duality and ignorance of categorial thought, or it means the post-meditative transformed particularity of transcategorial hermeneutic or meditative reason. In the latter case one is moved to a deepened reverence for Divine particularity and differentiation which flows in *śūnya* consciousness.

But here again, precisely *because* Nāgārjuna succeeds in taking us into the realm of the transcategorial hermeneutic, further questions are generated for the categorial sceptic. One naturally wonders, for example, how the silent hermeneutic of meditative reason can speak forth in *saṁsāric* form; how can the transparency of *śūnya* awareness become articulated in the determinate form of natural language ? How can non-dual reason manifest itself in the determinate logos of particularity ? These sorts of questions press for the further articulation of the Divine hermeneutic of transcategorial discourse. In effect, natural reason calls out for the further development of the logos in which the transcategorial universal can be non-different from the categorial particular.

Thus, our quest for the hermeneutic of WP has taken us to the frontier of transcategorial discourse. On the one hand we find that the contemplative tradition, which takes dualized *either/or* rationality to be absolutely given ends at the horizon of the "silence" of non-dual Logos. Categorial thought achieves its limits and encounters this realm as the *mystical*. Categorial reason becomes speechless here and inevitably ends in accepting an ultimate dualism of the dual (finite) and the non-dual (infinite). On the other hand, the meditative tradition takes the transparency of non-dual reason to be the absolute given and speaks forth from this hermeneutical realm to the fallen and bounded reason of categorial understanding. It seeks to awaken this slumbering consciousness to its enlightened form and devises a therapeutic logos to challenge and transform dualized life. This form of discourse out of the realm of "silence" naturally baffles the categorial mentality. Natural reason enters a dialectic which is the meeting ground of these two forms of speech. The dialogue between dual and non-dual discourse is the philosophical journey of human reason. And, in general, when discourse (dialogue) between different worlds (ontological languages) arises, the logos of transcategorial meaning comes forth. So the concerns of the Philosophy of Worlds require the hermeneutic of WP.

It appears, then, that both the contemplative and the meditative traditions take us to the frontiers of transcategorial discourse. It is here that we locate the future explorations of philosophy. The contemplative tradition is challenged to broaden its horizons in dialogue with the non-dual rationality, and the meditative tradition is required to expand its hermeneutic in a dialectical encounter with the rationality of categorial thought. The articulation of transcategorial reason is the inevitable challenge for natural reason in its evolution to WP.

The most pressing philosophical concern of our age (or of *any* age) is the challenge of WP. It should be clear that this hermeneutical concern is precisely the question of bondage and liberation, sin and salvation, ignorance and wisdom.

II

In this part I shall attempt to sketch the outlines of the transcategorial hermeneutic of WP. This requires first the articulation of the logical form of categorial thought (contemplative reason) as well as the explication of the meditative rationality of non-dual discourse. We will then be in a better position to further develop the main theme of this study, namely, the relevance of Indian Thought to the development of WP.

The Logical Form of Categorial (Dualistic) Rationality

Categorial thought is dual and dualistic in every way. It works from oppositional principles which at once structure consciousness (thought, meaning, discourse) and being. The primary opposition or differentiation is that between thought and object of thought, between consciousness (the thinker) and the object of consciousness (what is thought). This is the formal structure of contemplative reason. But this oppositional structure is inherent in the *objects* of consciousness as well, for to *be* an object is precisely to be differentiated from other entities. Such differentiation provides at the same time internal *identity*. So to be an object is to conform to the logic of *identity and difference*. Similarly, otherness is inherent in categorial *meaning* as well, and this is revealed in the isomorphism or "mirroring" between objects of thought and objects of being : meaning (sense or reference) is a matter of semantic *representation*—a name or referring expression is other than that which is named or designated. This is representational or dual meaning.[1]

The rationality of identity and difference emerges in the form of *predication.* To be an object is to be constituted in a predicative structure : an object (of thought) is a logical subject constituted by predicates. Stated ontologically, an object is a thing which is constituted by attributes. Apart from attributes a thing can have no differentiating marks, hence can have no internal identity (essence). Thus, categorial thought manifests itself in the logical form of predication.

But predication, too, is oppositional through and through. First, the logical subject "S" is differentiated from logical predicates "P". This reveals the dual structure of predication. And the formal principle of differentiation (otherness) applies to any possible object of thought, subject or predicate. To be a unique subject is to be differentiated, and the same holds for any possible predicate. In general, then, the essence of dual reason is the formal principle of difference (or identity):

> To be *S* is to be *other than* (differentiated from) *not-S*; to be *P* is to be differentiated from *not-P*

This formal principle of dual thought has been codified in the principles of thought (and being) articulated in classical Greek (Aristotelian) logic in the form of the principle of non-contradic-

1. For a more developed and systematic discussion of these and the immediately following points concerning the two types of opposition, categories, and ontological structures see the following papers:

(a) "Formal Ontology and Movement Between Worlds" *Philosophy East and West*, Vol. 26, No. 2 (April, 1976).

(b) "Formal Ontology and the Dialectical Transformation of Consciousness" *Philosophy East and West* 29, No. 1 (January, 1979).

(c) "Nagarjuna, Aristotle and Frege on the Nature of Thought" in Nathan Katz (ed), *Buddhist and Western Philosophy* (New Delhi : Sterling Publishers, 1980).

(d) "Comparative Ontology and the Interpretation of Karma" *Indian Philosophical Quarterly*, Vol. 6, No. 2 (January, 1979).

(e) "Comparative Ontology : Relative and Absolute Truth", *Philosophy East and West* (Forthcoming).

tion, excluded-middle and identity. In more familiar form the principle of intelligible rational thought is :

A given subject *S* cannot be both P and not-P (at the same time and in the same respect)

or

A given subject *S* must be either *P* or *not-P*

Let us review how this formal principle of opposition and duality defines categorial rationality. Any given term, subject or predicate—call it "*X*"—formally stands in opposition to its logical contrary *un-X*; the meaning of *X* is a function of its opposition to *un-X*. Logical contraries, taken together, constitute the *unit of meaning*, and we indicate such a polar term in brackets—*/X/* (="X-or-un-X"). For example, in ordinary English, the term "wise" stands in opposition to its contrary "un-wise"; "coloured" stands in contrary opposition to "colourless", "married" is bound in sense to its polar opposite "un-married", and so on. A polar term is called a "category", and a category specifies some domain of the world—it exhausts some range of meaning and being. For example, while "red" is a property term, the polar or category term "/red/" (="red-or-un-red") picks out a *feature* of the world. It must be stressed that polar terms are the units of meaning—any property term takes its meaning from its polar or category term. Thus, "wise" makes no sense apart from its contrary "un-wise", so the sense of "wise" derives from the sense of "/wise/".

It is crucial to distinguish between the contrary opposition of polar terms and another form of opposition called "complements" —the complement of "wise" is "non-wise", the complement of "coloured" is "non-coloured", and so on. Contraries are *internal* opposites while complements are *external* opposites. While contraries or polar terms specify some determinate feature of the world, some specific type of thing, complements designate the universal domain. For example, the polar term "/coloured/" specifies the feature of *colour* (i.e. all things that are or could be coloured or colourless), but the complements "coloured or non-coloured" exhaust the domain of all possible things in the world.

Another way to grasp the difference between these two forms of primitive opposition is to recognize that contraries are logical *privatives*—one contrary pole is the privation of the other—for example, that which is wise fails to be unwise, hence is potentially unwise (for *lacking* something presupposes that it could be acquired); again, that which is unwise lacks wisdom, hence is potentially wise. Privation and potentiality mutually entail each other, and this is the key to the definition of a category : only the things which are *potentially* wise can *become* wise, only the sort of thing that is potentially married can become married. This means that not all things are /wise/; for example, stones are neither wise nor unwise, for they are not of the appropriate category, nevertheless, they are either wise or non-wise : again, numbers are neither married nor un-married, though they are either married or non-married. So complementary opposites apply to any and all things regardless of its type or category, while polar contrary opposites apply only to the sort of type of thing which is of the appropriate category.

This logical feature of polar terms is the key to the formation of categorial meaning, for only terms of the appropriate categories may be meaningfully joined in predication. If inappropriate terms in a given language are joined then non-sense (category mistakes) result : for example, to say that "stones are wise" or "stones are un-wise" is nonsense, or to say that "numbers are married" or "numbers are un-married" is unintelligible. This is another way of making the point that the unit of meaning is the category-term, hence *categorial thought*.

Remembering that the logical features of categorial thought have their ontological analogues, it is timely to notice that the category constraints on the formation of meaning at the same time sets the bounds of rational understanding; we can understand only what is category-correct. This is why a particular category structure determines a system of meaning and thereby sets the bounds of human understanding for the ontology which it constitutes. Similarly, the intelligibility of process, change, becoming etc., is also determined by the structure of polar terms : since polar terms define potentiality, it follows that all intelligible processes must unfold between the poles of contraries. We cannot in categorial thought understand an alleged process which unfolds between distinct and unrelated categories—numbers can never become coloured, stones can never become married, etc. So reality itself, and all of its intelligible possibilities of transformation, is determined by category relations.

The appropriateness of terms for category-correct or meaningful predication is determined by the categorial structure of the terms which make up any language system. The categorial structure which constitutes a particular language is discerned when all of polar terms of the language are taken together in their predicative possibilities. That is, if we take all of the possible predicable terms of a language simultaneously and "mapped" their predicative possibilities we shall find that the categories of the language conform to a "pyramid" model, and those terms which form a continuous line may be significantly joined, while those which do not would form a category-mistake, if co-predicated. When the categorial structure of a language is discerned we have a conceptual map of its meaning possibilities as well as of its possible facts. Meaning in a predicative language, therefore, is governed by its particular categorial structure. The categorial structure of the Christian world would be different from the categorial configuration of the Buddhist world, etc.[1]

The above procedure explains how the formation of meaning of a given language *as a whole* is determined by taking the totality of the polar terms together in their mutual configurability. The meaning of a term is defined by its "location" on the pyramid structure, and one sense (univocity) means one location. This formal requirement of univocity is an important characteristic of categorial meaning—a given term has a principle of identity which defines its unique meaning in the language. If a term of the language is ambiguous or equivocal then it will have more than one location on the categorial map (and this means that they are really distinct terms). This logical feature of univocity is another form of the principle of identity and opposition which governs categorial thought.

The point to be stressed here is that what makes sense in one meaning system or categorial structure does not make sense in another. So, again, at the level of possible languages (taken as systematic wholes) we find the principle of identity and difference at work. Language systems are different categorial structures, different predicative possibilities, and since the meaning of any given term is a function of the meaning system as a whole, there can be no shared univocal terms between different

1. For a more detailed development of these points see "Formal Ontology and Movement Between Worlds", op. cit.

languages. This logical feature of categorial reason is reflected in the principle of *systematic ambiguity* of terms of different languages. Thus, for example, if a given term appears in two different categorial systems the principle requires that the term be judged systematically ambiguous, that is, it is not one term but two radically distinct and independent terms.[1]

These points may emerge with more clarity when we shift from the logical (meaning) import, for the categorial structure which defines a meaning-system thereby determines a world-system or ontology, as has been indicated earlier. Particular worlds are disclosed in determinate categorial configurations. Perhaps some further illustrations would be helpful. One world structure—the world of Cartesian dualism—holds that the two primary categories of being /thought/ and /extension/ are mutually exclusive and have no common terms. In the language system which displays this ontology we find that the sort of thing which /thinks/ is of a radically different nature or type from the kind of thing which is /extended/ (locatable in space). In this ontological language stones are /extended/ but non-thinking, while the ego or soul is /thinking/ but non-extended. It would be a category-mistake to say "the stone thinks" or to say "the soul is locatable". This ontology requires that the referent of the term "I" (the self or person) be a composite (dual) entity, for otherwise incoherence of meaning would result. This means that "I" is *equivocal* in reference—it refers either to the ego (a thinking thing which is non-extended) or to the body (a physical thing which is non-thinking); it cannot, without violating the sense structure of the language, refer to one unified thing which both /thinks/ *and* is /extended/. Strictly speaking, it is a category mistake to say in one utterance : "I am sitting in the chair and thinking about the future". For the term "I" here makes an equivocal reference. This shows that the meaning of the term "I" is governed by the categorial configuration of the language as a whole.

By contrast, if we work with another possible ontological language, one in which the categories of /thought/ and /extension/

1. Of course the opposition between distinct language systems or ontologies is not the same as contrary of polar opposition. Contrary opposition is intra-categorial only; polar terms (categories) are never opposed in contrary opposition, only in complementary (external) negation. Similarly, different worlds or language systems are not opposed as logical contraries.

are mutually configurable (co-predicable), we enter a different world in which the meaning possibilities (and factual possibilities) are altered. For example, one configuration is the language of *idealism* (Leibniz or Berkeley) in which the primary unifying category is /thought/ and the category of matter or /extension/ falls within or under it. In this language, the meaning of the categories themselves are radically revised from the Cartesian terms. In the idealist language anything which is /extended/ would also be /thinking/, since the former category is included within the latter. In fact, all things are potentially /thinking/ in the world of the idealist. In this categorial configuration it is possible for the term "I" to pick out one primitive individual entity which is both physical and conscious. In this language, then, the meaning of the term "I" is systematically different in sense from the term as used in the Cartesian language; and, in general, what makes sense in the idealist world does not make sense in the world of Cartesian dualism. And so on.

These are just brief glimpses of how categorial rationality in its oppositional dual structure leads to the formation of different worlds or systems of meaning and experience. For our present purposes it needs to be stressed that this rational mentality, and the formal predicative principles which govern it, are constituted in duality, determinacy, particularity and essential identity. Any given term or object in this hermeneutic of duality and opposition has inner identity and fixity or univocity of meaning. The identity of an object, the self, for example, reveals its essence, which defines its nature and form. To be is to have determinate essence, to have identity, to be an individuated discriminated object. In general, the essence of a particularized entity, for any possible world, is revealed in its unique ontological feature or category. Thus, it is important to see the necessary connection between being a determinate individual entity and the dual structure of categorial reason. In this respect categorial logic is the logos of essence and particularity. This point is, of course, recognized by "existentialists" who insist that an entity (the self) may exist prior to having determinate essence. For without determinate essence such an entity must be *nothing*; but this acknowledges its potentiality to become something—such a "nothing" still has /essence/. And this clearly acknowledges the principle that to be is to be /something/.

This point is crucial for us here for it is precisely this formal feature of categorial reason which is the focal point of the critique of meditative reason. In general, categorial life is a life of individuated identity, a life of radical finitude, potentiality, becoming (existence in categorial time). By its very nature, ego-centred life is life of ontological /sin/ (i.e. alienation from Infinite Being), /suffering/ and /mortality/. The Hindus call this form of existence "*saṃsāra*"—the dualized life of particularity which is caught between the oppositional poles of contrariety and alienated from the Infinite Being of the universal *Ātman*. Categorial existence is the life of bondage, fixity and determinacy from which the life of meditation brings ontological liberation.

Finally, it should be mentioned that the categorial hermeneutic provides one model of rationality—the logic of determinate pre-meditative understanding. This logic typically takes the form of a propositional (predicative) form of discourse which is concerned with facts and assertions which are true or false. This form of human understanding reaches its limits in *literal* discourse. Phenomena which are not factual in nature cannot be thought of or spoken of in this hermeneutic. This mentality, which is governed by the either/or principle, necessitates a choice one way or the other. This is so with particular (atomic) predications as well as with particular worlds. It requires that one world be true and the others false. In all of its forms it must conform to the principle of bivalence (true or false). It was this commitment of categorial rationality which disqualified it as an appropriate hermeneutic for WP.

Transcategorial (non-dual) Rationality : The Logic of Meditation

Having briefly outlined the logical form of pre-meditative or contemplative rationality we have taken the first step towards the sketch of the logic of meditation and non-dual meaning. For, as we have seen, the form of categorial (dual) reason is one of opposition, polarity, differentiation, univocity, and governed by the laws of identity and difference. In striking contrast to this, non-dual logos predictably flows in non-identity, non-difference, bi-polarity, relativicity, non-fixity and multivocity (metaphor).

To appreciate this it would be helpful to characterize some features of meditative reason. First of all, meditation is a *dynamic* self-transformation of reason. This dynamic power expands the understanding beyond any form of fixity and any fixity of form. And a key to entering this dynamic and organic reason is the expansion of *time* consciousness. It is not possible to approach the logos of meditation from the fixity of categorial time. If we begin with categorial time, the either/or logic of differentiation naturally follows. For within categorial time consciousness non-dual logos appears to be mere contradiction. There is a time element built into the formal principles of dual reason: "A given subject *S* cannot be both *P* and *not-P at the same time.*" But what appears to be a contradiction to categorial time is revealed to be the literal truth in meditative time. With this in mind let us examine the "form" of non-dual logos.

In meditative reason there is no differentiation (no logical space) between consciousness and object, no separation between sense and reference, no representative meaning, no differentiation between consciousness, word, idea, thought, name, object, meaning. Meaning is neither intensional nor extensional, and consciousness is not intentional. In meditative discourse there is only "self-reference" and predication is non-dual, that is, there is non-difference between subject and predicate, and predication is non-representational or non-descriptive—it does not picture facts or anything else. The logical atomism of meaning which structures categorial thought in terms of fixed essence and identity as well as rigid designation melts in the light of fluid organic reason. The meaning of any term grows out of the meaning of every term; the identity of any entity reflects the identity of every other object; the significance of any predication recursively projects, reiterates and echoes the significance of any other possible utterance. In the logical space of meditative reason polar opposition and differentiation evaporates into a bi-polarity (di-unity), and the fixity of essentialistic univocal meaning flows into multivocal unity of metaphor. This logical space turns upon itself in a virtuous circle in which the infinite distance in the point at which one begins : "here" is "everywhere," "now" is "everywhen" and "I" specifies everything and nothing. Process and development (becoming) moves in the stillness of non-dual "becoming". In short, the categorial particular shines forth with cosmic significance of the transcategorial universal. The space between the categorial finite and the transcategorial infinite is "closed" as one flows into the other.[1]

But let us slow down this high energy logos and trace in slow motion the infinite expansion of logical time and space, meaning and existence. For the categorial mind is naturally sceptical and legitimately asks how it can be possible to question the principle of identity and difference, and how it can be intelligible to question univocal, essential meaning and being. Of course, we are faced with a paradox of reason here. For what is coherent for categorial thought is incoherent for meditative logos, and *vice versa*. We must find a way for meditative reason to make itself intelligible to the categorial mentality.

A good device to show how rigid essentialistic meaning can begin to become fluid is *metaphor* : what appears metaphoric to categorial thought is literal in meditative awareness, a category-mistake for categorial thought is very likely to find a creative use in the poetry of meditative speech. The logical form of metaphor is *bi-polar* : in general, a metaphor is a symbol (non-dual) which unites opposites in a primitive unity, a special sort of unity which is foreign to the categorial mind.[2] For example, where categorial reason finds an irreconcilable opposition between polar terms (contraries), a metaphoric term reveals a *di-unity*; this is *not* an *identification* of opposites, but rather a preservation of the difference in a primitive unity. In the logos of meditation the categorial polar term " '*P*' " takes on transcategorial signification. And the principle of di-unity recurs on *all* levels for *all* dual distinctions. One striking example of di-unity is the Christ-being : the Christ is that primitive "unity" which is at once infinite *and* finite; /He/ negotiates the ultimate duality. From the point of view of the categorial hermeneutic we may say that the Christ is the paradigm metaphor. The Christ is a paradox for categorial understanding, and a paradigm for meditative

1. In this play on the spacial metaphor (logical space) it would be helpful to think of Einsteinian relativistic space. For a discussion of this see "Ontological Relativity : A Metaphysical Critique of Einstein's Thought", (forthcoming, Hofstra University Press, as part of an anthology celebrating Einstein's 100th Anniversary).

2. Metaphors appear to be like creative "category-mistakes" to categorial thought. It may be permitted in poetic discourse, (e.g. "Love is blue"), but not in propositional discourse.

meaning. It is the bi-polar principle of di-unity which heals the splits and suffering of categorial life.

Another meditative device which spans apparently unbridgeable dualities and distinctions of categorial thought is *analogy*. What appears to be a vague resemblance or similarity to dualized thought manifests itself as a unity and identity in meditation : analogy is the wings of meaning. It helps to disclose the ultimate synonymy of all names.

Perhaps, the most powerful instrument to aid categorial understanding in approaching the recursive fluidity of meaning is the principle of logical and ontological *relativity*. It is the easiest to appreciate the power of this principle in the context of the Philosophy of Worlds or Comparative Ontology. We saw earlier that the sense of a term (in categorial reason) is relative to the categorial language or ontology which is its original context. And the consequence of this is that any given term which occurs in different ontologies must be equivocal in meaning. For example, the term "I" as used in different world contexts is systematically ambiguous. Categorial thought is required by its either/or logical form to make bivalent judgments as to the "true" meaning of such a term, as well as the true or best categorial language. But if it can suspend judgment for a moment and work with the assumption that there is a plurality of possible and actual worlds, and if it is capable of recognizing that natural reason is *already* capable of inhabiting a multiplicity of worlds (in its expanded meditative form) then the way is open to ontological relativity. For in the meditative attitude it becomes possible to expand the horizon of meaning of a term across possible/actual worlds. Expanded understanding is not required to fix itself in one ontological language at a (categorial) time. In meditative time and space the plurality of distinct senses of a given term across worlds (its trans-world significance) becomes manifest in some kind of "unity." For example, the *meditative* meaning of the term "I" is precisely its relativistic multi-vocal sense for all possible world; the sense of this term in the Cartesian world, in Hume's world, in the world of Spinoza, in the language of Leibniz, in the Christian world, in the Buddhist world, in the Hindu world, etc., taken simultaneously (meditative time) constitutes its "true" meaning. Only when the fixity of essentialism, categorial identity and univocity is questioned, the way is open for the relativicity and multivocity) of meaning. The relativity of meaning (sense and reference) *and* identity (essence, name and form) opens the way to transcategorial significance.

We have been seeking ways to make meditative logos accessible to the sceptical categorial mind. The general challenge in each case is the same: wherever the categorial semantic assumes or affirms any sort of ultimate or primitive distinction or duality it must be shown how meditative meaning melts the opposition in bi-polar unity. Let us review some of these primitive oppositions : the distinction between thought and object, the distinction between a sign and its meaning, the distinction between name and object, the distinction between sense and reference, essence and existence, the distinction between subject and predicate, and so on. It is timely to illustrate how meditative discourse copes with these dualities.

A rich and familiar context for some relevant illustrations is found in Descartes' *Meditations*. Usually Descartes is interpreted in a categorial hermeneutic. I wish to suggest that the true significance and power of his discoveries and meditative experiments are missed in such a reading. Instead, I propose a *meditative* interpretation of his *Meditations*.

For example, if his utterance "I am, I exist" is taken in a meditative context, it truly defeats the evil demon and does silence the sceptical doubts. It does so because when he makes the utterance he has pressed categorial discourse to its limits where the logical space between sense and reference, saying and meaning, word and object, essence and existence, consciousness and object, subject and predicate, etc., have collapsed to one point. The utterance "I" is a self-referential meditative performance which does not make a categorial reference beyond itself. It is not a logical subject of categorial (dual) predication which can take differentiated, independent predicates, such as the "predicate": "exist". The meditative utterance "I" does not make reference to any sort of individuated or discriminated object; rather, it opens the horizon of the "transcendental" self. The term "I" is here a non-referential pronoun. There is no distinction possible in the utterance "I am" between affirmation (judgment) and the content of what is judged. For this reason there is no possibility of error and no room for deceit. The utterance cannot possibly be mistaken (is non-corrigible) because it is not the sort of thing that is either true or false : it is not a proposition or predication. If there is a "reference" in the utterance it is not a categorial reference but a special sort of "self-reference" to the performative utterance itself; the utterance is not a conclusion to a categorial argument, but a meditative performance which is self-validating, it is beyond the possibility of any supporting evidence. Furthermore, since the utterance *is* the object itself, there being no distinction between utterance and existence, the predicate in the utterance is non-different from the "subject", so existence (transcategorial) is immediately revealed in the meditative utterance. Again, there is no room for error or falsity, nor is there room for correctness or truth (categorial). Thus, if the utterance "I am" is taken as a propositional assertion, the demonstration is not successful; but if it is taken as a meditative utterance it is a powerful "ontological" disclosure.

This meditative reading takes on even greater force in interpreting the utterance "God exists". Here Descartes realizes that Divine nature is formally different from any finite creature. The perfection of Being (Infinite Being) is revealed only in the meditative context : It suffers no privation, so its attributes are all essences, beyond potentiality and accidents; it has no structure, so all of its attributes are synonymous (mutually entail each other); in its ontological perfection there can be no distinction between Divine "subject" and its "attributes"—the Divine Being is identical with any (essential) "attribute"; etc. Having meditated upon the meaning of Divine Perfection Descartes sees that necessarily *God exists*. Again, this is not a proposition that is being asserted in a modal context, but another meditative utterance, a pronouncement, a ritual performance, a declaration, a revelation. This "declaration" turns on the realization that there can be no distinction in Infinite Being between essence and existence, between name and object, between idea and thing. His demonstration of God's existence is not a propositional proof but a meditative transformation to the limits of categorial consciousness. In the meditative utterance, "God exists", there can be no distinction between Divine subject and Divine predicate; here "exist" is not a distinguishable predicate that is being affirmed of (attached to) the Divine Subject. Thus, again, if this utterance is taken as a propositional assertion the demonstration is faulty to say the least, but if taken as a meditative pronouncement it is a powerful "ontological" disclosure.

Finally, the dualism of mind and body which Descartes encounters in the Sixth Meditation is the inevitable conclusion for categorial thought, as was demonstrated earlier. If the categories of /thought/ and /extension/ and of /mind/ and /body/ are mutually exclusive, as he maintains, then there can be no categorial unity of the person (self, "I") which is at once both /thinking/ and /extended/. From the categorical point of view the term "I" is systematically ambiguous and the person is a composite (dual) entity. The resolution of the mind/body problem (the problem of rationally accounting for the primitive unity of the self with two radically distinct natures) presses categorial understanding to its limits. This problem requires a transcategorial resolution : in meditative discourse we have seen that two distinct natures may be primitively united in a bi-polar unity, as in Christ-being. In this respect Christ-being provides the paradigm for the existence and unity of the self. This transcategorial resolution provides a formula for understanding transformations between discrete categories, in this case the transformation (interaction, etc.) of mind into matter and *vice versa*, which is utterly inaccessible to categorial thought. Indeed, all transcategorial transformations (processes, etc.) become intelligible in the meditative hermeneutic.

These illustrations of meditative discourse should help us to see that meditative utterances are not propositional assertions. Rather, they are *ritual* performances which function solely to transform rational understanding beyond the bounds of categorial sense. This is why the Indian yogic tradition, for example, stresses the use of *mantras* and the concentration of sacred sounds in meditation.

Also, these illustrations should help us to understand the Scriptural remark that in the beginning was the Infinite Word. For the Infinite Word (Logos) is non-different from Infinite Being itself. And it may become more transparent that this Word may be incarnated in a (transcategorial) living form.

In concluding this brief sketch of meditative discourse, it is timely to return to the main theme of the hermeneutic of WP. It was indicated in Part I that the suitable hermeneutic of WP must be capable of negotiating the logical space between finite (dualistic) discourse and Infinite Logos (non-dual : it should be powerful enough to mediate dialectically between the categorial particular and the transcategorial universal; and it should be capable of acknowledging at once a plurality of actual worlds *and* that there is one and only one World. I wish to suggest that the rationality of meditative discourse meets this challenge. For the transcategorial discourse of meditative reason explodes the myth of essentialism (absolutism) and liberates the categorial mind from the bondage of rigid designation. It rescues consciousness from the fixity of finite particularly and reveals determinacy and individuation in its transfinite form. The particularity that is shown in meditative discourse overcomes the alienation of categorial finitude and flows in the transparent presence of the Infinite Word. Transcategorial particularity is worthy of honour, and *is* honoured in meditative discourse. The distinctions and determinations of dual thought are transformed and celebrated in transcategorial light. In the meditative logical space the differentiations of diverse worlds are recognized, but now in a context of transcategorial unity : there is, indeed, One World. But this unity is of a different nature from categorial unity : it is a unity beyond the category of quantity and number.

In this context, we begin to see the power of the ancient ideal of the Universal Logos; it is a trans-world (transcategorial) universality. Meditative reason recognizes that natural consciousness (natural reason, natural language) is *already* transcategorial; it remains perpetually ready for radical self-transformation.

It becomes clear that the categorial mind is neither hermetically sealed nor hermeneutically bound. The self-transformation power of meditative discourse is designed to liberate reason from categorial bondage. Indeed, liberation, salvation, is essentially a hermeneutical concern.

NOTES ON CONTRIBUTORS

PRATIMA BOWES is Reader in Religious Studies, University of Sussex, England. She is the author of several books including *The Concept of Morality*; *Is Metaphysics Possible?* *Consciousness and Freedom*; *The Hindu Religious Tradition*; *The Hindu Intellectual Tradition*.

SARASVATI CHENNAKESAVAN is (Retired) Professor of Philosophy, Sri Venkateswara University, Tirupati, India. She is a Fellow of the Royal Asiatic Society and is the author of *The Concept of Mind in Indian Philosophy*; *Perception*; *A Critical Study of Hinduism*; *Concepts of Indian Philosophy*.

P. T. RAJU is Professor Emeritus, College of Wooster, Wooster, Ohio, U. S. A. He has published over one hundred research papers and several books. His main books include: *Thought and Reality*; *The Idealistic Thought of India*; *The Concept of Man*; *The Philosophical Traditions of India*; *Introduction to Comparative Philosophy*.

K. B. RAMAKRISHNA RAO is Professor of Indian Philosophy and Head of the Department of Philosophy, University of Mysore, Mysore, India. He is the author of *Ontology of Advaita with Special Reference to Māyā*; *Theism of Pre-Classical Sāṅkhya*; *Advaita as Philosophy and Religion*; *Problems and Perspectives of Advaita*.

RAMAKANT SINARI is Professor of Philosophy and Head of the Department of Humanities and Social Sciences, Indian Institute of Technology, Bombay, India. As a Fulbright scholar, he did research at the University of Pennsylvania and studied in the State University of New York, Buffalo. His major publications include two books: *Reason in Existentialism* and *The Structure of Indian Thought*.

K. N. UPADHYAYA is Professor and Chairman of the Department of Philosophy, University of Hawaii, U. S. A. He has published several scholarly articles and is the author of *Early Buddhism and the Bhagavad gītā*; *An Outline of Indian Logic and Epistemology* (Hindi); and *Dadu, the Compassionate Mystic*.

DIPANKAR CHATTERJEE is Assistant Professor of Philosophy, University of Utah, U. S. A. He studied in Visvabharati University, Santiniketan, India and the University of Washington, Seattle, U. S. A. He has published several articles in American journals like *Philosophy East and West.*

KALIDAS BHATTACHARYYA is (Retired) Professor of Philosophy, Visvabharati University, Santiniketan, India. He was Director, Center for Advanced Study in Philosophy and also Vice-Chancellor (1966-70) of Visvabharati University. He has written a large number of articles and books. His most famous books include: *Alternative Standpoints in Philosophy*; *Object, Content and Relation*; *Philosophy, Logic and Language*; *Presuppositions of Science and Philosophy*.

RAM SHANKAR BHATTACHARYA is a traditional Indian scholar who lives in Varanasi, India. He is editing the *Sāṅkhya-Yoga* volume (with Gerald Larson of the University of California, Santa Barbara) in the monumental *Encyclopaedia of Indian Philosophies* series.

J. N. MOHANTY is George Lynn Cross Professor of Philosophy, University of Oklahoma, U.S.A. He was also the chairman of the Department of Philosophy, Graduate Faculty, New School for Social Research, New York and Director of the Husserl Archives. He has published several research papers and books including: *Edmund Husserl's Theory of Meaning*; *Phenomenology and Ontology*; *The Concept of Intentionality*; *Gaṅgeśa's Theory of Truth*.

BIMAL K. MATILAL is Spalding Professor of Eastern Religions and Ethics, Oxford University, England. He is the author of *The Navya-Nyāya Doctrine of Negation*; *Language, Grammar and Meaning in Indian Philosophy*, etc. He is also the Editor of The *Journal of Indian Philosophy*.

J. S. R. L. NARAYANA MOORTY teaches philosophy at Monterey Peninsula College, Monterey, California, U.S.A. He studied at the University of California, Berkeley, and has contributed articles to the Philosophy and Religion Volume of the *Telugu*

Encyclopaedia and papers to *Indian Philosophical Quarterly*, *Visvabharati Journal of Philosophy* and other magazines in India.

DEBABRATA SINHA is Professor of Philosophy, Brock University, Canada. He is the author of *The Idealistic Standpoint: A Study in the Vedantic Metaphysic of Experience*; *Studies in Phenomenology*; *Phenomenology and Existentialism: An Introduction.*

RAJENDRA PRASAD is Research Professor of Philosophy, Indian Institute of Technology, Kanpur, India. He has published several research papers in Indian and Western professional philosophy journals. He has co-edited *Proceedings of the International Institute of Philosophy*; *Bhagwandas Commemoration Volume and Marathi Encyclopaedia of Philosophy.* He was also editor of *Indian Review of Philosophy.*

DINESH C. MATHUR is Professor of Philosophy, State University of New York at Brockport. He has published several research papers in *The Journal of Philosophy*; *Philosophy and Phenomenological Research*; *Philosophy East and West.* He is the author of *Naturalistic Philosophies of Experience* (*Studies in James, Dewey and Farber against the Background of Husserl's Phenomenology.*)

N. K. DEVARAJA is U.G.C. Research Scholar, Lucknow University, India. He was a Senior Professor in the Department of Philosophy, Banaras Hindu University, India; Sayaji Rao Gaekwad Professor of Indian Civilization and Culture; and Director of the Center for Advanced Study in Philosophy, Banaras Hindu University. He has written several books, including *An Introduction to Śaṅkara's Theory of Knowledge*; *The Philosophy of Culture*; *The Mind and Spirit of India*; *Hinduism and the Modern Age*; and edited *Indian Philosophy Today.*

V. NARAYAN KARAN REDDY is Professor and Head of the Department of Philosophy, Osmania University, India. He is the author of *Sarvodaya Ideology and Acharya Vinobha Bhave*; *Thoreau, Gandhi and Vinoba*; *Universalism and Essentialism.*

N. S. S. RAMAN is Professor and Head of the Department of Philosophy, Banaras Hindu University. He studied at Mysore,

Rajasthan, Glasgow and Mainz. He was a Visiting Professor at the University of Mainz and wrote a number of research articles and a book on *Karl Jaspers* in German.

S. S. RAMA RAO PAPPU is Associate Professor of Philosophy, Miami University, Oxford, Ohio, U.S.A. He studied at the University of Delhi, India, and Southern Illinois University, U. S. A. He has published articles in Indian and American journals and has co-authored a book *Gandhi and America's Educational Future*.

ASHOK K. GANGADEAN is Associate Professor of Philosophy, Haverford College, Pennsylvania, U.S.A. He has published several research articles in *Philosophy East and West*.

INDEX

Abhinavagupta, 82
Absolute, 32f, 88f
absolutism, 110
action, classes of, 212f
ahiṃsā, 67f, 153
anekāntavāda, 197
Anikeev, N. P., 321f
anubhava, 133
anumāna, 188f, 195, 197, 283
ānvīkṣikī, 142
Aquinas, Thomas, 138
Aristotle, 64f, 77, 94, 123, 146, 157, 159f, 182f, 257, 372, 377
artha, 8, 165f
arthāpatti, 197
ātmalogy, 126, 132, 136
ātman, 6, 44, 47ff, 66f, 74, 133, 263, 327f, 333, 345; paradox of, 119
ātmanism, 112
atoms, 16
attitudes, 175
aum, 408f
Aurobindo, Sri, 58, 144, 173, 300, 318, 324, 328, 337, 350ff
Austin, J. L. 374
Ayer, A. J., 138, 374

becoming, 94f
Being, 74ff, 128, 200, 268; unity of, 110
Berkeley, G., 77, 126
Bhartṛhari, 97
Bhattacharya, Gopinath, 296f
Bhattacharyya, Kalidas, 258, 275
Bhattacharyya, K. C., 173, 275f, 296
Bradley, F. H., 102, 138, 319, 342, 347
Brahman, 6f, 14, 29, 51f, 67, 74, 80, 84, 120, 263, 327ff, 408f; as naturalistic, 328
Brahma-Sūtra, 135
Buddha, 102, 323
Buddhism, 13, 28f, 30ff, 67f, 181f, 217, 258, 262, 269; Chinese, 92
Burtt, E. A., 101ff

Cārvāka (Lokāyata), 4, 10, 13, 41, 49, 124, 151, 188ff
categories, 177, 184ff
Chan, W. T., 102
Chari, C. T. K., 304
Chatterjee, S. C., 137, 140
Chattopadhyaya, Debiprasad, 321f
Chubb, J. N., 296f
classification, 196
cogito, 120, 123
Collingwood, R. G., 375f
concepts, 32
Confucius, 91
consciousness, 22, 33, 50, 55, 117, 126, 177f, 352, 369; and ego, 130; states of, 56
contradiction, law of, 43
Coomaraswamy, Ananda, 101
creativity, philosophical, 309ff
criticism, 239f
culture, 5, 149; and philosophy, 273ff, 322ff

darśana, 9, 40, 118, 139, 142f, 235, 240f, 255ff, 294f, 298, 304; as therapeutic, 255f
Darwin, C., 324
Dasgupta, S. N., 137, 293
Datta, D. M., 137
definition, 246
democracy, 353f, 365
Descartes, 94, 123, 126, 214, 218, 257
detachment, 204f
Deussen, Paul, 95f
dharma, 7f, 45, 143f, 161, 226; nature of, 144; relation to *mokṣa*, 161ff
dharma-śāstras, 193, 209, 211
Dilthey, Wilhelm, 97
Divākara, Siddhasena, 12
dualism, 19

Edgerton, Franklin, 161
ego, 120f, 130, 200; and consciousness, 130
ethics, 85f, 156ff, 192ff, 264
existence, 127ff

facts, 194f
faith, 98
fallacies, logical, 198
Findlay, J. N., 132
Frankena, W. K., 156f
freedom, 201ff, 333f, 368; transcendental, 213f
futurology, 349ff

Gadamer, H. G., 379
Galileo, 153
Gandhi, M. K., 318, 323, 331f, 337, 346
Ganguly, S. N., 258
Gauḍapāda, 83